D·E·B·A·T·I·N·G R·A·T·I·O·N·A·L·I·T·Y

*Frank W. Pierce Memorial Lectureship
and Conference Series*

Number 10

DEBATING RATIONALITY

NONRATIONAL ASPECTS OF

ORGANIZATIONAL DECISION MAKING

EDITED BY

Jennifer J. Halpern

AND **Robert N. Stern**

ILR Press AN IMPRINT OF

Cornell University Press | ITHACA AND LONDON

Copyright © 1998 by Cornell University

All rights reserved. Except for brief quotations in a review, this book, or parts thereof, must not be reproduced in any form without permission in writing from the publisher. For information, address Cornell University Press, Sage House, 512 East State Street, Ithaca, New York 14850.

First published 1998 by Cornell University Press.

Printed in the United States of America

Cornell University strives to utilize environmentally responsible suppliers and materials to the fullest extent possible in the publishing of its books. Such materials include vegetable-based, low-VOC inks and acid-free papers that are either recycled, totally chlorine-free, or partly composed of nonwood fibers.

Cloth printing   10 9 8 7 6 5 4 3 2 1

Library of Congress
Cataloging-in-Publication Data

Debating rationality : Nonrational aspects of
organizational decision making / edited by
Jennifer J. Halpern and Robert N. Stern.
  p. cm. — (Frank W. Pierce memorial
lectureship and conference series; no. 10)
  Includes index.
  ISBN 0-8014-3378-9 (cloth : alk. paper)
  1. Decision-making—Congresses.
  2. Reasoning—Congresses.
  3. Management—Congresses.   I. Halpern,
Jennifer J., 1960–   . II. Stern, Robert N.,
1948–   . III. Series.
HD30.23.D377   1997
658.4'03—dc21   97-28828

To an obstacle that became

an opportunity

S N O W

Contents

Acknowledgments   ix

Abbreviations   xi

Introduction:

Beneath the Social Science Debate: Economic and Social
   Notions of Rationality
JENNIFER J. HALPERN AND ROBERT N. STERN   1

PART I THEORETICAL DISPUTES

1. Prescriptive Models in Organizational Decision Making
   ZUR SHAPIRA   21

2. Game Theory and Garbage Cans: An Introduction to the
   Economics of Internal Organization
   ROBERT GIBBONS   36

3. Behavioral Economics and Nonrational Organizational
   Decision Making
   COLIN F. CAMERER   53

4. Can Negotiators Outperform Game Theory?
   MAX H. BAZERMAN, ROBERT GIBBONS, LEIGH THOMPSON,
   AND KATHLEEN L. VALLEY   78

5. Playing the Maintenance Game: How Mental Models Drive
   Organizational Decisions
   JOHN S. CARROLL, JOHN STERMAN, AND ALFRED A. MARCUS   99

PART II NEW FOUNDATIONS OF RESEARCH

6. Organizational Contracting: A "Rational" Exchange?
   JUDI MCLEAN PARKS AND FAYE L. SMITH   125

7. Transaction Cost Economics and Organization Theory
   OLIVER E. WILLIAMSON   155

8. Toward a Psychology of Contingent Work
   BATIA WIESENFELD AND JOEL BROCKNER   195

PART III STRETCHING THE BOUNDARIES

9. Bonded Rationality: The Rationality of Everyday Decision Making
   in a Social Context
   JENNIFER J. HALPERN   219

10. Endogenous Preferences: A Structural Approach
    DAVID KRACKHARDT   239

    References   248
    Contributors   276
    Index   281

Acknowledgments

The worst snowstorm to hit Ithaca in twenty years trapped many of the participants at our conference "Nonrational Aspects of Organizational Decision Making." As the snow deepened, so did participants' thinking, and the ideas for this volume crystallized.

Many participants should be thanked for walking through three feet of snow. Our graduate students especially were undeterred. We are grateful to Deborah Connelley, Eric Rait, and Mario Scarselletta for their willingness to act as recorders for conference sessions, and for their help pitching in whenever we needed something. Amir Erez, who originally attended the conference as a member of the audience, ably managed the new logistics imposed by the storm. The conference would have frozen without his help.

Commentators at the conference helped shape the contents of the chapters in this book, and particularly the Introduction. Dick Thaler and Pamela Tolbert invested time and energy in considering the relationships among the papers. Steve Barley challenged the participants to change how they think about rationality, creating a lively, and at times loud, interdisciplinary exchange. His insightful comments led to the organization of the current volume.

Conference arrangements and the preparation of this volume depended on the substantial efforts of Krista Knout. We thank her for the skill with which she managed both projects, particularly amid university budget cuts and increasing workloads.

The conference was made possible by a grant from the Frank W. Pierce Memorial Lectureship and Conference Studies, at the School of Industrial and Labor Relations, Cornell University. The Teagle Foundation, Inc., generously supports this series. We thank Ronald Ehrenberg, research director, and the ILR Research and Publication Committee for the decision to support the conference. We also thank James March and anonymous reviewers for their editorial guidance.

J. J. H.
R. N. S.

Abbreviations

AFI   anticipated future interaction
INPO   Institute for Nuclear Power Operators
LBO   leveraged buy-out
NRC   Nuclear Regulatory Commission
RCT   rational choice theory

Beneath the Social Science Debate:
Economic and Social Notions
of Rationality

Jennifer J. Halpern and Robert N. Stern

Rationality is a magical quality that permeates the evaluation of every action in our society. Since the Renaissance we have aimed to perfect our understanding of the rational, and have valued reasoning and logic with rationality as the underlying premise. We have denigrated individuals for not arguing a point rationally and locked up those who are repeatedly irrational.

The notion of positive science is premised on a rational method, and social scientists have struggled continually with the concept of rationality, both in defending their methods and in describing human behavior.

The title of this volume, *Debating Rationality,* may strike some readers as odd: What is there to be debated when we discuss rationality? If rationality is a fundamental concept, practically an axiom, underlying models for understanding human behavior, especially decision behavior, it is assumed rather than debated. Considering the sometimes complementary and sometimes contradictory findings in the different disciplines, however, researchers will notice that there is a debate, at least about what is germane to the study of decision making.

These conference papers discuss both past and present ways in which rationality has been applied to organizational decision making. Since our society is now based on organizations as the institutionalized form for directing resources and accomplishing tasks, rationality becomes an even more critical concept for understanding human behavior and social organization.

This introduction provides a historical context for the papers presented at the March 1993 conference "Nonrational Elements of Organizational Decision Making" at Cornell's New York State School of Industrial and Labor Relations. The conference created an interdisciplinary exchange among scholars who could acknowledge their shared background on the basic "taken for granted" underpinnings of thinking on rationality but then debate their interdisciplinary differences. The debate produced a set of papers moving the field off this baseline knowledge and onto new ways of thinking about rationality in decision making. It was not a revolution overturning the framework for examining rationality; rather it was an extraordinary poke at a field bogged down in discipline-based assumptions. The debate drove the participants to examine these assumptions through cross-disciplinary lenses.

The resulting collection of papers takes the issue of rationality from its origins to current critical controversies. Individual contributions provide overviews of the basic literature relevant to their unique arguments. The historical development of the debate requires a different sort of explanation, however. The remainder of this chapter introduces the rationality issue and provides some common understandings of rationality from which to interpret the contributions of the conference participants.

The contributions of the conference participants are divided into three parts: Part 1: Theoretical Disputes, Part 2: New Foundations for Research, and Part 3: Stretching the Boundaries. These parts are organized to lay out the terms of the debate and then move it in new directions.

The Nature of the Debate

One side in the debate argues that the classical economists' model of rational decision making offers the best way to understand decision behavior. This model focuses on the value, or utility, of the decision outcome. Numerous researchers have been concerned about this focus on achieving "rational" outcomes because it de-emphasizes investigation of the decision *process.* In response, Simon (1990) characterizes the debate in terms of the classical economic model's lack of attention to decision processes, creating an incomplete picture of decision-making behavior.

> The desirability and usefulness of a procedural theory of decision making involves at least two separate issues. First, which kind of theory, substantive or procedural, can better predict and explain what decisions are actually reached? Second, are we interested only in the decisions that are reached, or is it the human decision making process that is the object of scientific curiosity? (Simon 1990, 17)

Researchers concerned with decision processes advocate identifying specific behaviors or concerns that characterize humans and incorporating their influences into the classical models.

A third approach to the debate advocates the inclusion of context, particularly social context, as an additional element influencing the decision maker (Greenhalgh and Chapman 1993; Halpern 1994; Carroll, this volume). As this third, more recent, approach develops, it may either extend or repudiate the classic model.

The following discussion describes these approaches to the rationality debate. Several of the book's chapters further explicate differing viewpoints within the debate.

Rational Behavior and the Self-Interest Criterion

When faced with a choice, most individuals do not merely decide blindly among alternatives; they try to make the *best* decision possible. This interest in achieving the optimum decision spawned decades of research investigating the characteristics and approach to reaching this "best decision." Researchers simplified the question by considering only *rational* outcomes, those made based on maximization of (expected) utility, unencumbered by external pressures or cognitive limitations.

Rationality, according to *Random House Unabridged Dictionary*, refers to the "possession of," "agreeableness to," or "exercise of reason." Reason, in turn, is a "basis or cause," or a "statement in justification or explanation of a belief or action." In philosophy, reason is defined as the "faculty or power of acquiring intellectual knowledge by direct understanding of first principles or by argument" (*Oxford English Dictionary*). Rational behaviors follow stable, consistent, and coherent beliefs or rules that enable individuals to understand what they are doing and why (cf. Velleman 1989). Most social scientists consider the elucidation of these rules per se to be sufficient for understanding behavior. How individuals come to understand their own behaviors and learn these rules was traditionally considered to be outside the purview of the study of rationality, but newer approaches consider this type of self-understanding.

The most clearly elucidated rules of rational behavior are based on self-interest. Self-interest is a philosophically comforting rule, simplifying the drawing of logical deductions about human behavior. It is based on the early philosophers' insights about hedonic relevance, the notion that people tend to seek pleasure and avoid pain. Material self-interest, however, is at best merely a quantifiable proxy for hedonic relevance: not all cultural traditions, and not even all Western traditions, dictate action in accordance with self-interest in all social situations.

This relatively simple anchor for understanding behavior spawned arguments almost immediately. The Hobbesian philosophy of survival of the financially fittest interpreted self-interest as preserving property, accumulating power, and authorizing a sovereign to act on one's behalf (a nice way to say accepting autocracy); (Mansbridge 1990, 4). Hobbesian self-interest was seen as an appalling principle by non-Hobbesians, who preferred self-rule to autocratic domination. The mid-seventeenth-century reaction to Hobbes was to redefine self-interest. Non-Hobbesians believed that a person, by the "light of nature and reason will do that which makes for his greatest advantage" (enlightened self interest) (cf. Mansbridge 1990, 5).

The redefined notion of enlightened self-interest persisted as a guide for understanding people's behavior for almost two hundred years. The companion observation to the notion of enlightened self-interest, that the common good is well-served by the free actions of self-interested agents in a market, was central to the rise of modern economics (Kahneman, Knetsch, and Thaler 1986a). By the late 1800s, Edgeworth, in *Mathematical Psychics,* asserted that the "first principle of Economics is that every agent is actuated only by self-interest." He specifically limited the application of his "economical calculus" to war and contract (Sen 1990). Nonetheless, Edgeworth's "first principle" of self-interest came to define the core of economic and political models.

Decision researchers (Simon 1947) found the notion of self-interest to be an incomplete means of understanding individual choice, and social science disciplines began to diverge in their research on rationality. On the one hand, anthropologists, clinical and social psychologists, and some sociologists moved toward incorporating more of the social context, an approach that is discussed below. Within economics a theory of rational choice developed, adding to the self-interest argument the notion of "revealed preferences" (Hogarth 1980, 65). By choosing and rejecting an object or action *y*, an individual "reveals" a preference for *x* over *y*. In this model, personal utility is a numerical representation of this "preference," with a higher utility assigned to a preferred alternative. The theory assumes that people are capable of expressing both consistent preferences (evaluative judgments) and consistent beliefs (predictive judgments concerning cause and effect). These preferences and beliefs are independent of each other, such that a person should not allow what she would like to have happen (that person's preferences) affect her beliefs about what she thinks is going to happen, and vice versa.

Rational Choice Theory in the Debate

The individual choice model combining self-interest with preferences has become known as *rational choice theory.* This theory supplies the underlying assumptions for most of the papers in this volume. It provides first principles for some authors and a target for others.

The theory of rational choice now embodies a number of commonsense principles. It suggests mathematically that a person's beliefs and preferences can be expressed by probabilities and utilities. Rational choice theory simplifies our understanding of decision making by offering maximization of expected utility (the expected value of benefit a factor offers an individual) as the sole criterion of a rational choice (Hogarth 1980, 64).

Among economists' approaches to rationality, game theorists have been particularly active in developing and clarifying the boundaries of rational choice theory, while economists in other subspecialties have applied the theory to a variety of research problems. From research which began in the 1950s (see, e.g., Luce and Raiffa 1957), game theorists have established parameters for economically rational, optimal behavior. The dominant research methodology consisting of highly controlled, situation-specific laboratory derivations of these parameters is, however, sometimes forgotten by researchers in other disciplines who use the rules in investigating human decision behavior outside the laboratory.

Limitations of Rational Choice Theory

It is possible to compare people's intuitive choices with those prescribed by rational choice theory in order to assess people's "rationality," but national choice theory has its limitations. A variety of empirical anomalies (e.g., Allais 1952; Ellsberg 1961) have demonstrated that the expected utility criterion was systematically misleading, and that people tended toward suboptimal decisions for a variety of non-"rational" reasons, such as concern for regret (cf. Tversky 1975).

Game theorists subsequently have identified other situations in which suboptimal behavior is likely. Economists often call these behaviors "deviations." because the behavior deviates from the rational model. In many cases, these deviations offer little cause for concern because market forces correct for them. Game theorists, other economists, and behavioral decision theorists have included the source of many of these deviations within the classical rational choice model. For example, concerns for "fairness," "social relationships," and, in a macro-economic example, "self-seeking with guile" have become incorporated into economic models (cf. Akerlof 1970; Loewenstein, Thompson, and Bazerman 1989; and Williamson 1975b).

The central assumptions of rational choice theory are powerful simplifications that describe the basis for and predict the optimal outcomes of an enormous scope of human behavior. This scope ranges from the trivial case of the behavior of a Las Vegas card counter, interested only in the probabilities expressed in the cards and not in the card dealer's social attentions, to the case of some American business deals, which may be made on a tightly calculated model that admits no interpersonal considerations.

Some researchers, however, have found rational choice theory's assumptions too constraining, its lack of attention to process too restrictive, and its calculation requirements too tortuous to describe behavior adequately. Tversky, a mathematical psychologist, observed: "Utility theory is normative, inadequate in descriptive terms as a theory of choice" (1975).[1] Arrow, a Nobel-prize winning economist, agreed: "[The rationality assumptions] . . . imply an ability at information processing and calculation that is far beyond the feasible and that cannot well be justified as the result of learning and adaptation" (1990, 25). Sen, another economist, observed that "too many economists assume that a person is given one preference ordering which is supposed to reflect his interests, represent his welfare, summarize his idea of what should be done, and describe his actual choices and behavior" (1990, 37). Sen questioned whether one preference ordering can do all these things.

> A person thus described may be "rational" in the limited sense of revealing no inconsistencies in his choice behavior, but if he has no use for these distinctions between quite different concepts, he must be a bit of a fool. . . . Economic theory has been much preoccupied with this rational fool decked in the glory of his one all-purpose preference ordering. To make room for the different concepts related to his behavior we need a more elaborate structure. (Sen 1990, 37)

More elaborate structures were subsequently designed jointly by economists and psychologists incorporating rational choice and psychological principles.[2] As a result, cognitive interpretations of rationality have become the contemporary state of the art in decision theory. The body of research based on this cognitive approach is often referred to as *behavioral decision theory.*

[1] Tversky further noted that this inadequacy restricts applications of the theory only to those aspects of psychology, economics, and so on that deal with decision making under risk (1975).

[2] Other economists also rose to the challenge. Harsanyi proposed a dual structure, permitting us to distinguish between what a person thinks is good from the social point of view (ethical preference) and what he or she regards as good from a personal point of view (subjective preference) (in Sen 1990). The structure falls short in describing what happens when a person deviates from his personal welfare maximization not through an impartial concern for society, but for a particular group, for example, a gang or work buddies. Sen himself proposed a meta-ranking system by which people can express a ranking of rankings of actions, allowing people to describe a particular ideology or system of class interests (1990). It can provide a format for expressing what preferences one would have preferred to have (his example: "I wish I liked vegetarian foods more"); or to analyze conflicts involved in addiction ("Given my current tastes, I am better off with heroin, but heroin leads me to addiction, and I would have preferred not to have these tastes") (Sen 1990, 39). These economists, however, were still working from the perspective of an individual reacting consciously to external stimuli, rather than admitting of any chance for noncalculative behavior to occur.

Cognitive Aspects of Rationality

Rational choice theory implies that their need to search for information and to calculate utilities when making decisions constrains decision makers. These constraints create difficulties for functioning in the real world, which doesn't permit the gathering of complete information or the unbiased weighting of alternatives. The first step in developing a new structure for decision theory research was, therefore, to address these difficulties. Psychologists, for example, had long argued for the primacy of affect over cognition. They also maintained that persuasion occurs via different cognitive routes depending on a variety of factors, including, for example, the nature of the message. Traditional rational choice theorists eschewed these considerations, in part because psychologists lacked techniques for quantifying these effects.

Simon's (1955) approach was an important step toward understanding some of these influences in a manner that could be quantified. He observed that human decision making is "boundedly rational": it is limited by our inability to process all the information that is available as well as by our inability to be consistent in our preferences.

> The assumption of a utility function postulates a consistency of human choice that is not always evidenced in reality. The assumption of maximization may also place a heavy computational burden on the decision maker. A theory of bounded rationality seeks to identify, in theory and in actual behavior, procedures for choosing that are computationally simpler, and that can account for observed inconsistencies in human choice patterns. (1990, 16)

As a result, people tend to "satisfice" or use a variety of heuristics (shortcuts) in their decision-making process. Simon noted that theories of bounded rationality can be generated by relaxing one or more of the expected utility theory assumptions:

> Instead of assuming a fixed set of alternatives among which a decision maker chooses, we may postulate a process for generating alternatives. Instead of assuming known probability distributions of outcomes, we may introduce estimating procedures for them, or we may look for strategies for dealing with uncertainty that don't assume knowledge of probabilities. Instead of assuming maximization of a utility function, we may postulate a satisfying strategy. (1990, 15)

Many of the "satisfying strategies" that people use are heuristics, cognitive shortcuts, or rules of thumb that simplify the sorting and analysis that decision making requires. While most of the time these heuristics lead to effective decisions, psychologists Tversky and Kahneman (1974) observed that heuristics could in some cases lead to systematic errors or biases. For example, they noted that people seem to use a reference point for making decisions under conditions of uncertainty. People act as though there is an S-shaped value function for decisions that constrains us to be risk-seeking to avoid losses and risk-averse in the domain of gains (Kahneman and Tversky 1979). As a result, how people "frame" questions as either issues of loss or gain (e.g., stating the outcome of a particular health policy decision during an epidemic in terms of how many people in a city will be *saved* in contrast to how many people there will *die*) has a strong—and nonrational—effect on the decision-making process. Other heuristics lead to similarly unanticipated outcomes. The availability bias, for example, leads us to judge a specific event as more likely to occur than is actually likely if there has been recent media coverage of a similar event (Tversky and Kahneman 1974).

Thaler, a behavioral economist, observed that economists can construct a rational explanation for any economic action, no matter how strange (1991, xvi). Nonetheless, research by some experimental economists and cognitive psychologists has demonstrated a contrast between the traditional economic models and some human choice behavior. These researchers found that the economic rationality-based discussions of decision-making behavior skirted a number of interesting and important phenomena about how people, rather than mathematical models, make decisions (Thaler 1991).

Thaler refers to these heuristics, and a variety of other regular, purposeful behaviors that seem to be systematically deviant from the rational choice theory axioms, as "quasi-rational" behaviors (1991). Thaler made predictions about behaviors that are independent of preferences. His concept of "mental accounting," which developed from his observation that people ignore sunk costs, helps account for a number of phenomena. For example, he uses the mental accounting concept to explain why gamblers who are ahead tend to become more reckless. He suggests that they imagine they could only lose the money they have just won (the "house money"). Thaler also can explain why people intentionally restrict their options when they think they later will regret specific behaviors (e.g., dieters don't keep desserts in the house; smokers who want to cut down buy cigarettes by the pack rather than by the box; and we force ourselves to save through pensions).

The cognitive/behavioral revolution in decision theory also presaged a shift in game theory, the core tool of rational choice models. Thaler and his colleagues found *behaviors* rather than outcomes per se to be of interest in the standard game theoretical paradigms. They observed, for example, that people were willing to turn down a good deal of money in an ultimatum game in order to punish an allocator perceived as too greedy. Kahneman, Knetsch, and Thaler

(1986a) also found evidence that people's conceptions of the fairness of a price change was affected by cognitive mechanisms relating to reference points: There are, for example, specific occasions on which people think it is more or less acceptable to raise or lower prices. As a result, judgments of fairness are susceptible to substantial framing effects, and there is reason to believe that firms have an incentive to frame the terms of exchanges so as to make them appear "fair" (Kahneman, Knetsch, and Thaler, 1986a, 217).

Thaler proposed that game theory should also reflect people's use of simplifying strategies and people's concerns about acting fairly and being treated fairly. Other game theorists agree: Gibbons and Camerer (this volume, chaps. 2 and 3) discuss some of the changes that game theory is experiencing. Their new "behavioral" game theory incorporates considerations of communication and some of the numerous shortcuts that people use regularly. Bazerman et al. (this volume, chap. 4) acknowledge, for example, that communication between players can lead to efficient outcomes where game theory predicts none.

The insights underlying the cognitively rational approach provide powerful modifications of rational choice theory. Behavioral decision theory thus is focused on the individual *acting alone,* or at most receiving additional information through a communication process. Most decisions, however, are made in a social context that has its own demands and ramifications, rather than in a social vacuum. The next section considers how models of rationality have been expanded to take context into account.

The Contexts of Rationality

The economists' preference for investigating rationality in a vacuum emerged from their tendency to study an ideal market with perfect competition, which functions without prolonged human or social contact (A. O. Hirschman 1986). Pre-existing social relationships produce complexity in a marketplace: they can lead to collusion or monopoly, or to forms of distribution other than those predicted by the model (Walzer 1983; Etzioni 1988; A. O. Hirschman 1986). It is not surprising, therefore, that studies examining quasi-rational behavior focused on self-interested strangers who were expected never to meet again (cf. Olson 1965; A. O. Hirschman 1986; and Hirsch 1990).

The critics of the classical rational choice structure, including anthropologists and some psychologists and sociologists, long had argued that decision making, even *economic* decision making, tends to occur in a social setting (Barley 1991; Nader and Todd 1978; Coleman 1990; Geertz 1963). Recently, researchers, including some economists have agreed that rationality has a social component (Walzer 1983; Etzioni 1988; A. O. Hirschman 1986). Some of the early work in the spirit of social rationality attempted to incorporate individuals' utility for fairness, friendship, and other social factors into the classical rational choice model. These factors constituted a "social utility function" that became part of the model's structure (Akerlof 1970; Loewenstein, Thompson, and Bazerman 1989). A particularly notable example of incorporating motives other than self-interest was provided by James Buchanan. In the same year that he received the Nobel Prize in economics for applying a "rational choice" model based on self-interest to politics, he repudiated the single motive of self-interest in favor of examining context in the political arena (1986; in Sen 1990). As he observed, politicians and bureaucrats pursue public interest, as well as their own pecuniary interest.

The social context creates pressures of its own, influencing the decision process and outcome. Moreover, as numerous anthropologists, philosophers, sociologists and others (cf. Coleman 1990; Velleman 1989; Yngvesson 1978; Halpern, this volume, chap. 9) have pointed out, what constitutes a "rational" outcome may be a function of the social context in which the decision is made. Arrow (1990, 25) acknowledged the importance of context in this observation:

> Rationality is not a property of the individual alone, although it is usually presented that way. Rather, it gathers not only its force but also its very meaning from the social context in which it is embedded. It is most plausible under very ideal conditions. When these conditions cease to hold, the rationality assumptions become strained, and possibly even self-contradictory.

John Stuart Mill (cited in Arrow 1990) argued that custom, not competition, governs much of the economic world. Mill added that the only possible "scientific" theory is that based on competition. Arrow responds: "There is no general principle that prevents the creation of an economic theory (of a market) based on hypotheses other than that of rationality" (1990, 25).

Other researchers, in the spirit of Arrow's argument, have used a different set of assumptions, creating another structure for understanding the rationality of individuals' decision making. This *socially rational* approach stresses the notion of shared understanding. The theory assumes that in making decisions, people strive to make sense of their behavior in the light of the common understandings or shared knowledge of their particular culture (cf. Velleman 1989, Yngvesson 1978; Coleman 1990).

Figure I.1 illustrates the basic differences in the forms of rationality. Economic rationality strongly addresses self-interest and the decision outcome, while social rationality can incorporate these, but also suggests explanations for social interests.

The development of theories incorporating social rationality posits an individual who maximizes "fit" with others, or with society, rather than maximizing individual utility alone. A recent theory utilizing these assumptions suggests

Concerns	Early economic rationality	Rational choice theory	Cognitive rationality	Social rationality
Self-interest	*	*	*	*
Revealed preferences	*	*		
Cognitive			*	*
Social/other				*
Prescriptive	*	*	*	*
Normative		*	*	*
Process-oriented			*	*
Context-determined				*

(* = characteristic of the theory)

Figure I.1. Models of rationality and their concerns

that people strive to maintain their relationships with others, whether these are positive (e.g., friendships) or negative (e.g., hostile) (Greenhalgh and Chapman 1993). Yet another theory suggests that the extent to which negotiators make self-interested as opposed to other-interested decisions is influenced by both their level of identification with that referent other, and by their perception of accountability toward that referent (Kramer, Pommerenke, and Newton 1993). These authors observe, for example, that it matters not only *whether* one is accountable to others, but also *to whom* one is accountable.

Anthropology provides the strongest impetus toward accepting the legitimacy of the social rationality perspective. The characteristics of different societies offer the clearest evidence of the diversity of rules by which people can organize their decision-making processes (Coleman 1990; Udy 1969; Nader and Todd 1978; Yngvesson 1978). A society that stresses profit-maximization as its standard operating procedure for commerce might teach its children self-interest as the basis for "rational" behavior. A society that considers itself in harmony with nature, such as the Sioux, teaches its children that considering the seventh generation to be born is the basis for "rational" decisions. The Australian aboriginal peoples consider the intent of their ancestors in the Dreamtime (when the world was created) as the basis for rational decisions. Even the meaning of something that seems so universally positive to U.S. eyes as gift-giving, or as commonsensical as the expectation of reciprocation for a favor done, may not in fact be so "clear"—so "rational"—to members of other societies (Mauss 1969; Benedict 1934). As an example, the French, whose Western European traditions of culture at first glance seem not so different from our own, regard the American taste for tit-for-tat reciprocity for favors among friends as somewhat gauche (R. Carroll 1987).

Empirical observations from the 1960s to the current day examining the effects of relationships on exchange are consistent with the social rationality argument. For example, Clark and Mills (1979) demonstrated that people who considered themselves to be in communal relationships had different expectations for reciprocation of favors than did those who perceived themselves to be in an exchange relationship. Friends are less self-interested in their interactions than are strangers, so tend toward a preference for equality in outcomes, and more generally use equality-based distribution rules than would strangers (Morgan and Sawyer 1967; Austin 1980).

Recent laboratory work, based on these earlier empirical observations, suggests that the social context exerts its effects even when there is no communication between transactors: Halpern (1992, 1994) observed repeatedly that even without communication, people thinking about transacting with friends agreed on prices for hypothetical items, while people thinking about transacting with strangers did not. Halpern (1997) also developed a measurement tool that indicates that friendship interacts strongly with the price of commodities, such that friendship favors the seller for more expensive items but favors the buyer for less expensive items. The result complements anthropological findings that non-U.S. cultures have different patterns for their transactions with friends and strangers: In the Philippines, for example, friends may give away even expensive items.

The social rationality argument could also be thought of as based on the functioning of norms (Coleman 1990). Norms specify what actions are regarded by a set of persons as proper or correct, or improper or incorrect. They are purposively generated, in that those persons who initiate or help maintain a norm see themselves as benefiting from its being observed or harmed by its being violated. People take norms and accompanying potential rewards or punishments into account, not as absolute determinants of their actions, but as elements affecting their decisions about what actions it will be in their interests to carry out (Coleman 1990). Coleman argues: "Some rational choice theorists, armed with maximization of utility as a principle of action, regard the concept of a norm as altogether unnecessary. To take this stance is to ignore important processes in the functioning of social systems and thus to limit the theory" (1990, 242).

Building a Science of Rationality

The development of research into decision making parallels the search for understanding in the social sciences. Initially, there was a quest for simplification and understanding of basic principles, followed by the realization that both the human mind and human society are more complex than a simplistic model would suggest. The pressures of the external world on the decision process were ignored as much as possible by the mainstream researchers to maintain simplicity. Eventually, however, even they felt the encroaching demands by science to explain actual human behavior, and thus they began to take into account the multifaceted complexities of "real life." At that point, research programs changed to accommodate the interaction of variables from noneconomic disciplines. The search for "deviations" from the predictions of the economic model, which first drove experimental research, became subordinated to the process of explaining the nature of social elements in decision making.

The study of rational decision making, which originated in philosophical concerns, became "scientific" when economists sought to predict optimal decision outcomes. When prediction failed, economists' focus was expanded to consider those cognitive limitations and human "foibles" that noneconomists had traditionally recognized as legitimate elements of social behavior.

Organizational Application of Rational Decision Making

The application of decision-making models to organizations parallels the development of general theories of rationality. When administrative theorists argued for the establishment of organizational science, they identified decision making as a fundamental activity of organizations. Analysis of organizational decision making began with the presentation of a prescriptive model for rational decisions. Writing in the first issue of *Administrative Science Quarterly*, Litchfield proposed a science of administration in which decisions might be both rational and irrational (1956, 13–14). He observed, however, that the tools for studying irrational decisions had not yet been developed. Neither were such models yet seen as interesting or possible. The discussion argued for general theory and included logico-deductive reasoning as a definition of a superior decision process.

Decision making was characterized as a relationship between alternative actions and consequences. For example, Victor Thompson (1976) described decision making in terms of mental processes. He suggested that people debate within themselves. "Course of action 1 leads to result A. Course of action 2 leads to result B. A is better than B. Therefore, choose course of action 1" (60). Of the four premises in the thought process, the first two are factual and the third is a value premise. The assumption is that the conclusion (choose #1) is a function of logical reasoning based on facts (premises 1 and 2) and a preference ordering of alternative outcomes (premise 3). Of course the preference ordering is subjective by nature, and, depending on who theorizes about the process, facts may be objective or subjective based on the decision maker's perceptions.

Organization theorists recognized that the factual premises depended on the availability of information and that the alternatives depended not only on that information but on the ability of an individual decision maker to process it. Simon (1947) provided the idea of the boundaries of this rational thinking based on the amount of information which could be obtained at reasonable cost, our ability to absorb it, and knowledge of the likely cause-effect linkages. Rational decision making occurred within these human limitations. The cost of seeking additional information and the limits of human processing capacity led to choosing the first of the alternatives which met situational requirements. That is, decision making was described as following logical process within the bounds of the information we have available and our ability to process it. Rationality was taken to mean the pursuit of a specific goal or objective through the decision and resultant action process.

Differing Views and Observations

Organizational decision making takes place within an environment of limited or scarce resources. For the organization theorist, the decision problem becomes immediately complex. The assumption that individuals have clear goals, and therefore identifiable preferences for outcomes, proved to be only partially true. Individuals might have clear goals, but in the organizational context there also were goals imposed by the collective nature of the enterprise. Or, the owner of the enterprise might have had a goal which differed from the individual goals of the employees. Thus, an agency issue develops which affects the logic of rational decision making. Whose goals are being evaluated in terms of alternative outcomes at any given time?

Early administrative theorists such as Taylor (1916) noted that a system could be designed that would optimize return to the owner. The challenge, as Taylor saw it, was that employees constantly acted in their own interest, and did not make decisions or take actions that a principal would consider rational. Taylor attempted to eliminate worker discretion entirely to avoid the actions of those with different goals from owners. He saw employees as irrational from the owners' perspective. The employees, however, were moving rationally toward their own goals.

It quickly became evident that employees were not sufficiently controlled by formal management systems. The existence and power of "informal organization" was recognized (Roethlisberger and Dickson 1964). Under the resulting organizational decision-making theories, workers' actions that were not consistent with management objectives were not seen as irrational. Instead, these actions were accepted as indicators of the existence of the workers' own goals and objectives. Sometimes these goals were work-group based.

Again Victor Thompson's systems view is instructive. He argued that the organization consisted of two systems. The artificial system is the tool designed by the owner and/or managers to accomplish a particular goal. The informal organization of social relationships constitutes a natural system whose goal is not entirely compatible with the artificial system's goal. The result is that the effectiveness of the artificial system is always limited by the natural one (1976, 2–26). A well-designed structural system would work if only there were no people in it. Competing preferences lead to the need to control behavior, and have spurred the development of principal-agent theory.

Preference ordering, however, is not the only issue concerning what appears rational to one party and nonrational to another (see above). Preferences may be determined by multiple dimensions. Calculated monetary outcome is but one of several goals that the decision maker has in mind. For example, social norms regarding factors other than money may enter into preference ordering. Even more interesting, however, is the possibility that there is less agreement on the factual premises and beliefs about cause and effect than appear on the surface.

Suppose that an individual examines the facts and concludes that action A (e.g., cheating) will result in a payoff X and the creation of a side effect P (distrust), while action B leads to a lower payoff Y and a side effect Q. Preference ordering now has multidimensionality, and the investigator must evaluate the salience or rank ordering of outcomes X/Y and P/Q. In the simple economic model, such outcomes would produce anomalies relative to predictions. Of additional consequence is the possibility that actors do not establish the facts the same way. One actor may come from a culture where cheating leads to distrust and is negatively valued. Another might come from a culture where cheating leads to confirmation of a cultural norm of behavior and reinforces a positive evaluation of actions (Belmonte 1989).

We are left to confront the possibility that many kinds of rationality exist and that the criteria among them overlap. Social rationality argues for the importance of norms and social structure in shaping preferences and beliefs about cause and effect. *Organizational rationality* incorporates the differences between collective and individual preferences, along with multiple levels of causality. Differences in beliefs about cause and effect, as well as clarity of objectives, receive serious attention within organizational decision analysis. For example, James Thompson (1967) constructs one of his omnipresent two-by-two tables with these dimensions and examines the nature of decision making under each of the possible conditions. Pfeffer (1981) shows that the more the ambiguity on goals or on means to accomplish them, the more likely is the exercise of political power in decision making.

Economic models offer a clean accounting system, placing monetary values on human action and the allocation of resources. The accounting system itself is reinforced by the societal economic system, and clear, parsimonious predictions of behavior are generated for testing.

Once the anomalies we have described began to appear in empirical work on the predictions of the rational model in economics, organization theorists began to build models that relaxed the rationality assumptions. Several organization theorists who were economists, including Akerlof (1970) and Williamson (1975), began creating decision models based on alternative assumptions. Other organization theorists produced perceptual models (Weick 1987) and process models such as the garbage can model (Cohen and March 1974).

As fundamental aspects of our character and science have become open to debate, economists, social psychologists, and organizational behaviorists have come to differ greatly among themselves. In that spirit, we organized a conference for February 1993. Little did we know that the weekend would see the worst snowstorm in more than a decade. Having trapped the participants inside the buildings of Cornell's School of Industrial and Labor Relations, the blizzard produced a more intense interdisciplinary exchange than we had expected. The result is this volume, in which we have organized the conference papers to reflect the flow of the debate as it developed.

Organizing the Debate

Part I, "Theoretical Disputes," opens the debate by examining the foundations of arguments from economic and social perspectives. What assumptions, beliefs, and models developed over time and provided fundamental academic perspectives? Zur Shapira (chapter 1) sets the stage by elaborating on a social psychological point of view that stands in fundamental contrast to the story of differing viewpoints within economics told by Robert Gibbons in chapter 2.

When the empirical evidence is placed alongside these theories over the limitations of initial models, researchers from several perspectives join the debate. Colin Camerer initiates this discussion (chapter 3) by reviewing the evidence from tests of economic theories that show the limits of prediction. Unexpected findings jar the simple model, and require changes in both the theory and the nature of testing economic rationality. Max Bazerman, Robert Gibbons, Leigh Thompson, and Kathleen Valley (chapter 4) carry out a similar analysis of experimental work on rational strategies in game situations. Again, the limitations of simple rational decision models become apparent, showing that long-run versus short-run thinking affects choices that what seems rational from one perspective appears irrational from another. John Carroll, John Sterman, and Alfred A. Marcus' study of nuclear power plants (chapter 5) considers how time perspectives affect rational decision making in a critical empirical case, and demonstrates the need to broaden the models used to predict decision-making actions.

Part I discusses the basic theories and their limitations. Part II, "New Foundations for Research," considers both theoretical and research responses. In chapter 6, Judi McLean Parks and fay smith review and further develop the social contracting perspective that both explains and reconceptualizes the social nature of rationality, decisions and exchange among contracting parties. Oliver Williamson (chapter 7) elaborates on the transaction cost alternative to the economics of a firm's decision making. His broadening of the decision-making perspective on rationality in economics significantly alters assumptions that supported initial rational models. Empirical work by Batia Wiesenfeld and Joel Brockner (chapter 8) pushes theory farther. Here, the long- versus short-run perspective of Carroll's analysis is applied to the issue of contingent workers and the response to workforce reductions. "Fairness" as an aspect of employees' rational evaluation of management decisions becomes a factor in both the ordering of preferences and the beliefs about cause and effect.

These models represent incremental changes in notions of rational behavior. Part III, "Stretching the Boundaries," considers some of the more radical approaches that are emerging. The final papers in this volume move toward altering the terms of the debate. Jennifer Halpern (chapter 9) supplies an alternative concept of the normative aspects of rationality. She argues that since individuals vary in objectives and value preferences, the altering of preferences by the addition of social criteria is itself important to the debate. Potentially more significant is the nature of collective social norms in altering the perceptions of the "factual premises" on which strategic decisions are made. Collectively held social facts enter the analysis of rationality in any situation, through what Halpern terms "social bonding." In the final paper, David Krackhardt (chapter 10) takes on the issue of how stable preferences really are, suggesting that what appears rational to an actor at one moment does not necessarily appear so later. Such shifting preferences are hypothesized to be a function of individuals' connectedness in social networks. Not only does Krackhardt question a critical assumption of economic models, but he hypothesizes a mechanism through which the shift occurs, and predicts changes in what will be seen as rational.

THEORETICAL DISPUTES

Prescriptive Models in Organizational Decision Making

Zur Shapira

Research on decision making has gone through several periods where the status of rationality has been debated. Since the publication of Von Neumann and Morgenstern's (1944) seminal work, the concept of maximizing expected utility became synonymous with rationality. Simon (1947), however, pointed out the inconsistency between the assumptions of modern utility theory and the actual behavior of individual decision makers. Simon's notions of satisficing and bounded rationality led to the development of the behavioral theory of the firm, which has had some impact on economics, primarily on institutional economics (Nelson and Winter 1982; Williamson 1975b). Save attempts by a few economists to elaborate on Simon's ideas regarding individual decision making (cf. Radner 1975) most economists preferred the mathematical elegance of Von Neumann and Morgenstern's formulation. Economists justified ignoring the empirical validity of their assumptions by pursuing the positive approach nicely described in Friedman's (1953) famous "as if" postulate, namely, assume that individuals behave as if they are utility maximizers and examine the testable hypotheses pertaining to aggregate market behavior.

Meanwhile, a review of the theory of decision making published by Edwards (1954) introduced psychologists to the literature on decision making in economics. A proliferation of psychological studies of decision making followed, culminating in a field now called behavioral decision theory. This body of research has been recently acknowledged by economists (cf. Arrow 1982a), primarily due to the work of Kahneman and Tversky (1979) on individual choice behavior.

Economists, philosophers and psychologists debate the nature of ultimate rationality, yet the question about the applicability of any notion of rationality to real-life decision making hinges on the degree to which decision makers find this question to be relevant.

In the following anecdote, an acquaintance of mine made sense of the world by using an approach that seemed rational to him. My acquaintance had four beautiful and talented daughters but wanted a baby boy. Over some casual conversation he noted that, since I was sort of a statistician, perhaps I could comment on his thinking. He was almost sure, he said, that since they had four daughters, their fifth would be a boy. He substantiated his argument with a reliance on the loosely defined "law of the chances." Responding with a bit of caution and recognizing that he was caught in the "gambler's fallacy," I said that I thought their chances of having a fifth beautiful and talented girl were higher, judging from their past success. I tried to base my argument on a simplified notion of the "law of large numbers," but my friend felt a little bit sorry for me and announced with a big smile that it was clear it would be a boy.

My friend indeed got a boy, and at the big party celebrating his son's birth, he commented to me, "I told you it was going to be a boy; you don't understand statistics."

This anecdote is a clear demonstration of the gambler's fallacy. It also illustrates the difference between the normative approach to decision making (e.g., Von Neumann and Morgenstern 1944) and the descriptive approach to decision making (March and Simon 1958 1993; Simon 1955; Kahneman and Tversky 1979). Initially, decision analysts thought that it would suffice to document people's biases, vis-a-vis the normative model, and point them out to decision makers. Once informed of the errors of their ways, decision makers would be able to correct their biases and follow the normative model. Unfortunately, such a remedial approach does not always succeed in eradicating departures from the normative rules of decision making. Some decision analysts made arguments for the development of a descriptive model of decision making. As Bell, Raiffa, and Tversky (1988) noted, however, in order to prescribe procedures and rules to decision makers, in the interest of improving organizational decision making, one needs to consider descriptive, normative and prescriptive aspects of decision making simultaneously.

The structure of this chapter reflects the same line of reasoning, and in its analysis of organizational decision making, deals with alternative notions of rationality, including a discussion of the notion of game rationality. The third section deals with rationality in context, and the final section discusses some potential prescriptions for organizational decision making. More than one form of rationality describes organizational decision making. Two distinct forms of rationality in organizational decision making can be described by the different time horizons they reflect: consequential choice, with its emphasis on future consequences; and rule following, which is focused on the past, on the interpretating organizations as dynamic systems whose "rationality" can be explicated in terms of traditions and rules.

Alternative Notions of Rationality

In their classical analysis of organizations, March and Simon (1958, 1993) argued that organizations should be viewed from a decision-making perspective. In subsequent writings, both suggested alternatives to the Von Neumann and Morgenstern (1944) notion of rationality. Simon's (1978) approach is a classical presentation of bounded rationality. March's (1978) is a classical exposition of the behavioral approach to rationality, consistent with the idea that decision making in organizations is described more by notions of attention and search than by calculation-based modes of choice.

Bounded Rationality

Simon's idea of satisficing (Simon 1955) constituted the first response to Von Neumann and Morgenstern's (1944) formulation of rationality as maximization. Simon's critique of the maximization principle was based on two issues. First, in order to maximize one has to have all the relevant information, and this usually is not the case. Second, people are limited in their ability to process information; hence, the chance that people would be able to maximize is rather small. Simon's (1955) framework of a behavioral model of rational choice is basically a search protocol. According to Simon's (1955) model, people select a subsample of the space of total relevant alternatives and search until they find a "good enough" alternative. Search is terminated when an alternative gets selected, and since the process does not continue to ensure the selection of the optimal alternative, it is defined as satisficing, which differs from maximizing.

In another paper, Simon (1978) emphasized the importance of the procedure of decision making rather than its outcomes. In a dynamic realistic decision situation, focusing on *substantive rationality* (defined as the degree to which appropriate choices are made) may be only partially relevant. In situations where there are constraints on the attention of decision makers, and where there are continuous changes in the membership of the subset of decision makers (i.e. situations that characterize organizational decision making), *procedural rationality* becomes more relevant. The more complex a situation becomes, the more people should be concerned with the procedural aspects of rationality

(Simon 1978, 8). Simon's approach emphasized the gap between a complex environment and the mind of a decision maker. According to Simon, this disparity could be dealt with only by mechanisms that are based on the nature (and limitations) of the human mind. Simon has long advocated the usefulness of artificial intelligence and computer simulations of human thinking processes. Of course, over-reliance on computers can pose problems in the question of how learning occurs in such situations. Indeed, the terms "intelligence" and "artificial" may be somewhat antagonistic. Yet, combining the capabilities of mind and machine might lead to better judgment and decision in certain situations.

It should be emphasized, though, that Simon's approach is not normative vis-à-vis the use of computers and expert systems. He (Simon 1987) clearly sought a system that would take advantage of both the mechanistic and human sides. Simon's (1987) discussion of the role of intuition left no doubt that these two resources are needed for improving decision making. Thus, the virtue of his discussion of procedural rationality is its attempt to examine the procedure rather than outcome. In so doing, he emphasized the role of attention as a scarce resource, and hence an important constraint on rational decision making.

Attention, Search, and Decision

In his discussion of complex decision situations, Simon noted that attention limitations and changes in the membership of the decision-making group make substantive rationality obscure. These ideas are reminiscent of March's notion of "organized anarchy" type decision situations and "garbage can processes" of organizational choice. As Cohen, March, and Olsen (1972) argued, organizational choice under conditions of ambiguity may resemble the organized anarchy type of decision making when the following properties apply:

1. *Problematic preferences.* This property characterizes a situation in which there is no coherent and consistent set of preferences and the organization seems to discover its preferences by action more than acting on the basis of stated preferences.
2. *Unclear technology.* This property implies that although organizations manage to survive and produce, members of the organization do not understand its processes and thus it operates on the basis of trial and error, based upon learning from accidents of past experience, and ad hoc inventions.
3. *Fluid participation.* This property signifies that participation and involvement vary among members and change along time. Therefore, the decision makers for different choices change, and the boundaries of the organization are uncertain and changing.

This framework was used to analyze decision-making processes in not-for-profit organizations, such as decisions in the domain of national security (Lanir and Shapira 1984).

In yet another celebrated analysis of bounded rationality, March (1978) suggested that rational choice consists of two guesses: guesses about the future consequences of current action, and choices and guesses about future preferences for these consequences. In the terminology of utility theory, the first guess pertains to probability and the second to the utility of outcomes. March (1978) proposed variants on the classical notion of calculative rationality. In addition to the notion of bounded rationality (Barnard 1938; Simon 1955), he suggested alternatives such as *limited rationality*, which describes the features of a process where decision makers try to simplify a decision problem because of problems associated with considering or anticipating all the alternatives and all the needed information. *Contextual rationality* highlights the effects of a social context where there are multiple other claims on decision makers' attention. *Game rationality* highlights the degree to which self interests and calculation guide the behavior of a decision maker, while *process rationality* is the extent to which decision makers focus on the process of making choices, rather than on the decision outcomes.

These notions were all variants on the idea of calculated rationality. March (1978) added three other notions of rationality: adaptive, selective, and posterior. The first, *adaptive rationality*, emphasizes the experiential learning of individuals or organizations and the way experience affects learning. *Selected rationality* refers to the process of selection through survival or growth, while *posterior rationality* refers to the discovery of intentions after actions have been taken. In more recent writings March (1994) distinguishes between two modes of choice in organizational decisions. The first is *consequential choice*, which highlights the consideration of alternatives in a calculated manner. The other mode is based on *rule following* and is akin to the last three notions of rationality mentioned above.

An important part of March's (1978) analysis is the treatment of tastes. Simon (1978) noted in passing that Stigler and Becker's (1977) notion of stability in taste may lead to an awkward definition of a commodity such as "music appreciation" (which is an investment in the capacity to appreciate music). Simon did not refer, however, to the essence of Stigler and Becker's (1977) argument regarding rationality in time preference. This approach was presented in its extreme form by Becker and Murphy (1990) in their rational theory of addiction. According to their approach, rational addiction is demonstrated when, in the aggregate, demand responds to changes in price. Thus, Becker, Grossman, and Murphy (1992) were able to show that consumption of goods such as alcohol went down when prices of alcoholic beverages went up. Rational addiction may be likened to increased consumption of a certain good along time, but with enough "elasticity" so that consumption responds to changes in price.

In contrast to the above approach, March (1978) noted that the second type of guess, that is, the guess about future preferences, may be rather ambiguous. Classical choice theory assumes that tastes are absolute, relevant, stable, consistent, precise and exogenous, with respect to the particular problem of choice. On the other hand, March (1978, 110) argued that we often manage our preferences, we construct them, treat them strategically, confound them, change them, expect them, and suppress them. The picture that emerges from March's (1978) analysis suggests two choice methods: *consequential* choice, where tastes are somewhat stable and endogenous, and *rule based choice*, where tastes are reconstructed and discovered through action.

Game Rationality and Organizational Decision Making

One should not interpret the gambler's fallacy example above to mean that people generally behave in a non-rational manner. The example suggests that people occasionally use heuristics inappropriately in judging probabilities (e.g., Tversky and Kahneman 1974). However, decision making in organizational settings can be examined by the degree to which procedural rationality (Simon 1978), contextual or process rationality (March 1978), or other forms of rationality are satisfied.

One of the many forms of rationality that March (1978) addressed is *game rationality*. Game theory has been advocated recently as the relevant form of rationality. This triggered a response from behavioral decision theorists, and among others, Bazerman, Gibbons, Thompson and Valley (this volume) attempt to show how negotiators, in experimental settings, do better than what game theory predicts. In particular, Bazerman et al. (this volume) argue that the behavioral literature on negotiation demonstrates that two assumptions of game theoretic approaches, namely self-interest and rationality, are not accurate.

Bazerman et al. (this volume) provide evidence about the "Acquiring a Company" problem in which one firm may offer to buy another. The problem, originally based on Akerloff's (1970) analysis of the "market for lemons," may lead to a demonstration of the "winner's curse." The situation is one of asymmetric information. The seller knows the exact value of the firm (for sale) while the buyer, in the absence of any additional information, assumes that all values are equally likely. If the potential buyer knows that the value of the firm he/she considers acquiring under current management is between $0 and $100, he/she is assumed to be willing to offer to pay the expected value of $50. An additional complication is that the buyer believes that under his/her management the acquired firm will be worth 1.5 times its current value. Thus, offers in the $50 to $75 range often are generated in experimental settings. The authors interpret these offers as suggesting that the ill-informed buyers have fallen victim to the winner's curse (Bazerman et al. this volume). The authors argue that a "social" form of this problem will eliminate the winner's curse if buyers and sellers "simply talk to each other." The authors claim that, in this way, one-sided private information negotiations outperform game theory predictions.

The moral of the above story is that when information is shared in negotiations one can expect more cooperative solutions that may prevent unfortunate outcomes such as the winner's curse and other biases. Indeed, in a series of experiments, Siegel and Fouraker (1960) demonstrated that the more information subjects shared, the more likely they were to reach an agreement, to the benefit of both parties.

Does the behavior in the social version of the "Acquiring a Company" problem demonstrate that people "outperform" game theory? The answer is not clear. First, non-cooperative game theory is clearly an adversarial way of conducting business. Game rationality focuses on situations of asymmetric information, when information is not shared. Thus, the experiments suggest that if information is shared the winner's curse is less likely to happen. In a sense it brings an option from the domain of "cooperative games" into the realm of non-cooperative games.

Second, can one generalize from these experiments to real-life situations? Clearly, the winner's curse is a phenomenon that still can be observed in situations of competitive bidding (Capen, Clapp, and Campbell 1971; Thaler 1988b). Situations of competitive bidding, such as auctions, are still used as ways of allocating scarce resources in several domains. It is very likely that collaborative effort may outperform individual game rationality in certain situations, but the general picture is more complex and may not warrant the dismissal of game theory as an approach for strategy in competitive decision situations.

Third, the requirements of the formal approach of game theory are indeed awesome. Perhaps they fit Simon's (1978) definition of the "omniscient economist" whose capabilities allow him/her to pursue Von Neumann and Morgenstern's (1944) framework. Yet in some recent work in game theory the rationality assumptions of the traditional game-theoretic approach are relaxed. Economists Dixit and Nalebuff (1991) analyze different phenomena in business strategy from a game-theoretic perspective. The frequent-flyer miles wars between the airlines are an example of a game where each party tries to anticipate its rival's moves. Would cooperation and information sharing lead to great profits for the airlines? Most likely yes, but these also would be met by allegations of anti-trust violations by the Justice Department. Dixit and Nalebuff's (1991) approach was based on

Von Neumann and Morgenstern's (1944) theory, but the practical message they are promoting is about strategic thinking about your rivals' moves. At times this may not necessarily imply a quantitative assessment of probability distributions; indeed, many times such analysis is not even possible. Such an approach was also advanced in Brams's (1993) new approach to political decision making, which he labeled the "Theory of Moves." In this theory, Brams (1993) advances the notion of dynamic games, that is, his theory assumes that actors can think about their moves, their opponents' countermoves, and their own counter-countermoves. Again, the theory does not require making quantitative calculations of probabilities but focuses on decomposing actions into discrete moves with clear outcomes.

The above discussion suggests that game theory may prove useful in situations that can be described as adversarial. These approaches do not assume that actors are capable of calculating complicated probability distributions. They do assume, however, that actors can think ahead, as most people do when they play the game of chess. Game theory may be a relevant approach to understanding rationality in specific contexts. Research needs to consider the applicability of game theory as an approach to studying rationality. For example (Bazerman et al. this volume), when the requirements are relaxed, game theory may prove to be a useful framework for strategic thinking.

The Assumption of Self-Interest in Decision Making

Most analyses of rationality in the game theoretic sense assume that parties' behavior can be subsumed to reflect self-interest. Bazerman et al. (this volume) raised the question of self-interest as a major assumption of game theoretic approaches, and argued that consideration of fairness on the one hand, and the norm of reciprocity on the other, nullify this assumption. They have further suggested a social utility function that incorporates elements of both utility to the self and the differences between one's outcomes and those of others.

The self-interest assumption is an integral part of the notion of competition that underlies not only game theory but many areas of economics. Indeed, even Williamson's (this volume) transaction cost analysis emphasizes self-interest with guile, which leads to opportunism. Such an assumption has implications for contracting, which should be a delicate task given the belief of opportunism. Bazerman et al. (this volume) review evidence showing that at times people will not behave in opportunistic ways. Note that the social utility function does not propose that there is some utility derived from the total welfare of a collection of people. Rather, this function refers to one's own utility in the context of social comparison. Thus, it still falls within the realm of standard economic assumptions, rather than in the realm of altruism.

Clearly, the assumption of self-interest is central to organizational decision making. On the one hand, it can be argued that there are situations in organizations where a utility for the outcomes of a social entity exist; that is, there are situations where one can talk about collective utility that is not necessarily the individual's utility in comparison to others. Second, in pursuing the idea of self-interest, contracting arrangements become a major issue. Indeed, the central theme of agency theory (Jensen and Meckling 1976) is the reconciliation of differential self-interests, albeit coupled with varying degrees of risk preferences. As will be argued later, the role of trust is of major importance in any form of organizational contracting.

Rationality in Context; Cognitive and Organizational Aspects

Rationality and self-interest were discussed in the previous section from a game-theoretic perspective. We now look at decision making from the contextual rationality perspective, following March's (1978) suggestion. The organizational context is a social context that is very salient in the way it affects decision making. Both the cognitive and the motivational aspects of rational choice may take on added meaning in the context of organizational decision making. Therefore, we shall discuss some cognitive aspects of choice, and then some motivational aspects of decision making in organizations.

Some Cognitive Aspects of Rational Choice

The "Acquiring a Company" problem again may serve as a good anchor, this time to examine the cognitive aspects of rational choice. Two cognitive considerations come into play. First, the decision maker involved in the transaction may consider the transaction to be part of a repeated choice situation; he or she may expect to make similar choices in the future. Second, the decision maker may anticipate future interaction with the same (other) party.

Single vs. Repeated Choices

From the normative perspective, the appropriateness of statistical principles as decision-making aids depends on whether choice is repeated. The usefulness of statistical measures to a single choice is less clear than in cases of repeated choice.

The "Acquiring a Company" simulation assumes that the buyer accepts for granted that "the firm's value under current management is *between* $0 and $100 with all *values* equally likely, the target *knows* its current worth *exactly*" (Bazerman et al., this volume, italics added). While an experimenter may direct the cognitions held by the buyer in this way, it may be presumptuous to think that real negotiators hold these assumptions. Clearly, even Akerloff's (1970) original analysis pointed out that sellers don't know the value of their used car *exactly*. They may know the particular problems that their car has, but may not be able to transform this knowledge into an *exact* value. Furthermore, instructions to the buyer that all values between $0 and $100 are "equally likely" as the "Acquiring Company" scenario states, may not properly represent the way decision makers in realistic situations perceive this information (this may be true also for the 50 percent value improvement under new management). Rather, in such settings decision makers may disregard the "normative" information given to them and focus on the idiosyncrasies of the situation as they perceive them and their own expertise. Evidence for the latter form of cognizing has been documented in Shapira's (1995) study of managerial perspectives on risk taking. In that study it was clear that managers tend to view risk taking as a longitudinal process wherein they can remedy the outcomes of bad choices. It is possible that if told that the value of the firm under the new management would be 50 percent higher, managers would feel that the value would increase even further under their own, idiosyncratic management. The statistical evidence that 95 percent of new small business ventures fail is commonly known (U.S. Small Business Administration 1991), but that information does not necessarily deter new entrepreneurs from going into the business.

The rationale that Bazerman et al. (this volume) provide for failure in the "Acquiring a Company" problem, namely, that subjects do not analyze the situation correctly and presumably calculate an expected value ($50) and add to it a 50 percent improvement factor, is reminiscent of Tversky and Kahneman's (1971) original study, where large sample statistics were erroneously applied to small samples.

Anticipation of Future Interactions

In their discussion of social heuristics, Bazerman et al. (this volume) noted that the assumption of future interaction leads to predictions of cooperative behavior. They cite research by Axelrod (1984) on the prisoner dilemma, and research on interaction and impression formation, and on tipping behavior. These results seem to be consistent across different tasks. It would be interesting to observe behavior in situations where there is an assumption of *no* future interaction. Game theory predicts that behavior will move away from cooperation when there is no expectation of future interaction. Experimental evidence shows that subjects move away from cooperation when it is announced that there is one more negotiation trial in a "prisoner's dilemma" type situation, though the move may not be as extreme as predicted by game theory (Murnighan 1991).

One possible explanation for behavior when future interaction is anticipated is the notion of fairness, yet future interaction and reputation are also good candidates for explaining such behavior. Even in situations where there is apparently no likelihood of future interaction, however, cooperation may still exist, as noted in Uzzi's (1994) study of inter-firm relations in the garment industry. It might be interesting to examine whether people really believe that there are situations with absolutely no chance of future interaction.

A related issue is the failure of game theory to predict behavior in ultimatum-type situations (see Bazerman et al., this volume). One can ask whether people believe in ultimatums in real-life situations, as opposed to controlled experimental settings. Many interpersonal conflicts can be modeled as some form of a game (Dixit and Nalebuff 1991). One salient issue in crafting a strategy to win a conflict is that of making credible threats. Unlike the situation in the prototypical case of the "game of chicken" (Murnighan 1991) where a driver eliminates the possibility of turning away at the last moment by throwing away her steering wheel, there are often questions as to when threats made in real-life conflicts are credible. In considering available statistics on conflicts in labor relations and political conflicts one may develop a belief that ultimatums are not actually enforceable. Scores of current international political conflicts demonstrate that deadlines are often extended and ultimatums are not enforced.

Anticipating a future interaction is not similar to but may be related to such phenomena. Interpretation of the above patterns conceivably may lead one to believe that conflicts and relationships do, in a sense, never end. If this is the case the old biblical statement: "Cast thy bread upon waters, for thou shalt find it after many days" (Ecclesiastes 11:1), may describe why people often select cooperative modes of rational choice.

The Organizational Context

There are some characteristics of organizational decision making that distinguish it from individual decision making (Shapira 1997).

First, unlike most studies of individual decision making, organizations often have only *ambiguous information* and ambiguous and unclear preferences. In contrast, most experimental studies of individual decision making present the subject with clear information in the form of probability distribution and often with monetary payoffs that "direct" the subject's preferences.

Second, decision making in and by organizations is embedded in a *longitudinal* context. That is, participants in organizational decision making are a part of ongoing processes. Even if they do not take on active roles in all phases of a decision, they are a part of the decision process and its consequences. In contrast, most studies of individual decision making are conducted in artificial settings (i.e., laboratory experiments) that are not connected to the subjects' real, ongoing activities.

Third, *incentives* play an important role in organizational decision making. Incentives, penalties, and their ramifications are real and may have long-lasting effects. These effects are even more pronounced due to the longitudinal nature of decisions in organization settings. In contrast, incentives used in experimental studies of individual choice behavior are meager and have no potential for lingering effects.

Fourth, many executives, especially in the middle levels of management may make *repeated* decisions on similar issues. Consider, for example, a loan officer who reviews requests for consumer house loans. Such a manager may develop a sense of using his or her *skills* (which may be faulty) and a sense of having *control* of the situation (which also may be faulty). Beliefs of having control and using one's skills are pervasive in managerial thinking about risk taking (Shapira 1995). It should also be noted that decisions on new loans are often made according to rule following rather than by employing pure information-processing modes (March 1994).

Fifth, *conflict* is pervasive in organizational decision making. Many times, power considerations and agenda setting, rather than calculations based on decision parameters, determine actual decisions.

Kahneman and Lovallo's (1993) study of forecasting and choice, March's (1994) analysis of decision making, Shapira's (1995) study of managerial risk taking, Staw's studies of escalation of commitments (Staw and Ross 1989) and Starbuck and Milliken's (1988) analysis of the Challenger disaster presented research illustrating some of the above characteristics.

Incentives, Conflict, Contracts, and Organizational Culture. The premises of the economic approach to the theory of the firm are:

1. Agents behave according to their self-interest.
2. Agents and principals differ in their risk preferences.
3. Agents and principals have asymmetric information.

The consequences of these assumptions have been developed in Williamson's (1975b) transaction cost theory and in agency theory (Jensen and Meckling 1976). The inevitable outcome of asymmetry in information, motivation and risk preferences is the drafting of contracts to minimize potential conflict between the different parties.

The problem with a contracting approach to understanding organizational decision-making is that economic contracting appears to be too narrow to account for decisions that are made. Furthermore, economists and lawyers acknowledge that the major problem of contracts is their incompleteness, due to human inability to foresee and anticipate all contingencies (Schwartz 1992). Economists have come to realize that contractual arrangements may be limited in the degree to which they can lead to investment in research and development (Arrow 1982b), defend proprietary knowledge (Winter 1987) or even solve ongoing problems between parties engaged in continuing economic agreements (Klein 1992). Thus, MacNeil (1985) proposed the notion that interpretation of contracts is an evolving process, an idea that was embraced by many organization theorists (see McLean Parks, this volume).

There is an emergent trend in economics that views the incompleteness of contracts as given. Researchers are proposing a variety of solutions to solve problems that eventually develop. Klein (1992), for example, suggests that firms attempt to minimize the probability of "hold-ups." He notes that several mechanisms, such as termination or non-renewal of contracts on the one hand, and reliance on market reputation on the other, may lead to a "self enforcement" mode. Such a mode, he argues, is a more efficient means of conflict resolution than the "court enforced" mode.

Klein demonstrated that "hold-ups" can never be completely eliminated. In his analysis of the conflict between General Motors and Fisher Body Corporation, Klein (1992) showed that even with a well-specified contract between the two parties, "hold-ups" were not eliminated. He analyzes the "hold-up" as a probabilistic possibility and rejects the notion that completely specified contracts can be written. Klein (1992, 151) does not think that self-interest or foolish preferences explain the "hold-up" "it is much too unlikely an explanation for the 'hold up' to rely on General Motors' naiveté or stupidity or on Fisher's guile . . . with ignorance and deception we can explain everything—and, therefore, nothing."

Organization theorists and perhaps some economists would like to introduce the term "trust" as a concept on which contracts may survive or break down. Trust is related to organizational culture when internal contracting is involved. Could one reduce the notion of what is conveyed by trust to a written contract that eliminates the need for trust? Perhaps this is the intent of the economic analysis of corporate culture (Kreps 1990). The alternative organizational view suggests that trust and organizational culture are embedded in norms and rules that cannot be easily formulated in contractual terms.

Organization Decision Making as Rule Following

In a recent book, March (1994) proposed that there are certain logics according to which decisions are made in organizations: Consequential choice is akin to the idea of limited rationality, or the general class of rationalities that can be grouped under the label "calculated rationality."

March (1994) suggests that rule following is based on the logic of *appropriateness*. According to this logic, decision makers deal with three issues:

1. Recognition, or, what type of a situation is this one?
2. Identity, or, what type of a person am I or what is the type of this organization?
3. Rules, or, what does a person or an organization (defined in question 2) do in this type of a situation (defined in question 1)?

According to the logic of appropriateness the process of organizational choice is systematic, consistent, and not trivial. It differs from rules of consequential choice by virtue of matching established rules to different situations, rather than by making explicit calculations. In his discussion of rules, identities, and actions, March (1994) deals with the issues of rule development and change, using the logic of appropriateness. He notes that the logic of consequential choice is based on the abilities of individuals and organizations to anticipate the future and establish a set of preferences to deal with future outcomes. The logic of appropriateness, on the other hand, depends on the abilities of individuals and organizations to learn from the past and establish useful identities. Both logics are forms of human reasoning and can be conceived as "rational" ways of pursuing human and organizational action.

March's (1994) analysis adds another layer to the discussion. According to his view, some see the two logics as complementary and others as contending. This might put the discussion of the term and role of trust in a wider perspective. Those who go by the logic of consequential choice will try to anticipate the future and, hence, define trust in a written contract. Those who believe in the logic of appropriateness will most likely continue relations with firms with whom they had successful interactions in the past. For them, trust would be a result of a fruitful collaboration in the past and, applying an appropriate "rule," they would most likely continue that relation into the future.

On Prescribing Rational Procedures for Organizational Decision Making

Simon's (1947) analysis of bounded rationality treated individual and organizational decision making similarly. The development of behavioral decision theory over the last twenty-five years, however, has focused more on the individual level of analysis. Recent attempts have been made to link the two and over the last decade relationships between these two levels of analysis have been explored (March and Shapira 1982, 1987, 1992; Kahneman and Lovallo 1993; Shapira 1997). As Bazerman et al. (this volume) noted, during the last decade the behavioral literature on negotiation and game theory literature on bargaining developed in parallel, and recently there seems to be more awareness of the potential interrelations between these two fields.

The purpose of this chapter is to develop the idea that there is more than one way to prescribe rational procedures for organizational decision making. The most salient "rational" protocol had been the expected utility principle, which has met with both negative and positive feedback. As Tversky and Kahneman (1986) noted, expected utility may be a good decision protocol under "transparent" conditions, but it may not work well under "opaque" scenarios where other models such as prospect theory may fare better.

Defining "nonrational" elements in organizational decision making depends therefore, in part, on the perspective held by the decision maker. For those who believe in expected utility there have been both confirming and disconfirming experiences. For the proponents of game theory there have also been instances of support, and others where the theory did less well (see Bazerman et al., this volume). It should also be noted that for those who advocate the market mechanism as an ultimate selection device among alternative decision protocols, the evidence shows that despite many efforts by decision engineers, managers did not embrace the expected utility paradigm as their preferred procedure. Since decision makers are not always willing to use a "rational" normative approach to decision making, researchers should also look at descriptive models of choice before coming up with a better prescriptive paradigm (Bell, Raiffa and Tversky 1988).

The picture that emerges from the literature reviewed in this chapter suggests that the question of what nonrational elements are in organizational decision making may not be easy to answer. Rationality in organizational decision making has many aspects such as game rationality, procedural rationality, posterior rationality and the like (cf. March 1978). What characterizes organizational decision making most likely is a mixture of different forms of rationality. Thus, in taking risks managers acknowledge the normative analysis of risk, but do not necessarily follow its canons (Shapira 1995). And, while on many occasions the economic principle of marginal analysis is pursued, at other times the sunk cost fallacy may lead to the escalation of commitment (Staw and Ross 1989), where the notion of consistency outweighs considerations of marginal analysis. These dual aspects of decision making exemplify March's (1994) two modes, the logic of consequential choice and the logic of appropriateness. The former depicts the anticipation of the future, and the latter refers to the interpretation of the past. These two aspects should both be considered for a sound prescriptive approach to organizational decision making.

Game Theory and Garbage Cans:
An Introduction to the Economics
of Internal Organization

Robert Gibbons

For two hundred years, the basic economic model of a firm was a black box: labor and physical inputs went in one end; output came out the other, at minimum cost and maximum profit. Most economists paid little attention to the internal structure and functioning of firms or other organizations.

During the 1980s, the black box began to be opened: economists (especially those in business schools) began to study the roles of information and incentives inside firms, often concluding that rational, self-interested organization members might well produce inefficient, informal, and institutionalized organizational behaviors. This conclusion differed from the implicit theory of organization seemingly underlying black-box economics[1], but was far from new to non-economist students of organizations—anthropologists, organization theorists, social psychologists, and sociologists had observed and analyzed such organizational behaviors for decades.

I am grateful to Bill Barnett, Steve Barley, Jim Baron, Mike Hannan, Ed Lazear, Joel Podolny, and seminar participants at Berkeley and Asilomar for helpful comments and to Cornell's Johnson School and the Center for Advanced Study in the Behavioral Sciences for financial support (the latter through a Fellowship funded in part by NSF grant SBR-9022192).
[1] In keeping with the lack of attention paid to the subject, I have been unable to find a description in the economics literature of the internal structure and functioning of black-box firms. Ironically, one seemingly apt description comes not from economics but from Merton's (1940, 561) characterization of Weberian bureaucracy in terms of "precision, speed, expert control, continuity, discretion, and optimal returns on input."

In this essay I introduce to non-economist students of organizations the five main theoretical ideas economists now use to analyze internal organization: incomplete contracts, agency theory, specific investments, strategic information transmission, and repeated games. To illustrate these ideas, I give fleeting descriptions of recent economic models of internal organization. These models also demonstrate economists' new interest in inefficient, informal, and institutionalized organizational behaviors.

Incomplete contracts appear in every model discussed below, because (as suggested by Coase 1937) there would be no need for an organization if it were costless to enforce a contract specifying all outcomes of interest as a function of all variables of interest. To illustrate the remaining four theoretical ideas, I discuss economic models of (1) pay for performance (to illustrate agency theory), (2) promotion decisions (to illustrate specific investments), (3) communication and decision making (to illustrate strategic information transmission), and (4) corporate culture and implicit contracts (to illustrate repeated games).

Economic models of the first three of these organizational issues—pay for performance, promotion decisions, and communication and decision making—provide examples of inefficient organizational behaviors, such as distortionary performance measures, up-or-out rules, and influence costs.[2] Economic models of corporate culture and implicit contracts provide examples of informal organizational behaviors. To provide examples of institutionalized organizational behaviors, I discuss a fifth class of economic models in which "herd behavior" emerges from the rational choices of individual decision makers.

All of these recent economic models are significant departures from the implicit theory of organization seemingly underlying black-box economics. To try to bridge the gap, I begin with a brief and selective history of the economics of internal organization.

Some History

Nineteen seventy-two saw two landmark publications in economics: Arrow and Hahn's *General Competitive Analysis* and Marschak and Radner's *Economic*

---

[2] In this paper, I use "inefficient" in a visceral, colloquial sense. Roughly speaking, I call a state of affairs "inefficient" if it is less than we would like it to be, even if it is also as good as we can make it. In the terminology of economics, the former is "first-best," the latter "second-best." The models described below produce second-best outcomes that depart from the first-best outcome in ways that seem to match decades of research on real organizations.

This distinction between first- and second-best (between ideal and best possible) could be used to defend black-box economics: one could argue that the production functions in the models through the 1960s and 1970s described best-possible rather than ideal practice. This is a coherent argument (indeed, production functions *should* represent best-possible rather than ideal practice), but I think it misses the point. To give but one example, I suspect that few (if any) black-box economists envisioned a production process as inefficient as the one Roy (1952) describes.

Theory of Teams. Both books began with elegant summaries of existing work and then progressed to the authors' new results.

Arrow and Hahn summarized two centuries of progress on the single largest research agenda in the history of economics. The central question had been posed by Adam Smith: Could the relentless pursuit of self-interest by hordes of tiny firms and consumers yield anything but chaos? Shockingly, the answer was that (under certain assumptions, including symmetric information, complete contracting, and perfect competition—all of which will be abandoned below) not only would there be an equilibrium rather than chaos, but it would be impossible to rearrange the allocation of resources in such an equilibrium to make all participants better off.

Marschak and Radner, in contrast, took a relatively new subject—the axiomatic single-person decision theory of von Neumann and Morgenstern (1944) and Savage (1954)—and applied it to a brand new area of economics. Before Marschak and Radner, the economics literature contained extremely little formal modeling of the internal organization and operation of firms. (In particular, the firms that appeared in the general-equilibrium models summarized and advanced by Arrow and Hahn were black boxes, as described above.) Marschak and Radner applied decision theory in "team" settings, where different agents have different information and control different actions but all agents share a common goal (such as maximization of the firm's profit).

Ironically, 1972 also saw the publication of the antithesis of team theory: "A Garbage Can Model of Organizational Choice," by Cohen, March, and Olsen. Whereas team theory envisions an organization whose members compute and execute optimal communication rules to achieve efficient decisions, a garbage can is "organized anarchy." Garbage cans are "collections of choices looking for problems, issues and feelings looking for decision situations in which they might be aired, solutions looking for issues to which they might be the answer, and decision makers looking for work" (1). For purposes of this brief and selective history, the crucial lesson from the garbage-can model (and from many of March's other contributions) is that it is often not useful to think of an organization as a single, unified, rational decision maker—as general-equilibrium models did for two hundred years, and as team theory continued to do.[3] Put more colorfully, *many organizations look more like garbage cans than like teams* (but note well the enormous middle ground between these polar extremes).

[3] As but one example of another of March's contributions along these lines, consider "Information in Organizations as Signal and Symbol" by Feldman and March (1981). I read this paper as a critique of team theory, *not* of economics in its entirety. Most of the organizational behaviors Feldman and March catalogue are inconsistent with formal theories of rational choice by *single* individuals—and so are inconsistent with viewing the organization as a single, unified, rational decision maker—but are entirely consistent with (say) simple game-theoretic models of signaling or free-riding.

Three developments allowed economic models to move away from team theory, toward garbage cans. First, the 1970s saw the growth of information economics, including Akerlof's (1970) and Rothschild and Stiglitz's (1976) analyses of adverse selection, Spence's (1973) paper on signaling, and Holmstrom's (1979) work on agency theory. Second, the 1980s brought new modeling approaches and equilibrium concepts in game theory, including Kreps, Milgrom, Roberts, and Wilson's (1982) model of reputation, Myerson's (1979) statement of the revelation principle, and Fudenberg and Maskin's (1986) articulation of the "folk theorem" for repeated games. Third, to return to the theme of landmark books, in 1975 Williamson published *Markets and Hierarchies*, launching the field of transaction-cost economics.

I imagine that the typical non-economist reader of this paper has had some exposure to information economics and game theory and perhaps somewhat more to transaction-cost economics. (I draw the latter inference from the many citations to Williamson's work in the organizations literature, but I am mindful that in 1972 Coase told economists that his 1937 paper had been "much cited and little used.") Indeed, some readers may wonder whether there is any difference between transaction-cost economics (TCE) and the economics of internal organization. To conclude this history, let me explain the difference I see.

Beginning with Coase (1937), TCE has emphasized inefficiencies that are separate from (and perhaps logically prior to) those discussed in this paper: the inefficiencies of the market in conducting certain transactions (from which it follows that an organization might be more efficient than the market at conducting such transactions), rather than the inefficiencies of the firm in its internal organization and operation. One of Williamson's (1975, 1985) important contributions to TCE was to elucidate the roles of specific investments and incomplete contracts in such subversions of market exchange. As a result, specific investments and incomplete contracts are two of the five main theoretical ideas underlying the economics of internal organization.

Another of Williamson's important contributions to TCE was to compare alternative governance structures, including ownership (e.g., vertical integration), imperfect contracts (i.e., short-run arrangements such as "hostages"), and relational contracting (i.e., long-run "implicit contracts" between non-integrated parties, as described below). In my opinion, TCE has explored these alternative governance structures more thoroughly between firms rather than within them. What distinguishes recent work in the economics of internal organization from TCE, therefore, is partly a difference in methodology (through the addition of agency theory, strategic information transmission, and repeated games to the modeler's tool kit) but more importantly a difference in focus: where transaction-cost economics has been more concerned with the boundaries of the firm than with its guts, the economics of internal organization reverses the emphasis.

Recent Models

This section offers fleeting descriptions of recent economic models of five organizational issues: pay for performance, promotion decisions, communication and decision making, corporate culture and implicit contracts, and herd behavior. As explained above, I chose these organizational issues for two reasons. First, they illustrate the five main theoretical ideas underlying the economics of internal organization: incomplete contracts, agency theory, specific investments, strategic information transmission, and repeated games. Second, they suggest rational-choice interpretations of three important ways that non-economist students of organizations often suggest that real organizations depart from economic models: inefficient, informal, and institutional organizational behaviors.

Agency Theory

In my view, the enormous literature on agency theory (now two decades in the making) should be construed as an attempt to progress beyond the adage, "You get what you pay for." That is, agency theory should address questions such as *what* should be paid for (i.e., what performance measures should be used) and *how* (e.g., whether there should be objective or subjective weights on these performance measures). From this perspective, Kerr's (1975) classic article "On the Folly of Rewarding A, While Hoping for B" is clearly relevant.

Unfortunately, not one of the hundreds of papers on agency theory written in the 1980s could even express the insight of Kerr's title, not to mention evaluate or extend it. Indeed, I know of no evidence that the economists writing these papers knew that work like Kerr's existed in the organizational-behavior literature. Instead, the agency-theory literature explored sophisticated variations on profit-sharing, emphasizing the trade-off between incentives and insurance that results if an agent's pay is linked to the organization's profit but factors beyond the agent's control make profit uncertain.

Recent work, on the other hand, has been very much in Kerr's spirit. In particular, Holmstrom and Milgrom (1991) and Baker (1992) can be read as independently discovering problems Kerr labeled "overemphasis on highly visible behaviors" and "fascination with an 'objective' criterion" (779–80), respectively. More generally, many economists have realized that the basic agency model abstracts from important dimensions of performance evaluation that make pay-for-performance systems terribly problematic for many firms. See Gibbons (1997a) for further discussion of both the basic agency model and these recent developments.

As one of many infamous examples of problematic pay-for-performance schemes, consider the H. J. Heinz Company: division managers received bonuses only if earnings increased from the prior year; managers delivered consistent earnings growth by manipulating the timing of shipments to customers and by prepaying for services not yet received (Post and Goodpaster 1981); such actions greatly reduced the firm's future flexibility, but the compensation system in no way addressed this issue. In keeping with the experience at Heinz, many new models have abandoned assumptions from the basic agency model that implied that the agent cannot "game" the performance-evaluation system. Instead, one of the central assumptions in many new models is that it is impossible to enforce a contract that makes pay (or anything else) contingent on a worker's *total* contribution to firm value; that is, these are incomplete-contract models. The rationale for this assumption is as follows: there are many ways that workers can help (or hurt) each other at a given point in time, and many ways that short-run performance can be a misleading forecast of long-run performance; as a result, a worker's total, long-run contribution to firm value typically cannot be measured precisely, especially if such measurements must be taken by a neutral outsider (say, a court) in the event of a contract dispute.

Specific Investments

Much of the work on specific investments (largely from a transaction-cost perspective) considers physical assets. Firm-specific human capital, however, is a fundamental concept in labor economics (Becker 1964). While analyses of physical assets often yield prescriptions about asset ownership (e.g., Grossman and Hart 1986) and hence focus on the boundaries of the firm, analyzing specific human capital naturally takes one inside the firm.

There are many ways that workers could increase their productivity with their current employer—learning more about some idiosyncratic aspect of the firm's production, marketing, or governance, for example. Consider the subset of such investments that are inexpensive (in terms of foregone productivity while the worker is devoting time to learning): the firm would like workers to undertake these investments, and would like to promise to reward those who do so.

Like any investment, an investment in human capital is valued for its future effects—for the increases in future productivity it yields. But if it is difficult for a court to determine a worker's *actual* contribution to firm value (as just argued in the context of agency theory), it is even more difficult for a court to determine a worker's *expected future* contribution to firm value. Thus, we are back to incomplete contracts: recent economic models assume that it is impossible to enforce a contract specifying pay or promotions based on a worker's investments in firm-specific human capital.

We have now reached the following two-sided incentive problem: the worker is concerned that the firm cannot be trusted to reward an investment in specific human capital properly, but the firm is concerned that the worker will not invest unless such rewards are anticipated. Prendergast (1993a) analyzes whether a promotion rule might solve this problem; Kahn and Huberman (1988) consider an alternative rule, "up-or-out."

Prendergast considers a two-job ladder with wages attached to jobs, as in some internal labor markets. The idea is that a court could enforce a contract specifying the wage to be paid in each job, even if it could not enforce contracts contingent on specific human capital. Each worker's career with the firm consists of two periods. The worker begins in the low-wage job in the first period and then is either promoted to the high-wage job or kept in the low-wage job for the second period. During the first period, the worker can invest in firm-specific human capital. At the end of the first period, the firm observes the outcome of each worker's investment and then chooses which, if any, workers to promote.

The workers can rely on the firm to promote those workers who are more *profitable* for the firm when assigned to the high-wage job, but there is an important difference between being more profitable and being more productive. Promoting a worker who is slightly more productive in the high-wage job reduce profits if the difference in wages between the two jobs is sufficiently large. For example, if the two jobs in question are really just two job titles sharing the same underlying production technology, then Prendergast's promotion rule (i.e., promote those who are more profitable in the high-wage job) will not solve the two-sided incentive problem because the firm gets just as much productivity by keeping the worker in the low-wage job. Consequently, workers have no incentive to invest. On the other hand, if the value of the worker's specific capital in the two jobs is sufficiently different, then this promotion rule does solve the two-sided incentive problem because there exist wages for the two jobs that are sufficiently far apart that workers are willing to incur the cost of investment in order to earn a promotion, but sufficiently close together that the firm finds it profitable to promote a worker who invests in specific capital.

Kahn and Huberman (1988) study the first of these two environments in which Prendergast's promotion rule does not solve the two-sided incentive problem: the two jobs are just two job titles sharing the same underlying technology. They show, however, that an up-or-out rule may solve the two-sided incentive problem (but also that such a rule may entail other costs), as follows.

An up-or-out rule is a promotion contract specifying that after some fixed probationary period the firm must either pay a worker a high wage or fire the worker. Again, this contract could be enforced by a court, even if contracts contingent on specific human capital could not. Under an up-or-out contract, the firm finds it in its interest to retain those who have made themselves sufficiently valuable (i.e., more valuable than the high wage) but to fire those who have not. The workers understand that the firm will promote or fire workers in this way, and so have an incentive to invest if the high wage is high enough. For some parameter values, an up-or-out rule solves the two-sided incentive problem completely; for others, it makes partial progress (i.e., it induces partial but not fully efficient investments in specific human capital).

An up-or-out rule also may have big costs, even if it solves the two-sided incentive problem. Suppose, for example, that workers who make the appropriate investment could realize any one of several different levels of specific human capital, from very low to very high. If some of the low realizations make the worker worth less than the high wage attached to the promotion, then these workers will be fired. Firing these workers wastes their specific capital. This is inefficient treatment of these particular workers, but a necessary part of Kahn and Huberman's solution to the two-sided incentive problem. In their model, a firm must choose between the inefficiency of firing valuable workers and the inefficiency of foregoing valuable investments. Thus, Prendergast's promotion rule would be more efficient than an up-or-out rule, provided the former solves the two-sided incentive problem. Consistent with this argument, up-or-out rules are often observed in accounting and law partnerships and in academics, where junior and senior jobs are often not so hugely different that Prendergast's promotion rule would not work, but seem less common in firms containing widely different jobs in a promotion ladder.

Strategic Information Transmission

The classic model of strategic information transmission is Spence's (1973) analysis of education as a job-market signal. In the ensuing two decades, signaling models have become commonplace virtually throughout economics (especially in industrial organization, labor, and macroeconomics) and in related fields such as finance, marketing, and political science; M. Meyer (1979) and Feldman and March (1981) sketch applications of signaling to organizational behavior.

Although signaling models have received much attention in the economics literature, other aspects of strategic information transmission may be more important for understanding the structure and functioning of organizations. One closely related class of models analyzes "cheap talk" rather than costly signals. Roughly speaking, an uninformed player simply talks to an uniformed player; more precisely, the informed player sends a costless, non-binding, non-verifiable message. Cheap-talk models were first studied by Crawford and Sobel (1982) and have since been applied in labor economics, macroeconomics, and political science—see Gibbons (1992, 210–18) for illustrations and references.

The key lesson of these models is that cheap talk becomes more credible, and hence can be used to communicate more information, when the parties' interests become more closely aligned. If the parties' interests are completely opposed, for example, cheap talk cannot communicate anything, but if the parties' interests are perfectly aligned, cheap talk can be perfectly informative.

An interesting question for research on organizations is under what circumstances it pays an organization to distort its structure and/or internal functioning, from the perspective of productive efficiency, so as to align members' interests and improve cheap-talk communication. In this spirit, Farrell and Gibbons (1995) suggest that in some settings unionization can improve social welfare, in spite of the employment distortion created by the union's wage demands, because it facilitates communication from the workforce to management. Under unionization, workers know they will receive a share of the pie, and so have incentives to develop and reveal information that enlarges the total pie. In a competitive labor market, in contrast, workers have incentives to hide information, much as described by Roy (1952).

Milgrom and Roberts (1988) provided the first economic model of a third aspect of strategic information transmission in organizations: influence activities. These are attempts to manipulate information to influence decisions to one's own benefit, even when one has no private information to signal. As an example of influence activities, consider Holmstrom's (1982) model of career concerns in labor markets: workers know that firms will use workers' outputs to draw inferences about workers' abilities, and that these inferences will in turn determine subsequent wage offers, so workers have an incentive to work hard to influence the firms' inference, even if the workers have no private information about their abilities. In Holmstrom's model, the workers' influence activities (hard work) are productive, but in many organizational contexts influence activities either distract organization members from productive tasks or merely change the distribution of organizational resources across members, without improving overall productivity.

Milgrom and Roberts suggest two ways that an organization could respond to the prospect of wasteful influence activities. First, an organization could eliminate influence activities by eliminating opportunities for influence, that is, by closing the relevant communication channels. Naturally, such a response has its costs. Second, an organization may also be able to eliminate influence activities by adjusting its structure and/or internal functioning away from what would otherwise be optimal, to eliminate members' incentives to manipulate information. That is, by sufficiently distorting the organizational design, it might be possible to create a Marschak-Radner team, in which all members share a common goal. Of course, an organization could go part way down either or both of these two roads. For example, an organization could commit to limits on its discretion, perhaps by limiting the time given for debate, or by imposing other rules that partially constrain the organization's ability to respond to information provided by its members. In this case, decision makers will have the benefit of some information, but organization members will also engage in some wasteful influence activities.

Recall that Kerr first articulated issues later modeled by Holmstrom and Milgrom and by Baker. Similarly, Crozier (1964, 45) lucidly described an organization that went quite far down the first of the two roads Milgrom and Roberts later proposed, toward shutting down communication entirely. In Gibbons (1997b), I construct a simple model of Crozier's ideas and discuss the potential value of such formal modeling.

Reputation in Repeated Games

The new work in agency theory described above emphasizes that it is often extremely difficult to measure the agent's total contribution to the firm, particularly if such measurements must be made by a neutral outsider in the event of a contract dispute. Economists describe this difficulty by saying that the agent's contribution to firm value is not *objectively measurable*. Even if the agent's contribution to firm value is not objectively measurable, it sometimes can be *subjectively assessed* by superiors who are well placed to observe the subtleties of the agent's behavior and opportunities. Such subjective assessments of an agent's contribution to firm value may be imperfect, but nonetheless may complement or improve on the available objective performance measures.

Using models of repeated games, economists have begun to analyze *implicit contracts* (i.e., agreements enforced by trust and reputation, rather than by the courts). The advantage of implicit contracts is that they can be based on subjective assessments, whereas explicit contracts must be based only on objective measures, and must have prespecified weights attached to these objective measures. The disadvantage is that implicit contracts must avoid creating (net) incentives for the parties to renege; they must be self-enforcing.[4]

Kreps (1990) develops a simple but influential model along these lines, using a repeated game to discuss corporate culture. In each period of the repeated game, the firm's "trading partner" (e.g., a worker, a supplier, or a customer) must choose whether to "trust" the firm (e.g., make a specific investment). The firm then chooses either to honor or to betray this trust. If the payoffs and in-

---

[4] The term "implicit contract" may be somewhat misleading, but is now standard in economics. One of the key lessons of this literature is that implicit contracts work best when they are clear, not vague. That is, one may want "implicit contracts" to be explicit, even if they cannot be enforced by a court. Hence, a better name might be "mutual understandings," which can be very clear between the contracting parties and yet not be enforceable by any outsider.

terest rate are such that betraying trust maximizes current profit but honoring trust maximizes the present value of current and future profit, then there exists an equilibrium in which the trading partner offers trust and the firm honors it (but the trading partner would cease to offer trust if the firm ever betrayed it).

Kreps interprets this abstract model in terms of the unexpected events that make contracts incomplete and culture potentially useful. When unforeseen problems or opportunities arise, the firm's culture may help all parties decide how to respond. The culture may indicate whether this is an instance in which the firm is meant to take the long view rather than maximize short-run profit, and hence also whether this is an instance in which the trading partner ought to trust the firm. Kreps's model seems consistent with Blau and Scott's (1962, 6) discussion of informal organization: "decisions not anticipated by official regulations must frequently be made ... [and] unofficial norms are apt to develop that regulate performance and productivity."

Bull (1987) constructs a similar model to analyze subjective performance evaluation. In each period, the agent chooses how hard to work; working harder makes high output more likely. If the agent produces high output, the firm is supposed to pay a bonus. Unfortunately, only the firm and the agent can observe the agent's output, so the firm can renege on the promised bonus if it chooses. Since the agent's output is already in the bank, the firm decides whether to renege by weighing the current cost of the bonus against the future profit from a smooth relationship with the agent. Shocks to the value of this relationship may cause the firm to renege unexpectedly.

One memorable example of the cost of reneging on an implicit contract involved a spate of departures from First Boston after Archibald Cox, Jr., having paid below-average bonuses the previous year, promised but then did not deliver bonuses on a par with those paid at comparable Wall Street firms (*New Yorker*, July 26, 1993). A similar storm may be brewing at Lincoln Electric—the firm that has gone "farther than any other large manufacturer in matching compensation to each employee's productivity" (*New York Times*, September 5, 1994)—because the firm is trying to cut its legendary bonuses even though profits have recently been at record levels.

Baker, Gibbons, and Murphy (1994) combine Bull's analysis of subjective (but non-distortionary) bonuses with Baker's model of distortionary explicit contracts. Using implicit contracts can ameliorate the distortions caused by explicit contracts; using explicit contracts can reduce the size of the bonus promised in the implicit contract, hence reducing the firm's incentive to renege. Such an analysis of the interplay between explicit and implicit contracts is a first step toward Blau and Scott's (1962, 6) observation that "it is impossible to understand the nature of a formal organization without investigating the networks of informal relations and the unofficial norms as well as the formal hierarchy of authority and the official body of rules, since the formally instituted and the informal emerging patterns are inextricably intertwined."

In a companion paper, Baker, Gibbons, and Murphy (1997) study the interplay between (formal) asset ownership and (informal) implicit contracts. They consider an upstream party who works with an asset to produce an input to a downstream party's production process. As in Grossman and Hart, asset ownership is a response to incomplete contracts: the owner of the asset decides how it will be used, and in particular what will happen to its output. When the downstream party owns the asset, the upstream party is called an employee (someone who works with the firm's asset and does not own the asset's output). When the upstream party owns the asset, she is called an independent contractor (someone who owns her own tools and can sell her output to the downstream party).

Baker, Gibbons, and Murphy (1997) analyze how asset ownership affects the feasibility of implicit contracts. (The key point is that when the downstream party owns the asset, then upstream must trust downstream to pay a bonus for good performance, as in Bull's model, whereas when the upstream party owns the asset, then downstream must trust upstream not to hold up downstream by threatening to sell the asset's output elsewhere.) They relate their results to Williamson's (1975) comparison between markets and hierarchies and to other social structures and organizational forms such as Macauley (1963) on "noncontractual relations," Granovetter (1985) on embeddedness, Williamson (1985) on relational contracting, and Powell (1990) on networks.

Herd Behavior and Institutional Theory

The previous four sub-sections illustrate agency theory, specific investments, strategic information transmission, and repeated games. All also involve incomplete contracts, so I have now introduced the five main theoretical ideas underlying the economics of internal organization. Furthermore, organizational issues such as distortionary performance measurement, up-or-out rules, and influence costs illustrate inefficient organizational behaviors, and corporate culture and implicit contracts illustrate informal organizational behaviors. All that remains is to say something about institutionalism.

Unfortunately, institutional theory is the part of organizational studies I understand least well, in part because it has several strands and interpretations. For example, DiMaggio and Powell (1991) distinguish between "old institutionalism," typified by Selznick (1949), and "new institutionalism," dating from Meyer and Rowan (1977); within the latter, DiMaggio and Powell (1983) describe "coercive," "mimetic," and "normative" isomorphism. Furthermore, there is recent work in economic history, political science, and economic sociology that has a very different flavor—roughly, that "institutions" can be efficiency enhancing, rather than constraints that perpetuate inefficient "institutional-ized" behaviors.[5]

I think the models of herd behavior I describe below speak to mimetic iso-morphism. Before turning to specific models, however, let me make two broad points—one concerning old institutionalism, the other new.

DiMaggio and Powell (1991) characterize old institutionalism as "straightfor-wardly political, . . . [exploring] the 'shadowland of informal interaction' (Selznick 1949, 260) . . . to illustrate how the informal structures deviated from and constrained aspects of formal structure and to demonstrate the subversion of the organization's intended, rational mission by parochial interests" (1991, 12–13). To my delight, this summary of the old institutionalism parallels the spirit of recent work in the economics of internal organization. I hope that a few of the papers sketched above suggest some of this flavor, even though the papers were chosen for other expositional purposes. In Gibbons (1997b) I go further in this vein, characterizing the economics of internal organization as not only "be-tween teams and garbage cans" but focused on "power and politics."

Ironically, while power and politics are central to some recent and much prospective work in the economics of internal organization, they seem almost to have disappeared from organizational studies. My guess, however, is that power and politics have not become less important in organizational life, they have only gone out of fashion in organizational research. Happily, DiMaggio and Powell seem to agree: "Power and interests have been slighted topics in in-stitutional analysis" (1991, 30).

The second broad point concerns the new institutionalism. To me, this litera-ture often seems vehemently anti-rational-choice. In many instances I find this vehemence entirely appropriate. In a few places, however, the anti-rational-choice fervor of the new institutionalism seems at odds with the literature's emphasis on what seem to me to be straightforwardly rational choices by orga-nizations. Meyer and Rowan (1977), for example, argue that "by designing a formal structure that adheres to the prescriptions of myths in the institutional environment, an organization demonstrates that it is acting on collectively val-ued purposes in a proper and adequate manner" ([1977] 1991, 50). Why is this not rational behavior by the organization? Observations similar to Meyer and Rowan's appear in Meyer (1979) and in Feldman and March (1981), accompa-nied by references to Spence's signaling model—a cornerstone of rational-choice modeling. Powell (1991) puts my question succinctly: "If organizations are rewarded for compliance with external demands, how can we argue that

[5] For examples, see North and Weingast (1989) on the genesis and effects of Parliament in Eng-land and Grief, Milgrom, and Weingast (1994) for a similar analysis of merchant guilds in early modern Europe.

conformity is not based on calculating behavior of those who are seeking legitimacy?" (1991, 190). Surely the interesting question is why organizations are rewarded for compliance, not why they comply.

Having demonstrated (at length!) that institutional theory is the part of organizational studies I understand least well, I now return to the *terra firma* of economic modeling, specifically the models of herd behavior, and their connection to mimetic isomorphism.

Banerjee (1992) analyzes a model with a sequence of decision makers, each facing identical choices. The kth decision maker's payoff depends only on whether she makes the optimal choice, not on any aspect of the others' choices (such as how many of them make the optimal choice, or how many of them make the same choice as k). Unfortunately, each decision maker lacks full information about which choice is optimal; instead, she begins with noisy prior information (shared by all the decision makers) and her own private but noisy signal. The key idea is that each decision maker observes the choices of those earlier in the sequence and so supplements her initial information with inferences about the signals held by earlier decision makers. The resulting *optimal* decisions can exhibit herd behavior (i.e., doing what others are doing rather than following one's own information).

The following example (paraphrased from Banerjee 1992, 798) shows how extreme the herd behavior might be:

There are two restaurants, A and B, that are next to each other. A publicly available restaurant guide suggests that the prior probabilities are 51 percent for A being the better restaurant and 49 percent for B. One hundred people arrive at the restaurants in sequence, observe the choices made by the people before them, and decide on one or the other of the restaurants.

In addition to knowing the prior probabilities and observing the choices made by people before them, each of these people also has a private signal (say, from a friend who has been to the restaurants) which says either that A is better or that B is better. The signal could be wrong, but is of high enough accuracy to outweigh the restaurant guide. That is, based on the prior information from the guide (which slightly favors A) and a signal that says that B is better, a person should go to restaurant B. The key question, however, will be what a person should do given (i) the prior information, (ii) a private signal in favor of B, and (iii) overwhelming evidence that other people have chosen A.

Suppose that of the hundred people, ninety-nine have received signals that B is better but the one person whose signal favors A chooses first. Since the restaurant guide and her signal both favor A, the first person will go to A. The second person will now know that the first person had a signal that favored A (because a signal favoring B would have outweighed the slight prior advantage of A).

The second person's signal favors B, but suppose that each person's signal has the same accuracy, so a person in possession of two conflicting signals (one advising A and another B) would ignore these two signals—they would cancel out. Thus, the second person's signal favoring B and the first person's favoring A cancel out, so the second person chooses A on the basis of the restaurant guide.

Of course, the second person would have chosen A had her signal favored A (because then the guide and the first and the second signals favor A). Thus, the third person can draw no inference about the second person's signal. The third person's situation is therefore exactly the same as the second person's was: the third person has the restaurant guide and her own signal (favoring B), and can infer the first person's signal (favoring A), so she makes the same choice that the second person made (again contrary to her signal favoring B). Indeed, everyone chooses A, even though given the aggregate information it is practically certain that B is better.

Banerjee's model seems very much in the spirit of DiMaggio and Powell's mimetic isomorphism, which operates when "organizational technologies are poorly understood ... [and] goals are ambiguous" ([1983] 1991, 69). More generally, Banerjee's model (and others like it, see below) should give pause to those who argue, or assume, that natural selection will produce efficiency. If one interprets the restaurant story as firms choosing technologies, for example, and supposes that firms that earn below-average profit will be selected out, then no firms go bankrupt even though no firm chooses the efficient technology.

Prendergast (1993b) develops a similar model, in which a "yes man" has an incentive to conform to the opinion of his supervisor. Extending the model to a multi-worker setting produces "group think," where individuals have an incentive to conform to the opinion of the group. A slight variation on Prendergast's one-worker model [in the spirit of Scharfstein and Stein (1990)] runs as follows.

Suppose a manager needs information from a worker, perhaps about a new production technology or marketing opportunity, but does not know the worker's ability in gathering the information (where a worker with higher ability is one who can gather more precise information about the underlying parameter of interest). Suppose also that the worker cannot simply pass along to the manager all the information she collects; rather, the worker can report only a point estimate of the parameter of interest. Will the worker report honestly (i.e., will she report the conditional expectation of the parameter based on all the information she has gathered) or will she bias her report toward what she thinks the manager expects to hear? If the worker's future wages depend on the manager's assessment of her ability, as seems sensible and follows from several models of the labor market, then the worker will bias her report, because the manager's assessment of the worker's ability is more favorable when her report is not wildly at odds with what the manager expects to hear. Roughly speaking, an outlandish report could be truth-telling by a very able worker, but is more likely to be the result of low ability.

Now suppose there are two workers. The same ideas apply, with an extra twist: what the manager considers to be an outlandish report from one worker now depends in part on the report from the other worker. Thus, each worker now wants to conform not only to what the manager expects to hear but also to what the other worker is expected to say. This does not bode well for communication and decision making in organizations.

The message of this essay has been that economists now appreciate the Marchian argument that it often is not useful to think of an *organization* as a self-interested, rational decision maker. As noted above, in Gibbons (1997b) I try to locate the emerging economics of internal organization more precisely than "between teams and garbage cans," arguing that the stage is set for a productive integration of new econonic models with work like Pfeffer's (1981) on power and politics. Where March, Pfeffer, and many other non-economist students of organizations may differ with the economic models described above, however, is over whether it is useful to think of an *individual* as a self-interested, rational decision maker. But even on this issue, economic and non-economic arguments have begun to converge; see Frank (1985) and Thaler (1985) for early examples of such "behavioral economics."

In terms of the economics of internal organization, perhaps the most exciting part of behavioral economics is "behavioral game theory," which not only imports cognitive models from behavioral decision theory into multi-person strategic problems, but also embeds insights from social psychology into economic analyses of such group interactions. Simply put, one can use well-established principles from social psychology to modify assumptions such as self-interest and rationality and then reinvestigate game-theoretic models such as repeated games or signaling; see Rabin (1993), Babcock and Loewenstein (1997), and Camerer (1997) for promising work in this direction.

While the first generation of models in the economics of internal organization feature self-interested, rational individuals producing inefficient, informal, and institutionalized organizational behaviors, I think the second generation may well feature individuals making purposive (i.e., not quite rational) choices in social (i.e., not quite self-interested) settings, producing even more dramatically inefficient, informal, and institutionalized organizational behaviors. One of many fascinating prospects along these lines would be convergence between second-generation models of the economics of internal organization and Zucker's (1983, 25) claim that "Institutionalization" (i.e., the process of becoming taken for granted) "is fundamentally a cognitive process."

Behavioral Economics and Nonrational Organizational Decision Making

Colin F. Camerer

My chapter focuses on behavioral economics, and some of its potential contributions to understanding behavior in organizations. First I define what makes economic analysis "behavioral," and then turn to two sorts of ideas about *systematic* departures from the conventional rationality assumptions in economics—experimental studies of game-playing behavior, and unorthodox assumptions about incentives and labor economics. (The game theory studies are a small part of a broad research program that will result. I think, in a very different sort of theory which is more descriptive than that of current theorizing.) The two strands are then loosely tied together in an alternative account of why LBO (leveraged buyout) restructuring of firms in the 1980s appears to have worked.

What "Positive Economics" Is, and
What Behavioral Economics Is Not

Behavioral economists like myself think that a fruitful direction for constructing better economic explanations is to search for empirically sound assumptions about individual behavior, which correspond to human psychology, to

Support from the Russell Sage Foundation during my visit there in 1991–1992, and from NSF grant 90–23531, is very gratefully acknowledged. Comments from the editors, from many conference participants, and from long talks with Chip Heath, Marc Knez, Martin Weber, and Daniel Kahneman (and other accomplices named in the paper), were very helpful.

serve as analytically tractable foundations for economic theorizing. This sounds so wholesome; who could possibly disagree?

In fact, most of the economics profession disagrees. Since the publication of Milton Friedman's influential *Methodology of Positive Economics* in the 1940s, economists have made assumptions about economic behavior which they know might be false, for example, that people are utility-maximizing. This standard argument in "positive economics," sometimes called the "F-twist" after Friedman's philosophical pirouette, states that assumptions should be judged *solely* by the validity of the predictions on which they are based. This argument has enabled economists to ignore criticisms of fundamental assumptions, and empirical evidence that people neither maximize expected utility nor obey Bayes's rule, and cannot imagine optimal lifetime consumption-savings plans. Consequently, economists feel free to ignore their own introspections and data generated by social scientists who study different levels of individual aggregation or work from fundamentally different assumptions, thus tearing their squares free from the quilt of social science.

The positive-economics strategy has been fruitful. By focusing attention on predictions, it forces a stiff empirical discipline on theorizing: Theories must make predictions, and inventors of theories must show how they could be proved false. But the research strategy positive economics encourages is inefficient and overly conservative, and has outlived its usefulness.

Inefficiency: Ignoring evidence on the validity of assumptions is inefficient because it throws away information. What justification can there be for *completely* ignoring data about the validity of a theory's assumptions? The standard defense is that testing the theory's predictions does, in fact, test its assumptions—indirectly. The problem is that if a theory based on a bundle of assumptions is rejected, its data often offer no special clues as to which of several underlying assumptions are false. Then one must turn to other sources of evidence, directly testing each assumption individually. Why not consider the evidence in the first place?

You build a bridge and worry about its strength. Do you test the bridge's components one-by-one before it collapses, or do you wait for it to collapse and then comb the wreckage for evidence of its structural weakness? Probably both.

Conservatism: The positive economics approach is conservative because there is a striking reluctance among economists, in practice, to cling to the core principles of rejected theories rather than consider new ones (V. Smith 1994, comments eloquently on this "Duheim-Quine" thesis). In practice, assumptions rarely *are* judged harshly when their predictions appear to be not-too-valid. Time is spent fussing over details and generating alternative explanations which are either implausible or insufficient, rather than boldly proposing explanations for evidence (and generating new testable predictions) based on new foundational assumptions. Conservatism has two rallying cries: "But the theory is useful!" and "There is no better theory."

"But the theory is useful" means the predictive glass is half-full. It certainly is, but then it is half-empty too. Surely science will progress faster if we concentrate on filling the empty half rather than just admiring the half that is filled.

"There is no better theory" is a sounder defense. It offers a legitimate reason for preferring current theory to poorly specified replacements, but it is hardly a reason to discourage the search for better alternatives.

Some Examples of Inefficiency and Conservatism of Positive Economics

There are many examples of conservative defense of elegant theories as anomalous evidence piles up. Let me give three.

1. Becker and Murphy (1992) explain addiction as rational consumption, given "metapreferences" in which the utility of current consumption depends on a stock of previous consumption, thus putting heroin addiction on an equal analytic footing with a taste for opera or single-malt scotch or Cuban cigars. Becker and Murphy's clever approach is predictive, and can explain some surprising facts, like the high sensitivity of demand to price changes—especially *predicted* price changes—for allegedly addictive goods like cigarettes. Nonetheless, this simple model cannot easily explain regrettable addictions in which people wish they had never started, or *chronic* cycles of binging and "cold turkey" quitting—smokers or overeaters who frequently quit then start again. (Smokers who rationally expected to start again later should never have quit the first time.) But chronic cycles can be explained if *two* consumption stocks are introduced.

2. There is persistent evidence against the combined assumptions of rational expectations and the "permanent income hypothesis," the idea that people plan optimal consumption over their lifetimes, given the income they expect (Deaton 1987). But rather than search for alternative assumptions rooted firmly in psychological evidence of how expectations formation or consumption planning might occur if people are boundedly rational (e.g., Shefrin and Thaler 1988), research attention has focused almost entirely on auxiliary assumptions that might explain the theory's failure, such as that consumption of durables (which provide service flows extending over several quarters, or years) happen quickly, or the idea that people do not consume optimally because they are liquidity-constrained cannot borrow against future income effectively (Zeldes 1989).

3. The post-1970 rise of information economics has contributed substantially to the conservative reluctance to take behavioral economics seriously. The problem is that allowing information to differ among economic agents now gives agents *two* distinct reasons for behavior—first, to satisfy their underlying preferences (the usual motive for behavior), and second, to reveal their information to a partner or hide it from a competitor. So an action which goes against fundamental preferences and appears irrational can be rationalized because it is potentially information-revealing.

Asymmetric-information models of strikes work this way: Temporarily foregoing the opportunity to profitably exchange labor for wages, workers or management strike to signal that they can be patient, or to invite outside opportunities. Scharfstein and Stein (1990) also explain managerial "herd behavior" this way. In their model, clever managers all do the same thing (because there is one right thing to do, and all the clever managers know what it is); less clever managers do that same thing too so they can pretend to be clever.

In this approach, incomplete information directly substitutes for various forms of irrationality in explaining apparently puzzling behavior, and behavioral explanations then must compete with information-asymmetry explanations. Competition is a good thing, but empirical data usually do not provide a sharp enough distinction between the two kinds of explanations. Moreover, I worry that economists have a natural tendency—a "sufficiency bias"—to consider a puzzle solved once a *sufficient*, though not *necessarily* true or easily testable, rationalizing explanation has been proposed. Furthermore, many such explanations push the source of irrationality aside without acknowledging that information asymmetry is a problem.

How to Do Behavioral Economics, and Why

The shift in methodology we behavioral economists have in mind is not so dramatic. We believe simply that the plausibility of a theory's assumptions should play in evaluating that theory, and that coherent, rich, testable theory *can* be constructed using more realistic assumptions than are typically used.

The replacement assumptions we have in mind will allow economic agents to be impulsive and myopic, to lack self-control, to keep track of spending and earnings in separate "mental accounting" categories, to care about the outcomes of others (both altruistically and enviously), to construct preferences from experience and observation, to sometimes misjudge probabilities, to take pleasure and pain from the difference between their economic state and some set of reference points, and so forth. Note that all these assumptions *sound* realistic, even innocuous. The big challenge is in finding systematic regularities in, say, the impulsiveness or altruism of agents, and in expressing these regularities formally within the structure of neoclassical economics to make better predictions than theory does now.[1]

One way to sharpen the difference between orthodox and behavioral economics is to define what we mean by "rationality." Our notion of rationality differs in three closely related ways from notions that are standard in economics: First, bearing in mind Simon's notion of "procedural rationality," as contrasted with "substantive rationality," we assume that agents obey some systematic decision-making procedures or algorithms, but that these procedures may lead them to violate substantively rational axioms (like completeness of preference, or dynamic consistency). Second, by focusing our attention on sensible procedures, we may use intuition and introspection about "how sensible people behave" to determine what those procedures are. Third, by defining rationality as procedural, evidence collected by other social scientists is admissible, and indeed, extremely useful, in helping establish what procedures people use. Taken together, these three standards imply that our model of rational choice will be the set of procedures that sensible people use, as observed by economists and other social scientists, chiefly psychologists and sociologists.

The Rest of the Chapter

Contained within this broad manifesto for a more behavioral approach to economics, are two specific components: the experimental study of behavior in simple games and our recent work with some co-authors on the psychology and economics of effort. The experiments I describe attacked the descriptive adequacy of game theory (cf. Bazerman, Gibbons, and Valley, in this book), with the intent of providing raw observations sufficient to construct a better, explicitly descriptive theory. The game-theoretic and effort strands of this paper are brought together by an informal behavioral-economics account of the LBO phenomenon of the 1980s.

The Behavioral Economics of Game Theory

Von Neumann and Morgenstern's seminal 1944 book on game theory was a bomb with a long fuse. It exploded in social science, particularly in economics, about thirty years after it was written. (Applications in political science, biology, philosophy, and other fields are growing too.)

---

[1] Some recent contributions which, impulsively, I cannot resist mentioning are Rabin (1993), Bowman, Minehart, and Rabin (in press), and Laibson (1997), who respectively incorporate fairness, loss-aversion, and hyperbolic discounting into economic theory.

Von Neumann and Morgenstern's building block was a noncooperative game in which players' moves were specified according to who moves first, whether random events occur and when, what moves are possible, and who earns what (not necessarily money) from a sequence of moves.[2] Until relatively recently (1980 or so), work in game theory consisted of exploring how players with varying degrees of rationality might play a specific game, or arrive at a given "equilibrium."[3]

Our work on behavioral game theory draws a parallel to "behavioral decision theory," which critiques the underlying assumptions of utility theory and Bayesian probability as descriptive principles. The formula for good behavioral decision theory is simple: construct choice or judgment problems in which normative principles provide unintuitive answers. Test how people actually solve these problems. If there is evidence in their answers of systematic deviations from the normative principles, use this evidence to make conjectures about the thinking processes that generate choices and judgments.

We took a similar approach in our experimental work on game theory. The idea was to study actual behavior in games in which modeling principles yield unintuitive equilibria, and to note any deviations from these principles that might provide raw material for more behaviorally realistic theory. Pioneering work along these lines has been done by many experimentalists; Neale and Bazerman (1991) and Camerer (1997) give recent summaries.

Table 3.1 shows a list of modeling principles that are used in deriving equilibria in games (left column), and recent experimental evidence of violation of each principle (right column). The table is neither even-handed nor exhaustive, but simply shows that *some* evidence exists to counter each principle. Theorists can judge which evidence is most persuasive and which principles need modification and, most important, how to modify them tractably.

Let me explain these principles and the evidence indicating how people systematically violate them.

Decision Principles

"Decision principles" describe assumptions about how people evaluate the payoffs of various move sequences, and how they form beliefs during a game. Most

[2] It is interesting, of course, to study how people *perceive* the games they play (e.g., Rubinstein 1991). Most game theory begins with the players' perceptions and studies their reasoning process from that point on. Work in managerial cognition on "cognitive communities" and firms' views of who their competitors are (which are sometimes asymmetric) might usefully inform game theory about perceived games.

[3] Recent work, happily, has shifted attention sharply from analyzing rational players to analyzing players who are limitedly rational but adaptive, or analyzing a population of players that evolves due to selection pressures.

Table 3.1. Game-theoretic modeling principles and experimental evidence

Selling Principles	Systematic Experimental Violations
Decision Principles	
Dominance	Prisoner's dilemma (Ledyard 1995)
Subjective expected utility	
a. description invariance (no framing)	Gain-loss asymmetry
	sequential bargaining (Camerer et al. 1993)
	Sunk cost relevance
	coordination games (Cachon and Camerer 1996)
b. additive beliefs	Ambiguity-aversion (subadditivity)
$P(A) + P(B) = P(A \cup B) - P(A \cap B)$	(Camerer and Karjalainen, 1993)
Independence of payoff utilities from . . .	
a. payoffs of others	Fairness concerns
	ultimatums, sequential bargaining
	(Thaler 1988; Roth 1994)
	social utility (Loewenstein et al. 1989)
b. path through tree	Nature vs. person difference
	ultimatums (Blount 1995)
Random mixing of strategies	Dependence on previous strategies
	Rapoport and Budescu 1992)
Choice-rating differences	Differential social comparison
(procedure-dependent preferences)	(Loewenstein, Blount, and Bazerman, in press)
Strategy Principles	
Irrelevance of labels & timing	Focal points & principles
	battle of sexes (Cooper et al. 1994)
Common prior beliefs	Egocentric, role-biased expectations
	arbitration (Neale and Bazerman 1985)
	pretrial bargaining (Babcock et al. 1995)
Mutual knowledge of rationality	
a. iterated dominance	False belief others violate dominance
	(Beard and Beil 1994; Schotter et al. 1994)
	"acquire-a-company" (Neale and Bazerman 1991)
	number game (Nagel 1995; Ho et al. in press)
	e-mail game (Camerer et al. 1994)
Backward induction	Underweight subgame payoffs
	sequential bargaining (Camerer et al. 1993)
	centipede game (McKelvey and Palfrey 1992)
Forward induction	Underweight foregone payoffs
	battle of sexes (Cooper et al. 1994)

of these principles grow out of decision-theoretic principles in theories of single-person decision making under risk (expected utility) or uncertainty (subjective expected utility theory).

For example, "dominance" means that an action which never yields a higher payoff, and sometimes is worse, than another action should never be chosen. Choosing to cooperate in a single play of the well-known prisoner's dilemma, which yields less money than defecting for *any* move by the other player, violates dominance. Of course, it is easy to explain away dominance violations by asserting that money amounts players are paid in experiments do not correspond directly to utilities; for example, a player may earn *more* utility, but *less* money, from cooperating. Then dominance becomes very difficult to falsify. For this reason, I think it is one of the least interesting modeling principles to study and, in practice, is least vulnerable to empirical attack.

The "independence" assumptions are more interesting. For example, in most experiments players are paid in dollar amounts and, for simplicity, we assume a player's utility depends only on her own payoff (the self-interest assumption[4]). If it does not, then fairness plays a complicating role.

Fairness

There is plenty of experimental evidence against the self-interest assumption. The simplest evidence comes from the "ultimatum game," first studied by Werner Güth and some of his German colleagues (see Camerer and Thaler, 1995, for reviews; and see Murnighan 1994). In the ultimatum game player 1 offers a division of an amount X to player 2, who can accept the division or reject it (then both get nothing). In most experiments, player 1 offers about 40 percent of X to player 2; if player 2 gets less than 20 percent or so, she often rejects the positive offer. Note that by rejecting the offer, player 2 indicates that she prefers getting nothing to getting a positive sum of money *when another player gets more*.

The ultimatum data also are interesting from a sociological point of view. Guth et al. published a paper in 1982 in the *Journal of Economic Behavior and Organization*, an eclectic journal which is not highly prestigious. Most of the flurry of replications that followed were deliberately "destructive," intended to test whether various aspects of the authors' experimental design—for example, the size of the stake X, blindness of experimenters to subjects' choices, verbal labels used to describe bargaining, how rights to propose and decide were determined—might have accounted for their results (they do not). Until recently, few of the replications were designed to advance our understanding of the psy-

---

[4] The self-interest assumption is by no means a crucial part of game theory (or economics; see Becker 1993, 385). Like the assumption of risk-aversion in utility theory it helps sharpen predictions, but rejecting it does not mean rejecting the whole theory.

chology or limits of the phenomenon, although some interesting ones have studied whether subjects know the amount being divided, and the gender and nationality of subjects. Here we see how conservatism in economic methods has slowed the pace at which we develop a true understanding of the phenomenon.

A related assumption, slightly weaker than pure self-interest, is that players do not care about the path through the tree (or sequence of moves) which leads to an allocation of payoffs. This assumption allows a player to care whether another player earns more or less than she does, but assumes that the first player does not care how the allocation came about. An ultimatum experiment by Blount (1994) casts doubt on this path-independence assumption as well.

In her experiment, one group of subjects plays a standard ultimatum game (for control), accepting or rejecting offers made by others. The average subject rejects $2.91 from a $7 total. Another group decides whether to accept or reject divisions of $7 between themselves and another person, which are determined by a computer that randomly generates offers. Then subjects reject only $1.20 on average. To some extent, people are punishing others who behave unfairly, rather than simply rejecting uneven allocations. (There is a clear link between Blount's elegant demonstration and the literature on "procedural justice," described by Brockner and Weisenfeld in their chapter in this book; they show that both fairness in process, and fairness in outcomes, matter to people.)

Fairness and Social Comparison

For an audience of skeptics who only study things with price tags, rejections in ultimatum games have established that fairness matters, that people will pay substantial amounts to punish those who treat them unfairly, and that therefore social comparison is an important part of fairness. Social comparison also plays a role in organizational behavior. For example, most accounts of social comparison revolve around A's comparing herself to some reference group. This simple assumption provides some firms scope to *manage* social comparison, or at least to influence it by affecting whom A compares herself to.

Job titles are one way to define reference groups. Consequently, the current trend toward "broad-banding"—coarsening job categories rather than refining them—is likely to increase A's reference group (Heath, Knez and Camerer 1993). If social comparison is asymmetric (Loewenstein, Thompson, and Bazerman 1989), in that people feel worse about being behind in their group than they feel good about being ahead and exhibit "social loss-aversion" — then broad-banding has a cost human-resource managers might not have considered (see also Akerlof and Yellen 1990, esp. 259).

Similarly, economic accounts of employee compensation (e.g., Milgrom and Roberts 1992, chap. 13) cannot explain the late 1980s uproar over CEO compensation in America, but social comparison theory can. Lower-paid employees compare themselves to CEOs, or at least are dissatisfied that CEOs earn, on average, nearly one hundred times as much as they do. The effect of social comparison is inflamed badly by giving stock options or shares to CEOs (the agency-theory panacea for reducing the mismatch between CEO and stockholder incentives). The problem is that CEOs rationally will sell shares, or exercise options to accumulate shares to sell, when they have private information that bad times are ahead, which is likely to happen just a step ahead of poor earnings and layoffs. The economic account therefore *predicts*, and in its normative use, encourages, this mismatch of the timing of CEO and employee benefits, in which the rich get very rich just when the relatively poor get laid off. Injecting a strong enough dose of social comparison into the model might reverse the standard advice that CEOs should be given heavy incentives such as shares they can sell, and options they can exercise freely.

Strategy Principles

Strategy principles are unique to games in which players weigh each other's moves. Let me mention one particularly interesting principle.

Mutual Knowledge of Rationality

A distinctly game-theoretic modeling principle, which does not exist in decision theory applications, is the amount of mutual knowledge of rationality two players have. Table 3.2 shows a game that illustrates this principle.

Table 3.2. A game testing mutual
knowledge of rationality

		Player 2	
		L	R
	T	−4, 4	−4, 4
Player 1			
	B	0, 1	6, 3

By choosing T, player 1 guarantees 4 for herself and 4 for player 2. Choosing B, however, represents a bet by player 1 on player 2's rationality: If 2 chooses L the payoffs are (0, 1) (0 for player 1, 1 for player 2); if 2 chooses R the payoffs are (6, 3).

For player 2, R weakly dominates L. Thus, if player 2 is rational she should choose R; if player 1 knows that player 2 is rational, she should choose B.

Schotter, Weigelt, and Wilson (1994) studied this game experimentally. They found that when the game was shown in a matrix ("normal-form"), about half the player 1's chose T. Virtually all the player 2's chose R. Thus, it appears that players are mostly rational—they maximize their own payoff—but half the players are not willing to bet that others are rational (see also Beard and Beil 1994).

An interesting question is how robust this general finding is: How high up the ladder of mutual-rationality reasoning do people tend to go in other games? A simple experiment which helps answer this question was conducted by Nagel (1993), and extended by Ho and Weigelt (1994).

In the "number game," N subjects choose a number from, say [0, 100]. Call the i-th subject's number n_i. The player whose number is closest to p times the average of all the numbers (including her own) wins a fixed prize \$X.[5]

The number game captures some of the features of games of timing or fashion. The choice of a number corresponds to how quickly an action is taken, and players are rewarded for being just ahead of the crowd—that is, for having chosen a "time" equal to p of the average time—but not too far ahead. Applied to organizations, the number game is a simple model of processes in which scarce resources are allocated, first-come-first-served, after a certain amount of pent-up demand, lobbying or pressure mounts. The trick is to not be too early—then one waits around for others to arrive, to create sufficient pressure—and not be too late, since then the scarce resources are gone to early-comers.

For behavioral game theory, the number game is more important as a diagnostic device to get a sharp measure of how much rationality people use, attribute to others, think others attribute to them, and so on.

The analysis proceeds as follows. If players are rational (they obey dominance), they know the average cannot be more than 100, so they should pick numbers between 0 and 100p. We cannot conclude much if a player chooses 50p, for example, but if she chooses a number in the interval (100p, 100] then she is clearly irrational, because choosing 100p dominates her choice. Furthermore, if players are rational and think others also are rational, then they will realize that the average will be between 0 and 100p (since others are rational and will choose numbers in [0, 100p] only), so they should pick numbers between 0 and $100p^2$. So we can conclude that anyone who picks a number in ($100p^2$, 100] either is irrational, or believes others are. Going one step further, anyone who chooses a number in ($100p^3$, 100] is irrational, or believes others are, or believes that others think she is irrational.

The same argument applies to higher levels of mutual rationality. Adding levels of mutual rationality reduces the interval of mutually rational numbers, so if we observe a subject choosing a number above a certain interval we can conclude

---

[5] If several people tie, they split \$X in any pre-announced division which gives everyone some part of, or some chance at, the whole amount.

that a corresponding level of mutual rationality fails to hold. By observing the numbers people pick, we get a direct measure of the degree of mutual rationality on which they are willing to bet, and how this varies in the population. Notice, by the way, that the *only* Nash equilibrium in this game is for everyone to pick 0. But since this equilibrium choice is the product of many levels of mutual rationality, it seems like, and is, a bad prediction of actual choices.

Nagel (1995) studied the game with twenty subject-groups and p = 2/3. About 10 percent of the subjects picked 25, 5 percent picked 33, and the average picked was 36.7. Further analysis shows that the average player is somewhere between thinking others are rational, and thinking that others think she is rational.

Ho, Camerer, and Weigelt (in press) extended Nagel's findings for three and seven-person groups, with p = 0.9 and other values. Figure 3.1 shows a times series of average numbers chosen, over ten rounds of the experiment. (At the end of each round, subjects learned the average number chosen in that round.) Numbers begin, on average, around 50 and decline steadily toward, but barely reach, the equilibrium of 0. Group size has the most interesting effect. One might presume that higher degrees of mutual rationality would hold in the smaller three-person groups (the open-box line) but instead the numbers chosen are higher, with consistently *lower* degrees of mutual rationality, than in seven-person groups shown with closed-box lines. Since the game-theoretic prediction makes the same wrong guess about actual choices—0—for all values of p < 1 and for all group sizes, regularities in Nagel's, and Ho et al.'s data represent interesting fodder for a behavioral modification that somehow takes limited *mutual* rationality into account (see Nagel, in press).

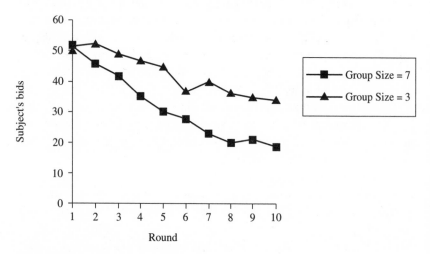

Figure 3.1 Subjects' average bids over time (p = 0.9)

There has been virtually no link drawn between mutual rationality and organizational behavior, but such a link seems useful and inevitable. Perhaps certain kinds of socialization, teamwork exercises, explicit communication of culture through mission statements, public rituals, and so forth, can be understood as devices to increase the amount of mutual rationality among workers (see also Camerer and Knez 1997). Conversely, the mutual rationality view points out that part of the cost of high worker turnover is the erosion of mutual rationality. The notion that the degree of mutual rationality may fall as groups increase in size (Ho et al.'s data notwithstanding) implies that strategic diseconomies of scale might keep optimal work group size surprisingly small for tasks in which trust is important. Finally, in many games increased mutual rationality *hurts*, because small amounts of "irrationality" are foundations on which players can build trust or profitable exchange. Examples of this phenomenon include the repeated prisoner's dilemma and its kin, the centipede game, studied experimentally by McKelvey and Palfrey (1992), and the "electronic mail game," which I studied with Blecherman and Goldstein (1994).

The examples of fairness and mutual rationality illustrate the general behavioral game theory approach. In both cases we take relatively simple games and use the games to isolate a simple modeling principle—Do people care what others earn? Do they believe others are rational?—and analyze how well the principle predicts what people choose. If we observe violation of a principle we try to check how big and systematic the violations are—across a subject pool, or in other games, and see whether repeating the game shrinks the rate of violations as people learn. If a principle is robustly violated, the search begins for a suitable, parsimonious replacement.

The Behavoral Economics of Effort and Incentives

George Loewenstein, Dick Thaler, and Robin Hogarth, and I have been exploring more realistic psychological assumptions about how workers' efforts respond to incentives. We hope to produce interesting new predictions about observable economic phenomena, and perhaps explain some current anomalies. Since these ideas run counter to much of the economic theory that underlies the vigorous "new theory of the firm," they should be of interest to students of organizational behavior. Let me offer a sketch of some of our ideas and findings—coming attractions, we hope, from papers yet unwritten.

Is Effort Utility Negative or Positive?

One of our ideas is that the standard assumptions used in the economic theory of incentives come from a manual-labor metaphor, which may be a poor metaphor to guide thinking about *managerial* effort. For example, the marginal utility of effort u(e) is thought to be negative (u'(e) < 0; people dislike work), and increasingly negative (u'''(e) < 0; the more they work, the more people dislike work). These assumptions seem to describe manual labor—the work is strenuous and painful, and increasingly painful as muscles tire and eyes glaze over—but may not describe managerial labor.

Managerial work is often interesting enough to produce positive u(e)—for example, people will work (some hours) for less than their opportunity wages because their jobs are fun.[6] And there is a range of work in which the "capital" one accumulates from previous work makes further work more pleasurable, so u''(e) > 0. For example, after collecting data, the work of analyzing it is often quite exciting. It is a fun way to spend time, and is more fun than the data collection stage which came before.[7]

The idea that work may be pleasurable, and increasingly so, has several unorthodox implications. First, financial incentive may not be necessary to motivate workers. Second, workers may work *too hard* from the firm's point of view. That is, even if u''(e) > 0 (work utility escalates, rather than satiates), productivity from marginal hours of work probably diminishes at the margin. Too much work may be disruptive to the workaholic employee, or to other employees, and can lower profits. Moving away from the manual labor metaphor suggests the possibility that managers might work too much, for example, delegating responsibility insufficiently,[8] rather than too little. This simple shift might help explain workaholism, worker burnout, and other modern phenomena which are hard to explain according to the manual-labor theory.

The obvious problem with a theory in which u(e) is positive is that it cannot explain why people do shirk in some work situations, whether manual-labor or managerial. I think we can get quite far with a small addition to the alternative theory which asserts that people like to work (u'(e) > 0) but dislike working

---

[6] Some people reading this paper are examples. Most business-school academics could work as part-time consultants, or managers, at substantially higher wages. If you are like me, you prefer academic work because its psychological rewards more than compensate for lower wages. Wageman and Baker (1992) put this assumption to work in an interesting analysis of interdependent tasks and rewards.

[7] However, it is important to note that the possibility that people like work, and like it more and more, only changes fundamental results derived from the standard manual-labor assumption if people like working throughout the entire range of hours they might work. If u'(e) > 0 for a small number of work hours e < e*, but changes to u'(e) < 0 for e > e*, then the standard theory works unless the firm's organizational setup makes hiring each worker for less than e* hours each particularly efficient.

[8] There are many examples of autocratic, workaholic CEOs who work almost as many hours as is humanly possible, and who seem to delegate insufficiently as a result (or perhaps as a cause). Wayne Huizenga (Blockbuster Video) and Jim Dutt (Beatrice Co., 1979–1986) are examples.

harder than others to whom they compare themselves, especially when working on a joint task. (Formally, we assume $u_i'(e_i, e_j) < 0$ if $e_i > e_j$).) The latter possibility introduces two interesting features: social comparison and multiple equilibria.

Social comparison arises because workers must decide whose effort level to compare their own efforts to.

Multiple equilibria arise because one can easily construct models in which everyone works hard if they expect others to (a good equilibrium), but everyone shirks if they expect others to (a bad equilibrium). This introduces scope for history, leadership, group norms, managerial decisions, and symbolism to fix an equilibrium or to push workers from the bad equilibrium to the good one (Camerer and Krez, 1997).

Do Higher Incentives Always Help?

The linchpin assumptions of the orthodox economic approach to effort are that (i) higher incentives raise effort; and (ii) higher effort improves performance (or does not harm it). We suspect the first is mostly true, and the second part less so. Too much effort, or misguided effort, *could* harm performance.[9]

For example, we studied free-throw shooting by basketball players from 1977 to 1991, during the regular season and in the playoffs (when incentives are presumably higher). All players who took twenty or more playoff free throws were included in the study. Shooting was *less* accurate during the playoffs (75.35 percent vs. 74.19 percent, t = 3.14, p = .0008). This finding is consistent with a large literature documenting "choking" in sports, and test-taking anxiety in educational psychology. These literatures indicate a belief that incentives create arousal, which may cause people to concentrate too much or concentrate on the wrong things. Professional basketball players may shoot most accurately when they are relaxed and executing their shots automatically rather than thinking too hard about the shooting process. Anxious students taking tests sometimes concentrate too much on themselves, or on the clock, which reduces their performance. Similarly, beginning teachers and students giving their first oral research seminars are highly motivated, but usually so inwardly focused that communicating with an audience, and understanding audience questions, is more difficult than at lower levels of incentives.

Evidence reported by Ehrenberg and Bognanno (1990) suggests our findings about professional basketball may generalize to men's professional golf, with an interesting twist. The authors studied whether more prize money improved players' scores. To understand their results, you need to know two facts: First, most tournaments last four eighteen-hole rounds; after the first two rounds the

[9] This notion is hardly original; it is familiar to psychologists as the Yerkes-Dodson law, published in 1908.

players with low scores are cut, and the rest play two more rounds. Second, successful veteran players are considered "exempt" (according to a complex set of rules), or able to qualify for future tournaments automatically. Most professional golfers in their sample are "non-exempt" journeymen for whom a single good performance could mean exemption; for them, the reward to playing well in a single round presumably is higher and the pressure is greater.[10]

In fact, both types of golfers *do* play better when total tournament prize money is larger (scores are 1.1 strokes per round lower for each $100,000 in total prizes), but the high-pressure non-exempt golfers do not respond to financial incentives quite as much as do low-pressure exempt golfers. Furthermore, only the exempt players play significantly better when the marginal financial return to moving up in the final round of the tournament is higher; on average, non-exempt players do not improve at all.

These results show a measurable incentive effect consistent with the orthodox economic view that money does improve scores, but one that is strongly moderated by exemption. Non-exempt players, less experienced and under greater pressure, *do not* play better when the stakes are greater. As in basketball playoff shooting, added financial pressure may have caused non-exempt players to "choke," offsetting the positive incentive effects evident among exempt players. Or exempt golfers, who are more experienced, may have adapted to a high-pressure play that causes younger non-exempt players to choke.

How Is Labor Allocated across Time?

Another study concerns intertemporal substitution of labor. In the standard theory, workers are given an allocation of time. They can spend their time working, which earns them wages with which they buy consumption goods, or they can "consume" leisure, using up hours without earning wages. In the standard account, workers allocate labor across various time periods to maximize the discounted expected utility of their leisure (nonwork) hours and the consumption bundles their wages can buy.

An important question is how the supply of labor varies with variation in wages. In the standard theory, workers work longer hours when real wages rise, and work fewer hours when wages fall. Workers who respond to wage changes this way are exerting labor when it pays the most to do so. (Put the other way

---

[10] Here my interpretation disagrees with Ehrenberg and Bonanno's: They assert that "[Because] the nonexempt players had to worry about qualifying for the next year's tour, the level and structure of prize money in a tournament may not be an accurate indicator of their marginal financial return to effort." They conclude that non-exempt players' scores might be *less* responsive to prize money, but I do not see how the added incentives non-exempt players face could make the responsiveness of their scores to prize money *lower* than responsiveness of exempt players (presuming their chances of qualifying rise with better scores).

around, they take time off when it is cheapest to do so—when the foregone wage is lowest.)

So the standard theory predicts that real wages and hours worked will be positively correlated. In fact, when the correlation is calculated using quarterly averages of wages and average hours worked, the correlation is close to zero, and is often negative (e.g., Mankiw, Rotemberg, and Summers 1985). This non-correlation is a *major* anomaly for macroeconomics. It casts doubt on available theories of business cycles, and hints at a deeper problem with the utility-maximization formulation that predicts the positive wage-hours correlation: How can it be that people do not work more when wages are high? A New York City cab ride in 1991 suggested a possible answer, and a research opportunity (Camerer, Babcock, Lowenstein, and Thaler 1997).

Many drivers lease their cabs for a twelve-hour shift (for about $78, plus gas), and keep all the fares they collect. We asked drivers how they decided how many hours to drive. Many said they set a target aspiration level, like earning $100 after buying gas and paying the lease fee, and drove until they reached the target. Drivers who use this decision rule drive *more* hours on days when wages are low, because it takes longer to earn the $100 target; similarly, they earn the target figure more quickly on high-wage days and drive *fewer* hours. This decision rule would produce data in which wages and hours were *negatively* correlated, contrary to the standard prediction (and in accord with the apparent facts).

Two ingredients are necessary to construct a more formal behavioral economics account of the drivers' labor supply decisions. First, drivers must choose a reference point (like the $100 target in our example) and value gains and losses from a reference point differently, reflecting loss-aversion (as in Tversky and Kahneman 1991). Loss-aversion would motivate them to drive until they reached the reference point, then quit, because the marginal value of each dollar toward the reference point is high and the marginal value of each dollar beyond it is low. Second, drivers must think somewhat myopically, rather than pooling their wages from a week (or months) and setting an aggregate reference point for the week. If they pooled wages in a week, say, then there is scope for them to drive longer hours on the highest-wage days in the week and drive less on the lowest-wage days, while still reaching the reference point. If they set a reference point each day, however, a stronger negative wage-hours correlation is induced by value-maximization with loss-aversion.

New York City cabdrivers fill out "trip sheets" documenting the starting and ending time of all the trips they take in a day, and the fares collected from each. The Taxicab Commission sampled thousands of these trip sheets for its factual studies of various issues (mostly related to fare increases). We obtained a sample of data culled from trip sheets.

The data show that the correlation between wages and hours is indeed negative and highly significant, corroborating the negative correlations observed in aggregated quarterly data, and supporting the behavioral theory of myopic value-maximimization rather than the standard theory of intertemporal utility maximization.

While our empirical conclusion is firm, perhaps our main point is methodological: We began with a psychologically compelling intuition that many drivers endorsed—namely, that drivers set reference levels for short periods, and act as if wages earned until the reference point is reached are more valuable than wages earned after that point. From that theory we derived a prediction which is opposite to the standard prediction, and appears to be true.

Notice that behavioral theory seems to satisfy all the criteria for good economic modeling. First, it can be easily formalized. Indeed, the standard theory can be cast as a special case of the more general behavioral one. In the behavioral theory, taxi drivers value gains and losses from a reference point, and choose a planning horizon. The standard theory corresponds to an extreme case where drivers use a reference point of zero (and maximize net wealth) and have an infinite planning horizon. Second, the behavioral theory has testable implications, which appear (so far) to be true and to explain a well-established puzzle about labor supply that the standard theory cannot explain. Third, the psychological roots of the theory are well established by other sorts of experiments, providing a loose unification of social science findings which we find pleasing, and which, to our puzzlement, many economists do not).[11]

Our theory of taxi driver labor supply has a close kinship to two other theories, one of which is especially relevant to organizations.

1. Benartzi and Thaler (1995) use the same key ingredients—myopia and loss-aversion—to explain the "equity premium puzzle" (the fact that, after inflation, long-term returns on stocks are much higher than returns on bonds). Their argument is that investors take a short-term investment horizon and dread the risk of losing money by investing in stocks, which causes investors to demand much higher average returns for holding stocks.

2. Kahneman and Lovallo (1993) discuss the apparent prevalence of both loss-aversion and myopia in organizational decision making. They note that firms appear to turn down a series of risky projects, fearing potential losses, even though *portfolios* of such projects appear acceptable. In their account, corporate myopia is cross-sectional rather than temporal: Firms choose projects one at a time, rather than considering portfolios of projects. At the same

---

[11] Social scientists often use the pointless term "ad hoc" to discredit a theory which appears unnatural or unconventional to them. The behavioral theory of labor supply may appear "ad hoc" (or unconventional) too because it is not grounded in the usual assumptions of utility maximization and infinite planning. In fact, it should be considered *less* ad hoc than the standard maximizing theory, because the standard theory is a special case of it, and there is better independent evidence for the components of the behavioral theory than for the standard theory.

time, massive overconfidence about project success, (based on "inside view" thinking that exaggerates idiosyncratic details of specific cases and shrugs off "outside view" failure frequencies estimated from similar cases) may be the main reason that myopic, loss-averse managers take any risks at all.

The Kahneman-Lovallo analysis suggests a rich way to understand nonrational organizational decision making as a corporate expression of the same loss-aversion, myopia, and inside-view overconfidence that individuals exhibit. Numerous questions spring to mind. Are myopia and loss-aversion features present in businesses that routinely take numerous low-probability high-payoff risks, like pharmaceutical research and development or venture capital? If myopia and loss-aversion are "cured," how do the cures work? Do risk-taking managers rise in an organization? Do organizational structure or culture counter individuals' natural myopia and loss aversion? Or does having responsibility for managing a broad array of projects impose a portfolio perspective that overcomes myopia and loss-aversion? Does organizational life create *greater* overconfidence than individual managers exhibit, perhaps licensing risk-taking, or more level-headed caution? It would also be good to know whether the apparent myopia and loss-aversion that managers display is a rational response to the way they are evaluated within their organizations and, if so, could a better evaluation system be designed? Essential to this project is an understanding of the organizational psychology behind assigning credit for successes and blame for mistakes; this, in turn, requires a deeper understanding of the psychology of regret (Loomes and Sugden 1987) and counterfactual thinking (Kahneman and Miller 1986).

There is an important normative lesson in these three stories about cabdrivers, investment in stocks and bonds, and capital budgeting by firms. In all three cases, the combination of myopia (in planning horizon, or the span of a corporate portfolio) and aversion to losses leads to systematic mistakes that, in principle, are easy to fix. Cabdrivers drive too much at the wrong hours (when wages are low, to avoid a "loss" on a slow day), people invest too little in stocks, and corporations take too few risks. At the same time, the approach promises to help social scientists describe cabdrivers, investors, and timid corporations, who routinely do things that look puzzling to those who expect their behavior to be farsighted and utility-maximizing.

The Behavioral Economics of Leveraged Buyouts

The behavioral approaches to game theory and labor economics can be applied speculatively, to help us understand some stylized facts about the many dramatic corporate reorganizations in the 1980s. The cornerstones of my account are: (i) *Self-control* problems, which explain why radical corporate restructurings were needed to get top managers to make difficult decisions they would not make otherwise—chiefly, downsizing firms in mature industries; and (ii) *loss-aversion*, which explains why the perceived cost of job loss to workers is so dramatic, and consequently, why managers are reluctant to downsize at all. I cannot claim that the stylized facts about corporate restructuring cannot be explained without these two behavioral features, but any orthodox explanation is strained and adds ad hoc assumptions that tend to serve the explanatory purpose of managerial self-control and loss-aversion.

What Is an LBO?

A leveraged buyout (LBO) occurs when a small group of investors, generally five to one hundred incumbent top managers and an outside LBO firm (like the well-known Kohlberg, Kravis & Roberts, or KKR) decide to take over a company and run it differently. Since such a small group of investors is not rich enough to buy all the shares with its own money, the group arranges to borrow a very large sum—assets of the firm as a kind of collateral, and its expected cash flow to make promised interest payments—and buys the shares using the borrowed sum and a smaller amount of their own money.

The LBO of the grocery-store chain Safeway (by KKR and a group of Safeway's top managers) is an interesting illustrative example. The LBO group bought the firm by using $120 million in equity and borrowing $5.1 billion in debt. Safeway had been generating "operating income" (earnings before paying interest and taxes) of about $600 million per year, and now had interest payments of about $400 million per year.

Generally, the banks or bondholders from whom money is borrowed demand a substantial repayment within two years of the LBO; this forces the firm to sell assets. (Post-LBO, Safeway sold $2 billion worth of stores, reducing their debt to $3 billion.) Even then, the required interest payments usually amount to a high proportion of the cash flow generated from operating businesses, because the interest payments on "high-yield" (or "junk") bonds of such highly leveraged firms are much greater in order to compensate bondholders for the increased risk of default or bankruptcy.

There are several stylized facts about the performance of LBOs like these—generally, LBOs worked—and several theories about why they worked.[12] I think

---

[12] An important third theory is the "contract-breaking" or "expropriation" view (Shleifer and Summers 1988). LBOs provide a way for managers to credibly break implicit contracts that govern the sharing of surplus between stockholders and workers (workers must accept lower wages or the debt-laden firm goes bankrupt). This account, too, has a behavioral economics underpinning:

Wages almost always rise with job seniority, even in jobs like a grocery checkout clerk where productivity does not rise much, or even falls, with age. As a result, older clerks are overpaid relative to their productivity, the theory goes, because the firm "banks" their wages as part of an implicit contract to provide job security and save money for workers' old age. In the behavioral economics view, it pays for workers to have firms save money for them, because they lack the self-control to do so themselves or simply prefer rising wage profiles. If LBOs are devices to break these contracts, we expect to see firms laying off "overpaid" workers. It is hard to get direct data to test this prediction, but in the Safeway case the union reported that the average age of workers fell ten years post-LBO (Faludi 1990).

the two main theories, down deep, rely on principles from behavioral economics to explain why LBOs have worked, even though most published discussions of LBO financial performance delicately couch the theories in the jargon of orthodox economics.

Three Stylized Facts about LBOs

At the risk of oversimplifying a complicated topic, let me suggest three stylized facts about LBOs that any good theory must explain (see Kaplan 1989; A. Smith 1990):

1. On average, LBOs worked well financially. Cash flow improved, bondholders experienced few defaults or bankruptcies, and shareholders (especially KKR and its partners) made money, without substantial drops in total employment or cuts in investment. Furthermore, most of the gains to shareholders did not come at the expense of previous bondholders (whose bonds were made riskier by the LBO, and thus less valuable) or from union wage concessions.
2. LBOs worked because incumbent managers, who generally stay with the firm post-LBO as equity partners, took actions they did not take, but could have taken, pre-LBO. In most cases LBO firms *did not* fire incumbent managers and hire new, better ones; nor did managers do anything after the LBO that they were legally prohibited from doing pre-LBO.
3. Some LBOs later went public—so-called "reverse LBOs"—by issuing shares to a large number of shareholders and using the proceeds to pay back most of the debt, thus restoring the firm's debt/equity ratio to its pre-LBO state (Muscarella and Vetsuypens 1990).

The Eclipse Theory

There are two widely discussed theories about why LBOs worked. The first theory, well articulated by Jensen (1989) in a famous article called "The Eclipse of the Public Corporation," is that the LBO is a better organizational form than the publicly-held corporation where share ownership is spread out and no single shareholder can discipline bad managers. The "eclipse" theory can explain the first fact (LBOs worked). Eclipse theory explains the second fact with the argument that top managers did not have enough financial incentive to take drastic actions—such actions are effortful (in a vague sense) and cause disutility—until the LBO restructuring promised to make them rich. But the eclipse theory clearly cannot explain the third fact. If the LBO is a better organizational form, why reverse the LBO and revert to a public corporation? The eclipse theory also cannot explain why the number of LBOs slowed to a trickle in the

1990s—the high-water mark was $60 billion in LBO volume in 1988, the year before Jensen's article was published, and receded to $4 billion in 1990—and the widely held public corporation is clearly still the predominant organizational form.

The Radical Surgery Theory

A second theory is that an LBO is a good vehicle for performing "radical surgery" and shrinking corporations, but is not a superior organizational form in general. The argument here is subtler, and fundamentally behavioral. The hardest fact to explain is the second one. What did managers do post-LBO that they couldn't have done pre-LBO? Perhaps the answer lies in a combination of self-control and loss-aversion. An analogy might help show how.

Imagine a group of pudgy children (four feet tall) standing in a deep pool in three feet of water. Suppose you want the children to tread water, in order to lose weight. A group of friends can coax them to do so. Or you can fill the pool with water until the level is above their heads, to six feet; then unless they tread water, they drown and treading water vigorously creates heat which evaporates water. In an LBO restructuring, top managers are lazy children; coaxing friends are ineffectual members of the board of directors; the fat the managers need to burn off is unproductive businesses (or employees); water is debt; evaporation of water from burned-off calories is reduction of debt by selling businesses; drowning is bankruptcy.

The pool analogy suggests what is both effective and risky about LBOs. If drowning is a worse fate than disappointing friends, then the "discipline of debt" may work well as a device to force managers to "lose weight" by shedding unprofitable businesses or laying off workers. For example, the president of Safeway said (post-LBO):

> We could not *have done what we did do* without going through the incredible trauma and pressure of the LBO. . . . Let's look at expense reduction. It's not easy to get your people to cut all the unnecessary expense they can when you are producing record profit. (Magowan 1989, 13–14)

At the same time, this "radical surgery" approach is risky because firms may sell businesses too cheaply, or the proverbial water level might be too high and bankruptcy occurs.

We now return to the crucial second fact, which raises the question, Why didn't managers take drastic post-LBO actions before? The orthodox economics view is that managers weren't paid enough money to exert the high-disutility effort necessary. That answer begs the deeper question of why selling businesses and laying off workers is so much more difficult than buying businesses and hiring workers. After all, shouldn't selling and buying take similar amounts of time, energy, and effort, and incur similar costs?

How Loss-Aversion and Self-Control
Make "Radical LBO Surgery" Necessary

Two ideas from behavioral economics, loss-aversion and self-control, are useful and perhaps necessary to answer this deeper question.

First, loss-aversion (Tversky and Kahneman 1991) suggests that selling and firing will be harder than equivalent amounts of buying and hiring. It is harder for managers to create losses, because managers inherit guilt and other emotions, including the frustration of being lobbied by frightened workers and division heads,[13] from workers who are loss-averse. Loss-aversion creates an "endowment effect" (Kahneman, Knetsch, and Thaler 1990) for workers' jobs; they prefer an object they own to an equivalent one they do not own. The existence of loss-aversion is not at odds with the orthodox economic explanation, but simply goes deeper, showing that the source of the extra "effort" selling and firing requires comes from the asymmetry between the managerial effort required to sell and fire and the effort required to buy and hire.

Many economists understand the special force of loss-aversion but are not familiar with that label, or with its empirical roots in psychology. For example, Jensen (1993, 847) writes: "Exit problems appear to be particularly severe in companies that for long periods enjoyed rapid growth, commanding market positions, and high cash flow and profits. In these situations, the culture of the organization and the mindset of managers seem to make it extremely difficult for adjustment to take place until long after the problems have become severe . . . there is an *asymmetry* between the growth stage and the contraction stage over the life of a firm" (emphasis mine).

What else could Jensen be alluding to, besides "corporate endowment effects" caused by loss-aversion?

Loss-aversion can explain why downsizing a firm is harder than growing it, but it does not quite explain why managers were unable to downsize the firm pre-LBO. The pool analogy, and Magowan's claim that "we could not have done what we did without the incredible pressure [of an LBO]" suggest the possibility that *incumbent* managers *voluntarily* take on heavy debt loads as a precom-

---

[13] Going one step further, firing is harder for managers than hiring (and thus is more costly for the firm in terms of diverted managerial attention) because workers will incur "influence costs" trying to keep their jobs (see Milgrom and Roberts 1992). But then why don't *prospective* workers lobby equally hard when managers are hiring? Again the answer seems to require loss-aversion: Viz., workers will spend more to keep their jobs than to get new ones.

mitment device to solve the self-control problem that led them to postpone difficult, painful decisions in the first place. (In the pool analogy, this is like jumping in the deep end to force your lazy self to tread water.) In this view, debt serves a self-control function similar to the use of excess income tax withholding as "forced saving," or making a precommitment to diet plans (cf. Thaler and Shefrin 1981).[14]

The "Overheated" LBO Market

A final stylized fact about LBOs also can, and must, be neatly explained by behavioral economics. Kaplan and Stein (1993) show that junk bonds used in LBOs were good investments in the early 1980s, and poor investments in the late 1980s. Later deals were organized to benefit LBO firms and large banks at the expense of junk bond investors, and bonds defaulted much more frequently. Kaplan and Stein conclude that the extent that junk bond investors miscalculated, they probably did so by focusing too much on stated coupon yields and past buyout successes, and too little on the subtle capital structure details of the deals in which they were investing (356). The mistaken extrapolation from past successes to future prospects is a familiar theme in behavioral studies of financial markets (e.g., DeBondt and Thaler 1985). Instead of having rational expectations, in the sense that subjective beliefs about junk bond returns were, on average, correct, junk bond investors appeared to have expectations that adapted to past observed success but failed to forecast changes that made future defaults more common and future returns lower. One can naturally wonder, could wise investors get quite rich at the expense of gullible investors who foolishly extrapolate trends? The answer is, yes; and LBO firms and smart bankers did just that.

In this sprawling chapter I have tried to illustrate behavioral economics in general, and in connection with three specific cases.

The hallmarks of economic analysis are methodological rather than substantive. Textbook definitions say something like "economics is the study of the allocation of scarce means to satisfy competing ends" (Becker 1971, 1), but political processes and cultural systems anthropologists study and allocate "scarce means" too. Perhaps it is more practical to define economics as a *style* rather than a subject.

[14] The problem managers face trying to "downsize" large firms is like the problem politicians face trying to cut budgets. Both have to overcome the endowment effects of people who have jobs or political "entitlements" (like Social Security payments or farm subsidies), which makes removing these entitlements particularly painful and causes people who feel entitled or endowed to lobby hard against cuts. Put this way, the balanced budget amendment exerts an extreme discipline akin to the cash-flow pressure of an LBO.

Economic analysis is the approach to social science that most values simple mathematical formalisms that make surprisingly accurate predictions about human behavior. Put this way, our hope is that behavioral economics is just good economics, a collection of modeling principles which can be expressed formally and which make *better* predictions than the orthodox approach that assumes stable preferences and equilibrium.

I have tried to sketch three domains of economic analysis that can be enriched behaviorally while maintaining the twin criteria of formalism and predictiveness.

1. By studying which game-theoretic modeling principles are most easily modified, like self-interest and high degrees of mutual rationality, we could, in principle, construct a more descriptively useful game theory. The search for tractable replacements for orthodox game-theoretic principles, however, has just begun.

2. Alternative behavioral assumptions about human motivation to do work could enrich labor economics, for example, people might come to enjoy the work increasingly over time, and myopically allocate their work hours to avoid daily losses relative to some reference point. The latter assumption can be formalized, and makes a surprising prediction which appears to be true: Across a sample of days, the average hourly wage of cabdrivers is *negatively* correlated with the number of hours driven, which implies that drivers are working longer on low-wage days and quitting early on high-wage days.

3. Perhaps of more interest to students of organizational behavior is the boom in leveraged buyout (LBO) restructurings of corporations in the 1980s. We suggest that, on average, the financial success of LBOs is due to top managers' use of high levels of debt to overcome a self-control problem, an unwillingness to sell business units or lay off workers because of their exaggerated aversion to losses, which induces "endowment effects." High levels of debt make sales and layoffs necessary to ward off bankruptcy.

Our claim is not that analyses like these are mature enough to replace standard analyses of economic behavior. We simply want such analyses to have a voice, and a sympathetic ear.

Can Negotiators Outperform Game Theory?

Max H. Bazerman, Robert Gibbons,
Leigh Thompson, and Kathleen L. Valley

It is an empirical question whether rational players, either jointly or individually, can actually do better than a purely formal game theory predicts and should consequently ignore the strategic principles produced by such a theory.

Thomas C. Schelling, *The Strategy of Conflict*

During the past decade, two parallel literatures emerged and flourished: the behavioral literature on negotiation, and the game-theoretic literature on bargaining. Abundant evidence from both literatures suggests that settlement terms predicted by game-theoretic models are not accurate descriptions of actual negotiated outcomes. Furthermore, the behavioral literature provides much evidence that two common assumptions in game-theoretic models, self-interest and economic rationality, also are not accurate. Both of these discrepancies between theory and evidence—in outcomes and in assumptions—primarily imply that actual negotiated outcomes are less efficient than those predicted by game theory. Evidence is beginning to emerge, however, that under certain conditions, negotiators reach *more* efficient outcomes than predicted by game-theoretic models.

The argument that individuals can outperform game-theoretic predictions is not new. In *The Strategy of Conflict*, Schelling suggests that social norms may lead actual negotiations toward more efficient outcomes than those predicted by formal game theory. Experimental results have supported this thesis. Axelrod (1984), in his work on the prisoner's dilemma game, focuses on the role of expected future interaction as an explanation for when interdependent parties can outperform the game-theoretic solution that dictates defection in a finite-period prisoner's dilemma game. Axelrod's empirical finding is consistent with the

The preparation of this chapter was supported in part by grants from the National Science Foundation, No. SES9210298 and PYI9157447 to Leigh Thompson.

theoretical work of Kreps, Milgrom, Roberts, and Wilson (1982), who develop a model that deviates from standard game theory by assuming a small probability that the other party either is not rational or is not self-interested, and so will not follow the rational pure defection strategy. Our goal is to show that the outperformance of game-theoretic predictions is possible in even a one-trial context, and to offer social and cognitive explanations for such outcomes.

This chapter begins with a whirlwind tour of the behavioral and game-theoretic literatures. Our survey reflects the existing literature's emphasis on inefficient negotiation outcomes. We then present some intriguing recent evidence suggesting that in some settings negotiators may be able to outperform game-theoretic predictions. Finally, we offer several potential explanations of when and why negotiators outperform game theory. We focus on evidence from negotiations with private information, for which game theory predicts inefficient outcomes but behavioral research finds that face-to-face communication promotes more efficient outcomes. Our explanations for these surprisingly efficient outcomes emphasize social-cognitive aspects of face-to-face interaction that game-theoretic models based on self-interest and economic rationality ignore. We conclude by suggesting that these psychological explanations be incorporated into game theoretic models of bargaining.

A Whirlwind Tour of Two Literatures

Game theory offers a mathematical analysis of behavior in tightly specified strategic settings. Bargaining games are extremely simplified relative to the rich context of most negotiations, but the controlled situation provides precise, testable predictions. The behavioral approach to negotiations, in contrast, often considers richer contexts but typically offers less precise predictions, such as the direction but not the magnitude of a predicted difference in behavior.

One fundamental difference between studies of bargaining from experimental economics and behavioral studies from the negotiations literature is the approach taken toward face-to-face interaction between bargaining parties. Face-to-face interaction introduces a multitude of factors that cannot all be identified, isolated or controlled in the manner required by a strict game-theoretic analysis. Therefore, experimental economics studies on bargaining games are usually conducted with anonymous players whose communication is restricted to choices among specified alternatives, or moves. Negotiations research, in contrast, assumes that face-to-face interaction is central to most negotiations, and experimental studies typically allow unrestricted communication, without necessarily identifying the various factors that operate in this condition. What experimental economics studies of bargaining and behavioral studies of negotiations have in common is that each approaches face-to-face communication in such a way that it eliminates the possibility of studying the effects of that communication.

The vast majority of game-theoretic analyses of bargaining begins with two assumptions: self-interest and economic rationality. Abundant evidence from the behavioral negotiations literature, however, suggests that neither of these assumptions is accurate. Contrary to the self-interest assumption, negotiators systematically fail to maximize their own outcomes because of social concerns such as fairness (Kahneman, Knetsch, and Thaler 1986a) and comparison with others (Loewenstein, Thompson, and Bazerman 1989). Contrary to the economic rationality assumption, it is well accepted that negotiators' thought processes differ from those typically assumed in game-theoretic (and other economic) models (Arrow, Mnookin, Ross, Tversky, and Wilson 1993). More specifically, negotiators tend to be inappropriately affected by the positive or negative frame in which risks are viewed (Neale and Bazerman 1985b; Bazerman, Magliozzi, and Neale 1985), to anchor their number estimates in negotiations on irrelevant information (Neale and Northcraft 1986; Northcraft and Neale 1987), to make errors as a result of inappropriate optimism (Kahneman and Tversky 1993), to rely too heavily on readily available information (Neale, 1984), and to be overconfident about the likelihood of attaining outcomes that favor themselves (Bazerman and Neale 1982; Kahneman and Tversky 1993). Negotiators are also overly disposed to assume that negotiation tasks are fixed-sum, and thereby miss opportunities for mutually beneficial trade-offs between the parties (Thompson and Hastie 1990; Bazerman, Magliozzi, and Neale 1985), to escalate commitment to a previously selected course of action when it is no longer the most reasonable alternative (Neale and Bazerman 1991), and to overlook valuable information that is available by considering the opponent's cognitive perspective (Samuelson and Bazerman 1985).

Complementary work in experimental economics has begun to catalogue discrepancies between negotiated outcomes and game-theoretic predictions in specific bargaining games (see Roth 1993, for a survey). The two leading examples are ultimatum games and two-stage, alternating-offer games. In the former, players 1 and 2 seek to divide a fixed pie. Player 1 makes an offer, which player 2 then accepts or rejects (in which case both players receive nothing). The game-theoretic prediction is that player 1 should offer epsilon (i.e., the smallest positive amount that can be offered) and that player 2 should accept, but a large body of experimental evidence refutes both these predictions. Instead, player 1 typically offers between a third and half the pie, and player 2 typically rejects offers near zero and occasionally rejects offers as high as a third (Roth 1993). Such rejections by player 2 are of course inefficient: Both players are worse off than if they had reached an agreement.

In two-stage, alternating-offer games, player 1 makes an offer, which player 2 accepts or rejects, but if player 2 rejects then 2 makes a counteroffer which 1 accepts or rejects (in which case both players receive nothing). The pie shrinks if player 1's offer is rejected—say, from $10 to be divided in the first period to $4 to be divided in the second. Game theory predicts that player 2 should offer epsilon in the second period, thereby earning nearly $4, so player 1 should offer $4 in the first period, and player 2 should accept 1's offer. These predictions are frequently refuted by the experimental evidence, in ways roughly consistent with the evidence on ultimatum games. Once again, if player 2 rejects player 1's initial offer, the outcome of the game is inefficient, regardless of whether 1 later accepts 2's offer, because the pie shrinks after 2's rejection. Furthermore, a new kind of behavior arises that is also inconsistent with the game-theoretic predictions: if player 2 rejects 1's offer, 2 often then makes a counterproposal that yields less cash for 2 than did 1's original offer, such as rejecting a 7-3 split and then offering 2-2.

In sum, ample evidence suggests that the great majority of existing game-theoretic bargaining models do not accurately predict negotiator behavior. Such models typically assume both economic rationality and self-interest, and there is substantial evidence that these underlying assumptions are false. One natural next step is to include robust behavioral findings in game-theoretic models (i.e., to depart in a well-specified way from at least one of the economic rationality and self-interest assumptions) and to test the predictions that result in simple bargaining games. Indeed, recent work has followed exactly this path (Bolton 1991; Rabin 1993).

This quick review might lead to the conclusion that human cognition and socialization inevitably impede the negotiation process. The departures from economic rationality described in the behavioral literature frequently lead to inefficient negotiation outcomes, and experiments involving two of the simplest bargaining games not only reject the point predictions from game theory but also find inefficient outcomes where game theory predicts efficiency. But there is also evidence that negotiators can be surprisingly effective, and in some contexts, negotiators systematically outperform the predictions of standard game-theoretic models. Thus, there appear to be functional, adaptive aspects of human behavior not accounted for by these models. We turn next to evidence that negotiators outperform game-theoretic predictions under specifiable conditions. Based on this evidence, we then develop a taxonomy of potential explanations.

Evidence That People Can Outperform Game Theory

In order for negotiators to outperform the game-theoretic prediction for a certain bargaining game, it is necessary that game theory's prediction for that game be inefficient, otherwise there is no room to improve. Almost every game-theoretic analysis of a bargaining game with complete information (i.e., no private information) predicts an efficient outcome (two notable exceptions are Crawford 1982 and Fernandez and Glazer 1991). In the ultimatum and two-stage, alternating-offer games, for example, game theory predicts efficient outcomes, so while experimental evidence can (and does) refute game theory's point predictions (i.e., the specific terms of agreement) for these games, evidence from such games can never show both negotiators outperforming game-theoretic predictions.

In bargaining games with private information, on the other hand, typical game-theoretic analysis predicts an inefficient outcome especially when there is two-sided private information. The intuition behind these predictions is that a player with private information will have an incentive to posture (e.g., be strategically deceptive about his or her interests), and will be willing to forego, or at least delay, trades with positive but small value to achieve more advantageous settlement terms in trades with large positive values.

In this section, we describe two classic models of bargaining with private information. The first of these models is Akerlof's (1970) analysis of "lemons," or the "winner's curse," a game with one-sided private information. The second is Myerson and Satterthwaite's (1983) study of bargaining with two-sided private information. In both cases, game theory predicts that the outcome will be inefficient. Yet in both cases, intriguing recent evidence suggests that face-to-face (or even telephone) communication may help negotiators achieve efficient outcomes.

One-Sided Private Information

Previous studies have suggested that, under asymmetric information, negotiators fail to consider the implications of information held by their opponents. This may result in negative payoffs—-the winner's curse (Samuelson and Bazerman 1985; Carroll, Bazerman, and Maury 1988). The most common documentation of the winner's curse in bilateral bargaining involves the "Acquiring a Company" problem, in which one firm (the acquirer) may offer to buy another (the target). While the acquirer knows only that the firm's value under current management is between $0 and $100, with all values equally likely, the target knows its current worth exactly. The acquirer does know, however, that the firm will be worth 50 percent more under the acquirer's management than under the current ownership. Thus, it would be efficient for a transaction to take place. What price should the acquirer offer for the target?

If the acquirer offers any positive value, $X, and the target accepts, the current value of the company is worth between $0 and $X, and any value in that range is equally likely. Therefore, the expected value of the target if an offer of

$X is accepted is $X/2. Since the company is worth 50 percent more to the acquirer, the acquirer's expected value is 1.5($X/2), which equals only 75 percent of the offer price. Thus, on average, the acquirer obtains a company worth 25 percent less than the price the acquirer pays when an offer is accepted. Considering all possible values of X, this analysis reveals the acquirer's best strategy is not to make an offer (i.e., X = 0).

The irony of the situation is that even though the firm is worth more to the acquirer than to the target, any offer above $0 leads to a negative expected return to the acquirer, because of the high likelihood that the target will accept the acquirer's offer when the firm is least valuable to the acquirer, i.e., when it is a "lemon" (Akerlof 1970). As a result, a "winning" bidder should expect to lose money, suffering the winner's curse.

In contrast to this game-theoretic prescriptive analysis, many studies have documented that buyers presented with this problem commonly offer between $50 and $75. This empirical finding is robust across a wide variety of subject populations, including many that have special training, knowledge, and skills (Samuelson and Bazerman 1985; Bazerman and Carroll 1987). In addition, this finding has been extended to contexts in which subjects were paid according to their performance and allowed multiple trials to learn the correct response (Ball, Bazerman, and Carroll 1991). How is this $50 to $75 decision reached? One common explanation is: "On average, the firm is worth $50 to the target and $75 to the acquirer. Consequently, a transaction in this range typically will be profitable to both parties." The buyers are not considering what the seller's potential acceptance of a bid implies about the value of the company.

In the studies reviewed above, all subjects act as buyer; that is, subjects are presented with the problem and asked to submit a bid rather than participate in a two-party negotiation. There is no opportunity to outperform game theory (i.e., multi-person decision theory) in this asocial, single-person version of the winner's curse problem. More recently, Valley, Moag, and Bazerman (1993) created a two-party, social version of this problem that allowed subjects to underperform, meet, or outperform the game-theoretic prediction.

Valley et al. developed the problem into a dyadic situation, with buyer and seller roles. The buyers were given the basic information from the earlier version. The sellers were told the structure of the problem and the true value of the firm to them (randomly assigned between 0 and 100), but were not told the degree to which the buyer's value for the firm would exceed their own (again 50 percent). The parties were then allowed to negotiate an acquisition price for the firm. Each party was told the objective was to make as much money as possible.

Valley et al. were intending to use this dyadic version of the winner's curse to study whether a relationship between the parties would protect the buyer from suffering the winner's curse. Accordingly, in two studies, the type of relationships between the parties was varied. They anticipated that without a relationship between the parties, the cognitive limitations suggested by the initial studies would again lead ill-informed buyers to be suckers and fall victim to the winner's curse, but that if parties with a pre-existing relationship were allowed to communicate directly, accurate information would be exchanged and the buyer would not fall prey to the winner's curse.

Unexpectedly, the majority of dyads in all conditions (including absence of a relationship) reached agreements that were mutually beneficial for both parties. Generally, information was openly and honestly shared, and this information sharing eliminated the winner's curse. The sellers did not take advantage of their superior information, despite the fact that they easily could have. Thus, the majority of dyads were able to reach an agreement that Pareto-dominated the impasse predicted by game theory: typically, both the buyer and the seller were better off than they would have been had trade not occurred.

After these studies, Valley et al. tentatively hypothesized that negotiators can solve the dyadic winner's curse simply by talking to each other. In a third study, they tested this hypothesis, manipulating whether the communication within the negotiation was verbal or written. In both conditions, the communication time was ample and the potential volume and content of communication unlimited. The dyads allowed to communicate verbally continued to solve the winner's curse. In the written condition, however, the winner's curse reemerged, and significant barriers to agreement were created. Valley et al. speculated that the verbal interchange created a relational bond which was a successful mechanism for increasing the amount of accurate information shared between the parties, thereby reducing or eliminating the winner's curse in bilateral bargaining. These findings suggest that verbal dialogue may have the potential to allow parties to outperform game-theoretic predictions in other settings.

Two-Sided Private Information

Myerson and Satterthwaite (1983) present a striking theoretical result: if a buyer and a seller have valuations (or "types") for a good that are privately known, independently distributed, and continuously distributed over intervals that at least partially overlap, then there is no game that all types of both parties would be willing to play that produces trade if and only if it is efficient. To be more concrete, consider a modified version of the "Acquiring a Company" problem, where the value of the firm under current management, V_s, is uniformly distributed between $0 and $100, and the value of the firm under the acquirer's management, V_b, is independently and uniformly distributed between $0 and $100. (The same impossibility result would hold if $0 and $100 become, say, $50 and $200 for V_b.) Myerson and Satterthwaite's result implies that whether one party makes a single, final offer, or the parties alternate in making offers until they quit or reach agreement, or the buyer and seller simultaneously make an offer and a demand, respectively, trading if the offer exceeds the demand, none of these games (or any other game) results in trade if and only if it is efficient (i.e., if and only if $V_b \geq V_s$).

Note that the intuition behind this result is quite different from that behind the winner's curse. In Akerlof's model, a low valuation for the seller implies a low valuation for the buyer. Here, in contrast, the buyer's and seller's types are independent, so the buyer cannot unknowingly get stuck with a lemon. Instead, the problem is that each side will posture, because sellers have an incentive to present the good as worth more to them than it really is, while buyers are motivated to present the good as worth less, thereby putting small-value trades at risk.

Myerson and Satterthwaite also prove a second result: for the uniform distributions we assumed in the modified "Acquiring a Company" problem (namely, 0 to 100), the game that maximizes the parties' expected gains from trade is a particular equilibrium of a double auction (or the "sealed-bid mechanism"). In this game, the buyer and seller simultaneously make an offer and a demand, and then trade at the average of the two if the offer exceeds the demand. Chatterjee and Samuelson (1983) analyzed many equilibria of this game, including one in which the parties' strategies are linear (e.g., the buyer's offer is a linear function of her valuation). In this linear equilibrium, trade occurs if and only if the acquirer's valuation exceeds the target's by at least $25. Thus, Myerson and Satterthwaite predict inefficiencies even under the most efficient of the possible bargaining games for this problem.

Experimental evidence suggests Myerson and Satterthwaite's pessimistic predictions are not supported when parties play games of two-sided private information in a face-to-face context. In one of a series of experiments, Radner and Schotter (1989) replaced the sealed-bid mechanism with face-to-face bargaining. Subjects in dyads were told they would bargain with one another for fifteen rounds. Both buyers and sellers drew envelopes dictating their valuations and costs, respectively, over the fifteen rounds. The distribution of possible values was skewed (up for the buyer and down for the seller, symmetrically) to increase the likelihood that the value to the buyer was greater than the value to the seller.[1] In each round, the pair could bargain for a maximum of five minutes. An administrator was present in the room to enforce a set of rules that stipulated that no values or costs could be revealed, no threats could be made,

[1] These skewed distributions result in an equilibrium of the sealed-bid mechanism where: buyers bid value if $V_b < 36$, and bid $20.25 + 0.438(V_b)$ if $V_b \geq 36$; sellers bid cost if $V_s > 64$, and bid $36 + 0.438(V_s)$ if $V_s \leq 64$.

no bargains could be contingent on future rounds, and no side payments could be made or promised. The transaction price was that agreed upon by the two parties. The surprising result was that when bargaining face-to-face, negotiators captured 99 percent of all available trades.

The experiments reviewed in this section suggest that face-to-face negotiation in bargaining games with private information includes social and cognitive factors that may lead to better outcomes than game theory predicts. More research is needed to isolate the factors that contribute to the success of face-to-face interactions. This analysis is best directed by developing a framework for considering how social and cognitive contingencies can affect standard game-theoretic predictions.

Potential Explanations for Why People Beat Game Theory

We have reviewed preliminary evidence suggesting that negotiators can systematically reach agreements that are Pareto-superior to those predicted by game theory. This section proposes a number of potential explanations for this evidence, organized into three broad categories. First, we explore non-traditional utility functions. Second, we explore the role of social heuristics based on psychological processes and assumptions. Finally, we look at how cognitive and behavioral limitations affect negotiations.

Non-traditional Utility Functions

Traditional economic models assume self-interest as the sole motive of actors, ignoring "social goals." More recent behavioral (and even economic) models, however, allow individuals to value other dimensions of outcomes, including concerns for others, disutility for deception, and preference for equality (e.g., Bolton 1991, Rabin 1993). These components appear to be part of the utility functions of individuals and may be incorporated into formal models. We review attempts to include these attributes in utility functions, and discuss how these revised utility functions may account for some of the evidence that individuals outperform game-theoretic predictions based exclusively on self-interest.

The Evidence

Fairness considerations account for some of the limitations of the explanatory power of economic models. Substantial evidence exists that individuals place utility on fairness in ways that are inconsistent with the self-interest assumption.

In a provocative set of experiments, Kahneman, Knetsch, and Thaler (1986a) asked subjects to evaluate the fairness of the action in the following situation:

A hardware store has been selling snow shovels for $15. The morning after a large snowstorm, the store raises the price to $20. Please rate this action as:

Completely Fair − Acceptable − Unfair − Very Unfair

The two favorable and the two unfavorable categories were combined to indicate the proportion of respondents who judged the action acceptable or unfair. Despite the (short-run) economic rationality of raising the prices on the snow shovels, 82 percent of the respondents considered this action unfair. These results may reflect concerns for fairness; if short-run supply and demand were the only considerations, raising prices would have been perceived as fair. Alternatively, the subjects' responses also are consistent with an entirely economic argument: The subjects may suspect that the firm has deviated from a long-run equilibrium of a repeated game, in which the firm has private information about supply and/or demand and is supposed to keep prices at non-gouging levels on average.

Fairness issues also arise in ultimatum games. A number of researchers have methodically studied how people respond to ultimatums (see Thaler 1988, for a survey). As noted above, game theory predicts that player 1 will offer player 2 only slightly more than zero, and that player 2 will accept any offer greater than zero. Empirical observation suggests, however, that individuals incorporate fairness considerations into their choices. Player 1 demands less than 70 percent of the funds on average, while individuals in the role of player 2 sometimes reject profitable but unequal offers, and accept zero only 20 percent of the time it is offered (Guth, Schmittbergh, and Schwarz 1982). However, distinguishing between the effects of fairness and self-interest here is difficult, given the observed behavior of player 2.

In recent work, Straub and Murnighan (1992) manipulated knowledge of the size of the pie in ultimatum games. When player 1 knew the size of the pie but player 2 did not, player 2s accepted lower offers and player 1s made lower offers. The latter evidence suggests that it is 1's evaluation of 2's requirement of fairness that drives 1's observed behavior when the size of the pie is common knowledge, rather than any absolute preference for fairness on the part of player 1. Since the players are assigned their roles at random, this conclusion about player 1's motives suggest that player 2's behavior is driven by a distaste for getting the short end of a deal, rather than by a symmetrical taste for fairness. Consistent with this, Loewenstein, Thompson, and Bazerman (1989) argue that the outcomes of others commonly act as a reference point in interpersonal decision settings, and that interpersonal comparisons can overwhelm concern for the absolute value of one's own outcome in rating potential resolutions of a dispute. For example, typical individuals rated $500 for self and $500 for another person as more satisfactory than $600 for the self and $800 for the other person.

Fairness considerations may be so powerful that players will be willing to pay to punish their opponent if their opponent asks for too much. In two-stage, alternating-offer bargaining games, Ochs and Roth (1989) found that 81 percent of rejected offers were followed by disadvantageous counteroffers, where the party who rejected the initial offer demanded less than he or she had just been offered. Ochs and Roth argue that the players' utilities for fairness may explain the results. They also note, however, that a simple notion of equality does not explain the data, since in most cases player 1 asks for more than 50 percent of the resources. Rather, as in ultimatum games, parties realize that the other side may very well refuse offers perceived as unfair, despite the economic rationality of accepting them. Thus, an offer closer to 50 percent than 100 percent maximizes player 1's expected payoff.

Ochs and Roth's argument also is consistent with Forsythe et al.'s (1991) results: Parties played either an ultimatum game or a "dictator" game in which player 1 could simply decide without player 2's approval how the resources would be split. Whereas many player 1s chose a fifty-fifty split in the ultimatum game, none proposed a 100 percent-0 percent split. In the dictator game, in contrast, 36 percent of the player 1s took 100 percent. Thus, when approval was required, proposals were more equal, consistent with 1's fear that 2 will judge an offer unfair. Even in the dictator game, however, 64 percent chose to give the other party some portion of the resources. The latter finding may be the best evidence that people place utility on being fair, rather than that they aim to maximize their own outcome by taking into consideration the other party's distaste for the short end of a deal. Even this evidence is open to questions as to whether the subjects anticipated repeated play, or even future interaction with the experimenter.

Modeling Social Utility

Probably the most well-accepted descriptive theory of decision making is Kahneman and Tversky's Prospect Theory (1979). A central idea of Prospect Theory is that people evaluate the utility of alternative courses of action relative to a reference point (Tversky and Kahneman 1981). Prospect Theory examines decision making in what Loewenstein et al. label *intrapersonal contexts*. In intrapersonal contexts, the outcomes of the decision affect only the decision maker, and the reference point is most frequently modeled as the current state (i.e., wealth) of the decision maker.

Intrapersonal contexts may be contrasted to *interpersonal contexts*, in which people's decisions affect their own and others' outcomes. In the latter contexts, the reference point does not simply represent the current state of the decision maker. Interpersonal contexts focus the decision maker on the comparison other, and the most likely comparison points are the outcomes obtained by the comparison other. Messick and his colleagues (Messick and Sentis 1985; Messick and Thorngate 1967) incorporate this concern by distinguishing between nonsocial utility (utility for own outcomes) and social utility (utility for the difference between own and others' outcomes).

Loewenstein et al. identified a utility function for decision making in interpersonal contexts that dealt explicitly with the comparison between outcomes to self and outcomes to others. The precise form of the estimated function, selected by goodness of fit tests over a variety of forms, was:

$$U = {}_1\text{self} + {}_2\text{posdif} + {}_3\text{posdif}^2 + {}_4\text{negdif} + {}_5\text{negdif}^2$$

where:

posdif = positive differences between one's own and the other's payoff (advantageous inequality);
negdif = the absolute value of negative differences between one's own and the other's payoff (disadvantageous inequality).

Loewenstein et al. found that disputants preferred equal outcomes over inequalities, so that the signs of both B_2 and B_4 were negative, but advantageous inequalities were preferred over disadvantageous inequalities, so that the absolute magnitude of B_4 was greater than that of B_2.

One could extend this type of analysis to predict that people place a disutility on lying. That is, people regulate their behavior in ways that enhance the correspondence between their self-presentation and how they truly think about themselves (DePaulo 1993). For example, the following adaptation of the regression in Loewenstein et al. might better capture the utility of negotiators:

$$U = {}_1\text{self} + {}_2\text{posdif} + {}_3\text{negdif} + {}_4\text{lying},$$

where lying refers to the disutility individuals place on telling a lie. By adding in such non-traditional attributes, a wide variety of utility functions could be specified and tested.

A central point of this section is that fairness, social comparison, equality, and the disutility of lying affect behavior in competitive contexts, and that they can be included in a model of bargaining behavior. The strength of such an approach is that potentially it empowers game-theoretic models to account for current anomalies. To the extent that individuals have utility for equality (Messick 1991) and negative utility for lying, the anomalies of dyads splitting the pie equally in an ultimatum game and people reaching mutually beneficial agreements in the Valley et al. task begin to be rational manifestations of people's true utility functions.

Social Heuristics

The previous subsection argued that alternative formulations of utility, incorporating non-traditional attributes, offer potential explanations for findings that cannot be explained by game-theoretic models based on self-interest. This subsection, in contrast, will suggest that some anomalies result not from utilities placed on potential *outcomes*, but instead from social heuristics guiding the negotiation *process*, and thus cannot be explained by game-theoretic models based on individual rationality. In a two-party negotiation, joint outcomes may exceed the game-theoretic prediction because of shared social heuristics guiding behavior. Social heuristics are the beliefs and assumptions about human behavior that individuals use to guide their own behavior when they are interacting with others; we will focus on these, rather than on the more commonly discussed cognitive heuristics that permeate the behavioral decision area (Dawes 1988; Bazerman 1990; Messick 1991).

Our hypothesis is that social heuristics held by both parties lead toward efficient dyadic outcomes in competitive situations, though applying these heuristics is not necessarily the best strategy for the individual negotiator. We believe that people tend to follow social heuristics in competitive, interactive bargaining situations. The use of these heuristics will be augmented to the extent that the bargaining situation allows individuals to interact in an unconstrained fashion. That is, to the extent that individuals may freely communicate and are in full view of one another, the heuristics are more likely to come into play than in situations in which communication is restricted. Thus, we argue that social heuristics help account for the communication effects observed by Valley et al. and by Radner and Schotter, and identify and review below some of the most powerful and pervasive social heuristics.

Assumption of Future Interaction

It is well known that individuals who expect to interact with someone in the future will behave differently than individuals who expect an interaction to be an isolated episode. People who foresee future interaction behave in ways they believe will affect or influence the other's future behavior. (Indeed, even game theory makes this prediction.) Acting under this heuristic, individuals often behave as if they were going to interact with a person again, even when they know the interaction is a one-shot situation. Thus, the heuristic departs from game theory's assumption of economic rationality. Studies of tipping behavior, for example, indicate that individuals frequently leave significant tips even when the probability of repeated interaction is extremely low.

In the context of bargaining, we might expect that negotiators will behave in one-shot interactions in ways that are more consistent with rational behavior under the assumption of future interaction. For example, Axelrod (1984), in his discussion of the prisoners' dilemma task, argued that cooperative behavior is more likely if people perceive they will interact in the future. In short, cooperative behavior operates as a signal to one's opponent that one will continue to act cooperatively in the future. If both parties act according to a social heuristic assuming future interaction, it becomes easier for the parties to reach agreement with incomplete information in the presence of only a small bargaining zone.

Concern with Reputation

According to this heuristic, people are concerned with maintaining their reputation even in situations where their reputation is not at stake, such as one-shot or anonymous bargaining situations. This concern obviously is closely related to the assumption of future interaction discussed above, but can apply more broadly. One's behavior in a dyad might affect one's reputation with a third party, for example. It is sensible and rational to act in ways that preserve and protect one's reputation when information about the self will be transmitted to others and will affect one's future dealings with others. However, reputation should not be a concern in bargaining situations where the parties will not meet again and/or the true identity of the opponent will not be revealed.

The concern for reputation results from the overgeneralization of a larger social motive, known as self-presentation or social desirability (Goffman 1959; Baumeister 1982). Social psychological research suggests that self-presentational concerns are often internalized. That is, it is not only important to the individual that he or she be seen by others in a favorable light, but also that he or she view himself or herself positively. A social heuristic that causes negotiators to maintain a concern for self-presentation or reputation, even in situations where such a concern may be irrational, may lead them to reveal information they otherwise might not reveal in isolated bargaining situations.

Belief in Simultaneous Causality

According to this heuristic, individuals believe that engaging in a behavior or action will increase the likelihood that another person will engage in the same behavior, even in situations where there can be no connection between the actions. That is, individuals behave as if their behavior at time 1 will make it more likely that other individuals also will engage in such behavior at time 1. A classic example of this faulty heuristic is the voter's belief that if he or she makes the effort to cast a ballot then others are more likely to vote. Note that this heuristic could have some validity if the voter's belief was that his or her vote at time 1 would affect the likelihood of voting by others in subsequent elections; it is more problematic to imagine that casting one's vote could simultaneously affect others' decisions to vote. Nevertheless, such beliefs pervade individuals' thinking. This type of thinking is part of a larger aspect of irrational thought, known as metamagical thinking (Hofstaeder 1983).

In bargaining situations, we might expect that individuals who choose to disclose information honestly will believe that a simultaneous disclosure by their opponent also is likely to be honest. Similarly, Shafir and Tversky (1992) found that a substantial portion of subjects would cooperate in a one-shot prisoners' dilemma game if they did not know the other party's decision, but would defect if they knew that the other party had already chosen either to cooperate or to defect. The subjects who knew the other party's decision made the payoff-maximizing choice, while the behavior of subjects who did not know the other party's choice suggests a belief in simultaneous causality.

Agreement-Is-Good Heuristic

According to this heuristic, individuals believe that reaching a mutual agreement is better than not reaching an agreement. (This belief could, of course, also be modeled as a non-traditional utility function.) In a bargaining context, individuals often lack a clear method of evaluating the utility of an outcome, and therefore may reason that if they reach an agreement with another person then the bargaining situation was successful; the failure to reach an agreement is regarded as unsuccessful. The agreement-is-good heuristic will lead negotiators to share more information than prescribed by a standard game-theoretic model, which is consistent with the empirical evidence reviewed above.

Norm of Reciprocity

Perhaps the most pervasive and robust social heuristic that guides human behavior is the norm of reciprocity (Gouldner 1960; Gergen et al. 1975). The generalized norm of reciprocity is extremely powerful and can lead individuals to reciprocate on dimensions that are out of proportion to the original offer. For example, individuals were more likely to support a confederate's request for buying raffle tickets that could help the confederate win a new convertible car when the confederate had previously bought the subject's cola (Regan 1968). Feelings of obligation are influenced by factors in the situation. For example, a larger favor is reciprocated more often than a smaller favor (Greenberg and Frisch 1972). People's attributions about the motives of the helper also matter. People are more likely to return a favor when the original help is perceived to be given intentionally and voluntarily (Goranson and Berkowitz 1966).

The generalized norm of reciprocity applies to the sharing of intimate or personal information among persons, or self-disclosure (Altman and Taylor 1973). Simply, if we share intimate information with other people, they are likely to respond with equally personal information. Extending the norm of reciprocity to a bargaining context, we would expect that an individual who offers information about his or her lowest selling price or highest possible offer will not only expect that such information will be reciprocated in kind, but also will be likely to receive such information from the opponent. This has the potential to result in more information exchange than accounted for by game theory, and this information exchange can account for mutually beneficial agreements that game theory would not predict.

Social Identity

Social identity theory asserts that the perception of the self is defined by social group memberships. Identifying with others reduces social and psychological distance, and increases our positive evaluations of them. Social identity is not a constant; it varies with the salience of the group context (Turner 1987). Orbell, van de Kragt, and Dawes (1988) found that an individual's sense of social identity with a specific group can be enhanced by communication with others in the group. More direct forms of communication that increase the perceptual salience of others, such as face-to-face or oral communication, should be more effective in increasing an individual's identification with the group.

Extended to bargaining situations, as individuals' social identities are heightened, they are less likely to focus on individual gains and less likely to deceive others (Kramer, Pommerenke, and Newton 1993). To the extent that an individual negotiator is evaluating himself or herself in terms of the group, social heuristics such as reciprocity, reputation concerns, and agreement-is-good should increase. Additionally, social identity perceptions of the self should increase the value one party places on joint outcomes, reducing the utility for rewards gained at the expense of the other party.

Norm of Commitment

The norm of commitment is the obligation that a person feels to comply or follow through with promises. Although communication between parties may lead to greater disclosure of truthful information in several ways, such as by enhancing social identity, as noted above, and creating a perceived relational bond (Kramer and Brewer 1984), the effectiveness of such communication in producing efficient agreements may be due in part to the actual verbal promises or commitments made during interaction. There is evidence that such discussion leads members of groups to make and keep promises to cooperate. For example, in studies of cooperation and defection in social dilemma tasks, Orbell et al. (1988) found that to the extent that members make promises during a discussion period, cooperation greatly increases during subsequent decision periods, even when fellow group members have no way of checking whether such promises are kept. Similarly, Braver and Wilson (1984) found that, controlling for future interaction and common knowledge, subjects who made promises during discussion were more likely to cooperate. Work in experimental economics is also beginning to consider the significant role of commitments in reaching negotiated agreements. Cooper (1990), testing the effects of promises in the Battle of the Sexes game, found that when one subject was allowed to make a single, nonbinding announcement about intended future behavior, subjects almost always reached a coordinated outcome.

Standard game theory treats unenforceable promises as signals that usually should be ignored by rational negotiators (though Farrell and Gibbons 1989 and Myerson 1989 propose that signals should be taken as true when they are consistent with the promisor's incentives). Yet the studies presented above suggest that when a party makes a verbal promise, she or he is likely to follow through with it, and the other party will assume this is true and adjust behavior accordingly. Thus, the norm of commitment may make promises binding on the parties, and thereby allow the dyad to coordinate behavior and, in some games, outperform expectations.

To summarize: We describe a set of social heuristics that serve humans quite well in most interactive situations. Like any heuristic, however, these social heuristics may lead to irrational behavior in some contexts. We argue that social heuristics lead individuals to engage in suboptimal behavior from an individual perspective, but may cause the quality of joint outcomes in games with private information to exceed game-theoretic predictions. To incorporate social heuristics into game-theoretic models requires that rationality be considered at the dyadic (or group) level, rather than at the individual level.

Cognitive and Behavioral Limitations

Despite the extensive evidence on the negative effects that cognitive biases have on negotiation (Neale and Bazerman 1991), we argue that there are certain cognitive limitations that benefit the dyad in competitive contexts. Two such limitations are especially important in environments with private information: limitations in individuals' ability to deceive and lie, and the illusory transparency of knowledge.

Limits on Deception and Lying

In discussing deception and lying, we move beyond our earlier suggestion that people place a disutility on lying, to the argument that there are limitations in our effectiveness as liars. A particularly important judgment that people make in many social interactions, especially in bargaining contexts, is evaluating when people are lying or otherwise fostering deception. One argument is that people will reveal deception through nonverbal cues, even when they are successful in lying verbally (Frank 1988). Ekman and Friesen (1974) argue that people attend more to what they are saying than to what they are doing with their bodies. People trying to deceive others, for example, may lie in a calm way, verbally, but reveal their true emotions through nonverbal cues. In Ekman's terms, there is "nonverbal leakage." That is, true emotions leak out even if a person tries to conceal them.

Liars often betray themselves through paralinguistic expressions of anxiety, tension, and nervousness. It is sometimes possible to tell when someone is lying by noting the pitch of the voice. Several studies (Ekman, Friesen, and Scherer 1976; Krauss, Geller, and Olson 1976) indicated that the average (or, more technically, fundamental) pitch of the voice is higher when lying than when telling the truth. The difference is small, and often one cannot tell by listening, but electronic vocal analysis reveals lying with considerable accuracy. In addition, shorter answers, longer delays in responding, more speech errors, and more nervous, less serious answers are all characteristic of people perceived as liars, or instructed to tell lies (Apple, Streeter, and Krauss 1979; Kraut 1978; Zuckerman, DePaulo, and Rosenthal 1981).

For our purpose, this research has two important implications: (1) people will be more accurate in detecting deception in face-to-face interactions and, therefore, (2) people will be less inclined to lie in face-to-face interactions with others. In terms of accuracy, subjects quite consistently perceive deceptive messages as less truthful than honest messages (see DePaulo 1993 for a review).

The research on lying and accuracy of lie detection suggests that bargaining contexts provide an arena that cultivates truthtelling and the accurate detection of deception. First, perceivers are more likely to be in a lie-detection mode. That is, in a negotiation situation, people are more "on guard" than in routinized social encounters. Second, a competitive situation provides good information about the likely motives of a potential liar. DePaulo, Stone, and Lassiter (1985) found that lies were easiest to detect when the sender of the lie had the greatest motivation to lie. In contrast, lies were harder to detect without any specific information about reasons to lie. It is clear how and why someone would use deception in a bargaining situation: sellers are expected to inflate their demands; buyers are expected to deflate their offers. These effects are enhanced when negotiators are in full view of one another and can take advantage of all the available non-verbal cues.

The Illusory Transparency of Knowledge

In this section, we argue that individuals often act as if another party (e.g., the opponent negotiator) has access to information the individual knows the other party does not possess. That is, we predict negotiators do not realize and achieve the full value of their private information. This prediction stems from work on the "curse of knowledge," which argues that in predicting others' knowledge, people are unable to ignore knowledge they possess, even when they know that others do not have access to the same information (Camerer, Loewenstein, and Weber 1989). Camerer (1992) argues that this curse explains the difficulty of teaching, since it is hard to imagine how little the students know, and the difficulty of product design, since it is hard for product designers to comprehend how tough it is for consumers to master high-tech devices. In our context, we argue that (1) a negotiator frequently acts in ways that would make more sense if the negotiator's opponent had the negotiator's private information, and (2) when both parties act as if the other party is better informed than is actually the case, this helps the parties achieve mutually beneficial agreements.

Keysar (1992) argues that individuals often assume that when they send an ambiguous message to another individual, their communicative intent will be magically understood by the other party, even when the content of the message is based on information that the receiver does not possess. Keysar had people read scenarios that provided them with privileged information about "David." They read that David followed a friend's recommendation for a particular restaurant and had dinner there. Half of the participants in the experiment learned that he really enjoyed the dinner, and the other half learned that he really disliked the dinner. In both cases, they read that David left the following note to the friend: "About the restaurant, it was marvelous, just marvelous." The participants in the study who knew that he enjoyed the dinner had a strong tendency to believe that the friend would take the comment as sincere. In contrast, participants in the study who knew that he disliked the dinner had a strong tendency to believe that the friend would take the comment as sarcastic. The result occurred despite the fact that both groups of participants knew that the friend had access to only the one note. Keysar argues that we believe an ambiguous message will be accurately received if we have the information to unambiguously interpret the message, even if we know that the recipient of the message does not.

Keysar, Ginzel, and Bazerman (1995) have recently extended these arguments to show that individuals ignore the privacy of private information in predicting the behavior of negotiators. In two experiments, subjects played the role of third-party observers of an adapted version of the Acquiring a Company problem. In the adapted version, all subjects were told that the seller sent a memo to the buyer stating that the firm is worth $80/share to the seller, and that the seller will accept $85/share. (Recall that the firm is worth 50 percent more to the seller.) The subjects vary, however, in terms of what they know about the true situation. One group was told that the true value of the firm is $20/share to the seller, and that the seller's agent (who sent the memo to the buyer) knew this. A second group was told that the value of the firm is again $20/share to the seller, but the seller's agent thought that the firm was worth $80/share. Finally, a third group was told that the value of the firm is $80/share to the seller, and that the seller's agent knew this. Keysar et al. found that (1) the subject's knowledge of the value of the firm to the seller dramatically affected the subjects' predictions of the buyer's behavior (even though the buyer had no access to information about the firm's value to the seller), and that (2) the subject's knowledge of the seller's agent's knowledge also had a dramatic influence on the subject's predictions of the buyer's behavior, independent of the true value of the firm to the seller. Thus, subjects acted as if the information that one negotiator had metamagically would be available to the other party.

The central point of this subsection on cognitive limitations is that if a negotiator acts as if his or her private knowledge is common, this will lead to behaviors that are more typical of the behaviors expected under a full-information condition, consistent with the high rate of mutually beneficial agreements found by Valley et al. and by Radner and Schotter. Thus, in contrast to the ample evidence that cognitive biases impede negotiation, this subsection suggests that certain cognitive limitations improve joint outcomes in negotiations.

Summary

Siegel and Fouraker (1960), discussing the vital role of social variables in face-to-face bargaining, conclude that "such variables should either be systematically studied or controlled in experimentation on bargaining. It cannot be assumed, as has often been done, that such variables may simply be neglected" (1960, 22). In the past, face-to-face communication has been treated by both game-theoretic analyses and behavioral negotiation research in ways that eliminated the possibility of identifying and testing the important effects of specific variables within that communication. The evidence presented at the beginning of this chapter suggests that in games of private information, where game theory predicts less than fully efficient outcomes, negotiators bargaining face-to-face outperform the predictions of game theory. We argue that the social, cognitive, and behavioral components of face-to-face communication may be keys to understanding why negotiators are able to outperform these game-theoretic predictions.

This chapter presents a three-part framework from which to build a systematic study of the vital effects of face-to-face communication in bargaining. First, face-to-face interaction affects the utilities of the parties, such that self-interest is only one variable in a utility function that includes preferences for equality, and disutilities for disadvantageous differences and lying. Second, social heuristics, beliefs and assumptions about human behavior that individuals use to guide their own behavior when they are interacting with others, increase tacit understandings between the parties that suggest that certain moves either are more or less acceptable in face-to-face bargaining. While these heuristics appear irrational at the individual level, they may be rational for the negotiating dyad. Finally, certain cognitive and behavioral limitations—limits on deception and lying, and the illusory transparency of knowledge—benefit the dyad in competitive contexts by reducing the ability of the individual parties to capitalize on private information. These conclusions are based on a limited body of research evidence. Future research is needed to replicate and extend these propositions, and to eliminate alternative explanations for efficient performance in games where inefficient agreements are predicted by game theory.

Schelling asserts that if bargainers "can do *better* than a purely deductive game theory would predict . . . even a normative, prescriptive, strategic theory cannot be based on purely formal analysis" (1960, 164). This chapter suggests Schelling's conclusion may be overly pessimistic. Game-theoretical analyses may be able to model some of the social variables leading to this superior performance, but they can only hope to do so if they begin to incorporate social and psychological variables into their analyses. Our objective is not to offer an alternative to game theory. Rather, we have developed a social-cognitive framework that provides a guide for future theoretical development and empirical analyses of behavior in competitive contexts. Models that include non-traditional utility functions, social heuristics, and cognitive and behavioral limitations may well be used to build more precise "normative, prescriptive, [and] strategic" theories of bargaining behavior.

Playing the Maintenance Game: How Mental Models Drive Organizational Decisions

John S. Carroll, John Sterman, and Alfred A. Marcus

Nature has equipped organisms with the ability to regenerate or repair themselves when damaged. If I cut myself, healing takes over without need of conscious direction. If I am hurt badly enough, the body's needs will make themselves known and tend to preempt voluntary activities. In this way, a balance between short-term interests (e.g., continuing to work or play) and long-term interests (staying healthy) is established on terms that derive from an evolutionary logic. Similarly, nature strikes a balance between parts and whole, for example, by diverting blood supply in cold weather to preserve the critical internal organs, although risking frostbite to the extremities.

Business decisions about short-term and long-term interests, and local and global interests, have no evolutionary logic or built-in process to rely upon. Instead, these decisions are based on the limited understandings, rules of thumb, and traditional practices of organizational actors (March and Shapira 1982). Research suggests that undue attention or decision weight may be given to the short term because the future is ambiguous or discounted (March 1978; Loewenstein and Prelec 1992). It is difficult for actors to understand the global and delayed consequences of local decisions and immediate actions (Senge and Sterman 1991; Sterman 1989a, 1989b), and

The writing of this paper was supported by the MIT International Program on Enhanced Nuclear Power Plant Safety, a research program of the MIT Energy Laboratory sponsored by an international group of nuclear power utilities and relevant institutions. John Sterman acknowledges the financial support of the MIT Organizational Learning Center.

this is particularly difficult in tightly-coupled (Perrow 1984) or highly inter-dependent organizations.

In this paper, we will present some evidence for the failure to give due consideration to preventive maintenance in organizational decisions taken by two companies in two different industries. In the short run, a plant can always cut preventive maintenance; the problems emerge later because preventive maintenance is an investment in the future. We suspect that the reasons for these decisions have some similarity. Further, we think that sparse allocation of resources to maintenance is not a rational strategy for the organization as a whole—it is a strategy that gets organizations deeper in trouble. Indeed, once recognized, organization members reject this pattern of behavior but have great difficulty overcoming it. There are some important psychological and organizational reasons why insufficient preventive maintenance may be locally rational in the sense of being in the best short-term interests of individuals who have limited understanding and/or concern for the longer-term and more global consequences.

As illustrated in the two case studies, underlying these maintenance issues are assumptions and understandings that we designate as the "mental models" of the organization participants. The term "mental models" is used in many ways (Gentner and Stevens 1983; Jungermann and Thuring 1988; Morecroft and Sterman 1994; Rasmussen 1979; Rouse and Morris 1986; Senge 1990) referring to the causal understandings people have about how a system works, the scripts they use to guide conduct and behave appropriately in various situations, and the deeply embedded cultural assumptions that condition behavior, attitudes, and perception. We use mental models to refer to beliefs and understandings at all levels of analysis: individuals "have" mental models, but portions of these mental models are shared across workgroups and professional specialties, and embedded in organizational or national culture. We argue that the local rationality and global irrationality of individual action arises because actors' mental models are simplifications that do not capture the fullness of complex, dynamic systems (Forrester 1961; Simon 1979).

We also describe the successful efforts of one company to improve organizational performance by focusing on new ways of learning about the dynamic interdependencies around the maintenance function. As we explore the way in which these decisions were made, we suggest ways that organizations can improve their decision making around maintenance and, indeed, around many important issues, by recognizing that decisions are based on incomplete, partially shared mental models whose coherence and comprehensiveness can be enriched through learning.

Maintenance at Du Pont

Du Pont, with 1991 sales of more than $38 billion and after-tax profits of $1.4 billion, is by far the largest U.S. chemical manufacturer.[1] Most of its chemical products are manufactured in continuous-processing plants, which theoretically run twenty-four hours per day, seven days per week, without shutting down or re-fitting for new batches of product. The goal is to maximize uptime (when the time the plant is in full operation); the shut-down and startup processes stress the plant and equipment, are energy-intensive, require operators and mechanics to work overtime under pressure, and could prevent Du Pont from delivering product to a customer on time.

Despite efforts to maximize uptime, the average chemical plant operates only about 83–95 percent of the time, depending on the particular type of plant. The remainder is downtime caused by critical equipment being serviced or awaiting service. The mean time between failures (MTBF) of equipment and the speed and quality of maintenance operations are therefore critical determinants of uptime and plant profitability.

Maintenance expenses account for 15–40 percent of production costs, depending on the type of manufacturing process. The amount of money Du Pont spent company-wide on maintenance in 1991 was roughly equal to its net income.

The Problem

In 1990 Du Pont undertook a competitive benchmarking study to measure the effectiveness of its maintenance programs relative to the top performers in the worldwide chemicals industry. The benchmarking study revealed an apparent paradox: Du Pont spent more on maintenance than industry leaders but got less for it (see table 5.1). Du Pont had the highest number of maintenance employees per dollar of plant value, yet their mechanics worked more overtime. Spare parts inventories were excessive yet the plants relied heavily on costly expedited procurement of critical components. Most disturbing, though, Du Pont's direct maintenance costs per dollar of plant value were 15 percent higher than the average of the industry leaders, yet availability of critical equipment and overall plant uptime lagged far behind.

[1] This description is taken from Sterman, Banaghan, and Gorman 1992. John Sterman acknowledges the assistance of Ellen Banaghan, Mark Paich, and Elizabeth Gorman; Winston Ledet, Mark Downing, Tony Cordella, and others at Du Pont are particularly acknowledged for generously sharing their efforts, data, and hospitality. This work was supported in part by the MIT Organizational Learning Center.

Table 5.1 Selected results of the Du Pont benchmarking study

Performance measures	Du Pont relative to industry leaders
Maintenance cost per $ of plant value, ERV (estimated replacement value)	+10% to 30%
Mechanics per $ of plant ERV	+23%
Maintenance planners per $ of plant ERV	−55%
Maintenance support staff per $ plant ERV	−15%
Flexibility of maintenance workforce (ability to do work outside of job categories)	−70%

Source: Flynn, V. (1992).

As in many industries today, chemicals producers are under strong pressure to reduce costs and improve productivity. Since 1970, the three worst recessions since the Great Depression caused widespread excess capacity. New competitors from the Pacific rim and the oil-rich nations of the Middle East have entered the market. Two severe energy crises wreaked havoc with input and operating costs. Environmental concerns and regulations continue to grow. Du Pont Chemicals responded to the intense cost competition with a series of cost-reduction initiatives over the past ten years; more recently, Du Pont (corporate) has undertaken a $1 billion cost reduction effort throughout its manufacturing divisions.

Maintenance, like other manufacturing functions, has come under pressure to improve its cost effectiveness. When maintenance departments are asked to cut expenses, nearly all of the cut has to come from activities such as planning and preventive maintenance rather than corrective maintenance, because breakdowns in critical equipment must be fixed. At the same time, cost cutting often results in other actions (e.g., postponing replacement of older, less reliable equipment or eliminating backup capacity) which increase the load on maintenance departments. With resources for preventive maintenance diminishing and maintenance needs increasing, a plant's equipment begins to break down more often. Maintenance managers must then shift more of their limited parts stocks and mechanics from preventive maintenance to corrective maintenance. Growing volumes of work orders for corrective maintenance further reduce resources available for preventive maintenance, leading to still more breakdowns, in a vicious self-reinforcing spiral.

Some Du Pont employees, observing this process unfold over several decades, had concluded that Du Pont had developed a culture of reactive maintenance. Unreliable equipment and frequent breakdowns had become an accepted occurrence. Organizational norms and routines for writing up work orders, scheduling maintenance effort and ordering parts had come to reflect a world of frequent breakdowns. Mechanics spent most of their time "fighting fires"; those mechanics who were scheduled for predictive or preventive work routinely were pulled off those jobs to do corrective work. Mechanics knew they could work overtime on a regular basis and considered overtime pay a part of their regular income. The "knowledge" that equipment was unreliable had even led to installation of backup pumps in many sites, embedding the low-reliability culture in the physical layout and capital costs of the plants.

Early Change Efforts Fail

The results of the benchmarking study served as "marching orders" for the corporate maintenance leadership team (CMLT), a group formed in 1988 with the objective of using effective maintenance operations to keep chemical plants running at near full capacity at a reasonable cost. The CMLT had created eight separate key pursuit field teams (planning and scheduling, predictive/preventive maintenance, materials management, contracted maintenance, competitive position assessment, human resource development, maintenance technology, and maintenance leadership) to identify strategies and products that could reduce maintenance costs, and "sell" these ideas to the plant operations managers. Based on the teams' recommendations, many plants began a variety of initiatives to reduce maintenance costs. But while some of the initiatives reduced maintenance costs and improved uptime in the short term, many gains were short-lived, and management began to question the value of these initiatives.

Meanwhile, the competitive position assessment (CPA) team was discovering that minimizing costs could backfire. A lack of resources in one area of the plant could put undue stress on other areas, causing additional expenses which outweighed the initial cost savings. For instance, cost-cutting reductions in spare parts supply handlers could easily raise costs: preventive maintenance might be delayed while the remaining supply personnel expedited emergency work orders, further delaying preventive work and causing increased breakdowns and additional costly expediting of replacement parts orders.

Deficient Mental Models

The CPA field team felt that while the benchmarking study provided an excellent assessment of Du Pont's relative functional performance, it did not indicate what actions needed to be taken to improve maintenance effectiveness. They felt that focusing on the correlates of maintenance success revealed little about the forces that produced and perpetuated low-maintenance productivity. Furthermore, the CMLT's approach to maintenance had previously been to focus on minimizing costs. The unquestioned underlying assumption was that minimizing maintenance costs would help minimize overall manufacturing costs, i.e., maintenance costs could be viewed as loosely coupled or independent from other functions.

The CPA team intuitively felt that maintenance was tightly linked to other functions through complex feedback relationships. Although some relationships were clear (e.g., more mechanics mean faster maintenance response time), considering the simultaneous effects of multiple variables quickly became too complex. Similarly, it was difficult to understand what would happen under alternative maintenance scenarios if the plant were subject to unanticipated production demands or cost pressures.

Maintenance at a Nuclear Power Plant

Peninsula Haven nuclear power facility is operated by the People's Power Company.[2] Like chemical process plants, nuclear plants are run continuously to generate electricity (other sources of electricity are easier to turn on and off and are used for the variable part of electricity demand). Nearly all the large-scale repairs and testing of nuclear power plants are performed during scheduled outages that take one to four months and occur less than once a year. Unlike chemical plants, nuclear plants do not directly compete with one another, but rather operate in the public interest with service areas and rate structures determined by public authorities (although approaching deregulation will change the structure of the industry). Further, the potential for catastrophic releases of radiation has led to intense public scrutiny and regulations that enforce a much higher level of attention to safety than in the chemical industry.

There are two separate nuclear power plants on site at Peninsula Haven: Colonial, which has operated for over a dozen years, and the newer Alexander Grant. The two plants have design differences that prevent moving licensed operating staff between units: for example, instrumentation and control is analog at one unit and digital at the other, and control rods come down at one unit and go up at the other. They also have had dramatically different performance records.

The Problem

When Colonial first started to produce power, and Alexander Grant was in the planning and construction stages, Peninsula Haven still had a "fossil mentality."

[2] This summary is based upon Marcus (1992). The names of the utility and the power plants have been disguised. Material in quotation marks is drawn from interviews or documents. This research was part of the MIT International Program for Enhanced Nuclear Power Plant Safety.

At fossil (coal and oil) plants, you "run a boiler and shovel coal into it till it falls apart." If a boiler was not maintained properly, it could be overhauled easily. Operators had considerable freedom to do what they wanted to keep a plant running. Protective systems did not exist, radiation was not a concern, and there were fewer codes and standards than at a nuclear plant. Employees operated on a very short time frame, a "month-by-month" basis. Thus, work practices developed around the reactive maintenance culture common to the fossil fuel industry.

An important safety incident took place in the mid-1980s when Colonial failed to shut down automatically in response to a problem; fortunately, an operator noticed the indicators calling for shutdown and initiated a manual shutdown. Responding to demands by the U.S. Nuclear Regulatory Commission (NRC) for an investigation, the utility found that a fundamental component had not been "prudently maintained." The NRC then brought in a team of investigators who unearthed numerous problems in how Colonial was "glued together" as an organization.

Change Efforts Fail

In response to a detailed action plan mandated by the NRC, and extensive recommendations by outside consultants hired by the utility, People's Power made many changes in their nuclear power operation and management. A major focus was on fixing procedures that did not work. They developed a procedure for how to write a procedure. They continued programs to create common procedures for the different units, modeling the standardization program after that of another large utility that had tried to establish common procedures for its plants.

Following recommendations to appoint an outsider as vice president of nuclear power generation, the utility hired a new vice president with a nuclear Navy background. His standards were "very high," and he wanted to make People's Power "among the best operating utilities in the world in five years." He made a "major, visible attack" on the traditional system of promoting anyone who simply "went along" and kept out of trouble. He introduced management by objectives, with indicators against which to judge key personnel. This system made plant management "more formal" and forced people to think "more" in terms of the "long term." He managed by "walking around" and expected other managers to follow his example—to be "out in the field" and close to their people. He brought in outside consultants who helped set up new hiring and discipline programs.

During this time, the CEO initiated an exhaustive productivity study to decrease costs at Peninsula Haven. Many cuts were made, including cuts at Colonial, although Alexander Grant "came out with additional resources."

The results of these changes were somewhat mixed. The new vice president's main accomplishment was starting up Alexander Grant on time and on budget. He changed the mindset from construction to operations. He created the departments and established a very "strong team," although he was less successful in bringing Colonial "up to speed." Judged just by quantitative indicators, Colonial was improving, but the vice president "did not build an infrastructure to survive him" after he left. The effort to create consistent procedures succeeded in radiation chemistry but failed elsewhere (e.g., operations) because the two units were so different and those with fossil backgrounds resisted a procedural compliance emphasis.

Change efforts continued after the vice president was replaced by his understudy. New plant managers were appointed, and were sent to the Harvard Business School to take the senior managers' course. Key people were moved from Alexander Grant to Colonial. The plant manager at Colonial had been an operations manager at Alexander Grant, and several other functional managers had worked at Alexander Grant. Emphasis was placed on the mission and on training in "reaching the vision" that included material on interpersonal skills, understanding people, and employee behavior. Revitalization was an "integrated program of procedure improvement and material upgrade." So far the emphasis had been on "general equipment and housekeeping," but making procedures "more correct" and taking into account "human factors" was part of the program.

To instill a culture of procedural compliance at Colonial, management had to do more careful "monitoring" and had to be certain that employees were being held "accountable." Management had to emphasize "quality," "assign responsibility," and "empower people," and its style needed to be "more brutal." Employees who did not adhere to procedures had to be "punished" to get a "commitment from them to do the right thing in the future." Yet, given the plants' "demanding schedule", it was necessary that employees be intrinsically motivated to get their jobs done in a "quality" way. While employees felt that they could not act without procedures, there were not enough procedures "to cover all bases." The procedure would say "push the stop button," and after pushing it the operator would feel that he had completed his task, even if the pump did not stop. Because of "rote" learning of procedures, employees did not have a "sense of connection" or understanding of the "system" as a whole.

Another "piece" of the revitalization program was backlog reduction. The maintenance backlog at Colonial was "above the norm for the industry," and there was "some money beyond the base budget" to bring in contractors to "clean up" the backlog. However, it was hard to reduce the maintenance backlog when so many spare part suppliers had gone out of business, despite efforts to keep a large inventory. Although the corrective maintenance backlog at both Colonial and Alexander Grant were similar to the average of the nuclear industry, overdue preventive maintenance was much higher at Colonial than at Alexander Grant, which was near the industry average (see table 5.2). Unless this preventive maintenance was unnecessary, such deferred maintenance eventually would lead to failures that would increase the corrective maintenance load over time.

Table 5.2 Maintenance backlogs at Peninsula Haven and in the nuclear industry generally

	Colonial	A. Grant	Industry
Corrective maintenance	50%	50%	50%
Preventive maintenance	25%	3%	3%

Source: "Comparative Performance Indicator Report" of Peninsula Haven. Exact numbers have been modified to maintain confidentiality.

The revitalization program also called for a systematic review of maintenance activities to determine where the "biggest bang for the buck" could be achieved in capital improvements, and the review determined that if equipment were replaced rather than repaired, it might reduce the amount of maintenance needed. The capital improvement program, though, was not yet in "full swing". When Peninsula Haven decided to replace obsolete systems, the engineering group chose to be cautious about design changes, and to work slowly. In any case, demanding outage schedules meant that it would be hard to implement change rapidly.

Despite continued efforts to improve, and numerous signs of improvement, Colonial did not achieve a sense of self-confidence. Colonial never seemed to be able to solve its problems before "even bigger and more demanding" problems came along and distracted it. Based on its troubled history, the NRC and INPO (the Institute for Nuclear Power Operators, an industry-wide support organization) continued to "senselessly beat" it, which hurt "morale" and discouraged people from doing better. The situation deteriorated, with "name calling" and the staff losing "incentive, impetus, and enthusiasm." Colonial needed two to three years of a "good, solid run" and "constant improvement" to change the "psyche" of "losing."

Colonial did have a "great" year: it achieved a capacity factor above 70 percent, it had no "personnel induced" forced shutdowns and was in INPO's best quartile for fewest reactor-forced shutdowns, and the number of personnel errors was "trending downward." The utility was "very happy" with its performance, and considered that further improvement would be facilitated if Colonial gained more confidence and stopped being perceived as a "loser."

A Severe Incident

A severe incident developed very quickly after many months of a good run. During a routine monthly test, three separate protection valves failed and caused severe damage to equipment, although safety systems were activated and functioned as expected. The faulty valves were found to have been "mechanically bound" because of "accumulated debris." The valve failures had not been detected in part because the vendor did not require their preventive maintenance, and industry focus was on safety systems that protected the reactor rather than the rest of the plant.

However, personnel at Colonial should have known of the potential for this type of failure. Three earlier events that involved similar protective equipment "not functioning as designed" had occured at other plants. These events had "not been recognized or addressed." Colonial also experienced a prior event in which the valves had functioned "erratically." Peninsula Haven had committed to replace its valves "during the next outage of sufficient duration," and to initiate preventive maintenance. Colonial had a mini-outage for maintenance purposes, but the "decision was made to defer the valve replacement" to an upcoming refueling outage. The valves had been tested during a reactor startup, and the test had indicated a "failure" of the protection system. The failure was attributed to "procedural problems," however, and "control room personnel decided to continue the startup without further probing or inquiry".

In retrospect, it was "easy to say so now" that judgment was poor, but at the time what was done made sense. During the Colonial mini-outage, employees completed "in excess of 1200 work requests to improve the safety and reliability of the plant," and the outage manager had to look at "thousands of things" that could have been done. These faulty valves were not in "category #1" because they were tested during a prior startup and were scheduled to be tested again during a future start-up. The outage work order did not provide for a complete assessment of downside risks. Plants had accommodated such events in the past without serious damage, so the commitment was to fix the valves during the next available outage of "sufficient duration." The decision makers "leaned on hope and were disappointed."

Nonetheless, policies for preventive maintenance had not developed rapidly enough. The previous vice president had started the reliability-centered maintenance program and was committed to it; but after he left, the budget was cut, programs were reallocated, and preventive maintenance declined in importance. It was difficult to gather data on past failures and reoccurrent maintenance problems and subject them to assessment. External industry data were hard to analyze: INPO alone had nine different programs, NRC had two, the vendors had seven, and there were three internal programs. The typical Colonial response to information about industry experience was that its own procedures were adequate. Colonial "missed the generic implications" and refused to acknowledge the problems. Alexander Grant, in contrast, responded directly and specifically to the questions raised by industry information.

Mental Models about Maintenance

The Du Pont and Peninsula Haven experiences suggested that good companies can get in trouble when their attention to maintenance (especially preventive maintenance) slips. In our research project examining safety issues in nuclear power plant management and organization (Carroll, Perin, and Marcus 1992), we have observed that the maintenance function is often given too little attention. Further, this is not just another item with which management must contend; it is unusually hard to fix the maintenance problem because its causes are subtle and systemic. We believe that difficulties in managing maintenance arise, in part, from limitations in mental models, as revealed in several observations about the Du Pont and Peninsula Haven maintenance stories.

First, managers in general, and perhaps U.S. managers with engineering backgrounds in particular, tend to think in terms of parts rather than wholes. They see a plant as a set of functional areas or parts in a machine; improvement programs start by creating separate task forces (such as the eight teams formed at Du Pont) that partition activities into components that are presumed to be separable. Although this decomposition strategy can be very effective, if the issues lie at the interfaces or interstices of highly interdependent components, such a strategy is unlikely to succeed. For example, the strongly-held separation of nuclear safety from worker safety, and the associated decomposition of the plant into reactor and balance of plant, can mask issues that cut across both. This observation is part of the argument made by Perrow (1984), who considered nuclear power plants to be "tightly coupled" (i.e., highly interdependent) relative to other manufacturing plants (in general, continuous-processing plants including chemical plants, are highly interdependent). The tendency to decompose tightly coupled systems is further reinforced by training and employment contracts that limit employees to specific jobs without cross-training, job rotation, or an understanding of how their work relates to the big picture.

Second, people have difficulty integrating events and relationships over time and, as a result, mental models tend to misperceive feedback and focus attention on the wrong things (Sterman 1989a, 1989b, 1994). Mental models often emphasize a succession of discrete events rather than underlying patterns of behavior (Axelrod 1976; Forrester 1971; Richardson 1991) and ignore or gloss over dynamic elements, including feedback loops, time delays, accumulations (stocks and flows) and nonlinearities (Axelrod 1976; Diehl and Sterman 1995; Funke 1991; Sterman 1989a, 1989b). The result is a focus on short-term and local, rather than long-term and global, issues. For example, at Du Pont neither management nor shopfloor employees really understood the linkages between the lack of planners and mechanics and the chronic corrective maintenance and high level of downtime. At Colonial, upgrading of procedures, management, housekeeping, training in achieving the vision, and so forth were done as separate improvements; no overall understanding directed attention at the deficiency in preventive maintenance and its potential impact.

The tendency to focus on short-term and local issues can be amplified by organizational factors. In the United States in particular, the reward structure in industry emphasizes annual or quarterly performance reviews and a person is judged by what they have done lately. This is partly because people expect to change jobs and even companies during their careers, and their activities have to create performances that can be associated with them in a timely way. The result, however, is lessened attention to and understanding of longer-term issues, and a lack of investment in activities that take time to produce results. The time horizon problem is exemplified in the cost-cutting pressures at Du Pont and Peninsula Haven that required each manager to look for redundant and less-productive activities to trim. Preventive maintenance is a prototypical activity that seems to be a low priority in the face of immediate demands to keep the machines running at lower cost, and the ultimate effects of deferred maintenance can be denied, ignored, or blamed on others.

Third, it is natural to focus attention on the people who seem responsible for the plant—the operators (and, in the airline industry, the pilots). Operators are the ones with their fingers on the switches. They must take action if anything goes wrong, so they are the last line of defense. Their errors are highly evident and dramatic (such as at Chernobyl, when the operators turned off all safety systems in order to test the reactor's behavior). For decades, they were the focus of human factors initiatives and expensive simulator training (Rasmussen and Batstone 1991). Maintenance as a concept is not as vivid within the "vision" of the organization: it is seen as a support rather than a core activity, part of the costs rather than the revenues, blue-collar rather than professional, and one can imagine power production without even thinking about maintenance. Only recently has attention shifted away from operations to other functional areas of the plant (e.g., maintenance), the desirability of a safety culture (IAEA 1991), and the management and organization of the plant as a whole.

Fourth, when management and organization are implicated in plant deficiencies and difficulties in the change process, the natural assumption is to look to leadership as the source of the problem and the source of solutions. Just as some baseball teams fire the manager after a bad season, nuclear power plants sometimes change top management (vice president of nuclear) as a strategy for changing a losing season. For example, Peninsula Haven turned to the nuclear Navy as the source of new leadership and, through the new leader, a new organization and culture. We have heard numerous times throughout the industry that a nuclear power plant tends to reflect the style of the vice president, unless the vice president is uninvolved, which is even worse. Programs for improvement, whether labeled revitalization, total quality management, empowerment, or whatever, then tend to flow from the top to the bottom. It is rare for the bottom of the organization to be the origin of programs. Because maintenance is *perceived* to be a support function staffed by nonprofessionals, their low status gives them a poor position to argue for resources and attention, despite their critical and costly role and management rhetoric insisting that employees take ownership of their activities.

Finally, associated with many of the above issues is the culture of individual blame and control that permeates industry. The reaction to incidents is to identify an error and blame someone for not following procedures or not paying attention (Carroll 1995; cf. the fundamental attribution error, Nisbett and Ross 1980). The typical response is to punish the offender with a few days off without pay, to tighten up training programs to emphasize self-checking, to tighten up procedures to include more detail and more checks, and to involve more people in quality assurance and oversight. Although these steps appear to create more barriers against accidents, they also create more pressure, narrowing of attention, alienation from work, distrust, lack of information flow, redundancy, and higher costs. These may interfere with the need to create a learning organization, which requires a free flow of information and an active, open, curious attitude on the part of all employees (Levitt and March 1988; Weick 1987).

Restructuring the Maintenance Game

Let us return to consider the situation at Du Pont. Clearly, they needed a method that could help them understand the dynamic complexity they faced—why past attempts had not worked, and how to design alternative policies—and they needed to find a way to explain these complex dynamics to the experienced plant operations and maintenance people who had to take action.

Developing New Mental Models

The Du Pont competitive position assessment team (CPA) began the development of a simulation model to capture the system-wide, dynamic benefits and costs of different maintenance initiatives. The model utilized the system dynamics metholodogy developed at the MIT Sloan School of Management (Forrester 1961; Richardson and Pugh 1981). It was developed interactively by the Du Pont team with the assistance of Mark Paich, an alumnus of MIT's program in system dynamics, now a professor and consultant. Using the model, the team attempted to quantify the net present value (NPV) of maintenance to the business as a whole, accounting for both the direct costs of each maintenance activity and the benefits it delivered over time in terms of increased uptime, more accurate and effective repairs, fewer breakdowns, more cost-efficient management of human resources and supplies, and so forth.

Recent theories of "modeling for learning" (Morecroft and Sterman 1994; Senge and Sterman 1991) have emphasized the heavy involvement of the client team as partners in model development. The model was used to create an environment for learning, a simulated plant or microworld in which the Du Pont team could experience the long-term effects of current practices, discover for themselves how the present system fails, and try out new policies. The team gradually developed an appreciation of the dynamic complexity of the maintenance system. For example, they realized that by creating eight separate teams, each focused on a distinct area, the CMLT had implicitly assumed that the maintenance function could be partitioned into separable components that did not interact. But clearly the eight areas investigated by the field teams were tightly intertwined, both with one another and with other aspects of plant operations. The best-practice companies, they reasoned, were most likely managing multiple initiatives so that they produced a reinforcing effect, or at a minimum, so that they did not undercut each other.

As an example, consider the ways improving scheduling can raise the productivity of the mechanics. If a team of mechanics is aware of pump maintenance needed on a given day, then the repairs can be performed faster and less expensively than if the work were unscheduled, since the work can be done during normal hours rather than overtime, and other work which might physically interfere with the pump maintenance can be avoided. Similarly, materials planning boosts the productivity of scheduled work by preparing kits of parts for scheduled jobs. Predictive maintenance (including vibration monitoring and failure trending) facilitates planning and parts procurement. More predictable demands for parts means less expediting and leaner parts inventories while improving part availability.

Reliability engineering was another dimension that was not being addressed adequately by the CMLT teams. Reliability engineering goes beyond preventing or predicting maintenance by redesigning machinery to be more robust (i.e., perform adequately for longer periods under more difficult conditions), thus reducing the creation of latent defects that ultimately can cause a breakdown. Investment in equipment reliability can reduce the machinery's normal failure rate and thus decrease the required maintenance effort. For example, upgrading to a more durable type of pump seal would improve reliability, allowing maintenance intervals to be lengthened and supplies of replacement seals in inventory to be reduced. The payoff to any of these initiatives is much greater when they are undertaken together rather than separately. Scheduling, for example, does nothing to benefit the unexpected outage.

The Manufacturing Game

The CPA felt that the simulation model and learning process helped them develop new perspectives on the maintenance problem that could improve the contribution of Du Pont's maintenance program to corporate profitability. Now their challenge was to implement the needed changes. In part, the challenge was technical—for example, to develop workable techniques to design more reliable components. In part, the challenge was managerial—for example, learning how to schedule predictive and preventive work. But fundamentally, the CPA had to recreate the learning process they had experienced throughout the plants, from top management to the lowest-grade mechanics. Their challenge was no less than to create a culture of defect elimination and preventive maintenance in place of the prevailing culture of reactive maintenance.

The Du Pont team's early efforts to communicate the results of their modeling work were mostly unsuccessful. They first tried to explain the model assumptions and show the simulations in traditional presentations, but found "it was difficult to compress the thinking that produced the model into a short period of time. . . .[T]he discussion of the assumptions was often frustrating to the modelers and confusing to the managers."[3] As noticed in other modeling studies (Senge and Sterman 1991), after going through a long process of learning facilitated by the modeling tools that changed their mental models and cultural understandings of the complex feedback dynamics created by interactions of maintenance with other functions in the organization, the modelers then implicitly expected others to accept these implications for policy after a short presentation. Such presentations are not only limited as a means for communication, but also may trigger resistance because the implied status differential between the new experts and the uninitiated may engage political conflicts and defensive routines (Argyris and Schon 1978).

The team decided that others must experience the learning process they, as modelers, had. One team member had attended an outside workshop on modeling where he played the "Beer Game," a board game illustrating how the in-

---

[3] Material in quotes relating to Du Pont was gathered in interviews by Ellen Banaghan and John Sterman.

ventory management policies of individual firms can create business cycles (Sterman 1989b). The team felt that a "maintenance game" experiential learning environment could enable plant personnel at all levels to discover for themselves many of the insights the modeling team had developed, but without the time-consuming modeling process. The team drew upon learning laboratories employing system dynamics simulations in designing the game and workshop (Sterman 1988, provides an example; Isaacs and Senge 1992; Kim 1989; Meadows 1989; and Senge and Sterman 1991, discuss the philosophy, design, and pitfalls of learning laboratories).

The day-long Manufacturing Game represents a typical continuous-processing plant on a board of about four by six feet. There are three players: the business services manager (who runs the parts store room), the maintenance manager (who plans, schedules, and allocates resources for maintenance work), and the operations manager (responsible for plant profitability and for meeting product demand). Chips represent equipment, product, parts, maintenance resources (such as mechanics), latent defects, and overtime or contractors. Equipment chips move through the operations sector. Each chip produces product and gradually accumulates latent defects. Eventually equipment with defects breaks down and enters a queue of equipment awaiting repair. Repairs can only be performed if maintenance resources (mechanics and parts) are available, requiring either coordination between the maintenance and stores managers or expensive overtime and expediting of parts procurement. The maintenance manager can also choose to attack defects through preventive maintenance. However, preventive maintenance requires that the operations manager take functioning equipment out of service (a planned outage) so the preventive work can be performed. Often, the operations manager refuses precisely because so much equipment is broken down that all remaining equipment is needed to meet demand, thus further deferring preventive maintenance and causing still more breakdowns.

Effective learning from a simulation game requires more than game play (Brehmer 1990; Diehl and Sterman 1995; Paich and Sterman 1992); the game experience must be embedded in a structured learning cycle including conceptualization, experimentation, reflection, and reconceptualization. The learning laboratory developed by the Du Pont team provides participants with a chance to share experiences and ideas about maintenance issues with colleagues from other functions; to develop skills in conceptualizing and representing their knowledge of maintenance dynamics, and to use these skills to develop and improve common mental models; to test programs and policies to improve maintenance (in the game) that they can not test in the real plants; and finally to learn how the insights developed in the learning lab can be implemented.

The response to the model, game, and learning lab has been enthusiastic. Thousands of Du Pont personnel have participated in the learning lab. Over thirty people are now qualified as facilitators to run the game and learning laboratory. For many Du Pont employees, the learning lab is their first chance to reflect on these issues and participate in the design of the structures, routines, incentives, and metrics that govern their work. The learning lab integrates the cognitive skills involved in understanding the dynamics of a complex feedback system with teamwork, group interaction and inquiry skills, and the emotions required for implementation and culture change. The learning lab now includes skits, games, and songs about eliminating defects as means to surface and legitimate discussion of the full range of issues important for successful plant-wide improvement of maintenance.

Implementing New Programs

After a team at a particular plant experiences the learning lab they are trained in an implementation program to translate the insights of the game into actual improvement. The pilot implementation program focused on pumps and was named "Pumps Running." Pumps were selected because they are common and important to the plants, consume a significant share of maintenance effort, and are subject to significant wear, suggesting a potential for large improvements in plant uptime by monitoring wear and investing in reliability engineering to examine the use of better parts (such as improved seals and bearings). The installation of duplicate pumps in response to poor pump reliability illustrates how a culture of low reliability and reactive maintenance had become so pervasive in some sites that the entire organization had adapted to it, at great cost, rather than correcting it. The presence of duplicate pumps also allowed the new proactive maintenance policy to be tested without adversely affecting production.

Results to date have been quite encouraging. More than ten different product lines in seven plants have participated in the learning laboratory and implemented the Pumps Running program. Table 5.3 shows the average improvement in MTBR to date among participating plants is about 17 percent per doubling of pump experience,[4] with maintenance costs during the same period falling by an average of 21 percent. Comparable nonparticipating plants have improved at a rate of only about 4 percent and have experienced a large increase in associated maintenance expenses.[5] It is noteworthy that one site, Plant

---

[4] The apparent rate of improvement was faster initially than later, reflecting the fact that the worst performing pumps, with the greatest scope for improvement, are likely to fail first and thus be enrolled in the program before intrinsically more reliable pumps. As the better-performing pumps gradually get added to the program the potential improvement falls. Such behavior is typical of improvement dynamics and reflects what Total Quality advocates call "picking the low hanging fruit."
[5] Plants enrolled in the program were not selected randomly; thus, plants choosing to participate may have been predisposed to change. Nevertheless, the differences in improvement rates and costs between participant and nonparticipant plants are large and highly suggestive of the benefits of the program.

C product line 6, decided to pursue a technical improvement program driven by the industrial engineering staff. This program, which did not explicitly address the issue of the culture or mental models of the workforce, has resulted in virtually no improvement while costs have increased dramatically.

Table 5.3 Improvement in mean time between repair (MTBR) for plants and product lines implementing the maintenance game and pumps running compared to control plants

Plants implementing the maintenance game and pumps running		
Plants/product lines	Improvement rate in MTBR[a]	Change in costs[b]
Plant A Product 1	16%	−16%
Plant A Product 2	14%	−13%
Plant A Product 3	23%	−43%
Plant B Product 4	16%	−25%
Plant C Product 1	18%	−10%
Plant D Product 5	13%	−23%

Comparison plants not using maintenance game/pumps running		
Plants/product lines	Improvement rate in MTBR[a]	Change in costs[b]
Plant C Product 2	8%	+5%
Plant C Product 6	0%	+70%

[a] The improvement rate is the percentage increase in MTBR per doubling of cumulative experience with pumps in the program.
[b] The change in costs is the total change in labor and materials costs associated with the maintenance of the pumps in the program.

The success to date of the maintenance game and pumps running program has generated its own challenges. In particular, although the maintenance game may alter mental models, the implementation of change generates its own dynamic reactions that may undermine the benefits. In essence, the maintenance game is not easily separable from a larger "organization game." The Du Pont team continually revises the game, learning lab, and implementation protocols as new issues come to light, such as:

Countervailing reward systems. For mechanics high on the priority list to receive overtime in their present work groups, transferring to a proactive maintenance group would mean losing lucrative overtime. The preventive/predictive maintenance manager at one plant said, "When an outage comes and [they] have a chance to work 14–16 hours per week overtime they say `to hell with this vibration [monitoring] stuff, I'm going to the outage area.'" A foreman noted, "I heard of a predictive maintenance guy getting kicked out of his group for taking a vibration reading on a down pump."

Turf and status. People are suspicious and biased about the skill sets, education and intentions of workers in other functions. For example, operators complained they could not get into the databases that record equipment histories and other information useful for planning and scheduling proactive maintenance. Some people in the plant believe if you allow operators or mechanics to add equipment histories to the data base "they'll mess it up." These issues involve turf, work rules, and status distinctions among different types of personnel in the plants. These suspicions would be alleviated if people understood the principle espoused by Will Rogers, not usually considered a management theorist: "Everybody is ignorant, only on different subjects."

Loss of challenging work. Mechanics who can handle the most difficult corrective situations are the heroes; proactive work is seen as less challenging and requiring less experience. A shift to preventive maintenance initially will be even more challenging and enjoyable, as preventive work uncovers additional latent defects. But as reliability improves, fewer latent defects will be created, and maintenance work will increasingly be planned and routine. Team members asked, "Could you get people to do inspections such that three-fourths of the time they'll find nothing?"

Job security and cost cutting. The leader of the Du Pont team noted, "Many of the mechanics are threatened by pumps running. If maintenance can be done with half as many mechanics, doesn't that mean the mechanics are being asked to work themselves out of a job?" The simulation model shows that it is more profitable for the business as a whole to keep a full complement of mechanics and incur greater costs in the maintenance function than to reduce costs by eliminating mechanics. Extra mechanics contribute more to plant uptime, and hence revenues, than they cost; reducing mechanics could cause a collapse in the commitment of plant personnel to the proactive maintenance program, and without slack, a run of bad luck means the remaining mechanics must be reallocated from proactive maintenance to reactive maintenance, which triggers the vicious spiral again. Yet the mental models of managers are strongly conditioned by cost-cutting pressure to pare back resources when there no longer appears to be a need. A team member worried that, "As soon as you get the problems down people will be taken away from the effort and the problems will go back up."

The concern that management would cease taking the medicine (maintaining slack in the maintenance function) once the symptoms of illness (a high breakdown rate) disappeared is well-founded: medical patients often stop taking the drugs that control their blood pressure after noting that their pressure has in fact dropped within normal levels (Caldwell et al. 1970); patients do not take the full regimen of antibiotics once they feel healthy; and so forth. Such behavior reflects a poor mental model of the relationships among symptoms, disease, and treatment. Indeed, the nuclear power industry is particularly concerned with complacency, which is the reduction in attentiveness when problems appear to have been solved (IAEA 1991). Changing the mental models of management and employees thus remains a major challenge for the team as the pilot programs generate results.

Differences between Chemical and Nuclear Power Plants

Although we have told the stories of Du Pont and Peninsula Haven in order to emphasize their similarities, Peninsula Haven and the nuclear power industry in general face some additional challenges in their efforts to improve their performance.

In the chemical industry a reliability data base that reveals information about mean time between failures and the mean time to repair has been very valuable in predicting failure probabilities for functions and systems. However, in the nuclear industry, this type of data base has only proved to be very useful in a few special cases, such as that of the small components used in instrumentation and control applications. In other cases where general performance statistics have been compiled to target corrective actions and refine preventive maintenance programs, maintenance specialists have found the data to be too simple and often inaccurate. The specialists have had to design carefully very elaborate reliability studies that take into account the mixture of modified and unmodified equipment used in plants, or the mixture of equipment of slightly different designs and vintages. The customizing of large components that exist in very small numbers makes the application of a typical reliability study in a nuclear context doubtful.

Colonial had difficulty reducing its maintenance backlog, in part because of the lack of spare parts inventory. Sales have dropped off for the vendors since plant construction halted in the United States, and many of them have gone out of business. Finding replacement parts of the same quality and type often is difficult. The use of slightly different replacement parts requires a time-consuming modification process involving design changes and approvals at many levels. If the repair is so big as to be designated a capital improvement, then even more layers of approval are necessary. Rather than go through the process of receiving approval for a request for a permanent modification, it is easier to get approval for a temporary modification and a time extension.

Japanese nuclear power plants are known for their preventive maintenance programs that are designed to guarantee long-term component and plant reliability, which contribute to low reactor trip and forced outage rates. The Japanese planned unavailability rate from 1979-1986 was high, about 35 percent, but their strategy was meant to reduce the forced shutdown rate to the lowest extent possible (it was below 5 percent). In contrast, Germany, France, and the United States had planned unavailability rates of about 20 percent, but their forced unavailability rates were higher: Germany at about 12 percent, France at 15 percent, and the United States at 20 percent.

The Japanese accomplish their low forced shutdown rate through ten-year maintenance plans which identify and schedule necessary preventive maintenance for essentially all plant equipment, and an industrial system that supports preventive maintenance practices (Carroll et al. 1992; INPO 1985; Yakura 1995). Their strong preventive maintenance programs depend on close relationship with the plant manufacturer, who is the prime contractor for annual outage inspection work. Manufacturing engineers are on site monitoring equipment conditions and making suggestions for improvements. The manufacturer plans and carries out major maintenance projects; after an unexplained shutdown, it is the manufacturer who organizes the special inspection team and determines the corrective actions. Subcontractor maintenance teams, which are involved in the original construction of a reactor, are usually hired for the lifetime of the plant to carry out all maintenance activities on the piece of equipment that they helped construct. These relationships are part of the Japanese industrial system that emphasizes long-term planning, long-term relationships among companies, long-term employment contracts and worker commitment, and a cooperative approach to government-industry issues including regulation. Cost-cutting pressures are far reduced: a Japanese nuclear industry is considered an essential national resource and utilites are allowed to charge generous rates to cutomers. The Japanese example demonstrates that a proactive maintenance culture with a long-term orientation is possible, and the result is indeed a reduction of corrective maintenance. The Japanese operating strategy, however, is supported by financial resources and cultural values that may not be sustainable as Japan undergoes social and political changes.

Conclusions

Mental Models

The Du Pont and Peninsula Haven stories have an underlying structural similarity or theme: it is difficult to establish and maintain preventive maintenance practices in the face of continuing pressure for immediate production and cost-cutting efficiencies. These difficulties are exacerbated by the mental models of employees from top to bottom of the organization, that conceptualize highly interdependent, dynamic processes as if they can be reduced to separable functions and discrete events. When things go wrong, the lessons learned do not penetrate these mental models, but are associated with a particular person who made an error, or with leadership deficiencies in the abstract. Because employees' mental models fit into the work practices, culture, career paths, and physical structure of the plant, there exists a system of assumptions and behaviors that is difficult to change. Indeed, expensive multi-year efforts to bring about improvements at both Du Pont and Peninsula Haven have not succeeded.

Rational and Irrational Decisions

It seems reasonable to conclude that neglect of preventive maintenance and other symptoms of incomplete, short-term mental models leads to decisions that are irrational from an organizational viewpoint. Information is available from which to design better strategies and practices, yet the strategic and operational levels of the organization do not easily integrate their concerns and feedback in order to improve. Both Du Pont and Peninsula Haven had organizational structures and incentives that made it seem rational for individuals (at least in the short run, and in terms of accepted logics within the organization) to preserve defective practices. To align individual and organizational rationality it may be necessary, first, to change mental models so as to create understanding of longer-term global issues and, second, to change work practices and organizations based on these new understandings.

Changing Mental Models

At Du Pont, the recent successful program to restructure the maintenance function did not stop with technical experts analyzing the problem and then designing a program to change work practices. Instead, Du Pont initiated an effort to change the way maintenance was understood from top to bottom of the organization. They have successfully changed mental models through an experiential game that provides a dynamic environment in which employees receive feedback on old and new practices in ways that encourage learning. As the manufacturing game alone is not sufficient to change mental models, it is used together with legitimate opportunities to share experiences and develop skills.

Changing Work Practices and Organizations

Perhaps most difficult of all is to translate changes of mental models into changes in work practice that produce operational improvements. New mental models are only the groundwork for the seeds of change; necessary but not sufficient. The success of Du Pont's pumps running program depended on the manufacturing game but added a well-crafted program that suited the organization. In a sense, implementation is an organization game within which the manufacturing game is played. As we have shown, resistance to changes in maintenance can emerge after initial success, due to employee motivations, career paths, power structures, and complacency.

NEW FOUNDATIONS OF RESEARCH

Organizational Contracting: A "Rational" Exchange?

Judi McLean Parks and faye l. smith

Contracting is ubiquitous in organizations. Some might claim that the process of contracting, perhaps even the norm of contracting, is one of the most pervasive in organizations and the organizing process (Rousseau and McLean Parks 1993). Contracting consists of an emergent and evolving series of decisions: decisions regarding the contracting partner(s), the content of the contract, and simply whether or not to honor a contract and its intent. The entirety of the contracting process is frequently assumed to be quite rational. However, this simply may not be the case. At least, it does not appear to be the case if one uses the "economically rational" model of man[1]—one in which the self-interested, utility maximizer is the metric against which rationality judgments are compared. For some types of contracts and contracting processes, pure self-interest is an invalid assumption.

The authors wish to acknowledge the direct and indirect contributions to this paper provided by Ed Conlon, Larry Cummings, Jennifer J. Halpern, Deborah Kidder, Denise Rousseau, Deborah Schmedemann, Robert Stern, and Linn Van Dyne. Each of these people has influenced our thinking on contracts. Parts of this paper were written while the first author was a visiting scholar at the Johnson Graduate School of Management, Ithaca, N.Y. Much of the conceptual work on this paper was completed while the first author was a Summer Scholar at the 1992 Summer Workshop on Conflict Resolution at the Center for Advanced Study in the Behavioral Sciences, Stanford, Calif., July–August 1992. The ideas presented in this paper benefited from the comments and the insights of the Summer Scholars. Funds for support of the Summer Institute were provided by the Andrew Mellon Foundation. We are most appreciative of their support. A previous version of this paper was presented at the Pierce Memorial Conference on Non-Rational Decision Making at Cornell University, Ithaca, N.Y., in 1993.

[1] Our use of the terminology "model of man" is meant in a nongender-specific sense. However, feminist theory might suggest that the economic rationality standard is, in fact, subscribed to by the "masculine" voice. See, for example, Gilligan 1982; Harding and O'Barr 1987; Harding 1987; Held 1990; or Mumby and Putnam 1992.

In this paper, we explore issues and assumptions about models of contracting that may be unduly restrictive by examining the characteristics of both the content and the social nature of the contract and the contracting process. This paper is part of a larger conceptual model drawn from the fields of economics, law, sociology and psychology (McLean Parks 1990; McLean Parks and Conlon 1989). Our paper is not intended to provide a comprehensive view of each topic area, but rather will highlight particular perspectives and ideas in an attempt to provoke thoughtful discourse and to generate alternative views of organizational contracts—views that may provide additional insights and a richer understanding of organizational contracts and the contracting process.

Within organizational contracting models, we find several implicit assumptions (or assumptions which have become implied through "benign neglect" in empirical and theoretical treatments). Specifically, many of our models of exchange and contracting assume the norm of balanced reciprocity; they assume that the parties are self-interested and behave "rationally" according to that metric; they assume that exchange is voluntary and power between the parties symmetric (or nearly symmetric). In this paper, we will briefly discuss alternatives to these implicit assumptions. We also will provide an overview of transactional and relational contracting, highlighting how different types of contracts may be grounded in different types of reciprocity, rationality, voluntarism and power symmetries, and how these differences may impact the creation, maintenance, and completion of organizational contracts.

In order to accomplish the goals of this paper, we will first highlight some of the current research on organizational contracts, and, reflecting our own training and intellectual heritage, will focus predominantly on the contracts between individuals and organizations. However, throughout our discussion, much of our logic can be applied at different levels of analysis: contracts between individuals, between individuals and collectives, and between collectives. Second, we discuss the components of contracts, in particular focusing on the contract dimensions that differentiate various forms of contract. Following this discussion, we will examine the norm of reciprocity, questioning whether such a norm is universal as suggested by Gouldner (1960), or if, in fact, there are different norms of reciprocity which characterize different types of contractual relationships. Reciprocity norms are one metric against which fairness and justice are assessed. Hence, we next will examine how different forms of justice are likely to be important in different contractual relationships, and how these forms of justice are likely to determine contractual outcomes, such as whether the parties breach the contract, comply with its terms, or go beyond the contract (i.e., organizational citizenship behaviors). We explicitly question the distribution of power in exchange relationships. Finally, we develop a contractual typology that is grounded in the power distributions and reciprocity norms, and discuss the implications of our typology for nonrational decision making.

Toward a Typology of Organizational Contracts

Social and Promissory Contracts

Contracts themselves are collections of commitments, duties and rights, which establish specific obligations and entitlements for each party (Farnsworth 1982). These commitments are created through one of two contractual mechanisms: promissory or social contracting (Cosmides and Tooby 1987). *Promissory contracts* are a form of economic exchange, where commitments of future behaviors, goods, services and money are exchanged, in addition to "a host of nonmonetizable factors such as loyalty and fidelity" (Rousseau and McLean Parks 1993). *Social contracts* comprise normative expectations regarding the appropriateness of particular behaviors, and provide the normative background against which promissory contracts are created, maintained and executed (Rousseau and McLean Parks 1993). The social contract forms the foundation for moral, as well as legal obligation, and thus is important in determining reactions to violations, as well as social norms prohibiting violation.

Although the social contract is not a focus of this paper, it provides a common basis for the parties' interpretation and execution of the promissory contract. The social contract, through implied norms and social imperatives, as well as in its expression through law, establishes the assumptions of the parties to the contract, their interpretation of the terms, their rights and obligations under the contract, as well as the constraints under which the contract is executed and enforced.[2] Against this backdrop, in this paper our focus is on

[2] The normative nature of the social contract (as articulated by the law) may vary (e.g., as a function of a particular culture). Yet recognizing the existence of the social contract and the constraints it provides is essential to understanding the nature of the promissory contract. For example, under different social contracts, expectations created by a simple oral promise may or may not be binding. As noted by Rousseau and McLean Parks (1993), the social contract in the former Soviet Union provided that oral promises have no meaning, while the social contract in Sweden ensures that oral promises are legally enforceable. In the United States, the social contract governing the legal enforceability of promises is more complex. Written contracts in U.S. law are not necessarily interpreted as a final agreement, and in fact, must not "be contradicted by evidence of any prior agreement or of a contemporaneous oral agreement" (Uniform Commercial Code, Article 2, Section 202). The Statute of Frauds (1677) and its subsequent repeal by Parliament in 1954, provided for oral contracts while mandating some exceptions, such as contracts for the "sale of lands, tenements or hereditaments, or any interest in or concerning them." Such contracts *must* be in writing for the law to provide remedies (virtually all states in the United States have enacted provisions modeled after the Statute of Frauds concerning contracts in consideration of land [Farnsworth 1982]). Further, U.S. law prefers not to distinguish between transactions which are *malum in se* and *malum prohibitum*. Under the former, agreements are absolutely void, with no claims or rights when the transaction itself violates the law (17A, Am Jur, 2d, Contracts, §309), and thus, at least in part, also violates the social contract. Yet the normative or perceived moral obligations encompassed by the social contract also go beyond its expression in law. For example, members of the underworld or gang members may enact contracts whose intent is illegal, and thus are provided no remedy by the courts, yet the fabric of their social contract still provides mechanisms to ensure the execution of the contract.

promissory contracts. We will argue that these promissory contracts can be classified according to two primary dimensions: the nature of the contract (transactional or relational), and the symmetry of the power between the contracting parties.

Organizational Contracts

Organizational contracts are simultaneously promissory and social in nature. They are social in that they are negotiated, maintained and executed under the "umbrella" of the normative social contract. They are promissory in that they create expected obligations and are one mechanism through which behaviors both within and between organizations are specified and reciprocated. Although organizational scholars have been interested in contractual relationships for some time, organizational contracts have received relatively little empirical or theoretical attention (a notable exception is that of the transaction cost economics perspective, inspired by the work of Williamson and others [e.g., Williamson 1985]). Recently, however, several scholars have begun to examine organizational contracts not just from the "macro" perspective represented by Williamson and his colleagues, but also from both a "micro" (the individual) and "meso" (the individual in an organizational context) perspective.

Building on earlier and frequently ignored work (Argyris 1960; Levinson 1962; Schein 1976; Weick 1979), these scholars have begun to examine the importance of psychological and implied contracts to the behavior of individuals in the organization, both theoretically (e.g., Graham and Organ 1993; Keeley 1988; Kidder 1993; McLean Parks 1990; McLean Parks 1992; McLean Parks and Conlon 1989; McLean Parks and Kidder 1994; Rousseau 1989; Rousseau and McLean Parks 1993), and empirically (Conlon and McLean Parks 1990; Guzzo, Nelson, and Noonan 1992; Leatherwood and Spector 1991; McLean Parks 1990; McLean Parks and Conlon 1991, 1995; McLean Parks and Schmedemann 1992 1994; Robinson, Kraatz, and Rousseau 1994; Robinson and Rousseau 1994; Rousseau 1990; Rousseau and Anton 1988; 1991; Rousseau and Aquino 1993; Schmedemann and McLean Parks 1994; Shanteau and Harrison 1991; Van Dyne, Graham, and Deinesch 1994; Weisenfeld and Brockner 1993).

The consequences of organizational contracts have also been explored less directly by such scholars as Brockner and his colleagues (Brockner 1988, 1990; Brockner and Greenberg 1990) and the researchers interested in extra-role (or extra-contracted) behaviors (e.g., Bies, Martin, and Brockner 1993; Organ 1988; Organ and Konovsky 1989; Smith, Organ and Near 1983; Van Dyne et al. 1994). Either directly or indirectly, the empirical research by these scholars has examined psychological and implied contracts from their creation (e.g., Conlon and McLean Parks 1990; McLean Parks 1990; McLean Parks and Conlon 1991, 1992; Robinson, Kraatz, and Rousseau 1994; Rousseau 1990) through their evolution or maintenance (e.g., Conlon and McLean Parks 1990; McLean Parks 1990; McLean Parks and Conlon 1991; 1992; Robinson, et al. 1991; Van Dyne et al. 1994) to their fulfillment (e.g., Amabile et al. 1986; Van Dyne et al. 1994; McLean Parks 1990; McLean Parks and Conlon 1991; Organ 1988; Organ and Konovsky 1989; Rousseau and Anton 1988; Shanteau and Harrison 1991; Smith et al. 1983) or their violation (e.g., Brockner 1990; Leatherwood and Spector 1991; Bies, et al. 1993; McLean Parks and Schmedemann 1992 1994; Robinson and Rousseau 1994; Rousseau and Anton 1988; 1991; Rousseau and Aquino 1991; Schmedemann and McLean Parks 1994; Shanteau and Harrison 1991; Weisenfeld and Brockner 1993).

At each stage of the contracting process, decisions are made. For example, contract creation involves decisions concerning the content of the contract and the identity of the contracting parties. Contract evolution involves decisions about contract modifications, and how severe a modification must be in order to warrant a "new" contract. Evolution also involves decisions about whether or not to repeat the contract, and if so, whether with the same or alternative contracting partners. Completion and violation involve decisions about whether or not to fulfill a contract by honoring the *letter* of the contract, by honoring its *intent*, or by violating the contract and bearing the costs of such violations. However, to understand these decisions, it is first necessary to understand the nature and character of the different forms of organizational contracts.

Resource Exchange and the Organizational Contract

Contracts are created to ensure fairness in transactions (Ouchi 1980), and involve the exchange of both material and intangible resources. In this section of our paper, we will briefly examine the types of resources exchanged, and review the transactional/relational contract continuum discussed by Rousseau and her colleagues (Rousseau 1990; Rousseau and McLean Parks 1993; McLean Parks 1992; McLean Parks and Kidder 1994), a view of contracting which forms the foundation of the contract typology presented in this paper. Specifically, Macneil (1985) suggested that organizational contracts can be conceptualized as lying along a continuum, ranging from the transactional contract to the relational contract. A review of the characteristics of the transactional and relational contracts, summarized in table 6.1, suggests that they can be placed into one of three broad categories (McLean Parks 1992): (1) the context in which the contract is negotiated and executed (including the operative norms of reciprocity); (2) those concerning the content and terms of the contract itself (i.e., timeframe, stability, tangibility and the governance mechanism provided by the contract); and (3) those concerning the social nature of the contracting parties (i.e., the focus of the contract, its scope, the identity of the parties, and the underlying norms of exchange). Yet one content aspect of the exchange relationship which has yet to be addressed in explicit detail is the implications of *what* it is that is exchanged, or the nature of the resources involved in the exchange relationship.

Table 6.1. From the transactional to the relational: Characteristics of the contractual continuum

	The context of the contract: Transactional contracts	Relational contracts
Social contract: Reciprocity norms	Balanced	Generalized
Model of human nature	Self-interested Instrumental	"Other" interested Expressive

	The terms of the contract: Transactional contracts	Relational contracts
Time frame	Close-ended Specific duration	Open-ended Indefinite duration
Stability	Static	Dynamic
Observability	Concrete/tangible Public Objective Easily observable	Intangible Private Subjective Understood
Type of resource	Universalistic	Particularistic

	The social nature of the contract: Transactional contracts	Relational contracts
Focus	Economic Extrinsic	Economic Socio-emotional Intrinsic
Scope	Narrow	Pervasive and comprehensive
Identity of the parties	Irrelevant	Important

Modified from Macneil 1985; Rousseau 1990; and Rousseau and McLean Parks 1993.

"What" Is Exchanged in Promissory Contracts?

Among the entitlements and obligations specified in a contract are the actual resources exchanged. However, whereas most of the dimensions of transactional and relational contracts have been fairly well explicated theoretically, few contract theorists have explicitly examined the congruence between the type of resource exchanged and the nature of the contractual relationship. Yet, certain types of resources clearly lend themselves better to one type of contract or another. In addition, as we will suggest later in this paper, the type of resource proffered may affect reactions to contract violation. The nature of these resources is also likely to impact the effectiveness of different governance mechanisms for the contracts, and hence is important to our discussion.

In their theory of social exchange, Foa and Foa (1975) note that resources have different characteristics which impact the relationship. Foa and Foa (1975, 3–4) suggest that most resources can be categorized into one of six basic resource classifications: (1) *money*, or "any coin, currency or token that has some standard unit of exchange value"; (2) *goods*, which are "tangible products, objects or materials"; (3) *services*, defined as "involv[ing] activities that affect the body or belongings . . . and often constitute labor for another"; (4) *information*, which includes "advice, opinions, instruction, or enlightenment", as well as expertise or specific knowledge; (5) *status*, which "indicates an evaluative judgment that conveys prestige, regard or esteem"; and (6) *affiliation/fidelity* (termed "love" by Foa and Foa), expressing "affectionate regard, warmth, or comfort" as well as respect and loyalty.

Foa and Foa (1975) suggest that these resources vary in terms of their particularism, as well as their concreteness or tangibility. Both dimensions are important in determining which types of resources are exchanged in any given form of organizational contract (i.e., transactional versus relational). Particularism can be thought of as the extent to which the actual identity of the individual is important to the resource exchanged. For example it does not matter nearly so much who one's bank teller is as who one's lawyer is (Foa and Foa 1975). In the latter case, identity is important, hence the services exchanged are more particularistic (Williamson has also noted the particularism or asset specificity dimension in resource exchange [1975b, 1985]). As noted by Foa and Foa (1975), it matters much from whom we receive affiliation and socio-emotional support; however, it matters very little from whom we receive money. Money is perhaps the most universalistic resource while affiliation/fidelity is the most particularistic. Goods and information are hypothesized to be less particularistic than service and status, but more particularistic than money.

The concreteness or tangibility of resources is particularly important when viewed through the lens of the agency contract and its emphasis on monitoring (and the observability of the resource exchanged, such as the efforts of the agent). Concreteness affects the degree to which the resource exchanged may, if observed by outsiders, be relatively unambiguously interpreted. In an exchange of money, an observer is easily able to discern the terms of the contract and the exchange; however, in an exchange of socio-emotional resources, it is more difficult for an observer to determine the terms of the exchange, and whether or not the exchange has been fair.[3] For example, money, which is fungible, is relatively low on particularism yet highly concrete. One dollar bill is generally substitutable for another in a specific transaction. The parties are unlikely to debate its worth, as an interpretation of its value can be relatively unambiguously assessed, and hence is high on observability. In contrast, one's status is always relative to that of another, and thus its interpretation is highly subjective *and* particularistic. In one context, a party may be of relatively high status and in another context may be low in status, although the identity of the party remains unchanged. This suggests that an exchange involving status is high in particularism but low in observability/concreteness.

Finally, Foa and Foa (1975) suggest that time is important in exchanging different types of resources. Some resources require more time than others to exchange. Foa and Foa (1975, 12) note that exchanging affiliation/fidelity "cannot be done in a hurry: it requires time and even some leisure. Money, to the contrary, can change hands very rapidly." This time element becomes important in determining what resources can reasonably be exchanged in each type of contract. Those resources that require more time in exchange will only be found in contracts negotiated for long time frames, where the parties expect to continue to interact. In contrast, resources that can be exchanged without the benefit of a long-term relationship will be found in contracts with short time frames (e.g., the "spot" contract).

The Nature of the Contract: Transactional versus Relational Contract

The type of resource exchanged, its characteristics in terms of particularism and its observability have implications in terms of the appropriateness of transactional or relational contracts. We briefly outline below the extremes of the transactional/relational contractual continuum, and how the nature of a contract may be more congruent with the exchange of one type of resource over another.

Transactional contracts. At the extreme, the transactional contract is of a specified, short duration, and consequently is static. Changes, when considered necessary, are implemented in the next contract, perhaps between entirely different

[3] The difficulty in determining the terms of an exchange of affiliative or socio-emotional resources is acknowledged in contract law. An implicit premise of contract law is that the "best" contracts are negotiated at arm's length, that is, between unrelated parties. This preference for the arm's length transaction is expressed by the legal system by its relative reluctance to enforce contracts between closely related parties (Hovenkamp 1988), where it is difficult for the courts to determine whether the exchange was fair when it involves such things as "love and affection," and whether or not the terms have been met.

parties. In the transactional contract, where the atctual identity of the parties is irrelevant to the exchange itself, contracting parties are regarded as substitutable (Macneil 1985; McLean Parks 1990, 1992; Rousseau and McLean Parks 1993). The assets or behaviors exchanged are well specified, tangible, and easily observed. The focus of the transactional contract is on economic or extrinsic benefit. Resources which are readily substitutable and easily measured will be exchanged, hence money, goods and well-specified services are likely to be among the resources exchanged in the transactional contract. The observability of the resources and terms of the transactional contract are likely to enhance the efficiency and effectiveness of governance mechanisms, such as third party governance (e.g., the courts) or behavioral or outcome control (e.g., monitoring of behavior or payment of contingent compensation; [cf. Conlon and McLean Parks 1990; Eisenhardt 1989; McLean Parks and Conlon 1995; Ouchi 1980]); as well as markets for reputations (e.g., Alchian and Demsetz 1972; Bull 1983; Dasgupta 1988; Klein, Crawford and Alchian 1978; McLean Parks 1990; Telser 1980). In addition, it may be easier for third parties to govern the contract and suggest remedies for breach when the resources are low in particularism (i.e., it is more difficult to determine the extent of damage for a highly particularistic resource because its non-substitutability makes a precise determination of damages inherently subjective). The extreme transactional contract, by its nature, is unlikely to be concerned with identity, and thus will involve exchanges of resources that are low in particularism. Due to its short-term nature, the resources exchanged are likely to be observable, so that contract performance can be unambiguously ascertained before exiting or renewing the relationship.

Relational contracts. In contrast, the relational contract, which may focus on non-pecuniary exchange, is likely to encompass the full range of resources, including those which are unobservable, but particularistic and highly particularistic. The extreme relational contract is characterized by diffuse obligations and concern for both the pecuniary and nonpecuniary benefits derived from the exchange relationship. These contracts typically are dynamic and quite flexible, and are characterized by a willingness to honor the intent of the contract, if not the letter, when circumstances warrant (McLean Parks 1990, 1992; McLean Parks and Conlon 1989, 1991; Rousseau and McLean Parks 1993). Relational contracts include open-ended time frames or long-term alliances (Macneil 1985; Rousseau 1989; Rousseau and McLean Parks 1993). The terms of the relational contract lack specificity, but rather tend to be subjective and mutually understood (Rousseau and McLean Parks 1993). At its extreme, the relational contract permeates the lives of those involved (e.g., McLean Parks 1990; McLean Parks and Conlon 1989; Rousseau and McLean Parks 1993). Finally, the parties to a relational contract are interested in maintaining the relationship itself, and thus they are *not* substitutable. In the relational contract, the identity of the parties is of paramount importance. Whereas any type of resource can be exchanged in a relational contract, unlike transactional contracts, relational contracts also lend themselves to the exchange of unobservable, intangible, or very particularistic and subjectively understood resources. Service, status, and affiliation (e.g., the marriage contract) can be exchanged in the relational contract. In addition, the benefits of "learning" the relationship comprise very idiosyncratic investments and benefits particular to that relationship (Eccles 1981), where something is irrevocably lost if the relationship is severed (McLean Parks 1990). Because of the highly particularistic nature of some of the resources exchanged in the relational contract, the continuity of the relationship is important. In addition, when highly particularistic resources are exchanged, they represent more of the individual. This personal involvement with the resource exchanged has two primary implications: first, individuals are likely to evaluate their own contributions more highly; second, if the contract is breached, then the loss felt will be more salient and personal, potentially creating stronger reactions on the part of the aggrieved party (as connoted by Congreve, *The Mourning Bride*, 3.8, "Heaven has no rage like love to hatred turned, nor hell a fury like a [lover] scorned.")

The Backdrop of the Social Contract

Most contracting models assume that the behavior of the parties is predicated on self-interest and a balanced norm of reciprocity. In this section of the paper, we will address these assumptions and offer an alternative perspective, one that regards the norm of reciprocity, as well as the "interest" (e.g., self-interest) of the parties as a contingency, rather than a presupposition.

Underlying all exchange relationships, of which contracts are one form, is the fabric of the social contract. Social contracts are the institutionalization of social expectations which at least implicitly provide rewards and sanctions for compliant and non-compliant behaviors (Dahrendorf 1970). Thus the social contract is the backdrop against which promissory contracts are created, maintained and executed, and includes information and beliefs about the appropriateness of behavior (Rousseau and McLean Parks 1993). These normative beliefs include norms of exchange and reciprocity and of good faith and fair dealing, which in turn can create constraints and obligations outside the parameters of the actual promissory contract (e.g., Kahneman, Knetsch, and Thaler 1986; Rousseau and McLean Parks 1993).

Reciprocity in Social Contracting

Norms of reciprocity are one component of the social contract, and are an important plank in the platform on which promissory contracts are built. Reciprocity norms are pervasive, and, as noted by Gouldner (1960), are universal. Reciprocity creates interdependencies and contingencies in exchange. What might otherwise be a single, discrete exchange from a classical economic viewpoint becomes contingent on what has gone (or been exchanged) before and what will occur (or be exchanged) in the future. Reciprocity norms form the basis for interpreting the actions of the parties (Rousseau and McLean Parks 1993), and may be particularly important when the promissory contract is violated or when the opportunity for violation exists. For example, assessments of fairness and obligation are measured against the metric provided by operative reciprocity norms, and the costs of such violations may be minimal or may be quite high, depending on the operative norms. When contracts are violated, the relationship upon which they are based is also damaged. Trust, which is measured and accumulated in the *absence* of violation, once lost, is not easily restored (Dasgupta 1988). Hence, reciprocity and trust are closely tied to one another.

Reciprocity norms may be relatively more important in regulating exchanges under adverse conditions than under conditions of relative munificence. Under such conditions, reciprocity norms are one form of survival strategy (e.g., Colson 1979), where there are two pressures towards compliance: pressures brought by the actual terms of the contract, as well as those brought by the social contract which provides the context in which contracts are executed. In general, norms of reciprocity have two primary implications: (1) one should help those who have provided help and (2) one should not harm someone who has provided help (Gouldner 1960).[4] Thus, fulfilling the terms of these normative social contracts, however inconvenient, can form the basis of an exchange of obligation (Malinowski 1932). Yet, reciprocity norms may vary as a function of the type of relationship in which the parties are engaged (e.g., a transactional or relational contract).

Although most economic models of exchange tend to focus on quid pro quo as a reciprocity norm, anthropologists and sociologists distinguish between different forms of reciprocity. For example, Sahlins (1972) suggests a tripartite view of reciprocity: generalized, balanced and negative. Generalized reciprocity is altruistic in flavor, where giving is characterized by a lack of concern over repayment in kind. Balanced reciprocity is based on the notion of quid pro quo, and negative reciprocity is characterized by a "taking"

---

[4] Neither of these implications follow from a pure self-interest perspective, especially when future exchanges are unanticipated.

orientation.[5] Not surprisingly, which reciprocity forms the basis of the social contract is largely a function of the type of relationship between the parties.

Sahlins (1972) suggests that exchanges between "close" parties are likely to be controlled by generalized reciprocity, while exchanges between "distant" parties are controlled by negative reciprocity norms. Sahlins views negative reciprocity as damaging; however, Macneil correctly points out that it may actually strengthen the relationship. Characterized as self-interest seeking, negative reciprocity encourages the parties to be "on guard" and consequently, they will "haggle" (Macneil 1985, 486). As Macneil notes, "haggling is a social process, and it is one that cannot help but convey information" which may be important to the exchange, thus enhancing the relationship. An important point here is that reciprocity must be congruent with the relationship—incongruent reciprocity can be destructive to the relationship (Macneil 1985). McLean Parks (1990) suggests that this congruency is a function of the "match" between the parties and their relationship; specifically, that if balanced reciprocity is *not* the norm, then negative reciprocity should be paired with generalized reciprocity, where one party expects to give and the other to receive.

Unlike Sahlins, Mitchell (1988), does not view reciprocity as lying along a continuum going from negative to balanced to generalized. Instead, he views positivity/negativity as an orthogonal dimension to Sahlins's balanced and generalized reciprocity, noting that reciprocity is both *positive* (giving something) and *negative* (taking something). Mitchell proposes four general types of reciprocity. Positive generalized exchange is analogous to Sahlins's generalized reciprocity. Similarly, positive balanced exchange is the analog of Sahlins's balanced

---

[5] Sahlins's description of generalized, balanced, and negative reciprocity is conceptually related to the individual difference variable, equity sensitivity (Huseman, Hatfield, and Miles 1987; Miles, Hatfield, and Huseman 1989). Specifically, Huseman and colleagues suggest that people are either (1) "benevolents", or those who are comfortable being under-rewarded relative to others; (2) sensitive to equity, motivated to restore equity whenever they perceive themselves to be either over- or under-rewarded (equity sensitives); or (3) "entitleds," those who are quite comfortable and in fact desire being over-rewarded relative to others. The benevolents would be most closely aligned with generalized reciprocity and the entitleds would likely subscribe to negative reciprocity. The equity-sensitivity construct is hypothesized to be a trait. Whether it is a trait or culturally determined is beyond the scope of this paper. Yet it is logical to assume that when the relationship between the parties relies on the social contract's norm of generalized reciprocity, even an "entitled" may moderate his or her behavior and move more towards an acceptance of a less unbalanced position (i.e., when dealing with a spouse or other in close "kinship"). In this paper, we refer to the norm of reciprocity subscribed to, rather than equity sensitivity as a trait, as individual differences in equity sensitivity as well as the orientation any individual has towards exchange are likely to be affected not only by the context of a particular situation (i.e. kinship distance) but also by the normative/cultural constraints provided by the fabric of the larger, social contract. If these norms are strong, they will create a "strong context" where the effect of individual propensities and orientations will be minimized (Mischel 1977).

reciprocity, where goods or other valued resources are given in exchange for one another. However, Mitchell suggests that negative generalized reciprocity is characterized by taking resources from a defined social unit (e.g., discriminatory behavior), while negative balanced reciprocity is characterized by taking resources from a specific "other" in order to get even (similar to "retributive justice"; Hogan and Emler 1980). Positive generalized reciprocity is exemplified by gift giving, positive balanced reciprocity by quid pro quo; in contrast, negative generalized reciprocity is characterized by gambling, and negative balanced reciprocity by revenge (Mitchell 1988). Thus Mitchell's perspective logically provides two implications of reciprocity norms in addition to those suggested by Gouldner (1960): (1) one should not help those who have harmed you; and (2) one should harm those who have harmed you.[6]

Rationality and Reciprocity

In this paper, we conceptualize rationality as answering the question, "Whose interests are served?" or "Who benefits?" Thus rationality provides a metric against which behaviors can be measured and compared. Classical economic thought, for example, assumes that rationality obtains when self-interest is served. In his treatise, *The Wealth of Nations*, Smith (1776) states, "Every individual intends only his own gain . . . [i]t is not from the benevolence of the butcher, the brewer, or the baker that we expect our dinner, but from their regard to their own interest." Similarly, Edgeworth (1881) stated that "the first principle of Economics is that every agent is actuated only by self-interest." In economic thought, self-interest is the driving force that motivates human behavior.

Yet, with the exception of positive balanced reciprocity, it is difficult to fit each of the forms of reciprocity that we have discussed within the context of the pure, classical economic contract (i.e., "spot" contracting) without relying either on the somewhat tautological nature of self-interest assumptions or the presence of additional constraints. The remaining forms of reciprocity imply a divergence from the notion of the purely self-interested, utility maximizer so familiar to classical economic thought. Negative generalized reciprocity may be associated with negative reputation effects, and thus does not fit neatly into notions of self-interested rationality unless one also assumes that information is

---

[6] Although it can be argued that this implication follows from Mitchell's discussion, the aversion with which many people regard such an implication is evidence, in and of itself, of the strength of the social contract addressing vengeance. As noted by Francis Bacon in his essay on revenge (1625), "In taking revenge, a man [*sic*] is but even with his enemy; but in passing it over, he is superior."

constrained. The rationality of altruism (positive, generalized reciprocity) has been a frequent source of debate among scholars, a debate that will not be repeated here; similarly, revenge (negative, balanced reciprocity) is regarded by some as irrational[7] and potentially damaging to the avenger.

The self-interest assumptions which form the foundation of many of our models of contracting are difficult, if not impossible, to test. However, it has been amply demonstrated that individuals can and do act *as if* they were motivated by *other-regarding* interests, and that they can and do exercise self-control. As observed by Cummings and Anton (1990), people do hold themselves accountable, in spite of a lack of "compelling economic reason[s] to . . . keep one's word" (Bhide and Stevenson 1991, 121).

Mumby and Putnam have recently unshackled rationality and expanded it to embrace emotionality (1992). Their concept of bounded emotionality fuses the emotional foundations of the social phenomenon, rationality, with the currently reified perspectives. The boundedness stems from each party's mutual respect for the other's space and dignity (a choice that a person makes) rather than the boundedness of rationality that is treated as a constraint without choice (Mumby and Putnam 1992). They suggest acknowledging the *emotionality* of rationality, in order to create an appreciation of "intersubjective understanding, community, and shared interests" (1992, 480), recognizing not only the cognitive, instrumental dimensions, but also the social dimensions of human behavior, in which emotions play an important role.

The very nature of the relational contract with its diffuse obligations and long-term horizons suggests that a collective or "other" interest may overpower pure self-interest assumptions. In a relational contract, the attributes of bounded emotionality could dominate performance. For example, one of the attributes of emotionality is a heterarchy of goals and values (Mumby and Putnam 1992), and in a relational contract we expect that contextual information on the current and future contracts will govern how the goals are ordered. In addition, the parties will be willing to accept more ambiguity in the contract's terms (another attribute of bounded emotionality) than if they were in a transactional contract. Relational contracts include *multiple* points of reciprocity, where the behavior being reciprocated is so embedded in the context of the relationship that it might not be easily identified by outsiders or the parties in the contract. In contrast, the transactional con-

---

[7] Witness the debate over capital punishment. The discussion of "retributive" justice by Hogan and Emler (1980) also is of interest. However, prior use of revenge also can provide a credible threat, thus fitting more easily into the self-interest assumptions; yet, once again, this requires additional assumptions either in terms of the repeated nature of the transaction, or in terms of the availability and quality of information.

tract, with its short time frames and emphasis on self-interest and pecuniary returns, creates an environment in which the costs of opportunism are small, promoting self-interested behavior.

Most perspectives on organizational contracts assume pure self-interest as the metric against which rationality is measured. However, cogent arguments have been made for regarding the standard metric of "rational" human behavior, as depicted by the self-interested, utility maximizer, as a contingency— when do organizational decision makers act in a purely self-interested manner and when do they act in the interests of others (e.g., Donaldson 1990; Kramer 1990; Perrow 1986)? Jencks (1990) suggests that all actions fall somewhere on a continuum between extreme self-interest and extreme "other"-interest, depending on how we weigh our own interests compared to those of others. Individual rationality may best be assessed by measuring human interactions against differing metrics of self-interest, depending on the nature of the relationship. Perhaps self-interest lies on a continuum that ranges from the most selfish/instrumental to the most altruistic, acknowledging the collective self-interest as one point along this continuum:

Individualism	Collectivism	Altruism
(self)	(collective group)	("other")

Such a continuum of individual rationality implies that pure self-interest, or a focus on the self as beneficiary of an action, is only one mechanism for motivating behavior. This view of rationality might best be termed individualism, where the question, "Who benefits?" is answered, "*I* do." However, one also may engage in collectivism as a metric of rationality. In this case, individual behavior is motivated by the belief that the beneficiary of the action will be a collective of which the individual is a part. The movement from individualism to collectivism along the rationality continuum implies that the focus on the self as beneficiary has become diluted or diffused as one becomes part of a group (or dyad),[8] developing sentient ties and an interest in what is best for the survival of the group rather than what is necessarily best for the self as individual. As rationality moves from pure self-interest to collective interest, the self is recognized as a component of a larger whole. Here, when asked, "Who benefits?" the decision maker will re-

[8] This is similar to the diffusion of responsibility effect found in the group literature. In this case, the diffusion effect is more of a diffusion or subrogation of self to the group, as the hedonic relevance of any particular decision moves from a focus on the individual to the larger group. This movement towards a collective rationality is closely aligned with a utilitarian philosophical perspective.

spond, "*We* do."[9] In this case, the self benefits as part of the collective group, so benefit still accrues through membership in the group, although less directly. As the interests of the self are diffused still more, we move towards altruism, where the question, "Who benefits?" is answered, "Someone *else.*" This form of rationality substitutes the interests of another for those of the self. At the extreme, pure altruism is based on putting another's interests ahead of one's own, where the benefits the self have been diffused completely or subrogated to the interests of the other (whether that other represents an individual or a group). Thus, we suggest that rationality has at least three different forms, each of which may prescribe a quite different answer to the question of who benefits from an action. Individualism prescribes that rational actions attempt to benefit to the self; collectivism prescribes that rational actions attempt to benefit the collective, which includes the self; finally, altruism prescribes that rational actions attempt to benefit someone other than the self, perhaps even eschewing benefit to the self. Each form of rationality is likely to be used as a metric under different circumstances and in different forms of contractual relationships.

Based on this discussion, we suggest that the transactional/relational contract continuum parallels the self/other rationality continuum outlined above. The rationality metric for the most extreme transactional contract is self-interest (or individualism), while the rationality metric for the most extreme relational contract is altruism. Given these forms of rationality, it is likely that the reciprocity subscribed to in any given contract will vary, with the balanced reciprocity commonly assumed representing only one form.

Justice in the Execution of the Contract

When a psychological contract has been violated, the contract moves along the contract continuum, and becomes more transactional (Robinson, Kraatz, and Rousseau 1994; Wiesenfeld and Brockner 1993). Notions of justice affect a person's response(s) to a violation (McLean Parks and Kidder 1994). Four types of justice correlate to our four types of contracts: distributive, procedural, interactional, and retributive (McLean Parks and Kidder 1994). Recent research has found that procedural justice is important in relational contracts and distributive justice is important in transactional contracts (Weisenfeld and Brockner 1993). We suggest that interactional justice is also important in relational con-

---

[9] This is not to say that actions are *decided* collectively. We intend the term "collective rationality/collectivism" to depict those situations where an individual makes a decision or takes an action in order to put the interests of the collective ahead of his or her own pure self-interest. The individual may or may not consult the collectivity before taking the action and may or may not be correct in the belief that taking such an action represents the preferences of the collective. Nevertheless, the action is selected on that basis, in the belief that it is the collective that benefits. For this actor, the question, "Who benefits?" will be answered by the actor, "We do." Other members of the collective may or may not agree.

tracts, and retributive (retaliatory) justice is important at some level in all contracts. Specifically, fairness in the transactional contract, with its focus on monetized exchange and self-interest, is likely to be measured in terms of distributions—did I get my fair share? In transactional contracts the emphasis on the fairness of outcomes is consistent with distributive and retributive justice. Distributive justice focuses on the positive side of allocations—what has been given; retributive justice focuses on the negative side—what has been, or can be, taken away (Hogan and Emler 1980).

In relational contracts, process is important, and since both procedural and interactional justice are associated with process, we expect them to be more closely associated with the relational contract. Process implies that time frames will be important characteristics in the contracts, and that there will be iterations of exchanges that will allow for mutual adjustments to contract violations. Procedural justice evaluates whether the procedure used to reach a decision has been fair, regardless of the fairness of the outcomes (Lind and Tyler 1988). Interactional justice examines whether the procedures are implemented in a respectful manner that maintains each party's dignity (Bies and Moag 1986; Moorman 1991). Fair procedures mean that in the long run (e.g., over repeated iterations), justice will obtain. Although one party may not benefit during the current time period, she or he may benefit more directly later (individualistic rationality). Alternatively, he or she may benefit indirectly through the benefits which accrue to dyad or group (collectivistic rationality). Finally, she or he may not benefit at all, knowing only that the other party has benefited (altruistic rationality). The time component of the relational contract creates not only multiple points of reciprocity, but also facilitates the use of multiple points of rationality[10] and a greater potential to secure perceived fairness and justice for the parties.

In contrast, in the transactional contract it is assumed that the relationship is of short duration, and thus procedural justice will be irrelevant, as justice will not obtain for the current contracting partners. The longer time frames of the relational contract facilitate assessing procedural justice once distributive injustice has been perceived. If violated, the parties will evaluate interactional issues. If interactional justice has been violated, then the parties will move to a more transactional type of contract. The cumulative total of the assessments of the different forms of justice may result in negative synergy. The outcome of the negative synergy could be covert violation of the contract and potential retribution.

[10] Relational contracts highlight both the potential tradeoffs between forms of rationality and the potential for coincident operation of multiple points of rationality. For example, editors of an academic book must trade off the three forms of reciprocity when making suggestions to authors. In suggesting that an author incorporate a specific literature into the theoretical framework, or in suggesting specific citations, editors may be using the benefit of all authors in the volume as a metric for rational action (collective rationality) or the improvement of the author's paper (altruistic rationality). From a pure self-interest perspective, the editors may have suggested that their own papers be cited. Forgoing such a suggestion expresses an element of altruistic rationality.

Power in Exchange Relationships

Many contracting models assume that the parties are equally powerful, hence voluntarism in transactions is ensured. However, in this section of our paper, we will draw from several literatures to show the importance of power asymmetries in organizational contracts, and how both the source of power and its relative strength may affect the type of contract which evolves between the parties.

Sociologists have long been interested in exchange, as well as the power created by exchange relationships. It was Blau (1964) who emphasized that exchange creates differentiation of status and power, extending the perspectives of Homans (1961) and Thibault and Kelley (1959). In order to examine larger social structures, exchange theory moved its focus to more complex networks of relationships, and has developed complex theory regarding exchange networks (e.g., Emerson 1962, 1972, 1981).

Emerson's theory of power dependence is the basis of the examination of networks of relationships (e.g., Emerson 1962, 1972, 1981), and even networks of contracts. Emerson suggested that power is actually a property of the *relationship* between two actors, rather than being vested in either one as individuals. Thus power is relationship-specific, not person-specific, and is a function of the reliance or dependency of one of the parties on the other. If dependence is symmetric, then power is balanced. If it is asymmetric, then power is out of balance, and the least powerful party will be motivated to restore balance by withdrawing, or attempting to find alternatives such as status emergence or coalition formation.[11] The less powerful party may also attempt to restore perceived control through actions such as shirking.

This view of exchange relationships suggests that the entire network or fabric

[11] Yet, as noted by Mechanic (1962), less powerful organizational members may not be powerless. The sources of power for lower participants include their expertise, willingness to exert effort, attractiveness, location in physical space and location in social space, coalitions, and knowledge of rules (Mechanic 1962). A person's expert knowledge in today's technologically advanced state makes her/him invaluable and difficult to replace, and offsets some of the formal power usually attributed to higher-ranking roles (Hickson, Hinings, Lee, Schneck, and Pennings 1971; Hinings, Hickson, Pennings, and Schneck 1974). In some instances, such as physicians in hospitals, the higher-ranking individuals are unwilling to direct their efforts to some tasks, and they delegate those tasks to lower participants by default. When this occurs, higher-ranking individuals become dependent on the lower participants who do perform the tasks and consequently obtain a level of power. In addition, a person's attractiveness, or similarity, to the higher-ranking person enhances her/his ability to gain access to people with formal power (Enz 1988; Schein 1985; Stinchcombe 1968). This allows the person to have greater propinquity (Feldman 1981; Ibarra and Andrews 1993; Lincoln and Miller 1979; Thibaut and Kelley 1959). Similarly, "powerless" parties may gain a measure of power through the use of coalitions, which may form along the many possible channels of power, both within an organization and externally (Provan, Beyer, and Kruytbosch 1980; Brass 1985; Gargiulo 1993; Pfeffer and Salancik 1978; Pfeffer 1981; Salancik and Pfeffer 1974; Thompson 1967). Finally, absolute compliance with the rules and norms of an organization is generally dysfunctional, but serves as a threat from lower participants when bargaining is necessary (Friedlander 1983).

of related exchanges in which contracting parties are involved is important. These networks themselves may control exchange relationships occurring within them, and also provide the potential for alternative contracting partners. An important implication of this view of contracts is that there will be power differentials between the contracting parties. Yet while few discussions of organizational contracts explicitly address power differences between contracting parties, power asymmetries do exist. These power differences affect the presumed voluntarism of the exchange relationship, dividing the parties into the broad categories of contract *makers* (relatively powerful) and contract *takers* (relatively powerless).

An explicit recognition of the role of power in contracting, unlike more classical economic views of contracts, emphasizes the fact that some parties only may be in a position to be "contract takers." These are the parties who are relatively more dependent on their contracting partner, and although their participation in the contract may be technically voluntary, they cannot exit the relationship as easily as the other party, and may not have many (if any) viable alternative contracting partners. In contrast, the less dependent party is in a better position to diversify and choose from among a potentially larger pool of alternative contracting partners, and as such can be regarded as a "contract maker": one who can extend the terms of the contract to the contract taker, with little accommodation to the contract taker's preferences being necessary (especially if the power asymmetry is large).

Earlier, we discussed the norms of reciprocity and their congruence. Congruence in terms of the norm of reciprocity to which *each* party subscribes has important implications for the power relationship between the parties (see table 6.2). In particular, when one party subscribes to negative reciprocity and the other to generalized reciprocity, the norms of reciprocity are congruent for both parties—one takes and one gives. However, when these norms are incongruent (e.g., one party subscribes to balanced, and one to negative, reciprocity), then the dynamics of the situation are changed, in particular if power is asymmetric. For example, when the contract maker (the more powerful party) subscribes to negative reciprocity, she/he may exploit the contract taker with compunction and little inhibition other than that provided by the normative, social contract. If the contract taker subscribes to negative reciprocity, however, then she/he will only exploit the contract maker when that exploitation is believed to be unobservable.

The Role of Power Distributions and Reciprocity Norms in Contracting

Based on the previous discussions, several broad generalizations can be drawn:

1. Most models of organizational contracting implicitly rely on the assumption of self-interest.

Table 6.2. Reciprocal congruence and power

Reciprocal congruence with symmetric power		
Party A:		
Party B:	Negative	Balanced	Generalized
Negative	"On guard" (mutual exploitation)	Balance "unstable" Party B may exploit Party A if future exchanges unanticipated	Party B exploits A (with A's acceptance)
Balanced	Balance "unstable" A may exploit B if future exchanges unanticipated	Reciprocity matched Mutual gratification	B takes advantage of A
Generalized	Party A exploits B (with B's acceptance)	A takes advantage of B	Mutual beneficence

Reciprocal congruence with asymmetric power		
Party A (Contract Maker):		
Party B (Contract Taker):	Negative[a]	Balanced	Generalized
Negative[b]	A exploits B B exploits A if "invisible"[c]	B exploits A if "invisible"[d]	B exploits A (with A's permission)
Balanced	A exploits B	Reciprocity matched	B explits A
Generalized	A exploits B	B exploits A if "invisible"	Reciprocity matched

[a] Normative or third party control may prevent A from exploiting B.
[b] Normative control, as well as contractual sanctions and rewards may prevent B from exploiting A.
[c] Elaborate monitoring systems may be instituted by the Contract Maker to observe the Contract Taker.
[d] Compensation contracts are likely to be outcome-based.

2. Most models of organizational contracting implicitly rely on notions of balanced reciprocity.

3. Organizational contracts are negotiated, maintained, and executed within the fabric of the larger, social contact.

4. Few models of organizational contracting explicitly recognize the variety of resources which may be exchanged (i.e., money or affiliation), and how the resource itself may impact the nature of the contract.

5. Most models of organizational contracting assume parties of equivalent (or nearly equivalent) power.

By examining these generalizations, we can explore a richer view of organizational contracts. These generalizations may be viewed as contingencies instead of assumptions and to a greater or lesser degree may apply to different types of contracts and different forms of contracting. In this section of the paper, we will discuss four possible types of organizational contracts, as well as the self-interest assumptions and reciprocity norms implied by each in its creation, fulfillment and violation.

A Contractual Typology

By juxtaposing the transactional/relational characteristics of the contract with symmetric and asymmetric power distributions it becomes possible to identify specific forms of organizational contracts. Each form of contract is grounded within a larger social contract of reciprocity norms and metrics of rationality, with different obligations and entitlements for the parties. As depicted in figure 6.1, we suggest that organizational contracts can be classified into one of four broad categories, defined by the transactional/relational continuum and the distribution of power between the parties. Specifically, we suggest that instrumental contracts are characterized by a transactional relationship in which the parties have symmetric power. Exploitive contracts are characterized by a transactional relationship in which the power between the parties is asymmetric. When the relationship between the parties is relational in orientation, the contract is either communitarian (symmetric power) or custodial (asymmetric power).

Table 6.3 expands this typology, to highlight how each form of contract suggests distinct implications in terms of ensuring contract fulfillment and the costs associated with contract violation, as well as the likelihood that the parties

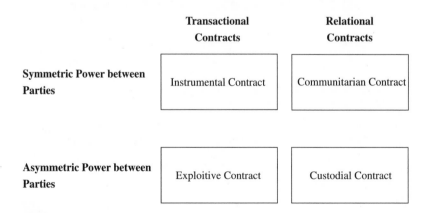

Figure 6.1

Table 6.3. Comparison of contract attributes and differences between contract makers and contract takers

Contracting between parties with symmetric power

	Communitarian contract (Relational)	Instrumental contract (Transactional)
1. Rationality	1. "collective" interest	1. self interest
2. Reciprocity	2. generalized or collective	2. balanced
3. Justice Metric	3. distributive, procedural & interactional	3. distributive
4. Time frame	4. open-ended or long	4. short/finite
5. Stability	5. dynamic	5. static
6. Scope	6. diffuse responsibilities	6. precise responsibilities
7. Resource offered	7. full range of resources	7. money, goods, services, information
8. Governance	8. internal market for reputations	8. external market for reputations

Contracting between parties with asymmetric power

	Custodial contract (Relational)		Exploitive contract (Transactional)	
	Contract maker	Contract taker	Contract maker	Contract taker
1. Rationality	1. "other" interest	1. self-/"other" interest	1. self interest	1. self interest
2. Reciprocity	2. generalized	2. negative	2. balanced or negative	2. balanced
3. Justice Metric	3. Interactional	3. distributive, procedural, & interactional	3. distributive	3. distributive
4. Time Frame	4. long	4. long	4. short/finite	4. short/finite
5. Stability	5. dynamic & adaptive	5. dynamic	5. static	5. adaptive
6. Scope	6. diffuse responsibilities	6. diffuse responsibilities	6. precise responsibilities	6. precise responsibilities
7. Resource offered	7. full range of resources	7. affiliation, status & perhaps service	7. service, money or goods	7. service
8. Governance	8. trust	8. trust	8. third parties	8. contingent contracts/monitoring

will be willing to go beyond the contract when unanticipated contingencies arise. In this typology, we associate self-interest with the transactional contract, and collective and altruistic rationality (emotionality) with the relational contract. Thus, in the view of Mumby and Putnam (1992), the transactional contract is considered instrumental and is characterized by calculative reasoning; in contrast, the relational contract is characterized by solidarity, mutual understanding and spontaneity. In the transactional contract, we might expect opportunism to rear its ugly head; in the relational contract, we would expect to find "other"-regarding behavior. This view is consistent with Rousseau and others' interpretation of Macneil's transactional/relational continuum (e.g., Rousseau 1989; Rousseau and McLean Parks 1993).

In this typology, we also suggest that power asymmetries, when they exist, carry with them responsibilities that are conferred on the more powerful party (the contract maker), and that are enforced predominantly through the fabric of the social contract. These responsibilities at least implicitly include a prohibition against exploitive behavior.[12] The enforcement power of these norms is likely to be greater in relational contracts, where the development of trust and norms of good faith and fair dealing are likely to be much stronger (Rousseau and McLean Parks 1993). Finally, it is important to note that the distribution of outcomes implies at least a minimal level of power; hence distributive justice is associated with the contract maker or symmetric power, whereas retributive justice is associated with both symmetric and asymmetric power, and consequently is one form of justice that is activated or imposed by the contract taker as well as by contract makers.

Instrumental contracts. Instrumental contracts are transactional in nature, and are characterized by parties of equal (or nearly equal) power. Instrumental contracts are predicated on self-interested behavior. Balanced reciprocity is the norm in instrumental contracts. Given short time frames and symmetric power, distributive justice is most important in determining fairness in the contractual relationship. These contracts are of finite (usually short) duration, and their terms are highly specific and quantifiable; consequently, they are easily observed by third parties. This ease of observation makes third-party enforcement (e.g., courts, arbitrators) of these contracts feasible, and enhances the effectiveness of the external market for reputations. An instrumental contract is exemplified by spot contracts such as the transaction between a buyer and seller in the market,

[12] Normative expectations surrounding the suppression of exploitation by (relatively) powerful parties in a transaction are exemplified by the outrage over excessive price gouging for necessities after hurricane Andrew or the Los Angeles earthquake, or by laws governing monopolistic power; similarly, in contract law, the precedent that favors interpretation according to the interests of the less powerful party when the intent of a contract cannot be unambiguously determined.

or by "outsourcing" employment contracts, with control of the employee vested outside the organization (Pfeffer and Baron 1988). Employees are hired to perform specific duties within a well specified time frame, and once their contract has been completed, will contract again with an alternative contracting party. The nature of these contracts suggests that the identity of the parties is irrelevant to the exchange itself, and future interactions are not anticipated.

Self-interest will motivate behavior in the instrumental contract, thus individualism is the metric of rational action. Consequently, violations of the contract and its terms will occur when economically rational, since there is no desire or need to preserve the relationship. For example, if the explicit costs of violation are less than the costs of compliance, it is likely that the instrumental contract will be violated. This implies that, in these contracts, violations will be negatively related to the perceived effectiveness of third party governance mechanisms (e.g., courts or arbitrators), the effectiveness of the market for reputations, and the strength of the potential penalties. The instrumental contract is static, and the parties are *un*likely to be willing to go beyond the contract (i.e., organizational citizenship behaviors; Organ 1988, 1990) in the event of unanticipated contingencies, preferring to renegotiate and demand recompense for previously unspecified contributions.

Exploitive contracts.[13] Like the instrumental contract, the exploitive contract also is transactional in nature and grounded in the cognitive, individualistic dimension of self-interest. However, unlike the instrumental contract, these transactional contracts are characterized by power asymmetries. Reciprocity is likely to be balanced, with components of negative reciprocity. Both parties subscribe to the instrumental metric of rationality, and thus, at the extreme, actions will be motivated by pure self-interest. The exploitive contract is characterized by the relationship between the migrant laborer and the farmer, the sweatshop owner and the garment maker, or between the temporary secretary and the office manager. Although grounded in self-interest, the exploitive contract and its power asymmetries can encourage the misuse or even abuse of power, moving this type of contract into the realm of negative reciprocity. The terms of the exploitive contract tend to be precise and clearly delineated (e.g., piecework). At the extreme, the lack of dependence of the contract maker on the contract taker suggests that the identity of the contract taker is generally irrelevant, and that contract takers may be considered to be substitutable.

---

[13] Our use of the term "exploitive" is similar to Williamson's (1975b) conceptualization of opportunism. Yet, Williamson envisions opportunism as a human factor separate from any explicit consequences of power. In our paper we emphasize the power asymmetries and the potential for both the use and abuse of power, rather than the power symmetries suggested by Williamson's exemplar of the bilateral monopoly.

Exploitive contracts may facilitate opportunism and the testing of the contract's limits by both parties. Like the instrumental contract, the short time frame of the exploitive contract suggests that fairness concerns will be judged by assessing distributive justice. Perceptions of fairness are one constraint on exploitive behavior (Kahneman, Knetsch, and Thaler 1986c). In the absence of sanctions from normative control (the social contract), however, the contract maker may exploit the contract taker. In the absence of effective control mechanisms, the contract taker may shirk, violating the terms of the contract, especially when violations are unlikely to be detected. Elaborate monitoring and performance systems may be implemented to ensure either behavioral or outcome control by the contract maker. Contract takers will be unable to enforce contract terms on the contract makers, and may instead resort to sabotage, or attempt to form coalitions when their contracts are violated (McLean Parks and Kidder 1994). Ensuring compliance by the contract maker requires strong normative control through third parties (e.g., the courts), and again, necessitates the establishment of systems that monitor the powerful contract maker's behavior within the context of the larger social contract. For example, regulatory agencies such as OSHA monitor contract makers (i.e., the organization) in order to enforce the social contract. In this case, the less powerful contract taker relies on the larger fabric of the social contract to ensure compliance by the contract maker. Like parties to an instrumental contract, those involved in static exploitive contracts are unlikely to go beyond delineated terms when there are unanticipated contingencies. Instead, they generally choose to honor the letter of the contract, and incorporate important contingencies in future contracting periods. It should be noted, however, that unanticipated contingencies may provide the contract makers impetus for exploitation or coercion, due to the power asymmetry in this form of contract. Similarly, with asymmetric power, the timeframe of the exploitive contract may be implicitly lengthened: the contract taker may be more dependent on the contract maker and may be unable to find alternative contracting partners, making exit from the relationship difficult.

Communitarian contracts. Communitarian contracts are relational contracts between parties of equal (or nearly equal) power. At the extreme, these contracts can be characterized as an exchange between close friends or colleagues with generalized or collective norms of reciprocity, where the parties to the contract expect to interact for an indefinite time period. Law partnerships, as well as relationships between academic co-authors at different universities exemplify the communitarian contract. These contracts are characterized by the parties' long-term commitments to each other. The communitarian contract's is focused both on pecuniary and nonpecuniary benefits. The communitarian contract is likely to include socio-emotional benefits, and identification with the collectivity will be a motivating factor. Communitarian contracts are closely related to the clan control of Ouchi (1980), or the covenants discussed by Graham and her colleagues (e.g., Graham 1991; Graham and Organ 1993; McLean Parks 1992; Van Dyne, et al. 1994). Communitarian contracts are characterized by diffuse obligations and long-term commitments, by a focus on maintaining and extending the relationship into the future, and by preserving and enhancing the collectivity's well-being.

Communitarian contracts imply solidarity and "other"-regarding, rather than purely self-interested behavior. Reciprocity is likely to be generalized, and actions are motivated by a collective form of rationality. Communitarian contracts are dynamic and adaptable. When unanticipated contingencies arise, the parties to a communitarian contract will honor the *intent* of the contract, making mutual adjustments in order to maintain and enhance the relationship. Thus, in the communitarian contract, there is a greater likelihood that the parties will go beyond delineated requirements in order to create solidarity and ensure continuing the relationship into the future. Immediate outcomes (distributive justice) may be less salient, as it is assumed that fairness will obtain in the long run. Consequently, procedural and interactional justice are likely to be considered in assessing contract outcomes.

Due to the evolutionary and continuous nature of a communitarian contract, its parties can establish among themselves reputations, or patterns of reliable trustworthy behavior. Over time, trust develops through repeated interactions, and thus these contracts are likely to be governed by trust. Trust itself is characterized by the formation of an emotional bond between the parties, where the emotional costs incurred by violating the trust are assumed to be greater than the potential gains (Luhman 1979). If violated, trust is not easily restored, and a violation is likely to result in the severance of a relationship, or a more "transactional" orientation (McLean Parks and Kidder 1994; Robinson and Rousseau 1994; Rousseau and McLean Parks 1993). Under such circumstances, solidarity and the communitarian nature of the contract are likely to be irrevocably damaged.

Custodial contracts. Custodial contracts are relational contracts between parties of unequal or asymmetric power. From the perspective of the contract maker, these contracts are "mothering"[14] (Held 1990) in nature, and are exemplified by a parent and child relationship, or that between mentor and protégé, or between a large corporation and its entrepreneurial spin-off (e.g., Honeywell

---

[14] Held does not associate a gender with "mothering" but rather suggests that the "mothering" person is one who puts another's interests first, and performs a nurturing role.

and Alliance Technologies). Highly maternalistic/paternalistic organizations exemplify custodial contracts, and such employment relationships are characterized by a high degree of involvement, both on the part of the contract taker (i.e., the employee, who identifies closely with the organization and treats it as an extension of family) and the contract maker (e.g., the "company town," exemplified by Pullman Palace Car Company in the late 1890s [Guzzo, Nelson, and Noonan 1992]). In custodial contracts, the contract taker is highly dependent on the contract maker. The high level of involvement and the nature of the custodial contract broaden the scope of the contractual exchange relationship. In the case of Pullman Palace Car Company, the contract permeated every aspect of the contract takers' lives.

Custodial contracts are grounded in notions of generalized reciprocity and "other-interest." The custodial contract maker looks out for the interests of the contract taker, and derives little direct, measurable benefit from the arrangement. Ties between the parties are socio-emotional. They are custodial on the one hand, and dependent on the other. The contract maker's contributions are predicated not on a notion of fair return, but rather on a collective or altruistic rationality. In addition, the norms of the social contract prohibit exploitation. In relational contracts, however, such exploitation may be quite difficult to govern, and thus there is a strong reliance on the "other" orientation of the contract maker.

In custodial contracts, the contract maker is held accountable for the interests of the contract taker, and his or her external reputation (as well as self-concept) is tied to the successes (or failures) of the contract taker. The contract takers' interests are protected, and in this sense this type of exchange is characterized by "other-regard" that is somewhat unidirectional. Although the contract taker may, in fact, return this "other-regard," it is not a primary motivator of the contract maker's behavior. This type of exchange might be found at the relational extreme of the contract continuum and will be controlled by very general rules and diffuse obligations. Thus, the metric of rationality in such contracts may simultaneously cover the full range of rationality: the individualistic self-orientation of the protégé who "takes" from the mentor; the collective interest of both parties in attempting to ensure the continuity of the relationship, and finally, the "other" interest of the mentor in attempting to protect and enhance the performance of the protégé.

These contracts are dynamic. It is common in the custodial contract to observe the parties going beyond their delineated obligations and making adjustments when contingencies arise. As in the communitarian contract, procedural and interactional justice are quite important. However, procedure delineation tends to be associated with power, and hence primarily is the prerogative of the contract maker. Thus, we suggest that interactional justice will be particularly important in custodial contracts. If the custodial contract is violated, it is unlikely that it can be repaired, as the combined violation of trust and the potential abuse of power may evoke a strong, emotional response, severing the tie between the parties. As the relationship dissolves, parties may then use retributive justice to settle accounts.

Implications for Non-rational Decision Making

In this paper we have criticized the implicit assumptions in many of our exchange models that suggest symmetric power, self-interest, and balanced reciprocity. We have suggested that there are important differences between power-symmetric and asymmetric contracts. In addition, the reciprocity norms to which individual contracting parties subscribe may be grounded in quite different metrics of rationality. We have asserted that the commonly-used metrics of self-interest and balanced reciprocity should be viewed as contingencies. We argue the importance of determining what metric of rationality is "in use" by an actor, and how that actor answers the question, "Who benefits?" Metrics of rationality other than self-interest (individualistic rationality) are plausible, and are likely to underlie quite different forms of reciprocity operating in different types of exchange relationships. We have suggested that multiple points of reciprocity and rationality may operate in different forms of contracts. These points may operate exclusively, or simultaneously. In particular, we have suggested that rationality can be conceptualized as a continuum, ranging from an individualistic orientation where the motivator of actions, is to benefit self; to collectivist rationality, where individual decision makers choose actions based on what they believe will benefit the collective; to altruistic rationality, where a decision maker chooses an action based on the interests of another party (and at the extreme, potentially sacrificing her or his own self-interest). The form of rationality underlying each form of organizational contract may vary, both as a function of the type of relationship between parties, and as the distribution of power between them. Consequently, the "rationality" of such behaviors can only be measured against the metric intended by the parties, a metric that we suggest can be predicted as a function of the type of contract which governs the exchange relationship between the parties.

When contracting parties decide whether to violate a contract, execute its terms, or go beyond the contract into the realm of supra-role behaviors, they will not always be measuring the potential benefits of these decisions against a metric of pure self-interest. We suggest that relational contracts in particular are grounded in collective or altruistic forms of rationality, where the intangible and non-quantifiable benefits of the relationship itself may dictate a preeminent concern for the outcomes of the other party in the exchange relationship.

In addition, we have argued that particular attention should be paid to the notion of voluntariness and power in exchange relationships. We do not assume that contract takers can easily abandon an organizational contract if they are dissatisfied. Rather, they may be more likely to stay and shirk, steal, or engage in sabotage in order to even the status quo and regain a sense of control and perceived equity in the relationship (McLean Parks and Kidder 1994). Finally, we have suggested that different forms of justice are important to different forms of contract. This has implications for how contracting parties handle situations where the terms of a contract *cannot* be met, or for how they can renegotiate a contract without violating perceptions of justice. It is particularly important to realize that the parties to a contract, regardless of their power, may have different criteria for evaluating the fairness of an outcome or process. For instance, parties to a contract may have differences about what behavior should be judged more valuable. These perceptions and socially constructed attitudes and behaviors about "appropriate" outcomes and processes will affect judgments of fairness. Gilligan and her colleagues suggest that such behavior choices appear to be the result of two different types of morality: justice (decision maker is more detached and emphasizes equity and rights) and care (decision maker is more empathetic and concerned for others) (Gilligan 1982; Gilligan, Ward, and Taylor 1988). The grounding of the justice view of morality may range from individualistic to collectivistic rationality, while the grounding of the care perspective on morality may range from collectivistic to altruistic assessments of rational action. Quite simply, the choice of acting to execute, violate or go beyond an organizational contract depends on the contracting parties' metrics of rationality, the norm of reciprocity to which they subscribe, their view of justice, and the relative power between different parties to the contract.

Conclusion

In this paper, we have provided a platform for enriching our views of organizational contracts and the contracting process. We have presented alternatives to three of the implicit assumptions found in much of our research on organizational contracting: (1) that contracting parties are "rational," where rationality is defined in terms of the self-interested, utility maximizer; (2) that exchange is governed by norms of balanced reciprocity, or quid pro quo; and (3) that exchange is generally voluntary, entered into by parties of symmetric power. Although the alternatives generated in this paper are by no means comprehensive, they provide insight into types of contracts and contracting processes which may not be apparent because of the particular lens through which we examine exchange relationships. Rather than regarding each of these postulates as assumptions, it is more appropriate to regard them as *contingencies* and to ask: (1) When and under what conditions is the self-interest metric of rationality appropriate, and when and under what conditions might the metric of emotionality (which encompasses collective and altruistic rationality) be more accurate? (2) When and under what conditions does balanced reciprocity predominate, and when and under what conditions do other reciprocity norms control exchange relationships? (3) When and under what conditions is power between contracting parties symmetric, and when and under what conditions will it be asymmetric? In a related vein, when and under what conditions does the employee become the contract maker, and the employer the contract taker? And finally, (4) What are the implications of each of these contingencies for organizations and the individuals who comprise them? By addressing questions such as these, we hope to incorporate and highlight aspects of organizational contracts that currently are overlooked or trivialized.

Transaction Cost Economics and Organization Theory

Oliver E. Williamson

Economic and sociological approaches to economic organization have reached a state of healthy tension. That is to be contrasted with an earlier state of affairs in which the two approaches were largely disjunct, and hence ignored one another, or described each other's research agendas and research accomplishments with disdain (Swedberg 1990, 4). Healthy tension involves genuine give and take. Neither the obsolescence of organization theory, to which Charles Perrow has recently alluded (1992, 162), nor the capitulation of economics, about which James March (tongue-in-cheek) remarked,[1] is implied.

A more respectful relation, perhaps even a sense that economics and organization are engaged in a joint venture, is evident in W. Richard Scott's remark that "while important areas of disagreement remain, more consensus exists than is at first apparent" (1992, 3), in game theorist David Kreps's contention that "almost any theory of organization which is addressed by game theory will do more for game theory than game theory will do for it" (1992, 1), and in my argument that a science of organization is in progress in which law, economics, and organization are joined.[2]

This paper has benefited from oral presentations to the Macro Organization Behavior Society at the October 1992 meeting at Northwestern, the Stanford Center for Organizational Research, and the Institutional Analysis Workshop at the University of California, Berkeley.
[1] James March advised the Fourth International Conference of the Society for the Advancement of Socio-Economics that economics had been so fully reformed that the audience should "declare victory and go home" (Coughlin 1992, 23).
[2] Richard Posner comes out differently. He argues that "organization theory . . . [adds] nothing to economics that the literature on information economics had not added years earlier" (1992, 28).

155

Joint ventures sometimes evolve into mergers and sometimes unravel. I do not expect that either will happen here. That merger is not in prospect is because economics, organization theory, and law have separate as well as combined agendas. A full-blown merger, moreover, would impoverish the evolving science of organization—which has benefitted from the variety of insights that are revealed by the use of different lenses. I expect that the joint venture will hold until one of the parties has learned enough from the others to go it alone. Progress attended by controversy is what I project for the remainder of the decade.

This paper focuses on connections between transaction cost economics and organization theory, and argues that a three-part relation is taking shape. The first and most important of these is that transaction cost economics has been (and will continue to be) massively influenced by concepts and empirical regularities that have their origins in organization theory. Second, I sketch the key concepts out of which transaction cost economics works, and to which organization theorists can (and many do) relate productively. The triad is completed by an examination of phenomena for which rival interpretations have been advanced, and which remain unresolved and provoke controversy.

At the suggestion of the conference organizers, I begin this paper with some background on institutional economics, both old and new. Next, a three-level schema for studying economic organization is proposed in section 2. Some of the more important ways in which transaction cost economics has benefited from organization theory then are examined in section 3, and the key concepts in transaction cost economics are sketched in section 4. Empirical regularities, as discerned through the lens of transaction cost economics pertinent to organization theory are discussed in section 5. Contested terrain is surveyed in Section 6 and concluding remarks follow.

1. Institutional Economics

Older Traditions

Leading figures in the older institutional economics movement in the United States were Wesley Mitchell, Thorstein Veblen, and John R. Commons. Although many sociologists appear to be sympathetic with the older tradition, there is growing agreement that that approach was "largely descriptive and historically specific" (DiMaggio and Powell 1991, 2) and was not cumulative (Granovetter 1988, 8).

Criticisms by economists of the old institutional economics have been scathing. Thus, George Stigler remarks that "the school failed in America for a very simple reason. It had nothing in it except a stance of hostility to the standard theoretical tradition. There was no positive agenda of research" (Stigler

1983, 170). Similar views are expressed by R. C. O. Matthews (1986, 9031. Ronald Coase concurs that the work of American institutionalists "led to nothing. . . . Without a theory, they had nothing to pass on except a mass of descriptive material waiting for a theory or a fire. So if modern institutionalists have antecedents, it is not what went immediately before" (Coase 1984, 230). My general agreement with these assessments notwithstanding, I would make an exception for John R. Commons. For one thing, the institutional economics tradition at Wisconsin is still very much alive (Bromley 1989). Also, Commons and his students and colleagues had enormous influence on public policy. Andrew Van de Ven's summary of Commons's intellectual contributions is pertinent to the first of these:

> Especially worthy of emphasis [about Commons] are his (1) dynamic views of institutions as a response to scarcity and conflicts of interest, (2) original formulation of the transaction as the basic unit of analysis, (3) part-whole analysis of how collective action constrains, liberates, and expands individual action in countless numbers of routine and complementary transactions on the one hand, and how individual wills and power to gain control over limiting or contested factors provide the generative mechanisms for institutional change on the other, and (4) historical appreciation of how customs, legal precedents, and laws of a society evolve to construct a collective standard of prudent reasonable behavior for resolving disputes between conflicting parties in pragmatic and ethical ways. (1992, 14)

Albeit in varying degree, transaction cost economics is responsive to Commons in *all four of these respects.*[3]

During and after the Great Depression Commons and his colleagues and students were influential in politics in shaping social security, labor legislation, public utility regulation, and, more generally, public policy toward business. Possibly because of its public policy successes, the Wisconsin School was remiss in developing its intellectual foundations. The successive operationalization—from informal into preformal, semiformal, and fully formal modes of analysis—that I associate with transaction cost economics (Williamson 1993a) never materialized. Instead, Commons' institutional economics progressed very little beyond the informal stage.

[3]Briefly, the transaction cost economics responses are: (1) institutions respond to scarcity as economizing devices, (2) the transaction is expressly adopted as the basic unit of analysis, (3) conflicts are recognized and relieved by the creation of credible commitments/ex post governance apparatus, and (4) the institutional environment is treated as a set of shift parameters that change the comparative costs of governance. Although these may be incomplete responses, the spirit of the transaction cost economics enterprise nevertheless makes serious contract with Commons's prescription.

The New Institutional Economics

The New Institutional Economics comes in a variety of flavors and has been variously defined. The economics of property rights, as developed especially by Coase (1959; 1960), Armen Alchian (1961), and Harold Demsetz (1967), was an early and influential dissent from orthodoxy that advanced an evolutionary, as opposed to a technological, approach to economic organization. According to this approach, new property rights were created and enforced as economic needs arose, if and as these were cost effective.

The definition of ownership rights advanced by Eirik Furubotn and Svetozar Pejovich is broadly pertinent: "By general agreement, the right of ownership of an asset consists of three elements: (a) the right to use the asset . . ., (b) the right to appropriate the returns from the asset . . ., and (c) the right to change the asset's form and/or substance" (1974, 4). Strong claims on behalf of the property rights approach to economic organization were set out by Coase as follows (1959, 14): A private enterprise system cannot function unless property rights are created in resources, and when this is done, someone wishing to use a resource has to pay the owner to obtain it. Chaos disappears; and so does the government except that a legal system to define property rights and to arbitrate disputes is, of course, necessary. As it turns out, these claims overstate the case for the property rights approach. Not only is the definition of property rights sometimes costly—consider the problems of intellectual property rights—but court ordering can be an expensive way to proceed. Therefore a comparative contractual approach, rather than a pure property rights approach, has a great deal to recommend according to this approach, court ordering thus becomes only one of several options, and an extreme one at that, for governing contractual relations (MacNeil 1974 1978; Williamson 1979 1991a). Assessing the comparative efficacy of alternative modes of governance is a microanalytic undertaking in which the attributes of transactions and organizations, as well as property rights, matter. Much of the New Institutional Economics, however, is concerned with rules and constraints rather than the governance of contractual relations. Thus Douglass North defines institutions as "the humanly devised constraints that structure political, economic, and social interactions. They consist of both informal constraints (sanctions, taboos, customs, traditions, and codes of conduct), and formal rules (constitutions, laws, property rights)" (1991, 97). Elsewhere he argues that "institutions consist of a set of constraints on behavior in the form of rules and regulations; a set of procedures to detect deviations from the rules and regulations; and, finally, a set of moral, ethical behavioral norms which define the contours and that constrain the way in which the rules and regulations are specified and enforcement is carried out" (North 1986, 8).

Relatedly, Allan Schmid defines institutions as "sets of ordered relationships among people which define their rights, exposures to the rights of others, privileges, and responsibilities" (1972, 893); Daniel Bromley contends that institutions fall into two classes: conventions, and rules or entitlements (1989, 41); and Andrew Schotter defines institutions as "regularities in behavior which are agreed to by all members of a society and which specify behavior in specific recurrent situations" (1981, 9). According to Eirik Furubotn and Rudolf Richter, "Modern institutional economics focuses on the institution of property, and on the system of norms governing the acquisition or transfer of property rights" (1991, 3), although they subsequently make significant provision for governance. Although many of the phenomena with which the New Institutional Economics has been concerned has been at the governance level, as had much of the predictive content and most of the empirical research, (Matthews 1986, 907), analysis is needed at both the institutional environment and institutions of governance levels. Indeed, the two are complementary, as the two-part treatment proposed by Lance Davis and Douglass North suggested:

> The *institutional environment* is the set of fundamental political, social and legal ground rules that establishes the basis for production, exchange and distribution. Rules governing elections, property rights, and the right of contract are examples.
>
> An *institutional arrangement* is an arrangement between economic units that governs the ways in which these units can cooperate and/or compete. It[can] provide a structure within which its members can cooperate . . . or [it can] provide a mechanism that can effect a change in laws or property rights. (1971, 6-7; emphasis in original)

2. A Three-Level Schema

Transaction cost economics is concerned mainly with the governance of contractual relations. Governance, however, does not operate in isolation. The comparative efficacy of alternative modes of governance varies with the institutional environment on the one hand and the attributes of economic actors on the other. A three-level schema is therefore proposed, according to which the object of analysis, governance, is bracketed by more macro features (the institutional environment) and more micro features (the individual). Feedbacks aside (which are underdeveloped in the transaction cost economics setup), the institutional environment is treated as the locus of shift parameters, changes in which the comparative costs of governance shift, and the individual is located where the behavioral assumptions originate.

Roger Friedland and Robert Alford also propose a three-level schema in which environment, governance, and individual are distinguished, but there the emphasis is very different. They argue that "An adequate social theory must work at three levels of analysis—individuals competing and negotiating, organizations in conflict, and institutions in contradiction and interdependency" (Friedland and Alford 1991, 240). "These levels of analysis [are] nested, where organization and institution specify progressively higher levels of constraint and opportunity for individual action" (1991, 242).

There is a lot to be said for a nested approach, especially if the relevant action is at the level of the individual. If, however, the governance structures of organizations are the object of analysis, then the causal model proposed by W. Richard Scott (1992, 45), as well as that which I propose, have advantages.

There are three main effects in my schema (see figure 7.1). These are shown by the solid arrows. Secondary effects are drawn as dashed arrows. As indicated, the institutional environment defines the rules of the game. If changes in property rights, contract laws, norms, customs, and the like induce changes in the comparative costs of governance, then a reconfiguration of economic organization is implied.

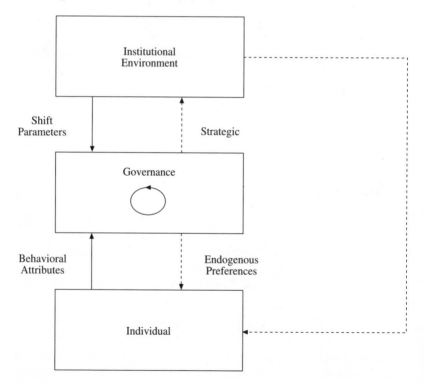

Figure 7.1

The solid arrow from the individual to governance carries the behavioral assumptions within which transaction cost economics operates, and the circular arrow within the governance sector reflects the proposition that an organization, like the law, has a life of its own. Although behavioral assumptions are frequently scanted in economics, transaction cost economics subscribes to the proposition that economic actors should be described in workable realistic terms (Simon 1978; Coase 1984). Physicists, as opposed to economists, have insisted that a better understanding of human agents' actions requires more self-conscious attention to the study of how men's minds work (Bridgeman 1955, 450; Waldrop 1992, 142). Herbert Simon concurs:

> Nothing is more fundamental in setting our research agenda and informing our research methods than our view of the nature of the human beings whose behavior we are studying. It makes a difference, a very large difference, to our research strategy whether we are studying the nearly omniscient *Homo economicus* of rational choice theory or the boundedly rational *Homo psychologicus* of cognitive psychology. It makes a difference to research, but it also makes a difference for the proper design of political institutions. James Madison was well aware of that, and in the pages of the *Federalist Papers* he opted for this view of the human condition (*Federalist*, No. 55):"As there is a degree of depravity in mankind which requires a certain degree of circumspection and distrust, so there are other qualities in human nature which justify a certain portion of esteem and confidence."—a balanced and realistic view, we may concede, of bounded human rationality and its accompanying frailties of motive and reason. (1985, 303)

Transaction cost economics expressly adopts the proposition that human cognition is subject to bounded rationality, where this is defined as behavior that is "intendedly rational, but only limitedly so" (Simon 1957, xxiv), and interprets the "degree of depravity" to which Madison refers not as "frailties of motive and reason," which sound like peccadilloes, but as *opportunism*.

Opportunism can take blatant, subtle, and natural forms. The blatant form is associated with Machiavelli. Because he perceived that the economic agents with whom the Prince was dealing were opportunistic, Machiavelli advised the Prince to engage in reciprocal and even pre-emptive opportunism, and to breach contracts with impunity whenever "the reasons which made him bind himself no longer exist" (Machiavelli 1952, 92). The subtle form is strategic and has been described elsewhere as "self-interest seeking with guile" (Williamson 1975, 26-37; 1985, 46-52, 64-67). The natural form involves tilting the system at the margin. The so-called dollar-a-year men in the Office of Production Management, of which there were 250 at the beginning of World War II, were of concern to the Senate Special Committee to Investigate the National Defense

Program because (McCullough 1992, 265): "Such corporate executives in high official roles were too inclined to make decisions for the benefit of their corporations. 'They have their own business at heart,' [Senator] Truman remarked. The report called them lobbyists 'in a very real sense,' because their presence inevitably meant favoritism, human nature being what it is."

Feedback effects from governance to the institutional environment can be either instrumental or strategic. An example of the former would be an improvement in contract law, brought about at the request of parties who find that extant law is poorly suited to support the integrity of the contract process. Strategic changes could take the form of protectionist trade barriers against domestic and/or foreign competition. Feedback from governance to the level of the individual can be interpreted as "endogenous preference" formation (Bowles and Gintis 1993), due to advertising or other forms of "education." The individual is also influenced by the environment, in that endogenous preferences are the product of social conditioning. Although transaction cost economics may relate to these secondary effects, other modes of analysis are often more pertinent.

More generally, the Friedland and Alford scheme, the Scott scheme, and the variant that I offer are not mutually exclusive. Which to use when depends on the questions being asked. To repeat, the main case approach to economic organization that I have proposed works out of the heavy line causal relations shown in Figure 7.1, to which the dashed lines represent refinements.

3. The Value Added of Organization Theory

Richard Swedberg (1987, 1990), Robert Frank (1992), and others have described numerous ways in which economics has been influenced by sociology and organization theory. The value added to which I refer here deals only with those aspects where transaction cost economics has been a direct and significant beneficiary.

The behavioral assumptions to which I refer above—bounded rationality and opportunism—perhaps are the most obvious examples of how transaction cost economics has been shaped by organization theory. But the proposition that organization has a life of its own (the circular arrow in the governance box in Figure 7.1) is also important. And there are additional influences as well.

4. Intertemporal Process Transformations

Describing the firm as a production function invites an engineering approach to organization. The resulting "machine model" of organization emphasizes intended effects to the neglect of unintended effects (March and Simon 1958, chap.3). But if organizations, like the law, have a life of their own, and if the usual economic approach is unable to relate to the intertemporal realities of organizations, then—for some purposes at least—an unusual economic approach may be needed.

Note that I do not propose that the economic approach be abandoned. Rather, the "usual" or orthodox economic approach gives way to "unusual" or nonstandard approaches. That is very different from adopting an altogether different approach such as, for example, neural networks.

As it turns out, the economic approach is very elastic and increasing numbers of economists aspire to deal with economic organization "as it is," warts and all, whereupon all significant regularities, intended and unintended alike, come within the ambit. Moreover, the farsighted propensity that economics ascribes to economic actors permits the analysis of regularities to be taken a step further. Once unanticipated consequences are understood, they will thereafter be anticipated and their ramifications folded back into the organizational design. Unwanted costs will then be mitigated, and unanticipated benefits enhanced. Better economic performance ordinarily will result.

Unintended effects are frequently delayed and are often subtle. Deep knowledge of the details and intertemporal process transformations that attend organization therefore is needed. Because organization theorists have wider and deeper knowledge of these conditions, economists ought to defer to them. Four specific illustrations are sketched here.

(a) Demands for control. A natural response to perceived failures of performance is to introduce added controls. Such efforts can have both intended *and* unintended consequences (Merton 1936; Gouldner 1954).

One illustration is the employment relations, where an increased emphasis on the reliability of behavior gives rise to added rules (March and Simon 1958, 38-40). Rules, however, serve not merely as controls but also define minimally acceptable behavior (Cyert and March 1963). Managers who apply rules to subordinates in a legalistic and mechanical way invite "working to rules," which frustrates effective performance.

The wider peripheral vision of organization theorists will pick up on these unintended consequences. But in the spirit of farsighted contracting, the argument will be taken a step further. Once apprised of these consequences, the farsighted economist will take them into account by factoring them into the organizational design. (Organization theorists might respond that this last point is fanciful and unrealistic. This can be decided by examining the data.)

(b) Oligarchy. The Iron Law of Oligarchy holds that "It is organization which gives birth to the dominion of the elected over the electors, of the mandatories

over the mandators, of the delegates over the delegators. Who says organization, says oligarchy" (Michels 1962, 365). Thus, good intentions notwithstanding, initial leadership (or its successors) will inevitably develop attachments to its office. The leadership, being strategically situated, will predictably entrench itself by controlling information, manipulating rewards and punishments, and mobilizing resources to defeat rivals. Even worse, the entrenched leadership will use the organization to promote its own agenda at the expense of the membership. One response to this situation might be to eschew organization in favor of anarchy.

The polar choices of anarchy or oligarchy do not, however, exhaust the alternatives. The better and deeper lesson is to take all predictable regularities into account at the outset, whereupon it may be possible to mitigate foreseeable oligarchical excesses at the initial design stage.[4]

(c) Identity/capability. The proposition that identity matters applies both in general and with respect to particular transactions. The latter is a transaction cost economics argument and is developed further below.

One way to unpack the "capabilities" view of a firm is to ask what is needed to describe the firm's capabilities in addition to an inventory of its physical assets, an accounting for its financial assets, and a census of its workforce. Transaction cost economics would respond that the contractual relations between the firm and each of its constituencies all matter, but set these aside. Features of organization that arguably are important include the following: (1) the communication codes that the firm has developed (Arrow 1974); (2) the routines that it employs (Cyert and March 1963; Nelson and Winter 1982); and (3) the corporate culture that has taken shape (Kreps 1990). What do we make of these?

One response is to regard them as spontaneous features of economic organization. A rival response is to interpret them as intentional. Institutional theory in sociology holds that "organizational structures, procedures, and decisions are *largely ritualistic and symbolic,* especially so when it is difficult or impossible to assess the efficacy of organizational decisions on the basis of their tangible outcomes" (Baron and Hannan 1992, 57; emphasis added).

---

[4] Oligarchy is usually applied to composite organization, but it applies to subdivisions as well. Whether a firm should make or buy is thus a matter for which oligarchy has a bearing. If the decision to take a transaction out of the market and organize it internally is attended by subsequent information distortions and subgoal pursuit, then that should be taken into account at the outset (Williamson 1975, chap. 7; 1985, chap. 6). Not only do operating costs rise but a constituency develops that favors the renewal of internal facilities. An obvious response is to demand high hurdle rates for new projects, thereby to protect against the unremarked but predictable distortions (added costs; advocacy efforts) to which internal (as compared with market) procurement is differentially subject. The argument applies to public sector projects as well. Because of the deferred and undisclosed, but nevertheless predictable, distortions to which "organization" is subject, new projects and regulatory proposals should be required to display large (apparent) net gains.

To take the intentionality view is to regard capabilities as (partly) subject to strategic determination. If the benefits of capabilities vary with the attributes of transactions, which arguably they do, then the cost effective thing to do is to *shape* culture, *develop* communication codes, and *manage* routines in a deliberative (transaction-specific) way. Implementing the intentionality view will require that the microanalytic attributes that define culture, communication codes, and routines be uncovered, which is an ambitious exercise.

(d) Bureaucratization. As compared with the study of market failure, the study of bureaucratic failure is rather poorly developed. A well-considered theory of organization will make provision, however, for failures of all kinds and all failures need to be assessed comparatively.

The bureaucratic failure literature is vast, partly because purported failures are described in absolute rather than comparative terms. Unless a superior and feasible form of organization to which to assign a transaction (or related set of transactions) can be identified, however, the failure in question is effectively irremediable. One of the tasks of transaction cost economics is to assess purported bureaucratic failures in comparative institutional terms. Most of the remediable bureaucratic failures are related to time (as with oligarchy) or complexity (Williamson 1975, chap. 7; 1985, chap. 6).

Adaptation

The economist Friedrich Hayek maintained that the main problem of economic organization was adaptation, and argued that this was realized spontaneously through the price system. Changes in the demand or supply of a commodity give rise to price changes, whereupon "*individual* participants . . . [are] able to take the right action" (Hayek 1945, 527; emphasis added). Such price-induced adaptations by individual actors will be referred to as adaptations (A), where (A) denotes autonomy.

The organization theorist Chester Barnard also held that adaptation was the central problem of organization. But whereas Hayek emphasized autonomous adaptation of a spontaneous kind, Barnard was concerned with cooperative adaptation, hereafter referred to as adaptation (C), that was accomplished in an intentional way. Formal organization, especially hierarchy, was the instrument through which the "conscious, deliberate, purposeful" cooperation to which Barnard called attention was accomplished (Barnard 1938, 4). Barnard's insights have had a lasting effect on organization theory. They can and should have a lasting effect on economics as well.

Transaction cost economics (1) concurs that adaptation is the central problem of economic organization, (2) regards adaptations of both autonomous and cooperative kinds as important, (3) maintains that whether adaptations to disturbances ought to be predominantly of type A, type C, or a mixture thereof varies with the attributes of the transactions (especially with the degree to which the investments associated with successive stages of activity are bilaterally or multilaterally dependent), and (4) argues that each generic form of governance—market, hybrid, and hierarchy—differs systematically in its capacity to adapt in autonomous and cooperative ways. A series of predicted (transaction cost economizing) alignments between transactions and governance structures thereby obtain (Williamson 1991a), which predictions invite and have been subjected to empirical testing (Joskow 1988; Shelanski 1991; Masten 1992).

Politics

Terry Moe (1990) makes a compelling case for the proposition that public bureaucracies are different. That is partly because the transactions that are assigned to the public sector are different, but Moe argues additionally that public sector bureaucracies are *shaped by politics*. Democratic politics requires compromises different in kind from those posed in the private sector, and poses novel expropriation hazards. Added "inefficiencies" arise in the design of public agencies on both accounts. The inefficiencies resulting from compromise are illustrated by the design of the Occupational Safety and Health Administration (OSHA) (Moe 1990, 126): "If business firms were allowed to help design OSHA, they would structure it in a way that it could not do its job. They would try to cripple it. This is not a hypothetical case. Interest groups representing business actually did participate in the design of OSHA, . . . [and] OSHA is an administrative nightmare, in large measure because some of its influential designers fully intended to endow it with structures that would not work."

To be sure, private sector organization is also the product of compromise. Egregious inefficiency in the private sector is checked, however, by competition in both product and capital markets. Note that with reference to the latter the voting rules in the private and public sectors are very different. The private rule is one share-one vote, and shares may be concentrated through purchase. The public rule is one-person-one vote, and the "purchase" of votes is much more cumbersome. Moreover, because, the gains that result from improved efficiency accrue (in the first instance, at least) to private sector owners in proportion to their ownership, private incentives to concentrate ownership and remove inefficiency are greater.

Even setting compromise considerations aside, however, there is another factor that induces politicians to design agencies inefficiently. Incumbent politicians who create and design bureaus are aware that the opposition can be expected to win a majority and take control in the future. Agencies therefore

will be designed with reference both to immediate benefits (which favors responsive mechanisms) and to possible future losses (which favors crafting iner-
tia into the system). A farsighted majority party, therefore, will design some
degree of (apparent) inefficiency into the agency at the outset, the effect of
which will be to frustrate successor administrations' efforts to reshape the purposes served by an agency.[5]

Embeddedness and Networks

Gary Hamilton and Nicole Biggart (1988) take exception to the transaction cost
economics interpretation of economic organization because it implicitly assumes that the institutional environment is everywhere the same as that of
Western democracies, and most especially that of the United States. Hamilton
and Biggart observed that large firms in East Asia differ from United States corporations in significant respects, and they explained that "organizational practices . . . are fashioned out of preexisting interactional patterns, which in many
cases date to preindustrial times. Hence, industrial enterprise is a complex
modern adaptation of preexisting patterns of domination to economic situations in which profit, efficiency, and control usually form the very conditions of
existence" (Hamilton and Biggart 1988, S54).

The evidence that East Asian corporations differ is compelling. The argument that transaction cost economics has no application to East Asian
economies goes too far, however.

The correct argument is that the institutional environment matters and that
transaction cost economics, in its preoccupation with governance, has neglected
that. Treating the institutional environment as a set of shift parameters—
changes in which induce shifts in the comparative costs of governance—is, to a
first approximation at least, the obvious response (Williamson 1991a). That is
the interpretation advanced above and shown in Figure 7.1.

The objection could be made, nevertheless, that this is fine as far as it goes,
but that comparative statics, a once-for-all exercise, does not go far enough. As
Mark Granovetter observes, "More sophisticated . . . analyses of cultural influences . . . make it clear that culture is not a once-for-all influence but an *ongoing
process*, continuously constructed and reconstructed during interaction. It not

[5] That is an interesting and important argument. Politics really is different. But it is not as
though there is no private sector counterpart. The more general argument is this: Weak property
rights regimes—both public and private—invite farsighted parties to provide added protections.
The issues are discussed further in conjunction with remediableness (see section 4, below). Note,
as a comparative institutional matter, that secure totalitarian regimes can, according to this logic,
be expected to design more efficient public agencies. That is neither here nor there if democratic
values are held to be paramount—in which event the apparent inefficiencies of agencies under a
democracy are simply a cost of this form of governance.

only shapes its members but is also shaped by them, in part for their own strategic reasons" (1985, 486).

I do not disagree, but would observe that "more sophisticated analyses" must be judged by their value added. What are the deeper insights? What are the added implications? Are the effects in question really beyond the reach of economizing reasoning?

With reference to this last question, consider the embeddedness argument that "concrete relations and structures" generate trust and discourage malfeasance of noneconomic or extraeconomic kinds:

> Better than a statement that someone is known to be reliable is information from a trusted informant that he has dealt with that individual and found him so. Even better is information from one's own past dealings with that person. This is better information for four reasons: (1) it is cheap; (2) one trusts one's own information best—it is richer, more detailed, and known to be accurate; (3) individuals with whom one has a continuing relation have an economic motivation to be trustworthy, so as not to discourage future transactions; and (4) departing from pure economic motives, continuing economic relations often become overlaid with social content that carries strong expectations of trust and abstention from opportunism. (Granovetter 1985, 490)

This last point aside, the entire argument is consistent with, and much of it has been anticipated by, transaction cost reasoning. Transaction cost economics and embeddedness reasoning are evidently complementary in many respects. A related argument is that transaction cost economics is preoccupied with dyadic relations, whereupon network relations are given short shrift. The former is correct,[6] but the suggestion that network analysis is beyond the reach of transaction cost economics is too strong. For one thing, many of the network effects described by Ray Miles and Charles Snow (1992) correspond very closely to the transaction cost economics treatment of the hybrid form of economic organization (Williamson 1983, 1991a). For another, as a discussion of Japanese economic organization reveals, transaction cost economics can be, and has been, extended to deal with a richer set of network effects.

Discrete Structural Analysis

One possible objection to the use of maximization/marginal analysis is that "parsimony recommends that we prefer the postulate that men are reasonable

---

[6] Interdependencies among dyadic contracting relations and the possible manipulation thereof have been examined, however (Williamson 1985, 318-319). Also see the discussion of appropriability in section 4, below.

to the postulate that they are supremely rational when either of the two assumptions will do our work of inference as well as the other" (Simon 1978, 8). But while one might agree with Simon that satisficing is more reasonable than maximizing, the analytical toolbox out of which satisficing works is incomplete and very cumbersome compared with maximizing apparatus. Thus, if one reaches the same outcome through the satisficing postulate as through maximizing, and if the latter is much easier to implement, then economists can be thought of as analytical satisficers: They use a short-cut form of analysis that is simple to implement. Maximization gets the job done, albeit at the expense of realism in assumptions.

A different criticism of marginal analysis is that it glosses over first order effects of a discrete structural kind. Oskar Lange's conjecture (1938, 109) that inefficient resource allocation posed a less serious danger to socialism than bureaucratization is illustrative. Bureaucratization posed a discrete structural hazard (a difference in kind), whereas Lange was convinced that socialism could implement the relevant marginalist rules (mainly marginal cost pricing) for efficient resource allocation. More generally, if alternative forms of governance are *syndromes of attributes that differ in discrete structural ways*, and if the first order economizing problem is to choose the right structure and the second order problem is to tune it up, then it is important to keep the priorities straight and to address the discrete structural issues at the outset.

Friedland and Alford's recent treatment of institutions is in this spirit. They contend that "each of the most important institutional orders of contemporary Western societies has a central logic—a set of material practices and symbolic constructions—which constitutes its organizing principles and which is available to organizations and individuals to elaborate" (1991, 248). Purposive differences are what mainly concern them:

> The institutional logic of capitalism is accumulation and the commodification of human activity. That of the state is rationalization and the regulation of human activity by legal and bureaucratic hierarchies. That of democracy is participation and the extension of popular control over human activity. That of the family is community and the motivation of human activity by unconditional loyalty to its members and their reproductive needs. That of religion, or science for that matter, is truth, whether mundane or transcendental, and the symbolic construction of reality within which all human activity takes place. (Friedland and Alford 1991, 248)

Transaction cost economics does not disagree, but maintains that discrete structural differences supported by distinctive logics exist within, as well as between, institutional orders. Within the institutional order of capitalism, for example, each generic mode of governance—market, hybrid, and hierarchy—possesses its own logic and distinctive cluster of attributes. Of special importance is the proposition that each generic mode of governance is supported by a distinctive form of contract law.

As developed elsewhere (Williamson 1991a), transaction cost economics holds that classical contract law applies to markets, neoclassical contract law applies to hybrids, and forbearance law is the contract law of hierarchy. Among these three concepts of contract, classical contract law is the most legalistic, neoclassical contract law is somewhat more elastic (MacNeil 1974, 1978), and forbearance law has the property that hierarchy is its own court of ultimate appeal. But for these contract law differences, markets and hierarchies would be indistinguishable in fiat respects.

Recall in this connection that Alchian and Demsetz introduced their analysis of the "classical capitalist firm" with the following argument that (1972, 777) "It is common to see the firm characterized by the power to settle issues by fiat. . . . This is delusion. The firm . . . has no power of fiat, no authority, no disciplinary action any different in the slightest degree from ordinary market contracting."

That is a provocative formulation and places the burden on those who hold that firm and market differ in fiat respects *to show* wherein those differences originate. The transaction cost economics response is that courts treat interfirm and intrafirm disputes differently, and serve as the forum of ultimate appeal for interfirm disputes while *refusing* to hear identical technical disputes that arise between divisions (regarding transfer prices, delays, quality, and the like). Because hierarchy is its own court of ultimate appeal (Williamson 1991a), firms can and do exercise fiat that markets cannot. Prior neglect of the discrete structural contract law differences that distinguish alternative modes of governance explains earlier claims that firms and markets are indistinguishable in fiat and control respects.

5. Transaction Cost Economics, the Strategy

The transaction cost economics program for studying economic organization has been described elsewhere (Williamson 1975, 1981, 1985, 1988a, 1991a; Klein, Crawford, and Alchian 1978; Alchian and Woodward 1987; Davis and Powell 1992). My purpose here is to sketch the general *strategy* employed by transaction cost economics, adding the suggestion that organization theorists could adopt (some already have adopted) parts of it.

The five-part strategy that I describe entails (1) a main case orientation (transaction cost economizing), (2) choice and explication of the unit of analysis, (3) a systems view of contracting, (4) rudimentary tradeoff apparatus, and (5) a remediableness test for assessing "failures."

The Main Case

Because economic organization is complex and our understanding of it is primitive, there is a need to sort the wheat from the chaff. I propose for this purpose that each rival theory of organization should declare the *main case* out of which it works and develop the *refutable implications* that accrue thereto.

Transaction cost economics holds that economizing on transaction costs largely dictates the choice of one form of capitalist organization over another, and applies this hypothesis to a wide range of phenomena. These include vertical integration, vertical market restrictions, labor organization, corporate governance, finance, regulation (and deregulation), conglomerate organization, technology transfer, and, more generally, any issue that can be posed directly or indirectly as a contracting problem. As it turns out, large numbers of problems which on first examination do not appear to be of a contracting kind turn out to have an underlying contracting structure. Examples are the oligopoly problem (Williamson 1975, chap. 12) and the organization of the company town (Williamson 1985, 35-38). Moreover, comparisons with other rival or complementary main case alternatives are invited.

Three of the older main case alternatives mainly explain economic organization by (1) technology, (2) monopolization, and (3) efficient risk bearing. More recent main case candidates are (4) contested exchange between labor and capital, (5) other types of power arguments (e.g., resource dependency), and (6) path dependency. My brief responses to the first three case alternatives are that (1) technological nonseparabilities and indivisibilities explain only small groups and, at most, large plants, but explain neither multiplant organization nor which technologically separable groups/activities should remain autonomous and which should be joined; (2) monopoly explanations require that monopoly preconditions be satisfied, but most markets are competitively organized; and (3) although differential risk aversion may apply to many employment relationships, it applies less to trade between firms where portfolio diversification is more easily accomplished and where smaller firms (for incentive intensity and economizing, but not riskbearing, reasons) are often observed to bear inordinate risk). I develop responses to the last three case alternatives developed more fully below, but my brief responses are these: (4) The failures to which contested exchange refers are often irremediable, (5) resource dependency is a truncated theory of contract, and (6) although path dependency is an important phenomenon, remediable inefficiency is rarely established.

To be sure, transaction cost economizing does not always operate smoothly or quickly. Thus we should "expect [transaction cost economizing] to be most clearly exhibited in industries where entry is [easy] and where the struggle for survival is [keen]" (Koopmans 1957, 141).[7] Transaction cost economics never-theless maintains that later, if not sooner, inefficiency in the commercial sector invites its own demise, all the more so as international competition has become more vigorous. Politically imposed impediments (tariffs, quotas, subsidies, rules), however, can and have delayed the reckoning;[8] and disadvantaged parties (railroad workers, longshoremen, managers) may also be able to delay changes unless compensated by buyouts.

The economizing to which I refer operates through weak-form selection, according to which the fitter, but not necessarily the fittest, in some absolute sense, are selected (Simon 1983, 69).[9] Also, the economizing in question works through a private net benefit calculus. That suits the needs of positive economics rather well, but public policy needs to be more circumspect. As discussed below, remediableness is the relevant test of whether public policy intervention is warranted.

These important qualifications notwithstanding, transaction cost economics maintains that economizing is mainly determinative of private sector economic organization and invites comparison with rival main case hypotheses.

Unit of Analysis

A variety of units of analysis have been proposed to study economic organization. Simon has proposed that the *decision premise* is the appropriate unit of analysis (1957a). "*Ownership*" is the unit of analysis for the economics of property rights. The *industry* is the unit of analysis in the structure-conduct-performance approach to industrial organization (Bain 1956; Scherer 1970). The *individual*

---

[7] The statement is a weakened variant on Tjalling Koopmans'. Where he referred to "profit maximization," "easiest," and "keenest," I have substituted transaction cost economizing, easy, and keen.

[8] Joel Mokyr observes that resistance to innovation "occurred in many periods and places but seems to have been neglected by most historians" (1990, 178). He nevertheless gives a number of examples in which established interests, often with the use of the political process, set out to defeat new technologies. In the end, however, the effect was not to defeat but to delay machines that pressed pinheads, an improved slide rest lathe, the ribbon loom, the flying shuttle, the use of Arabic numerals, and the use of the printing press (Mokyr 1990, 178-179). That, of course, is not dispositive. There may be many cases in which superior technologies were in fact defeated, of which the typewriter keyboard is purportedly an example. Assuming, however, that the appropriate criterion for judging superiority is that of remediability, I register grave doubts that significant technological or organizational efficiencies can be delayed indefinitely.

[9] The Schumpeterian process of "handing on"—which entails "a fall in the price of the product to the new level of costs" (Schumpeter 1947, 155) and purportedly works whenever rivals are alert to new opportunities and are not prevented by purposive restrictions from adopting them—is pertinent. The efficacy of handing on varies with the circumstances. When are rivals *more* alert? What are the underlying information assumptions? Are there other capital market and/or organizational concerns?

has been nominated as the unit of analysis by positive agency theory (Jensen 1983). Transaction cost economics follows John R. Commons (1924, 1934) and takes the *transaction* to be the basic unit of analysis.

Once a unit of analysis is selected, the critical dimensions according to which that unit of analysis differs need to be identified. Otherwise the unit will remain nonoperational. Also, a specific problem to which the unit of analysis applies needs to be described. Vague applications signal potential bankruptcy. Table 7.1 sets out the relevant comparisons.

Table 7.1 Comparison of units of analysis

Unit of analysis	Critical dimensions	Focal problem
decision premise	role; information; idiosyncratic[a]	human problem solving[b]
ownership	"eleven characteristics"[c]	externality
industry	concentration; barriers to entry	price-cost margins
individual	undeclared	incentive alignment
transaction	frequency; uncertainty; asset specificity	vertical integration

[a] Simon (1957).
[b] Newell and Simon (1972).
[c] Bromley (1989, 187–190).

Not surprisingly, different units of analysis have application to different phenomena. Vertical integration is the representative problem with which transaction cost economics deals. That is, when should a firm make rather than buy a good or service? More generally, transaction cost economics is concerned with the governance of contractual relations, which bears a resemblance to the "going concerns" to which Commons referred, but with some differences. Whereas Commons described different classes of transactions—authorized, authoritative, etc.—and described the working rules of different sectors, I examine the organization of (very nearly) identical transactions by alternative governance structures, all within the industrial sector.

The dimensions to which I refer—uncertainty, frequency, and, especially, asset specificity—affect the complexity of contracting. The predictive action turns on the following proposition: Transactions, which differ in their attributes, are aligned with governance structures, which differ in their costs and competence, in a discriminating, mainly transaction cost-economizing, way.

The arguments are familiar and are developed elsewhere. Suffice it to observe here that empirical research in organization theory long has suffered from the lack of an appropriate unit of analysis and the operationalization, or dimensionalization, thereof.

Farsighted Contracting

Economists' preoccupation with direct and intended effects, to the neglect of indirect and often delayed unintended effects, is widely interpreted as myopia. In fact, however, most economists are farsighted, and the problem is one of limited peripheral vision.

Tunnel-vision is both a strength and a weakness. Its strength is that a focused lens can be very powerful, provided that it focuses on core issues. Its limitation is that the main case is not the only case, and important regularities might be missed or, even worse, dismissed.

Transaction cost economics relates to these limitations by drawing on organization theory. Because organization has a life of its own, transaction cost economics (1) asks to be apprised of important intertemporal phenomena, whereupon (2) given the prospectve effects of these phenomena, it asks what are the ramifications for efficient governance. Unanticipated effects (from organization theory) are joined with farsighted contracting (from economics).

Lest claims of farsightedness be taken to hyperrationality extremes, transaction cost economics concedes that all complex contracts are unavoidably incomplete. That concession has both practical and theoretical significance. The practical lesson is this: All relevant contracting action cannot be concentrated in the ex ante incentive alignment, and some spills over into ex post governance. The theoretical lesson is that organization form loses significance under a comprehensive contracting setup, because any form of organization then can replicate any other (Hart 1990).

Transaction cost economics combines incompleteness with farsighted contracting by describing the contracting process as one of "incomplete contracting in its entirety." But for incompleteness, the above-described significance of ex post governance would vanish. But for farsightedness, transaction cost economics would be denied access to one of the most important "tricks" in the economist's bag, namely, the assumption that economic actors have the ability to look ahead, discern problems and prospects, and factor these back into the organizational/contractual design. "Plausible farsightedness," as against hyperrationality, will often suffice.

Consider, for example, the issue of threats. Threats are easy to make, but which threats are to be believed? If A says that it will do X if B does Y, but if after B does Y, A's best response is to do Z, then A's threat will not be perceived as credible to a farsighted B. Credible threats are those for which a farsighted B perceives that A's ex post incentives comport with its claims because, for example, A has made the requisite kind and amount of investment to support its threats (Dixit 1980). That is not a demanding prescription.

Or consider the matter of opportunism. As described above, Machiavelli worked out of a farsighted rather than a myopic logic. Rather than replying to opportunism in kind, the farsighted Prince is advised to look ahead and take potential hazards into account by redesigning the contractual relation, often by devising ex ante safeguards to deter ex post opportunism. Rather than reply to opportunism in kind, the wise prince is advised to give and receive "credible commitments." That too is feasible.

To be sure, it is more complicated to think about a contract as a triple (p, k, s)—where p refers to the price at which the trade takes place, k refers to the hazards associated with the exchange, s denotes the safeguards within which the exchange is embedded, and price, hazards, and safeguards are determined simultaneously—than as a scalar, where price alone is determinative. The simple schema shown in figure 7.2 nevertheless captures much of the relevant action.[10]

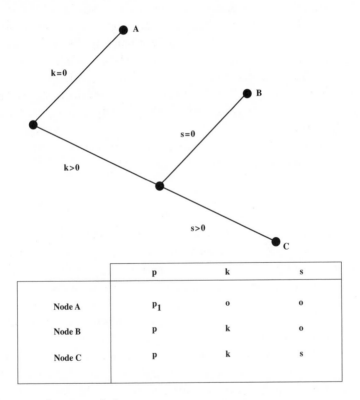

	p	k	s
Node A	p_1	0	0
Node B	p	k	0
Node C	p	k	s

Figure 7.2 Simple contractual schema

It will facilitate comparisons to assume that suppliers are competitively organized and risk neutral. The prices at which product will be supplied therefore

[10] The remainder of this subsection is based on Williamson 1993b.

reflect an expected break-even condition. The break-even price associated with Node A is P_1. There being no hazards, $k = O$. And since safeguards are unneeded, $s = o$.[11]

Node B is more interesting. The contractual hazard here is k. If the buyer is unable or unwilling to provide a safeguard, then $s = O$. The corresponding break-even price is p.

Node C poses the same contractual hazard, namely k. In this case, however, a safeguard in amount s is provided. The break-even price projected under these conditions is p. It is elementary that p < p.

Note that Jeffrey Bradach and Robert Eccles contend that "mutual dependence [i.e., $k > O$] between exchange partners . . . [promotes] trust, [which] contrasts sharply with the argument central to transaction cost economics that . . . dependence . . . fosters opportunistic behavior" (1989, 111). What transaction cost economics says, however, is that because opportunistic agents will not self-enforce open-ended promises to behave responsibly, efficient exchange will be realized only if dependencies are supported by credible commitments. Wherein is trust implicated if parties to an exchange are farsighted and reflect the relevant hazards in terms of the exchange? (A better price (p < p) will be offered if the hazards ($k > O$) are mitigated by cost-effective contractual safeguards ($s > O$).)

As it turns out, the farsighted approach to contracting has pervasive ramifications, some of which are developed below in figure 7.2.

Tradeoffs

The ideal organization adapts quickly and efficaciously to disturbance of all kinds. That turns out to be an impossible prescription. Thus, where more decentralized forms of organization (e.g., markets) support high-power incentives and display outstanding adaptive properties to disturbances of an autonomous kind, they are poorly suited to cooperative adaptation. Hierarchy, by contrast, has weaker incentives and is comparatively worse in autonomous adaptation but comparatively better in cooperative adaptation.

Simple transactions (for which $k = O$)—in intermediate product market labor, finance, regulation, and the like—are easy to organize. The required adaptations here are preponderantly autonomous and the market option is efficacious (so firms buy rather than make, use spot contract labor, use debt rather than equity, eschew regulation, etc.). Problems with markets arise when the need for cooperative adaptations builds up in bilateral dependencies. The

[11] Another way of putting it is that (transition problems aside), each party can go its own way without cost to the other. Competition provides a safeguard.

least-cost form of organization thus varies transaction attributes (especially asset specificity, which is largely responsible for bilateral dependency).

More generally, the point is that: informed choice among alternative forms of organization entails tradeoffs, since otherwise everything would be organized by a single, dominant form. Identifying and explicating tradeoffs is key to the study of comparative economic organization. Social scientists—economists and organization theorists alike—as well as legal specialists need to come to terms with that proposition.

Remediability

Related to this last point is the concept of remediability. If all feasible forms of organization are flawed (Coase 1964), then references to benign government, costless regulation, omniscient courts, and the like are operationally irrelevant. Hypothetical ideals can be useful as a reference standard, but such a standard is artificial. Is unbounded rationality the relevant standard? How about perfect stewardship, in which event opportunism vanishes? Or, turning to the physical realm, why not alchemy?

Lapses into ideal but operationally irrelevant reasoning will be avoided by (1) recognizing that it is impossible to do better than one's best, (2) insisting that all organization form competition finalists meet the test of feasibility, (3) symmetrically exposing the weaknesses as well as the strengths of all proposed feasible forms, and (4) describing and costing out the mechanisms of any proposed reorganization. Such precautions seem to be reasonable, transparent, even beyond dispute, yet all frequently are violated.

Note that in this connection "inefficiency" is unavoidably associated with contractual hazards. The basic market and hierarchy tradeoff incurred upon taking transactions out of markets and organizing them internally substitutes one form of inefficiency (bureaucracy) for another (maladaptation). Other examples are (1) decisions by firms to integrate into adjacent stages of production (or distribution) in a weak intellectual property rights regime, thereby mitigating the leakage of valued know-how (Teece 1986); (2) decisions by manufacturers' agents to incur expenses over and above those needed to develop the market, if these added expenses strengthen customer bonds in a cost-effective way, thereby detering manufacturers from entering and expropriating market development investments (Heide and John 1988); and (3) the use of costly bonding to deter franchisees from violating quality norms (Klein and Leffler 1981). The form of organization also influences parties' bargaining power and the distribution of rents. Thus, organizations sometimes forego efficiency to maximize bargaining power. For example, concern over losing bargaining power to suppliers often influenced the large U.S. automobile industry firms' decision to vertically integrate into parts (Helper and Levine 1992). When the Big Three automakers had a tight oligopoly, the product-market rents they had to protect were largest. Thus, it is unsurprising that the level of vertical integration was most extensive at that time. Similar arguments arise in considering how the presence of rents affects employees' desire to unionize and companies' opposition to unions.

To be sure, any sacrifice of organizational efficiency, for oligopolistic rent protection reasons or otherwise, poses troublesome public policy issues. A remediability test is nonetheless required to ascertain whether public policy should influence the oligopoly power in question. Will net social gains be realized if oligopoly power is upset?[12] These issues are discussed further below in relation to path dependency.

Added Regularities

It is evident from the foregoing that the comparative contractual approach out of which transaction cost economics works can be and needs to be informed by organization theory. Transaction cost economics, however, is more than a mere user. It pushes the logic of self-interest seeking to deeper levels, of which the concept of credible commitment is one example. More generally, it responds to prospective dysfunctional consequences by proposing improved ex ante designs and/or alternative forms of governance. Also, and what concerns me here, transaction cost has helped to discover added regularities that are pertinent to the study of organization. These include (1) the fundamental transformation, (2) the impossibility of selective intervention, (3) the economics of atmosphere, and (4) an interpretation of Japanese economic organization.

The Fundamental Transformation

The fundamental transformation is the principal transaction cost economics response to the proposition that "identity matters."[13] It helps to explain how firms take on distinctive identities and why identity matters.

Economists of all persuasions recognize that the terms upon which an initial bargain will be struck depend on whether noncollusive bids can be elicited from more than one qualified supplier. Monopolistic terms will obtain if there

---

[12] This has public policy ramifications. As between two oligopolies, one of which engages in rent-protective measures while the other does not, and assuming that they are identical in other respects, the dissolution of the rent-protective oligopoly will yield larger welfare gains.

[13] This subsection is based on Williamson 1985, 61–63.

is only a single highly qualified supplier, while competitive terms will result if there are many. Transaction cost economics fully accepts this description of ex ante bidding competition but insists that the study of contracting be extended to include ex post features.

Contrary to earlier practice, transaction cost economics holds that a condition of large numbers bidding at the outset does not necessarily imply that a large numbers bidding condition will obtain thereafter. Whether ex post competition is fully efficacious or not depends on whether the good or service in question is supported by durable investments in transaction-specific human or physical assets. Where no such specialized investments are incurred, the initial winning bidder realizes no advantage over nonwinners. Although it may continue to supply for a long period of time, this is only because, in effect, it is continuously meeting competitive bids from qualified rivals. Rivals cannot be presumed to operate on a parity, however, once substantial investments in transaction-specific assets are put in place. Winners in these circumstances enjoy advantages over non-winners, which is to say that parity at the renewal interval is upset. Accordingly, what was a large numbers bidding condition at the outset is effectively transformed into one of bilateral supply thereafter. Significant reliance investments in durable, transaction-specific assets introduce contractual asymmetry between the winning bidder on the one hand and non-winners on the other because economic values would be sacrificed if the ongoing supply relation were to be terminated. Faceless contracting is thereby supplanted by contracting in which the pairwise identity of the parties matters. Not only would the supplier be unable to realize equivalent value were the specialized assets to be redeployed to other uses, but a buyer would need to induce potential suppliers to make similar specialized investments were he to seek least-cost supply from an outsider. Such parties, therefore, have strong incentives to work things out rather than terminate. More generally, farsighted agents will attempt to craft Node C safeguards ex ante. The progression is from markets to hybrids and, if that does not suffice, to hierarchies. Given its bureaucratic disabilities, hierarchy is the organizational form of last resort.

The Impossibility of Selective Intervention

Large established firms purportedly have advantages over smaller potential entrants because: "the leader can at least use [inputs] exactly as the entrant would have . . ., and earn the same profit as the entrant. But typically, the leader can improve on this by coordinating production from his new and existing inputs. Hence [inputs] will be valued more by the dominant firm" (Lewis 1983, 1092)

That argument has the following implication: if large firms, through replication, can do as well everywhere as a collection of smaller firms, and can sometimes do better through selective intervention, then large firms ought to grow without limit. That is a variant of the Coasian puzzle, "Why is not all production carried on in one big firm?" (1937, 395).

The simple answer to that question is that replication and/or selective intervention are impossible. But that merely moves the argument back one stage. How are these impossibilities explained?

The underlying difficulty is that the integrity of rule governance is unavoidably compromised by allowing discretion (Williamson 1985, chap. 6). Accordingly, any effort to combine rule governance (as in markets) with discretionary governance (hierarchy) leads to tradeoffs. The proposal to "implement the rules with discretion" is simply too facile.

That comes as no surprise to those who approach the study of governance in discrete structural terms, whereupon each generic form of governance possesses distinctive strengths and weaknesses and movements between them entail tradeoffs. The answer to the puzzle of limits to firm size has nonetheless been elusive for fifty years or more (Williamson 1985, 132–135), and still occasions confusion.

Atmosphere

The unintended effects described in 3.1 above are more local than are the atmospheric effects.[14] Atmosphere refers to interactions between transactions that are technologically separable but joined attitudinally, with systems consequences.

Thus, suppose that a job can be split into a series of separable functions. Suppose further that differential metering at the margin is attempted with reference to each. What are the consequences?

If functional separability does not imply attitudinal separability, then piecemeal calculativeness can easily be dysfunctional. The risk is that pushing metering at the margin everywhere to the limit will have spillover effects from easy-to-meter onto hard-to-meter activities. If cooperative attitudes are impaired, then transactions that can be metered only with difficulty, but for which consummate cooperation is important, will be discharged in a more perfunctory manner. The neglect of such interaction effects is encouraged by piecemeal calculativeness, that is to say by an insensitivity to atmosphere.

A related issue is the matter of externalities. The question may be put as follows: ought all externalities to be metered which, taken separately, can be metered with net gains? Presumably this turns partly on whether secondary effects obtain when an externality is accorded legitimacy. All kinds of grievances may be "felt," and demands for compensation made accordingly, if what had hith-

---

[14] This subsection is based on Williamson 1993a.

erto been considered to be harmless byproducts of normal social intercourse are suddenly declared to be compensable injuries. The transformation of relationships that will ensue can easily lead to a lower level of felt satisfaction among the parties than prevailed previously—at least transitionally and possibly permanently.

Filing claims for petty injuries influences attitudes toward other transactions. My insistence on compensation for A leads you to file claims for B, C, and D, which induces me to seek compensation for E and F, etc. Although an efficiency gain might be realized were it possible to isolate transaction A, the overall impact can easily be negative. Realizing this to be the case, some individuals will be prepared to overlook such injuries. But not everyone is so constituted, and society will be rearranged to the advantage of those who demand more exacting correspondences between rewards and deeds if metering at the margin is everywhere attempted. Were the issue of compensation to be taken up as a constitutional matter, rather than on a case-by-case basis, a greater tolerance for spillover would commonly obtain (Schelling 1978).

Also pertinent is that individuals keep informal social accounts and find the exchange of reciprocal favors among parties for whom uncompensated spillovers exist to be satisfying (Gouldner 1954). Transforming these casual social accounts into exact and legal obligations may well be destructive of atmosphere and lead to a net loss of satisfaction between the parties. Put differently, pervasive pecuniary relations impair the quality of "contracting," even when metering transactions is costless.

The argument that emerges from the above is not that metering ought to be prohibited, but that the calculative approach to organization that is associated with economics can be taken to extremes. An awareness of attitudinal spillovers and nonpecuniary satisfactions serves to check such excesses of calculativeness.[15]

6. Unresolved Tensions

The healthy tension to which I referred at the outset has contributed to the better and deeper understanding of a variety of phenomena. The matters that concern me here—power, path dependence, the labor managed enterprise, trust,

[15] The buying of "rounds" in English pubs is an example. Would a costless meter lead to a superior result? Suppose that everyone privately disclosed a willingness to pay and that successive bids were solicited until a breakeven result was projected. Suppose that the results of the final solicitation either are kept secret or posted, depending on preferences, and that rounds are thereafter delivered to the table on request. Monthly bills are sent out in accordance with the breakeven condition. How is camaraderie effected?

and tosh—are those where differences are great between transaction cost economics and organization theory.

Power/Resource Dependence

That efficiency plays such a large role in the economic analysis of organization exists because parties to a contract are assumed to consent to it, and do so in a relatively farsighted way. Such voluntarism is widely disputed by sociologists, who "tend to regard systems of exchange as embedded within systems of power and domination (usually regarded as grounded in a class structure in the Marxian tradition) or systems of norms and values" (Baron and Hannan 1992, 14).

The concept of power is very diffuse. Some specialists, unable to define power, report that they know it when they see it (Pfeffer 1981, 3). This has led other students of power to conclude that it is a "disappointing concept. It tends to become a tautological label for the unexplained variance" (March 1988, 6).

Among the ways in which the term power is used are: the power of capital over labor (Bowles and Gintis 1993); strategic power exercised by established firms in relation to extant and prospective rivals (Shapiro 1989); special interest power over the political process (Moe 1990); and resource dependency. Although all are relevant to economic organization, the last is distinctive to organization theory.[16]

Two versions of resource dependency can be distinguished. The weak version is that parties who are subject to dependency will try to mitigate it. That version is unexceptionable and is akin to the safeguard argument advanced above, with two significant differences: (1) resource dependency nowhere recognizes that price, hazards, and safeguards are determined simultaneously; and (2) resource dependency nowhere remarks that asset specificity (which is the source of contractual hazard) is actively chosen because it is the source of productive benefits.

The strong version of resource dependency assumes myopia. The argument here is that myopic parties to contracts are victims of unanticipated and unwanted dependency. Because myopic parties do not perceive the hazards, safeguards will not be provided and the hazards will not be priced out.

Questions regarding evidence pertinent to the myopic versus farsighted view of contract include the following: (1) Are suppliers indifferent in choosing between two technologies with identical investments and identical (steady state) operating costs, although one technology is much less redeployable than the other? (2) Is the degree of nonredeployability evident ex ante or is it revealed only after an adverse state realization (which induces defection from the spirit of the agreement) has materialized? (3) Do added ex ante safeguards appear as

---

[16] Friedland and Alford (1991, 235) identify resource dependency as one of the two dominant theories of organization (the other being population ecology).

added specificity builds up? And (4) Does contract law doctrine and enforcement reflect one or the other of these concepts of contract? Transaction cost economics offers the following answers to these questions: (1) the more generic (redeployable) technology will always be used whenever the cetera are paria; (2) nonredeployability can be discerned ex ante and is recognized as such (Palay 1984, 1985; Masten 1984; Shelanski 1993); (3) added ex ante safeguards do appear as asset specificity builds up (Joskow 1985, 1988); and (4) because truly unusual events are unforeseeable and can have punitive consequences if contracts are enforced literally, various forms of "excuse" are recognized by the law, though excuse is granted sparingly.[17]

Path Dependency

Transaction cost economics not only subscribes to the proposition that history matters but relies on that proposition to explain the differential strengths and weaknesses of alternative forms of governance. The Fundamental Transformation, for example, is a specific manifestation of the proposition that history matters. (Transactions that are not subject to the Fundamental Transformation are much easier to manage contractually.) The bureaucracy problems that afflict internal organization (entrenchment; coalitions) are also the product of experience and illustrate the proposition that history matters. Were it not that systems drifted away from their initial conditions, efforts to replicate markets within hierarchies (or the reverse) and selectively intervene would be much easier—in which event differences between organization forms would diminish.

The benefits that accrue to experience also are testimony to the proposition that history matters. Tacit knowledge and its consequences (Polanyi 1962; Marschak 1968; Arrow 1974) attest to that. More generally, firm-specific human assets—of both spontaneous (e.g., coding economies) and intentional (e.g., learning) kinds—are the product of idiosyncratic experience. The entire institutional environment (laws, rules, conventions, norms, etc.) within which the institutions of governance are embedded is the product of history. And although the social conditioning that operates within governance structures (e.g.,

---

[17] Because contracts are incomplete and contain gaps, errors, omissions, and the like, and because the immediate parties may not be able to reconcile their differences when an unanticipated disturbance arises, parties to a contract will sometimes ask courts to be excused from performance. Because, moreover, literal enforcement can pose unacceptably severe contractual hazards, the effects of which are to discourage contracting (in favor of vertical integration) and/or to discourage potentially cost effective investments in specialized assets, some relief from strict enforcement recommends itself. How much relief is then the question. Were excuse to be granted routinely whenever adversity occurred, then incentives to think through contracts, choose technologies judiciously, share risks efficiently, and avert adversity would be impaired. Accordingly, transaction cost economics recommends that (1) provision be made for excuse but (2) excuse should be awarded sparingly, which evidently it is (Farnsworth 1968, 885; Buxbaum 1985).

corporate culture [Kreps 1990]) is reflexive and often intentional, this too has accidental and temporal features.

That history matters does not, however, imply that only history matters. Intentionality and economizing explain a lot of what is going on out there. Also, most of the path dependency literature emphasizes technology (e.g., the QWERTY typewriter keyboard) rather than the organizational consequences referred to above, Paul David's recent paper (1992) being an exception. I am not persuaded that technological, as against organizational, path dependency is as important as much of that literature suggests. Many of the "inefficiencies" to which the technological path dependency literature refers are of an irremediable kind.

(a) Remediable inefficiencies. As described above, transaction cost economics emphasizes remediable inefficiencies—that is, those conditions for which a *feasible* alternative can be described which, if introduced, would yield *net gains*. That is to be distinguished from hypothetical net gains, where the inefficiency in question is judged by comparing an actual alternative with a hypothetical ideal. To be sure, big disparities between the actual and hypothetical sometimes signal opportunities for net gains. But a preoccupation with hypotheticals comes at a cost (Coase 1964, 195; emphasis added): Contemplation of an optimal system may provide techniques of analysis that would otherwise have been missed and, in certain special cases, it may go far to providing a solution. But in general its influence has been pernicious. It has directed economists' attention away from the main question, which is how *alternative arrangements will actually work in practice.* Consider Brian Arthur's (1989) numerical example of path dependency in which the payoffs to individual firms upon adopting either of two technologies (A or B) depend on the number of prior adoptions of each. Technology A has a higher payoff than B if there are few prior adoptions, but the advantage switches to technology B if there have been many prior adoptions. The "problem" is that if each potential adopter consults only its own immediate net gain, then each will select A and there will be "lock-in" to an inferior technology. A tyranny of micromotives thereby obtains (Schelling 1978). As S. J. Liebowitz and Stephen Margolis observe of this argument, however, whether choice of technology A is inefficient or not depends on what assumptions are made about the state of knowledge (1992, 15). Also, even if individual parties could be assumed to know that technology B would become the more efficient choice after 30 or 50 adoptions, the added costs of collective action—to deter individuals from choosing technology A—would need to be taken into account. If it is unrealistic to assume that individuals possess the relevant knowledge to ensure that a switchover (from A to B) will occur upon 30 or 50 adoptions, or if, given that knowledge, that the costs of orchestrating col-

lective action are prohibitive, then the inefficiency in question is effectively irremediable through private ordering.

Sometimes, however, public ordering can do better. The issues here are whether (1) the public sector is better informed about network externalities, (2) the requisite collective action is easier to orchestrate through the public sector (possibly by fiat), and/or (3) the social net benefit calculus differs from the private in sufficient degree to warrant a different result. Absent *plausible* assumptions that would support a prospective net gain (in either private or social respects), the purported inefficiency is effectively irremediable.

That is regrettable, in that society would have done better if it had better knowledge or if a reorganization could have been accomplished more easily. Hypothetical regrets—the "nirvana economics" to which E. A. G. Robinson (1934) and Harold Demsetz (1969) referred—are neither here nor there. Real costs in relation to real choices is what comparative institutional economics is all about.

(b) Quantitative significance. Path dependency, remediable or not, poses a greater challenge if the effects in question are large and lasting rather than small and temporary. It is not easy to document the quantitative significance of path dependency. Arthur provides a series of examples and emphasizes especially the videocassette recorder (where VHS prevailed over the Beta technology (1990, 92)) and nuclear power (where light water reactors prevailed over high temperature, gas cooled reactors [1990, 99]). But while both are interesting examples of path dependency, it is not obvious that the "winning" technology is significantly inferior to the loser, or even, for that matter, whether the winner is inferior at all.

Much the most widely cited case study is that of the typewriter keyboard. The QWERTY keyboard story has been set out by Paul David (1985; 1986). It illustrates "why the study of economic history is a necessity in the making of good economists" (David 1986, 30).

QWERTY refers to the first six letters on the top row of the standard typewriter keyboard. Today's keyboard layout is the same as that devised when the typewriter was first invented in 1870. The early mechanical technology was beset by typebar clashes, and these problems were mitigated by the QWERTY keyboard design.

Subsequent developments in typewriter technology relieved problems with typebar clashes, but the QWERTY keyboard persisted in the face of large (reported) discrepancies in typing speed between it and later keyboard designs. The Dvorak Simplified Keyboard (DSK), which was patented in 1932, was so much faster than the standard keyboard that, according to U.S. Navy experiments, the "increased efficiency obtained with DSK would amortize the cost of retraining a group of typists within the first ten days of their subsequent full-time employment" (David 1986, 33). More recently, the Apple IIC computer included a built-in switch that instantly converted its keyboard from QWERTY to DSK: "If as Apple advertising copy says, DSK 'lets you type 20-40% faster,' why did this superior design meet essentially the same resistance?" (David 1986, 34).

There are several possibilities. These include nonrational behavior, conspiracy among typewriter firms, and path dependency (David 1986, 34-46). David makes a strong case for the last, but there is a fourth possibility, subsequently raised and examined by Liebowitz and Margolis (1990): neither the Navy study nor Apple advertising copy can support the astonishing claims made on their behalf. Upon going back to the archives and examining the data, Liebowitz and Margolis conclude that "the standard history of QWERTY versus Dvorak is flawed and incomplete. . . . [The] claims of superiority of the Dvorak keyboard are suspect. The most dramatic claims are traceable to Dvorak himself, and the best documented experiments, as well as recent ergonomic studies, suggest little or no advantage for the Dvorak keyboard" (1990, 21). If that assessment stands up, then path dependence has had only modest efficiency effects in the QWERTY keyboard case. Such effects could easily fall below the threshold of remediable inefficiency.

Recent studies of the evolution of particular industries by sociologists also display path dependency. Population ecologists have used the ecological model of density-dependent legitimation and competition to examine the evolutionary process, both in particular industries (e.g., the telephone industry [Barnett and Carroll 1993]) and in computer simulations. Glenn Carroll and Richard Harrison conclude from the latter that "chance can play a major role in organizational evolution" (1992, 26).

Although these simulations do suggest that path dependency has large and lasting effects, Carroll and Harrison do not address the matter of remediability. Until a feasible reorganization of the decision process for choosing technologies can be described, the effect of which is to yield expected net private or social gains, it seems premature to describe their experiments as a test of the "relative roles of chance and rationality" (Carroll and Harrison 1992, 12). Large but irremediable inefficiencies nevertheless do raise serious issues for modeling economic organization.[18]

(c) Perspectives. David contends, and I am persuaded, that "there are many more QWERTY worlds lying out there" (1986, 47). An unchanged keyboard

[18] I have argued that dominant firm industries in which chance plays a role do warrant public policy intervention (Williamson 1975, chap. 11), but whether net gains would really be realized by implementing that proposal (especially as international competition becomes more intensive) is problematic.

layout does not, however, strike me as the most important economic attribute of typewriter development from 1870 to the present. What about improvements in the mechanical technology? What about the electric typewriter? What about personal computers and laser printers? Why did these prevail in the face of path dependency? Were other "structurally superior" technologies (as defined by Carroll and Harrison) bypassed? If, with lags and hitches, the more efficient technologies have regularly supplanted less efficient technologies, shouldn't that be featured?

Possibly the response is that "everyone knows" that economizing is the main case: "It goes without saying that economizing is the main case to which path dependency, monopolizing, efficient risk bearing, etc. are qualifications."

The persistent neglect of economizing reasoning suggests otherwise. Thus the "inhospitality tradition" in antitrust—with which Coase (1972) and others (Stigler 1968; Williamson 1968, 1985) have taken exception—proceeded with sublime confidence that nonstandard and unfamiliar business practices had little or no efficiency rationale, but mainly had monopoly purpose and effect. Similarly, the vast inefficiencies that brought down the economies of the Soviet Union and Eastern Europe may now be obvious, but that could never have been gleaned from the postwar literature on comparative economic systems or from CIA intelligence estimates. The preoccupation in the area of business strategy with clever "plans, ploys, and positioning" to the neglect of economizing is likewise testimony to the widespread tendency to disregard efficiency (Williamson 1991b). And the view that the "effective organization is (1) *garrulous*, (2) *clumsy*, (3) *superstitious*, (4) *hypocritical*, (5) *monstrous*, (6) *octopoid*, (7) *wandering*, and (8) *grouchy*" (Weick 1977, 193–194; emphasis in original) is reconciled with economizing only with effort. More recent "social construction of industry" arguments reduce economizing to insignificance.[19] If economizing really does get at

***

[19] The "new sociology of organization" holds that "outcomes can vary dramatically even for the same economic problems and technologies, if the social structure, institutional history and collective action are different" (Granovetter 1988, 28). The "social construction of industry" argument is developed in a major book by Patrick McGuire, Mark Granovetter, and Michael Schwartz on the origins of the American electric power industry. That book has been described as follows:

Building on detailed historical research, . . . this book treats the origins of the electrical utility industry from a sociological perspective. The idea that industries, like other economic institutions, are 'socially constructed,' derives from Granovetter's work on 'embeddedness' (1985) and presents an alternative to the New Institutional Economics, which contends that economic institutions should be understood as the efficient solutions to economic problems. (McGuire, Granovetter, and Schwartz 1992, 1–2)

We believe that the way the utility industry developed from its inception in the 1880s was not the only technologically practical one, nor the most efficient. It arose because a set of powerful actors accessed certain techniques and applied them in a highly visible and profitable way. Those techniques resulted from the shared personal understandings, social connections, organizational conditions and historical opportunities available to these actors. This success, in turn, triggered the fundamentals, then that condition ought to be continuously featured. Some progress has been made (Zald 1986), but there is little reason to be complacent.

Worker-Managed Enterprises

> John Bonin and Louis Putterman define a worker-managed firm as a productive enterprise the ultimate decision-making rights over which are held by member-workers, on the basis of equality of those rights regardless of job, skill grade, or capital contribution. A full definition would state that no non-workers have a direct say in enterprise decisions, and that no workers are denied an equal say in those decisions. This definition does not imply that any particular set of decisions must be made by the full working group, nor does it imply a particular choice rule, such as majority voting. It says nothing about financing structures other than that financiers are not accorded direct decision-making powers in the enterprise by virtue of their non-labor contributions, and it does not say anything about how income is distributed among workers. On all of these matters, all that is implied is that ultimate decision-making rights are vested in the workers, and only in the workers. Thus, the basic definition centers on an allocation of governance rights, and is simultaneously economic and political. (1987, 2)

This definition does not preclude hierarchical structure, specialized decision making, a leadership elite, or marginal product payment schemes.[20] It merely stipulates that finance can have no decision rights in the labor-managed enterprise. The question is whether these financial restrictions come at a cost. Putterman evidently believes that they do not, since he elsewhere endorses Roger McCain's proposal that the labor-managed enterprise be financed in part by "risk participation bonds," where these purportedly differ from "ordinary equity" only in that "its owner can have no voting control over enterprise decisions, or over the election of enterprise management" (Putterman 1984, 189). Since "the labor-managed firm whose objective is to maximize profit-per-worker, having both ordinary and 'risk participation' bonds at its disposal, would 'attain the same allocation of resources as would a capitalist corporation, under comparable circumstances and informationally efficient markets'" (1984, 189), Putterman concludes that the labor managed firm is on a parity.

The argument illustrates the hazards of addressing issues of economic organization within a framework that ignores, hence effectively suppresses, the role

---

pressures for uniformity across regions, even when this excluded viable and possibly more efficient alternative technologies and organizational forms.

Our argument resembles that made by economists Paul David and Brian Arthur on the 'lock-in' of inefficient technologies (such as the QWERTY keyboard), but draws on the sociology of knowledge and of social structure.

[20] This subsection is based on Williamson (1996, 244–245).

of governance. Operating, as he does, out of a firm-as-production-function framework, McCain (1977) is only concerned with examining the marginal conditions that obtain under two different setups, under both of which the firm is described as a production function.

Governance issues never arise and hence are not amenable to analysis within this orthodox framework. If, however, a critical—indeed, I would say, the critical—attribute of equity is the ability to exercise contingent control by concentrating votes and taking over the board of directors, then McCain's demonstration that allocative efficiency is identical under standard equity and risk participation bonds is simply inapposite.

Indeed, if risk participation finance is available on more adverse terms than standard equity because holders are provided with less security against mismanagement and expropriation, then the constraints that Bonin and Putterman have built into the worker-managed firm come at a cost. To be sure, the worker-managed firm may be able to offset financial disabilities by offering compensating advantages. If those advantages are not uniform but vary among firms and industries, then the net gains of the worker-managed firm will vary accordingly.

I submit that firms that can be mainly financed with debt are the obvious candidates for worker-management. Thus, if there is little equity-like capital at stake, then there is little reason for equity to ask or expect that preemptive control over the board of directors will be awarded to equity as a contractual safeguard. The question then is, what types of firms best qualify for a preponderance of debt financing?

As discussed elsewhere, peer group forms of organization can and do operate well in small enterprises where the membership has been carefully screened and is committed to democratic ideals (Williamson 1975, chap. 3). Also, the partnership form of organization works well in professional organizations, such as law and accounting firms, where the need for firm-specific physical capital is small (Hansmann 1988). There being little need for equity capital to support investment in such firms, the control of these firms naturally accrues to those who supply specialized human assets (Williamson 1989, 24–26). These exceptions aside, "third forms" experience serious incentive disabilities.[21]

[21] The limits of third forms for organizing *large* enterprises with *variegated* membership are severe in both theory and fact. To be sure, some students of economic organization remain sanguine (Horvat 1991). The evidence from Eastern Europe has not, however, been supportive. Maciej Iwanek (1991, 12) remarks of the Polish experience that "except [among] advocates of workers' management, nobody believes that the . . . governance scheme of state-owned enterprises [by workers' management] creates strong incentives"; Manuel Hinds (1990, 28) concludes that "absenteeism, shirking, and lack of initiative are pervasive in the self-managed firm"; Janos Kornai (1990, 144) counsels that "it would be intellectually dishonest to hide the evidence concerning the weakness of third forms."

Trust

There is a growing tendency, among economists and sociologists alike, to describe trust in calculative terms: both rational choice sociologists (Coleman 1990) and game theorists (Dasgupta 1988) treat trust as a subclass of risk. I urge that calculative trust is an oxymoron, and concur with Granovetter that to craft credible commitments (through the use of bonds, hostages, information disclosure rules, specialized dispute settlement mechanisms, and the like) is to create functional substitutes for trust (Granovetter 1985, 487). Albeit vitally important to economic organization, such substitutes should not be confused with (real) trust.

Spontaneous processes in economics (Hayek 1945), sociology (Selznick 1949), and political science (Michels 1962) are subtle, important, and comparatively neglected. The ongoing social relations to which Granovetter ascribes real trust are also spontaneous. Spontaneous processes are often embedded in planned structures in which intentionality and discriminating alignment are featured.[22]

If, for example, the integrity of trade at a particular interface is perceived to be especially important, and if greater confidence can be realized by assigning managers to this interface who are perceived to be more highly principled, then the spontaneous development of trading-trust can be, and presumably will be, promoted by assigning principled managers to this rather than to a lesser trading interface. The evidence, moreover, is corroborative (Palay 1981, 105, 117, 124).

As I have argued elsewhere (Williamson 1993a), relations that are subject to continuous Bayesian updating of probabilities based on experience are thoroughly calculative. Because commercial relations are invariably calculative and because the concept of calculative trust is a contradiction in terms, I propose that the concept of calculated risk (rather than calculated trust) be used to describe commercial transactions.

Continuous experience rating need not obtain everywhere, however. Indeed, because some personal relations are unique and because continuous updating, even if only of a low-grade kind, can have corrosive effects,[23] certain personal relations are treated in a nearly-noncalculative way. That is accomplished by a discrete structural reclassification, according to which personal relations are dealt with on an all-or-none, rather than a continuous updating, basis. The upshot is that personal trust relations and commercial/calculative risk relations

---

[22] Note, moreover, that the trust that Granovetter ascribes to ongoing relations can go either way, frequent suggestions to the contrary notwithstanding. That is because experience can be either good (more confidence) or bad (less confidence), which, if contracts of both kinds are renewed, will show up in differential contracting (Crocker and Reynolds 1993).

[23] Not only can intendedly noncalculative relations be upset by Type I error, according to which a true relation is incorrectly classified as false, but calculativeness may be subject to (involuntary) positive feedback. Intendedly noncalculative relations that are continuously subject to being reclassified as calculative are, in effect, calculative.

differ in kind. Commercial relations are in no way denigrated as a result (Robbins 1933, 179–180).

Tosh

Lon Fuller distinguished between "essentials" and "tosh," where the former involves an examination of the "rational core" (Fuller 1978, 359–362) and tosh is preoccupied with "superfluous rituals, rules of procedure without clear purpose, [and] needless precautions preserved through habit" (Fuller 1978, 356). According to Fuller, to focus on the latter would "abandon any hope of fruitful analysis" (Fuller 1978, 360). I think that this last goes too far: a place should be made for tosh, but tosh should be kept in its place.[24] Consider in this connection the Friedland and Alford interpretation of Clifford Geertz's description of Balinese cockfights (Friedland and Alford 1991, 247–248; emphasis added): "Enormous sums of money can change hands at each match, sums that are *irrational* from an individualistic, utilitarian perspective. The higher the sums, the more *evenly matched* the cocks are arranged to be, and the more likely the odds on which the bet is made are even. The greater the sum of money at stake, the more the decision to bet is not individualistic and utilitarian, but collective—one bets with one's kin or village—and status-oriented."

That there are social pressures to support one's kin or village is a sociological argument. Absent these pressures, the concentration of bets on evenly matched cocks would be difficult to explain. It does not, however, follow that it is "irrational" to bet enormous sums on evenly matched cocks. Given the social context, it has become nonviable, as a betting matter, to fight unevenly matched cocks.

Thus, suppose that the objective odds for a proposed match are 4:1. Considerations of local pride may reduce the effective odds to 3:2. Such a match will not attract much betting because those from the village with the lesser cock who view it from an individualistic, acquisitive perspective will make only perfunctory bets. Accordingly, the only interesting matches are those where social pressures are relieved by the even odds.[25] The "symbolic construction of reality"

---

[24] The evolution of cooperation between opposed armies or gangs that are purportedly engaged in "deadly combat" is illustrated by Robert Axelrod's examination of "The Live-and-Let-Live System in Trench Warfare in World War I" (1984, 73–87). Interesting and important as the live-and-let-live rituals were, these nonviolent practices should not be mistaken for the main case. Rather, these rituals were the exception to the main case, which was that British and German troops were at war.

[25] Richard M. Coughlin contends that the "essence" of the socio-economic approach proposed by Amitai Etzioni is (1992, 3): "Human behavior must be understood in terms of the fusion of individually-based and communally-based forces, which Etzioni labels the *I and We*. The *I* represents the individual acting in pursuit of his or her own pleasure; the *We* stands for the obligations and restraints imposed by the collectivity." That is close to the interpretation that I advance here to interpret the Balinese cock fights.

to which Friedland and Alford refer thus has real consequences. It delimits the feasible set within which rationality operates; but rationality is fully operative thereafter.

One interpretation of this is that tosh has discrete structural effects and that rationality, operating through the marginal calculus, applies thereafter. Indeed, that seems to fit the Balinese cockfight example rather well. Whether the social construction of reality has such important consequences more generally is then the question. My sense is that it varies with the circumstances.

Tosh is arguably more important in noncommercial circumstances—state, family, religion—than in the commercial sector, although the Hamilton and Biggart (1988) examination of differences in corporate forms in Far East Asia might be offered as a contradiction. Hamilton and Biggart, however, go well beyond tosh (as described by Fuller) to implicate the institutional environment—to include property rights, contract law, politics, and the like.

Thus although both tosh (superfluous rituals) and the institutional environment refer to background conditions, the one should not be confused with the other. Tosh is a source of interesting variety and adds spice to life. Core features of the institutional environment, as defined by North (1986, 1991) and others (Sundaram and Black 1992), are arguably more important, however, to the study of comparative economic organization.[26]

Conclusions

The science of organization to which Barnard made reference (1938, 290) over 50 years ago has made major strides in the past 10 or 20 years. All of the social sciences have a stake in this, but none more than economics and organization theory.

If the schematic set out in figure 7.1 is an accurate way to characterize much of what is going on, then the economics of governance needs to be informed both from the level of the institutional environment (where sociology has a lot to contribute) and from the level of the individual (where psychology is implicated). The intertemporal process transformations that take place within the institutions of governance (with respect to which organization theory has a lot

[26] This is pertinent, among other things, to the study of the multinational enterprise. As Anant Sundaram and J. Stewart Black observe, MNEs "pursue different entry/involvement strategies in different markets and for different products at any given time" (1992, 740). Their argument, that transaction cost economics "is inadequate for explaining simultaneously different entry modes because . . . asset specificity . . . [is] largely the same the world over" (1992, 740), assumes that the governance level operates independently of the institutional environment under a transaction cost setup. That is mistaken.

to say) are also pertinent. The overall schema works out of the rational spirit approach that is associated with economics.[27]

This multilevel approach relieves some—perhaps much—of the strain to which Baron and Hannan refer: "We think it important to understand the different assumptions and forms of reasoning used in contemporary sociology versus economics. These disciplinary differences represent major barriers to intellectual trade between economics and sociology" (1992, 13). If, however, deep knowledge at several levels is needed and is beyond the competence of any one discipline, and if a systems conception can be devised in which intellectual trade among levels can be accomplished, then some of the worst misunderstandings of the past can be put behind us.

I summarize here what I see to be some of the principal respects in which the healthy tension to which I referred at the outset has supported and prospectively will support more, intellectual trade.

Organization Theory Supports for Transaction Cost Economics

(a) Behavioral assumptions. Organization theory's insistence on workably realistic, as opposed to analytically convenient, behavioral assumptions is a healthy antidote. Transaction cost economics responds by describing economic actors in terms of bounded rationality and opportunism.

(b) Adaptation. The cooperative adaptation emphasized by Barnard is joined with the autonomous adaptation of Hayek, with the result that transaction cost economics makes an appropriate place for *both* market and hierarchy.

(c) Unanticipated consequences. The subtle and unintended consequences of control and organization need to be uncovered, whereupon provision can be made for these in the ex ante organizational design.

(d) Politics. Because property rights in the public arena are shaped by democratic politics, provision needs to be made for these in the ex ante organizational design of public sector bureaus.

(e) Embeddedness. The first-order response to the proposition that embeddedness matters is to regard the institutional environment as a locus of shift parameters, changes in which change the comparative costs of governance.

[27] I borrow the term "rational spirit" from Kenneth Arrow (1974, 16). The rational spirit approach holds that there is a *logic* to organization and that this logic is mainly discerned by the relentless application of economic reasoning (subject, however, to cognitive constraints). The rational spirit approach is akin to but somewhat weaker (in that it eschews stronger forms of utility maximization) than the "rational choice" approach associated with James Coleman (1990).

(f) Discrete structural analysis. Each generic form of organization is described as a syndrome of attributes and possesses its own logic. These discreteness features need to be discovered and explicated—both within and between sectors.

Transaction Cost Economics Supports for Organization Theory

(a) Unit of analysis. Any theory of organization that fails to name the unit of analysis out of which it works, and thereafter fails to identify the critical dimensions with respect to which that unit of analysis varies, is nonoperational at best and could be bankrupt.

(b) The main case. All rival theories of organization are asked to nominate the main case, develop the refutable implications that accrue thereto, and examine the data. Economizing on transaction costs is the transaction cost economics candidate.

(c) Farsighted contracting. Looking ahead, recognizing hazards, and folding these back into the design of governance is often feasible and explains a very considerable amount of organizational variety.

(d) Tradeoffs. Because each mode of governance is a syndrome of attributes, the move from one mode to another involves tradeoffs. The key tradeoffs need to be stated and explicated.

(e) Remediability. Relevant choices among *feasible* forms of organization are what the analysis of comparative economic organization is all about.

Toward a Psychology of Contingent Work

Batia Wiesenfeld and Joel Brockner

U.S. companies are increasingly employing temporary, part-time, and con-tractual workers rather than full-time, permanent employees. Between 1982 and 1992, the number of temporary workers grew from 400,000 to 1,456,000 (Ansberry 1993). Recent statistics indicate that 24 percent of the 1.6 million new jobs created between February 1992 and February 1993 were part-time. Another 24 percent represent growth in self-employment, many of whom are temporary or contract workers (Castro 1993). Reports of the prevalence of temporary, part-time, and contract workers vary, but former Labor Secretary Robert B. Reich estimated that about 30 percent of the American workforce is composed of these types of workers, prompting him to state that "the entire [employment] system has fragmented" (Kilborn 1993). Temporary work is now pervasive at all levels. About 24 percent of temporary workers are "elite"—profes-sionals or other highly skilled workers—up from 14 percent in 1981 (Diesenhouse 1993).

This growing phenomenon has been labeled the rise of the contingent workforce (Freedman 1986), and appears to be driven by employers rather than workers. Organizations prefer to use contingent workers to meet their staffing requirements because of the increased efficiency and flexibility they afford (Appelbaum 1991). Contingent workers are less costly; for example, companies typically do not provide fringe benefits to them. In addition, the re-liance on contingent workers may help companies avoid both the wrenching psychological pain of laying off long-term employees and the potentially severe financial cost of layoffs (e.g., severance pay and outplacement counseling).

Given that the employment of contingent workers is becoming an ever-increasing human resource strategy, it is important to understand its implications for behavior in organizations. What is the experience of being a contingent worker? Moreover, what effect does the experience of contingency have on employees' work attitudes and behaviors? To address these questions it is necessary to take a psychological approach to the study of contingent work. This chapter provides such an approach. We begin by offering a psychological definition of contingent work (perceived contingency). We also explore the effects of perceived contingency on employees' attitudes and behaviors. A key axiom in the present analysis is that perceived contingency influences individuals' values, thereby affecting their definitions of rationality.

A Psychological Definition of Contingent Work

Economists were among the first to recognize the growing presence of contingent workers in the labor force. They have directed substantial research toward quantifying the contingent workforce and exploring its composition and public policy implications. One result of this research is the inclusion of questions about contingent work in a recent revision of the monthly survey of the Bureau of Labor Statistics, signaling official recognition of this growing phenomenon.

To facilitate the measurement of the contingent workforce, economic research has defined contingent work according to the terms of the explicit employment agreement. Perhaps the central component of the economic definition of contingent work is the absence of a long-term employment contract (Polivka and Nardone 1989).

How is the absence of a long-term employment contract likely to influence contingent workers' perceptions of their relationship with an organization? Several factors are likely to shape the experience of contingent workers. For example, because they generally do not receive benefits such as job training or promotion (Quiroz, Auerbach, and Coles 1991), health insurance (Rasell, Connerton, Himmelstein, and McGarrah 1991), unemployment insurance (Wayne, Hartmann, and Spriggs 1991) or retirement benefits (Hushbeck, Gottlick, and Shaffer 1991), evidence indicates that they perceive themselves to be relatively "peripheral" to the organization and their coworkers (Barker in press). In combination, these characteristics of contingent work assignments are likely to lead workers to focus on the short-term nature of their relationship with the organization. The belief that one's relationship with the organization is short-term—i.e., that a valued future with the organization cannot be expected—forms the psychological definition of contingent work.

In response to feeling the lack of a valued future relationship with the organization, contingent workers are likely to have different priorities than their less contingent counterparts. That is, individuals' perceptions of their contingency should affect their definition of rationality. The values of those who see themselves as more contingent should differ from those who are themselves as less contingent along two dimensions: (1) the time frame in which rewards are meaningful to them, and (2) the nature of the rewards that are meaningful to them.

Time Frame

Most people work in exchange for rewards that they receive in the present *and* anticipate receiving in the future. Thus, the total reward value of a job is some combination of the present benefits that it dispenses and the future ones that it promises. For example, "fast-track" jobs are highly coveted because the incumbents believe that they will be handsomely rewarded over time, even if their current level of reward is not very high. Alternatively, "dead-end" jobs are unappealing because of their negative implications for future rewards.

Contingent workers view their long-term relationship with the organization as unpredictable (at best) or nonexistent (at worst). As a result, it is not rational for them to attach much significance to the "promise" of the rewards to be obtained in the future. Relative to their less contingent counterparts, they should be much more concerned with the rewards received in the present. For example, current levels of economic remuneration might be expected to have a greater impact on the job satisfaction of employees who see themselves as more contingent. This is not to say that the less contingent workers do not care about the level of their present rewards. Compared to those who see themselves as more contingent, however, their belief that they have a longer-term relationship with the organization leads them to assign greater importance to anticipated future outcomes. Put differently, those who see themselves as relatively noncontingent can afford to be somewhat less concerned with the favorability of their current rewards because they believe that future benefits are forthcoming.

Nature of the Rewards

Most people work in exchange for a variety of economic and social/psychological rewards. Thus, people want jobs that enable them to satisfy their material needs. In addition, according to social identity theory (Tajfel and Turner 1979), people want jobs that fulfill their needs for self-esteem, self-identity, and belongingness, to name a few. Ongoing organizational affiliations and social relationships, such as those provided in the workplace, are a major source of these social/psychological rewards. Thus, human behavior in organizations is motivated in part by social or psychological rationality, as opposed to economic rationality.

The social/psychological benefits of group membership are less meaningful, however, when the relationship entails little sense of a future. Indeed, the experience of being a group member depends not only on one's present status as a part of the group, but also on the anticipation of remaining with the group. It is perfectly rational for employees with little sense of future membership in an organization to remain at the periphery; after all, who wants to invest energy in a relationship that is not likely to persist over time? When individuals feel unattached to collectives in the workplace, their chances of deriving the social/psychological rewards of group membership are diminished.

This reasoning suggests that workers are likely to attach differential importance to the potential rewards to be received from their organizational affiliations as a function of their perceived contingency. Among those who see themselves as contingent, the perception that they lack a valued future relationship will lead them to assign less importance to social/psychological rewards, relative to their less contingent counterparts. Said differently, those who see themselves as relatively contingent should be more concerned with the economic benefits of the job. In fact, the relative scarcity of social/psychological rewards for those who define themselves as contingent may force them to justify their job incumbency as being primarily economically motivated.

In summary, we hypothesize that perceived contingency influences workers' preference structures and hence their conceptions of rationality. Those who define themselves as less contingent are more apt to feel that they have a valued future with their organizations. As a result, they will attach importance to present rewards *and* the anticipation of future rewards; moreover, they are motivated by economic *and* social/psychological rewards. Those who see themselves as contingent do not anticipate a valued future with the organization. Consequently, they will be much more concerned with the favorability of their *present* outcomes, and in particular, those that are *economic* in nature.

Traditionally, contingency has been defined as an attribute of jobs. Individuals in occupations in which there is little sense of a valued future relationship comprise the contingent workforce (e.g., temporary or contractual employees). The psychological approach to the study of contingent work views contingency status as residing within individuals: the more employees believe that they cannot depend upon having a valued future relationship with their organizations, the more they are psychologically contingent. The psychological approach to contingent work explicitly recognizes that employees need not be temporary or contractual in order to have the psychological experience of contingency. Permanent workers also may perceive that they lack a valued future with the organization. Indeed, an important consequence of the large-scale layoffs in the 1980s and 1990s is an upsurge in job insecurity among the employees who retained their jobs (the "survivors").

An additional implication of the present analysis is that contingency should be treated as a continuous variable. Traditional definitions of contingency, which viewed it as an attribute of jobs, have conceptualized contingency as a categorical variable.

The remainder of the chapter is divided into two sections. First, we shall provide initial empirical evidence that psychological contingency is associated with different conceptions of rationality. Second, we will consider the implications of theory and research on the psychological approach to contingent work.

Psychological Contingency and Conceptions of Rationality

Employees who define themselves as relatively contingent are less apt to believe that they have a valued future with the organization. Thus, those who see themselves as contingent should attach greater importance to the current economic outcomes which they receive from their employers, relative to those who view themselves as less contingent. One way to evaluate the perceived importance of an outcome is to assess the effect of the outcome on individuals' work attitudes and/or behaviors. The greater the significance of the outcome, the more of an effect the outcome should have on employees' reactions. If perceived contingency leads employees to put a premium on their current economic outcomes, then the level of said outcomes should have a greater impact on the behaviors and/or attitudes of those who see themselves as more contingent.

Numerous studies have been conducted that directly or indirectly bear on this hypothesis. In all of the studies employees' attitudes (e.g., organizational commitment) or behaviors (e.g., work performance) were assessed as a function of: (a) the level of current economic outcomes they were receiving, and (b) perceived contingency. Current economic outcomes included levels of pay, benefits, or other concrete forms of compensation. Perceived contingency was operationalized in a variety of ways across studies: (a) the extent to which people saw themselves as having a future with their employers, (b) the perceived threat of future job loss, and (c) procedural unfairness.

Perception of the Future

Individuals who believe that the future with their current employers holds little for them should experience greater contingency. In a recent study (Wiesenfeld, Brockner, and Petzall 1994), we asked individuals who had survived layoffs within their respective organizations to indicate their degree of endorsement of the following statement: "I don't have much of a future with this organization." Presumably, those who agreed with the statement to a greater extent view themselves as more contingent. The level of current outcomes was assessed by having participants respond to the following question: "Overall, just how bad was this layoff for you?" The dependent variable was their current affective state.

The results of a multiple regression analysis yielded an interaction between their perception of their future with their employers and the outcomes associated with the layoffs ($p < .01$). To illustrate the nature of the interaction we performed a median split on the two independent variables; the mean level of their affective state was computed for each of the four groups that emerged from this 2×2 classification scheme. As can be seen in table 8.1, those who felt that they did not have much of a future with their current employers exhibited a relatively strong relationship between the perceived level of outcomes and their affective states; that is, the more they felt that the outcomes of the layoffs were bad for them, the more negative was their current affective state. Table 8.1 reveals that the relationship between outcomes and affective state was not nearly as pronounced among those who felt that they had a relatively promising future with their employers.

Table 8.1. Negative affect as a function of belief in a valued future and level of current outcomes

		Level of current outcomes	
		Low	High
	High	1.50	1.34
Belief in valued future			
	Low	2.02	1.49

Note: Scores could range from 1 to 4. Higher scores reflect more negative affect.

Perceived Threat of Future Job Loss

When employees believe that the threat of future job loss is high, it is rational for them to become more concerned with the favorability of the *current* outcomes they receive. After all, the threat of future job loss renders unpredictable (at best) the outcomes that they can expect to receive from the organization over time. The threat of future job loss should induce the perception of contingency and thereby heighten the importance that employees attach to the current outcomes which they receive from the organization.

This hypothesis has been evaluated among two different samples of layoff survivors. Participants in one study (Wiesenfeld, Brockner, and Martin 1994) were longtime employees in a manufacturing facility that was undergoing repeated layoffs. Layoffs had occurred within the past six months and employees had been told that more could be expected in the future. All survivors indicated the likelihood that they would be laid off in the future; it was expected that those who believed that they were more likely candidates for job loss would experience greater psychological contingency. The level of economic outcomes was determined by having participants rate the generosity of the organization in providing concrete assistance to the layoff victims, such as severance pay, continuation of health benefits, and assistance in finding another job through services such as outplacement counseling. Although these outcomes were provided to the laid-off workers and not to the participants themselves, those who viewed themselves as likely candidates for job loss should view such economic information as quite self-relevant. The dependent variable was organizational commitment.

Regression analysis revealed a marginally significant interaction (p < .10). To interpret the nature of the interaction we conducted median splits on the two independent variable dimensions and computed the mean level of organizational commitment for the four groups emanating from the 2 × 2 classification scheme. The results are shown in table 8.2: as predicted, the organizational commitment level of those who viewed themselves as more likely to lose their jobs was more strongly related to the perceived level of concrete caretaking provided to the most recent group of layoff victims.

Table 8.2. Organizational commitment as a function of perceived threat of future job loss and concrete caretaking

		Concrete caretaking	
		Low	High
	Low	4.67	5.83
Threat of future job loss			
	High	4.13	6.06

Note: Scores could range from 1 to 7. Higher scores reflect greater levels of organizational commitment.

In a second study, layoff survivors reported their work performance as a function of the threat of future layoffs and outcome favorability (Brockner, Grover, Reed, and DeWitt 1992). Outcome favorability was assessed by having participants indicate how much the concrete support offered to the most recent layoff victims—i.e., severance pay, continuation of health benefits, and assistance in finding another job—would provide for *their own* needs, were they to lose their jobs in a future round of layoffs. Regression analysis yielded an interaction effect (p < .05). Among those who perceived the threat of future layoffs to be high (i.e., those who should have been more apt to feel contingent) there was a positive relationship between outcome favorability and work performance. No such relationship existed, however, for the survivors who believed that the threat of additional layoffs was relatively low.

Procedural Unfairness

According to our psychological perspective on contingent work, perceived contingency is determined by the factors that affect individuals' beliefs of whether they have a valued future with their employers. Obviously, if employees believe that they cannot depend upon keeping their jobs, they are likely to experience contingency. The experience of contingency is not limited, however, to those who believe their jobs are not permanent. Incumbents of full-time, permanent positions also may be subjected to factors that cause them to feel that they do (or may) not have a valued future with the organization; the greater the presence of such factors, the greater their experience of contingency.

One such factor is procedural justice: the fairness of the procedures used by the organization to make or implement a resource allocation decision. Whereas distributive justice (e.g., Adams 1965) is concerned with the fairness of the content of the decision (i.e., the *what* of the decision), procedural justice refers to the legitimacy of the methods used to make the decision (i.e., the *how* of the decision). In their initial theorizing, Thibaut and Walker (1975) suggested that workers' perceptions of procedural justice influence both their reactions to the outcomes they receive and their evaluations of those responsible for the resource allocation decision. Thibaut and Walker's work focused on the structural aspects of procedural justice. They suggested that the degree to which the individual is permitted to affect either the deliberations leading to the decision (process control), or the actual rendering of the decision (decision control) will determine perceptions of procedural fairness.

Leventhal, Karuza, and Fry (1980) further specified the structural components of procedural justice. They suggested that the following six factors influence perceptions of procedural justice: (1) consistency (the use of consistent procedures), (2) bias suppression (the absence of self-interest), (3) accuracy (the use of accurate information), (4) correctability (the presence of opportunities to correct the decision), (5) representativeness (all concerned parties adequately represented), and (6) ethicality (adherence to moral and ethical standards).

Most recently, research has focused on the social or interpersonal component of procedural justice (Bies and Moag 1986; Folger and Bies 1989; Tyler and Bies 1990). This research has isolated another component of procedural fairness called interactional justice, which is primarily concerned with: (1) how clearly and adequately the reasons underlying the resource allocation decisions were explained, and (2) whether those responsible for implementing the decision treated those affected by the decision with dignity and respect.

Procedural justice should affect employees' perceptions of contingency because it contains diagnostic information about the organization. The structural and interactional components of procedural justice provide information about the "rules of the game," the standards or norms of the organization's treatment of its members. When the organization is perceived as procedurally fair, workers are more likely to believe that they can trust the organization to dispense the economic benefits it promises in the future, and they also are more likely to feel reassured that the organization stands for values that are important to them (Lind and Tyler 1988). When managerial actions are seen as procedurally unfair, however, workers are likely to believe that they cannot depend upon the organization to provide them with economic or psychological benefits in the future.

In short, procedures provide information about the relatively enduring aspects of life within the organization. Fairness is a commonly understood standard. When procedural fairness is absent, the standard that workers rely upon is reduced or eliminated. Unfairness is unreliable; it may be expressed in a variety of ways. Without fairness as a standard, workers lose the ability to predict organizational actions over time. Thus, procedural unfairness creates uncertainty about the longer term benefits, both economic and psychological, that employees can expect to receive from the organization.

Workers' response to procedural unfairness may be to withdraw from the organization. Without leaving their jobs and sources of livelihood, workers may put psychological distance between themselves and the organization by objectifying the relationship. Short-term, tangible economic rewards may come to replace long-term economic and psychological attachment as the basis for workers' involvement in the organization, making the relationship more psychologically contingent.

This reasoning suggests that the lack of procedural fairness accompanying significant organizational events causes workers to become psychologically contingent. That is, they will attach greater importance to outcomes that are short-term and tangible, relative to when procedural fairness is present. One implication of this reasoning is that procedural unfairness should moderate the relationship between current tangible outcomes and worker attitudes/behaviors. Specifically, the work attitudes/behaviors of individuals who view the organization to be procedurally unfair should be more influenced by their perception of current tangible outcomes relative to those of workers who believe that the organization behaves in a procedurally fair manner.

Table 8.3 summarizes nine studies that examined the moderating effect of procedural fairness on the relationship between current tangible outcomes and

Table 8.3. Summary of studies showing the interaction between procedural unfairness and the current tangible outcomes

Study	Critical event	Sample	Dependent variables	Independent variables: Current tangible outcomes	Procedural unfairness
Brockner, Konovsky, Cooper-Schneider, Folger, Martin, and Bies (1994)	Layoff	150 bank employees who survived a layoff	Organizational commitment	Severity of the layoff (by department)	Clarity of layoff explanation, Interactional justice
Brockner, DeWitt, Grover, and Reed (1990)	Layoff	597 employees of a retail store chain who survived a layoff	Organizational commitment	Adequacy of caretaking such as severance pay, job placement assistance, etc.	Clarity of layoff explanation, Interactional justice
Brockner, Wiesenfeld, and Martin (1995)	Layoff	271 employees of a large telecommunications organization who survived a layoff	Organizational commitment	Severity of the layoff for respondent	Interactional justice
Cropanzano and Konovsky (1995)	Institution of drug testing policy	195 laboratory employees	Perceived fairness of drug testing procedure	Perception of how those who test positively are treated	Six procedural practices, including advance notice, voice, and explanation clarity
Greenberg (1993)	Institution of smoking ban	732 credit and data processing employees	Acceptance of smoking ban	Amount respondents smoke prior to the ban	Thoroughness and social sensitivity of announcement of the ban

Daly and Geyer (1993)	Relocation	171 employees—7 organizations	Organizational commitment	Perceived cause of relocation: decline vs. growth	Fairness of decision process
Schaubroeck, May, and Brown (1994)	Pay freeze	173 manufacturing employees	Turnover intention, Organizational commitment, Job satisfaction	Perceived economic hardship caused by pay freeze	Interactional justice
McFarlin and Sweeney (1992)	Pay and performance review	675 bank employees	Organizational commitment; Subsequent performance (evaluated by supervisor)	Perception of fairness of rewards received	Fairness of communication of feedback
Trevino (1993)	Punishment event	97 employees of 19 orgaizations	Subsequent performance (evaluated by supervisor); Organizational citizenship behaviors	Perceived harshness of punishment event	Procedural practices, including explanation clarity, privacy, arbitrariness

employees' attitudes/behaviors. In each study, an organization-wide or individually-targeted event had occurred. In three studies the organization-wide event was a layoff in which the reactions of survivors were examined (Brockner et al. 1990, 1994, 1995). Other organization-wide events that have been studied include the institution of a new drug-testing policy (Cropanzano and Konovsky 1995), a smoking ban (Greenberg 1993), a pay freeze (Schaubroeck, May, and Brown 1994), and relocations (Daly and Geyer 1993). Studies also have looked at individually targeted events such as pay and promotion reviews (McFarlin and Sweeney 1992) and punishment incidents (Trevino 1993). The dependent variables are operationalized in different ways across studies, but seem to share the same conceptual foundation: workers' willingness to act or think in ways that promote the organization's goals. Some specific operationalizations of this construct are the willingness of punished workers to expend effort on behalf of the organization (Trevino 1993), acceptance of the limitations imposed by the new drug-testing and smoking policies (Greenberg 1993, Cropanzano and Konovsky 1995), and organizational commitment (Schaubroeck et al. 1994).

The independent variables in all studies were: (1) outcome favorability and (2) procedural fairness. Outcome favorability refers to the concrete consequences of the decision. For example, operationalizations of outcome favorability include the amount of cigarettes smoked prior to the smoking ban, with the heaviest smokers likely to experience the most negative outcomes in response to a smoking ban (Greenberg 1993); the severity of the punishment (Trevino 1993); the adequacy of a pay raise (McFarlin and Sweeney 1992); and the adequacy of severance pay and other tangible benefits in the case of layoffs (Brockner et al. 1990). Procedural fairness was operationalized in a variety of ways including the provision of advanced notice, the clarity of managers' explanations for the organizational actions, the degree to which workers were treated with dignity and respect, and workers' participation or voice in the process.

In all nine studies, the interaction between procedural unfairness and outcome favorability took the same form. When procedures were unfair—i.e., when employees should have perceived themselves as more contingent—their reactions were more strongly related to current tangible outcomes than when procedures were fair (see figure 8.1). For example, Schaubroeck et al. (1994) examined the relationship between the degree of economic hardship imposed by an organization-wide pay freeze and employees' organizational commitment. As might be expected, these two factors were inversely related. The inverse relationship between felt economic hardship and organizational commitment was moderated, however, by the procedural fairness with which the pay freeze was introduced; the relationship was much more pronounced when procedural fairness was relatively low.

In summary, several operationalizations of perceived contingency—employees' beliefs about the value of their future with their organization, the perceived

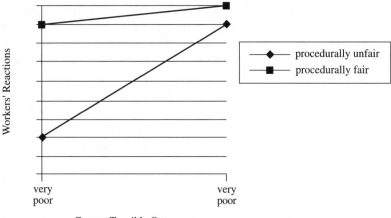

Figure 8.1

threat of job loss, and procedural unfairness—led employees to be more affected by the economic outcomes associated with a current resource allocation decision. Such findings suggest that perceived contingency leads people to assign greater importance to the current economic outcomes of a decision. (For more on the interactive relationship between procedural unfairness and outcome favorability, see Brockner and Wiesenfeld (1996)).

One implication of the theory and research on the psychology of contingency is that those who see themselves as relatively contingent should be less interested in information about how they are likely to be treated by the organization over the longer term. As mentioned previously, procedural fairness is one factor that organization members are apt to consider when trying to determine their expected future outcomes. Thus, not only will those who see themselves as relatively contingent be *more* affected by current economic outcomes, as reported above, but also their work behaviors and attitudes may be *less* influenced by procedural fairness.

To test the latter hypothesis we recently surveyed a group of layoff survivors. The studies described above (in tables 8.1 through 8.3) suggested that psychological contingency was associated with the tendency to assign significance to current economic outcomes. Thus, we employed the following item as a proxy for perceived contingency: "My attachment to this plant is primarily due to the pay and benefits I receive." Procedural fairness was assessed by an item asking, "To what extent was concern shown for the rights of those laid off?" The dependent variable was a self-report measure of work performance.

Multiple regression analysis revealed that contingency status interacted with procedural fairness to influence work performance ($p < .05$). To illustrate the nature of the interaction we performed median splits on the two independent variables. The mean level of work performance for the four groups emerging from the median split-based classification scheme is shown in table 8.4. As can be seen, procedural fairness was less strongly related to the work performance of those who viewed themselves as more contingent. These findings complement the previously reported findings in that they suggest what perceived contingency is *not* associated with: the tendency for workers to attach significance to information having implications for how they are likely to be treated over time. Said differently, the results in table 8.4 elaborate upon the notion that perceived contingency affects people's definition of rationality.

Table 8.4. Work motivation as a function of contingency status and procedural justice

		Procedural justice	
		Low	High
	Non-contingent	5.64	6.45
Contingency status			
	Contingent	6.31	6.49

Note: Scores could range from 1 to 7. Higher scores reflect greater levels of work motivation.

Implications

The present chapter argues that the traditional definition of contingent work based on the terms of the explicit employment contract needs to be supplemented with a psychological definition based on workers' perceptions of the value of their future with the organization. In the remaining pages we discuss the relationship between perceived contingency and related constructs in organizational behavior, as well as some implications of the psychological approach to the study of contingent work.

Distinguishing Perceived Contingency from Related Constructs

Greenhalgh and Rosenblatt (1984) suggested that job insecurity was comprised of two factors: (a) the perceived threat of job loss (perceived threat), and (b) the perceived ability to control or counteract the negative effects of job loss (perceived control). According to this two-factor model, job insecurity is most pronounced when perceived threat is high and perceived control is low. More recently, Ashford, Lee, and Bobko (1989) suggested that the perceived threat could be to the valued features of the job, and not simply to the job itself. Psychological contingency is similar to Ashford et al.'s expanded definition of the perceived threat component of job insecurity. Unlike Ashford et al., however, the present paper discusses an important consequence of perceiving a threat to valued features of one's job: the significance attached to present economic outcomes will far outweigh the significance attached to anticipated future outcomes. Empirical evidence described above, moreover, illustrates the implications of the values associated with perceived contingency for employees' thoughts, feelings, and actions.

According to Mowday, Porter, and Steers (1982), organizational commitment consists of three components: (1) belief in the organization's goals and values, (2) willingness to work hard to further those goals, and (3) tendency to remain with the organization. More recently, commitment theorists have suggested that it is important to identify the underlying motivational bases for individuals' levels of commitment. For example, consider the third component of commitment: the tendency to remain with the organization. People may have very different reasons for doing so. Some may want to remain with the organization because they have internalized the organization's values. Others may need to remain with the organization because the costs associated with leaving would be severe. Thus, the motivational bases for individuals' commitment may be intrinsic or extrinsic; the former is called affective commitment, whereas the latter has been dubbed continuance commitment (Meyer and Allen 1984).

How does perceived contingency relate to organizational commitment? We see at least two connections. First, perceived contingency may be one of the factors that affect individuals' organizational commitment. Commitment is reciprocal. The more people feel that their employers are not committed to providing them with a valued future—i.e., the more contingent they feel they are—the less committed they should be to the organization. Second, the psychology of perceived contingency seems similar to that of continuance commitment: in both instances individuals are motivated by extrinsic reasons. Still, there is a subtle difference in the extrinsic motivation exhibited by individuals who are high in continuance commitment versus perceived contingency. Continuance commitment is based upon individuals' not wanting to give up tangible rewards that have been built over time. For example, employees may remain with their employers because they would be forfeiting an attractive pension if they were to leave. Perceived contingency, in contrast, gives rise to a concern with current economic outcomes. For example, the work motivation of those who see themselves as more contingent should be more influenced by the level of their current pay. The extrinsic motivation underlying continuance commitment is based on history: individuals' past actions have enabled them to receive certain benefits (and/or have established their "credit" for the receipt of future benefits). Thus, they remain committed in order not to lose those benefits. The extrinsic motivation accompanying perceived contingency requires no history. Rather, those who view themselves as contingent assign value to the concrete outcomes that they receive in the here and now; the greater the outcomes, the more favorable their response.

Implications for the Study of Contingent Work

The psychological approach has at least two implications for the study of the growing phenomenon of contingent work in organizations. First, workers' perceptions of their relationship with the organization may supplement the explicit contract as a basis for classifying contingent workers. One implication of the psychological perspective is that managerial actions, such as procedural fairness, are important determinants of perceptions of contingency. However, many other factors may influence workers' perceptions of contingency. For example, social cues from coworkers are likely to affect contingency perceptions. In addition, when coworkers perceive that promotions are unlikely, employees will be more likely to believe that their future with the organization is not promising, and they therefore will perceive themselves as more contingent. Certain organizational realities also may make workers feel contingent. For example, full-time workers in an organization on the verge of bankruptcy may believe that they do not have a valued future with their employer, and thereby may become contingent. Further research is needed to specify additional antecedents of perceived contingency.

Second, the present research indicates that certain workers whose full-time, permanent employment contracts suggest that they are noncontingent may perceive themselves as contingent workers (e.g., survivors of a procedurally unfair layoff). Perceptions of contingency, moreover, will have important implications for the way that workers think, feel, and behave. For example, the determinants of job and organizational commitment may differ for workers as a function of their perceived contingency. As the previously reported studies suggest, those who see themselves as more contingent are more influenced by current outcomes, and less affected by procedural justice.

We have suggested that contingent workers have a more short-term, economic attachment to the organization relative to their less contingent counterparts. We might ask: If not to their organizations, then to what are contingent workers attached? Recent evidence suggests that the prototype of the "organization man" of the 1950's and 1960's is being replaced by workers who are committed to their own long-term career goals rather than to any single organization (Hall and Richter 1990). These individuals may have well-defined career goals, and a strategy for achieving them, which guides their involvement in organizations. They may evaluate the benefits of participation in any single organization according to whether the specific short-term opportunity in that organization is congruent with their long-term career goals. Alternatively, attachment to the organization may be replaced with increased commitment to other aspects of workers' lives, such as their families. The fact that the "organization man" is very likely to be a working mother lends some support to the latter speculation.

Implications for the Study of Psychological Contracts

At first blush, the psychological approach to the study of contingent work may appear to be only a reiteration of the psychological contracts literature because perceived contingency is synonymous with the notion of a transactional psychological contract (Rousseau and Parks 1993). However, the present research reinforces and extends the study of psychological contracts by exploring the characteristics, as well as consequences and antecedents, of transactional psychological contracts.

For example, the current definition of a transactional psychological contract is multifaceted, including both the perception that the relationship is short-term and the focus on economic rewards. The present analysis suggests a possible causal relationship between these two factors. Contingent workers' focus on economic rewards may be a *consequence* of the belief that their relationship with the organization is short-term. It may be a form of withdrawal, a strategy for objectifying the relationship.

Furthermore, by considering the antecedents of perceived contingency, the present research sheds some light on the process of change in the nature of the psychological contract. We speculate that the function of critical events is to make the psychological contract salient, providing a fertile context for change. These events may be organization-wide (e.g., layoffs) or not. That is, individually relevant events such as performance evaluations and punishments also may lead workers to evaluate or re-evaluate the work relationship. Organization-wide and individually relevant events differ in several important ways. During and following organization-wide (but not individually relevant) events, there may be a *collective* effort for workers to determine how their relationship with the organization has changed, because the event affects an entire class of people simultaneously. As a result, there is great potential for social influence processes to shape workers' perceptions, resulting in some form of consensus about the organization's relationship to its workers. Further research is needed to explore possible differences in workers' reactions to organization-wide or individually relevant events that have implications for their contingency status.

The importance of individually relevant events in psychological contract change suggests that workers' perceptions of the psychological contract must be managed on a more constant basis. That is, far-reaching organizational changes (which are relatively infrequent) are not required for the psychological contract to become salient; even regularly scheduled decisions (e.g., pay raise and performance reviews) can set the stage for change.

By itself, an important event provides the context for change in the psychological contract. However, it is the fairness or unfairness of the event that seems to determine the nature of workers' subsequent perceptions of the employment relationship. Specifically, procedurally unfair managerial actions apparently make the work relationship more short-term, economic, and (therefore) transactional.

Implications for Justice Research

Research on procedural justice (Bies 1987) suggests that following a perception of injustice workers will be morally outraged and angry. As a result they will take active steps to even the score, such as sabotage or revenge. Due to their precarious position in the organization, contingent workers may be unable to express anger in these ways. If so, then their anger may surface through some other response. For example, they may withdraw, or try to distance themselves from the perpetrator of unfair treatment. In several of the studies reviewed in table 8.3, distancing may have been accomplished by workers' attempts to change the basis of their relationship with the organization from one of identification to one based on an objective, monetizable exchange. It is important to understand the relationship between these responses to injustice and, if applicable, under what conditions, or for whom, the withdrawal response is more likely to be exhibited than the revenge response.

The psychological approach also suggests an interesting asymmetry in the relationship between procedural justice and perceived contingency. While it seems that procedural unfairness creates perceptions of contingency, procedural fairness may not be as effective in reducing feelings of contingency. Procedural unfairness is a violation of workers' trust in the organization. Reparation of violated trust may require an extended period of time, since trust is based upon repeated acts of fairness which prove that the organization is reliable. Trust seems to be much easier to destroy than to (re)build.

Organizational Implications

Extracting performance and commitment from workers who perceive themselves to be contingent will be quite challenging from a managerial perspective. If an organization does not recognize its employees' perceptions of their contingency status, it may institute inefficient compensation programs. Specifically, if we assume that workers provide effort according to their expectation of compensation, and that those who see themselves as relatively contingent do not value deferred compensation, their work will be affected only by the portion of their compensation which is paid currently. Their effort may not vary as a function of the value of future-oriented inducements such as expectations of promotion which are often meaningful components of full-time, permanent jobs. "Tournament" models of worker effort (Lazear and Rosen 1981), which suggest that employees exert effort in any period to increase their probability of moving to a higher level of the organization in the following period, may be ill-suited to explain the behavior of workers who see themselves as contingent.

Employees' unwillingness to defer rewards poses a particularly acute problem for organizations that have instituted layoffs, pay cuts, or other cutbacks. Such organizations are generally strapped for resources in the short term, but require a great deal of effort and commitment from employees to achieve a long-term performance reversal. They need employees who are willing to forego current rewards for the expectation of future benefits, and they cannot afford to spend scarce resources on long-term programs or benefits that will not be appreciated by those who define themselves as contingent. Ironically, firms that lay off workers require a committed surviving workforce willing to provide effort in the present for benefits to be paid when performance improves. Layoffs also may lead workers to infer that they are contingent, particularly when the layoffs are procedurally unfair, and that they should not be willing to make such a trade-off. Thus, an organization's survival after a downsizing may ultimately depend upon its ability to manage its employees' perceptions of the work relationship.

Sutton and Callahan (1987) provide corroborating evidence of how such a scenario may unfold in firms that file for bankruptcy protection. In order to reorganize and re-emerge successfully after filing for bankruptcy, firms require that stakeholders be willing to defer rewards. Sutton and Callahan document, however, that just the opposite occurs. Stakeholders of the four firms they examined behaved as if the firm would not exist in the future. For example, suppliers shipped defective goods and yet required immediate cash payment because they were unconcerned with the long-term consequences of such actions on their relationship with the bankrupt firm. In effect, expectations for the future were treated as completely valueless, and stakeholders maintained a transactional or contingent relationship with the organization, guaranteeing the firm's rapid destruction.

Contingency and the Definition of Rationality

Both the theoretical perspective and the empirical results in the present paper have important implications for various conceptions of rationality. Economic rationality refers to behavior performed in exchange for a tangible or concrete reward. Human endeavors may or may not be motivated by economic considerations. Whenever people are intrinsically motivated—in that the very doing of the activity serves as its own source of reward—they are psychologically (but not necessarily economically) rational. A subset of psychological rationality is social rationality. For example, studies of altruism have shown that people may act to benefit others "simply" because it feels good to do so. In short, people can undertake certain activities as a means to concrete ends (in which case they may be economically rational), or as ends in their own right (in which case they are psychologically or socially rational).

The two prevailing theories of procedural justice provide an example of the distinction between various conceptions of rationality. Originally, Thibaut and Walker (1975) asserted that people prefer procedural fairness for instrumental or economically rational reasons. When procedures are fair, that is, when people are allowed to participate in the decision process, people believe that they have a reasonable chance of receiving desired material benefits from the present decision and/or related ones in the future. More recently, Lind and Tyler (1988) suggested that people prefer procedural justice because it provides the psychological and social benefits of group membership (e.g., enhanced self-esteem, a clearer sense of self-identity, and a feeling of belonging). Lind and Tyler's group value model views procedural fairness not as a means to some economic end, but as a desired end in its own right. Put differently, group value theory posits that people prefer procedural fairness for reasons that are socially or psychologically rational, not simply for reasons that are economically rational.

Often a counterproductive relationship exists between the proponents of economic versus social/psychological rationality. The division between the two camps is manifested in such questions as, "Which perspective can explain more of the variance in individuals' beliefs and behaviors?" A more fruitful discussion between the economic rationalists and social/psychological rationalists may be promoted when there is an *interactive* relationship between outcome negativity and procedural fairness. That is, both outcome negativity and procedural fairness influence individuals' beliefs and behaviors, supporting economically rational and socially/psychologically rational arguments, respectively. Importantly, however, the spate of studies reviewed in table 8.3 reveal that the impact of outcome factors depends upon the level of the procedural variables, and vice versa. Outcomes matter much more when procedures are unfair than when they are fair. Moreover, procedures matter much more when economic outcomes are relatively unfavorable. In short, the economic rationalists need to acknowledge that the impact of their "most favored variables"—i.e., outcomes—is moderated by a socially/psychologically rational factor: procedural justice. Moreover, the social/psychological rationalists must take into account the fact that the effect of procedural justice is affected by an economically rational factor: outcomes. Thus, the interactive relationship between economic outcomes and procedural fairness has implications, not only for the psychology of contingent workers but also for the long-standing (and often not entirely healthy) tension between economically rational and socially/psychologically rational theories of behavior.

P·A·R·T III

STRETCHING THE BOUNDARIES

Bonded Rationality: The Rationality of Everyday Decision Making in a Social Context

Jennifer J. Halpern

$\mathbf{M}$arkets can operate successfully in a social vacuum, but people must understand each other in order to interact effectively. Mutual understanding requires that we be able to anticipate how the other person reasons. Clearly, we do this most of the time. It is therefore surprising that so much research into human decision processes has been interpreted as demonstrating nonrational behavior. If people saw others as not rational, they would find it difficult to understand each other in ordinary social interactions, including during transactions.

This chapter examines the place of rationality in human decision processes. Rationality, as the term is used in rational choice theory, requires that people's choices between pairs of alternatives follow specific rules, or axioms. This chapter argues that people generally are rational in this logical sense. The fact that many people do not make decisions that correspond to contemporary economic norms is likely due to the fact that people understand and describe alternatives in a personal way. Such "personalizations" of the alternatives may be based on misunderstandings, misperceptions, personal experience or cultural demands. These personal perceptions may not always conform with objective reality. However, these perceptions do depend upon cognitions and on social and cultural perspectives shared among transaction partners. Just as human

This paper could not have been written in a social vacuum. Thanks are due to J. David Velleman (University of Michigan, Department of Philosophy) and Paul F. Velleman (Cornell University, Department of Social Statistics) for invaluable conceptual discussions and assistance with the paper's logical exposition. James March, Ishak Saporta, Zur Shapira, and the UC Berkeley Student Group also provided very helpful comments.

cognitive limitations on our ability to process and use information lead us to have "bounded rationality" (Simon 1957b), so also do our shared limitations on information processing and on our understanding of the evaluation of alternatives lead us to a "bonded rationality" based on our need to interact effectively with other people.

Bonded rationality is a model of human interaction that argues first, that we share ways of evaluating alternatives that may not be objectively optimal, and second, that we reason rationally about these shared evaluations. It follows that we should study evidence of suboptimal transaction behavior as elucidating shared ways of valuing alternatives rather than as evidence of nonrational reasoning (cf. Halpern 1997).

Most modern theories of choice assume subjective assessments of probabilities and values, so this idea is well-grounded. We need to go further, however: We need to study how people and partners with whom they interact understand each other, not just how one person makes decisions in the presence of another person. The key to understanding bondedly rational decisions lies in discovering and describing the shared influences that drive personal subjective assessments.

This chapter accepts the axioms of rational choice theory as a working basis for defining "rational" decision making. Then, rather than considering how people *ought* to reason, it proposes bonded rationality as a descriptive model of how people *do* reason when they make decisions.

The first section of this chapter considers the limitations of contemporary decision research. A discussion of a missing piece—personalization as a function of an individual's alternatives and choices—follows. A review of the axioms of rational choice theory and the additional assumptions that accompany applications of rational choice theory comprises the next section. A subsequent section offers a discussion of how personalization of alternatives occurs, and how we prevent ourselves from reasoning in a non-rational way. The next section describes how bonded rationality facilitates social interaction: how we reason in a bondedly rational fashion, and how we can understand others' personalizations. A formal model of bonded rationality follows. Lastly, some research directions are outlined.

Decision Research

Until recently, social scientists generally have studied decision making as some researchers argue it ought to be, based only on financial and other utilitarian considerations, and isolated from its social context. This normative approach has been valuable for understanding idealized outcomes. However, rather than considering the decision maker realistically within a social context, this normative approach instead regards the decision maker as a reasoning black box.

The drawback of limiting the study of decision making to a normative approach is well understood. For example, Tversky (1975) observed that decision theory based on rational choice theory (RCT) is concerned only with the consistency of preferences, not with justifying them. He warned that we "cannot accept the evaluation of consequences as given and examine only the consistency of preferences" (Tversky 1975, 172).

The normative approach also has encouraged social scientists to apply simplifying assumptions or value judgments to their interpretations of behavior that may not be shared by the participants in an experiment (Perrow 1984). Subjects isolated from a social context by the experiment's design are deprived of important cues and background information that they ordinarily would employ in making decisions. Virtually all research that demonstrates deviations from rationality assumes a particular valuation of the alternatives, and then demonstrates that the subjects' choices turn out to be inconsistent in terms of this valuation. As a result, experiment subjects may be labeled nonrational even when their reasoning follows rationally from their personalization of the alternatives available.

Rational decision making can be defined formally by the axioms of rational choice theory (RCT; e.g., Luce and Raiffa 1957). Many studies of human decision making have imposed additional constraints on RCT in order to focus on specific aspects of decisions. For example, researchers concentrating on economic behavior assume that subjects should wish to maximize expected monetary return, and that they should ignore non-monetary concerns such as regret and sunk costs. Another example of an added constraint is the assumption that subjects want to win made in experiments based on game theory. And almost all experimenters assume that subjects do not value the time they spend as experiment subjects.

A decision maker may perceive alternatives incorrectly. The perceptions may result from the decision maker's application of heuristics to simplify complex alternatives. They may include (or exclude) aspects that others would not include (or exclude). Studies of perception and judgment errors, and of how people tend to understand alternatives, have shown a remarkable consistency among people's decision-making behavior, even when the shared judgments and understandings lead to suboptimal returns. These studies thus are productive avenues of research. The findings, however, are not evidence of nonrational behavior.

Rather than considering how people *ought* to reason to achieve a particular goal, this chapter proposes a model of how people *do* reason when they make decisions. This chapter does not present a prescription for rational decision making, nor does it try to evaluate alternative decision-making strategies. The focus here is to examine the decision makers' understanding of alternatives as she or he makes decisions in real world contexts. Such an examination allows us to understand human decision-making behavior as the normative rational application of consistent rules to alternatives, as these alternatives are understood by the decision maker. As a theory of behavior, the model developed here is inevitably imperfect. It describes general trends of behavior, but not necessarily the behavior of particular individuals. Nevertheless, it synthesizes many disparate results under a consistent point of view, provides valuable insights, and suggests new lines of research.

Alternatives and Choices

The argument of this article requires a clear distinction between an individual's personal understanding, description, and individuation of alternatives, and her choices between pairs of alternatives as she understands them. An individual's act of understanding an alternative can be called *personalization.*

Personalization considers how the individual describes the alternatives both objectively (e.g., as measured in pecuniary terms on the open market), and subjectively. The subjective meaning of the alternative may include psychological or social rewards or punishments. It may be affected by errors the decision maker has made in understanding aspects of the alternative. The context in which a decision maker considers an alternative also contributes substantially to the subjective meaning of the alternative.

For an individual's choices between alternatives (however she or he understands these) to be "rational," they must be governed by the axioms of RCT, namely transitivity, monotonicity, independence, and continuity. The next section outlines these briefly.

Rational Choice Theory

Rational choice theory (RCT) is an axiomatic system that provides a benchmark for understanding decision behavior. The axioms of RCT define rationality.[1] These axioms consider choices between pairs of alternatives. According to RCT, all that is needed for a person's preferences to be rational is that these preferences satisfy the four axioms described below. Simple examples are provided in Appendix A.

1. Transitivity: If you prefer payoff A to payoff B, and prefer payoff B to payoff C, then you prefer A to C.

---

[1] Other definitions may be possible, but should have little effect on the argument.

2. Monotonicity: In choosing between two lotteries involving only a most and least preferred alternative, you will select the lottery that renders the alternative you prefer most probable. Lottery $[pA_1, (1 - p)A_r]$ is preferred or indifferent to $[p'A1, (1 - p'A_r)]$, if and only if $p > p'$.

3. Independence: If you prefer payoff A to payoff B, and this preference is not affected by whether some outcome p is true, then, for any other payoff, C, you should prefer the chancy option {A if p, C if not p} to the option {B if p, C if not p}. That is, you should prefer a chance of getting A to an equal chance of getting B provided the "consolation prize" is the same in either case.

4. Continuity: If you prefer payoff A to payoff B and payoff B to payoff C, there is some contingency p such that you are indifferent between B and the gamble "A if p and C if not p." That is, the path from "payoff A for certain," through "a 50/50 gamble between payoff A and payoff C" to "payoff C for certain" is continuous in the sense that it must include a gamble that is equivalent in preference to any other payoff, B, that we would value between A and C.

Preferences that satisfy these axioms are said to be *coherent*, and the holder of such preferences is said to be rational. It can be shown that coherent preferences always can be represented by a utility function whose value is maximized by holding those preferences.[2] The injunction to "maximize your utility function" is redundant. If your preferences are coherent, then they maximize your utility function; if they are not coherent, then you have no utility function to maximize.

There are a number of other arguments to which researchers refer when they discuss rationality. As the following section indicates, these are additional assumptions that specific groups have added to simplify their research programs, but which have little to do with the axiom-based rationality discussed here.

Additional Assumptions

Some economists who are interested in transactions, and particularly in teaching people how to maximize monetary return, assume that every alternative has a monetary value that can be used for comparing alternatives. They then add to the basic axioms of RCT the prescription that one should maximize monetary return. Some game theorists augment RCT similarly, using success or points in the game as a standard scale for comparing alternatives. These prescriptions introduce what Edgeworth (1881) called the "first principle of economics"— self-interest. Many researchers now regard these additional prescriptions as a natural part of rational decision making.

[2] See Luce and Raiffa (1957, pp. 31 *ff*) for a discussion of the relationship of RCT axioms to utility functions.

As Simon (1990) observed, however, while such assumptions are convenient, "providing the basis for a very rich and elegant body of theory, . . . they are assumptions that may not fit empirically the situations of economic choice in which we are interested" (15). However, the assumption that outcomes are characterized fully by relevant monetary values cannot be derived from normative considerations, and is not part of RCT (Tversky 1975). According to RCT it is the *coherence* of the preferences that defines rationality, not whether the resulting utility function conforms with external standards. The consistent masochist is rational if his or her preferences are coherent.

One reason for assuming that outcomes are fungible is to provide a consistent standard of comparison across decision makers. This chapter argues that decision makers operate on their personal understanding and individuation of outcomes, and that *this* is key to interpreting their decision making.

Personalizing Alternatives

It is always possible to recast formally a collection of alternatives so that any particular set of preferences is coherent. For example, if an individual prefers alternative A to alternative B, and B to C, but prefers A to C (thereby appearing to violate the transitivity axiom), we need only assert that "alternative A when compared with alternative B" is different from "alternative A when compared with alternative C" to restore coherence. Of course, recasting alternatives in this mechanical way makes RCT vacuous, because the same alternative never appears in two different comparisons.

However, people inevitably recast alternatives as part of their attempts to individuate them. If a person can describe how he or she individuates the alternatives in such a way that the person's preferences are then coherent, we would judge this person rational, though we might disagree with how he or she saw the alternatives, or even find his or her description of the alternatives bizarre. Rationality depends only on the coherence of preferences after the alternatives have been individuated.

Of course, if each individual's subjective personalizations of alternatives were entirely idiosyncratic, we would be in the same bind as with the mechanical recasting of alternatives. Rational choice theory then would be essentially vacuous as a basis for understanding human decision making. However, there is concrete evidence (which is discussed in later sections) that while people do personalize alternatives, they do so in similar ways *even though these personalizations may incorporate errors or be influenced by social and cultural context that at first might seem to be irrelevant.* The bonded rationality perspective argues that all that is needed for negotiations and transactions to be possible is that people share similar individuations of alternatives and reason rationally about them, even if these individuals do not objectively value alternatives "correctly."

The critical issue in the bonded rationality framework is that because we observe that people *do* engage in transactions successfully, we can infer that they must share similar personal understandings of alternatives. If we observe that these personalized understandings incorporate errors and social context, then we must ask how the transactors come to understand each other.

Much previous work in decision making has failed to incorporate the fact that shared understanding is necessary for social groups to operate. Central ideas about the importance of social context on the decision process generally are found in the voluminous research on interdependence and social influence. However, these have not been incorporated into decision theory. Decision research tends not to address how it is possible for there to be successful social interaction if people are biased in their decision making. If my decision making were not rational, it would be difficult for others to understand my choices. If I reason rationally (by the rules of RCT), but with personal understandings of the alternatives that are idiosyncratic, then, again, others cannot understand my choices. In either case, negotiations and transactions would be nearly impossible because the two sides would be talking about essentially different things.

It is possible that social groups communicate because everyone understands alternatives "correctly." For example, all people might possess the natural ability to reason with probabilities according to the mathematical laws of probability, and with neither a distaste nor a preference for taking chances. Evaluations of chancy alternatives would then be agreed upon by all. But research has shown that people generally do *not* evaluate probabilities of events correctly; rather, they make common errors in reasoning about even simple combinations of chancy events (Kahneman and Tversky 1996).

Thus, we can infer from the (usual) success of social interaction that people generally reason rationally about their personal perceptions of alternatives and that these perceptions, while possibly not entirely correct, incorporate shared ways of perceiving the world. We might even say that they incorporate shared ways of misperceiving the world. For example, our perceptions are affected by our limited abilities to process information (which limitations lead us to use simplifying heuristics), by cognitive illusions (which lead us to evaluate alternatives incorrectly), by misunderstandings and misestimations of probability, by the inclusion of aspects (such as regret and sunk costs) that (from an independent perspective) are extraneous to the choice at hand, by the social context of the decision, and by our cultural background.

Personalizing may lead to decisions that do not appear optimal to an independent observer (or researcher) who does not share the individual's subjective context, or who imposes an external measure of success (such as maximizing pecuniary return) that is not shared by the decision maker. Nevertheless, because they reflect behaviors that are common (both in the sense of being shared by others and in the sense of occurring frequently), these personalizations can be understood by others who will recognize rational decisions about them as being rational even if they are suboptimal.

Bonded rationality derives from the fact that our personalizations can be understood by others, and that we wish these personalizations to be understood by others. The decision maker who is bondedly rational is usually understood (although not necessarily agreed with) by peers because his or her personalized perceptions share common cognitive bounds and contextual references. Bonded rationality thus both derives from, and facilitates, social interaction.

People usually exhibit bonded rationality, reasoning rationally about personalized alternatives that share common perceptions. This perspective of bondedly rational reasoning synthesizes previous work in nonrational decision making by focusing on the fact that these personalizations harbor shared perceptions. This focus suggests much about human psychology, social relations, and cultural influences.

Social Interaction and Rationality

To facilitate social interaction we must be bondedly rational.

- We must understand how others personalize the alternatives at hand;
- We must personalize the alternatives ourselves in a way that can be understood by others;
- We must usually reason rationally about our personal understandings of alternatives, and
- We must assume that others reason rationally as well.

When decision making is seen as nonrational, the importance of understandable personalizations can be missed.

Understanding Others' Personalizations

If everyone saw the world objectively, there would be no need to develop the skills of understanding how others evaluate alternatives. However, we know that this is not the case. Some of the biases in evaluating alternatives that people exhibit are due to the cognitive limitations of the human mind, and can be understood simply by assuming that others use the same simplifying heuristics that we use. To the extent that these heuristics derive from a natural over-application of patterns that any intelligence capable of abstraction is likely to perceive (Nisbett and Ross (1980) discuss many of these), the assumption that others use the same heuristics enhances understanding. When the heuristics are learned from our families or others in our society, the assumption may work only for interactions with members of that society.

Other biases are the result of social and cultural influences. We usually can assume that other members of our social and cultural group are "like us." But if we use such an assumption when dealing with people from different backgrounds we may fail to understand how the other decision maker personalizes alternatives. We thus may find this other decision maker to be nonrational.

It is important to remember that we need not *agree* with a decision maker's personalizations to consider that reasoning rational, or to engage in a transaction. As long as we can anticipate that our transaction partner will reason rationally, we only need to *understand* the partner's personalized alternatives in order to continue an interaction. Integrative solutions are possible when the parties to a transaction personalize the alternatives on the table differently but can understand each other's personalizations. The different personalizations may reveal issues valued by one party that are of less value to the other, potentially creating opportunities for an agreement satisfactory to both sides.

However, if we find another's *reasoning* to be nonrational, we are likely to be uncomfortable. There is no way to predict how this person might respond to anything we say or do. We tend to avoid interacting with people whom we see as nonrational. However, we usually have little trouble interacting with others with whom we disagree on the relative values of alternatives.

Thaler (1991), Neale and Bazerman (e.g. 1991), and other writers on "nonrational decision making" identify as "biases" deviations from "rational" decision making (which they define as choosing alternatives that maximize expected return). These authors suggest that by identifying and "debiasing" (correcting) these errors, decision makers can become more nearly "rational."

From a bonded rationality perspective, however, these authors are identifying common personalizations of alternatives rather than instances of nonrational reasoning. Their principal contribution is to help readers understand how their transaction partners personalize alternatives. The bonded rationality perspective differs from their approach in arguing that these biases only appear as personal evaluations of alternatives and not in the rationality of the reasoning applied to the personalized alternatives.[3]

Nevertheless, elucidation of common biases is valuable. A person who recognizes these biases can notice when her transaction partner's personalizations reveal a willingness to accept a lower pecuniary return, or can suggest a higher value for a contextual aspect of the available alternatives. She can then take advantage of

---

[3] Writers on nonrational decision making pin much of the charge of nonrationality on the observation that personal evaluations of alternatives often do not maximize expected pecuniary value. As we have noted, this is only not rational if the economic prescription is added to the axioms of rational choice theory.

that personalization if she values the higher pecuniary return (as these authors assume she will), or is willing to sacrifice the contextual aspect to achieve agreement.

Indeed, readers of these authors form a minor subculture, sharing personalizations that may not be shared by other members of their broader home cultures. Many MBA students have had the experience of moving a joint decision-making process along by identifying a factor as a "sunk cost." With no more than those two words, the colleague accepts the situation, and the discussion proceeds as if that cost had never been incurred. These two words recall several pages of discussion and examples from MBA courses and real-life experiences. Yet to one not versed in these matters, the phrase is cryptic and the concept is (as Thaler notes) not natural.

Even without reading about decision making, members of a social group understand how others commonly personalize alternatives. It is natural to know which factors other members of our own group value in these personalizations, if only because we credit others with thinking much the way we do ourselves. Thaler observed that "it is often viewed as an embarrassment to the basic theory [of economics] that people vote, do not always free ride, and commonly allocate resources equitably to others and to themselves when they are free to do otherwise" (1991, 221). The behaviors that embarrass mainstream economists do not surprise other members of society, however, because we *expect* other people to value fairness, social obligation, and other non-economic aspects in personalizing alternatives.

Bonded Rationality

As social creatures, we seek connections with others. In fact, rational behavior among individuals striving for the same ends in a context of scarce resources is thought by utilitarian philosophers to explain the existence of society (cf. Udy 1969).

Members of a society share understandings that range from what constitutes good and evil, to which side of the road to drive on, to how much one should tip at a restaurant you'll never visit again. There are norms for politeness that help direct interactions and manage conflict (Mikula and Schwinger 1978). These norms not only guide our own behavior, they help us know what to expect the other person to do. The rules of rational decision making similarly allow a transaction partner or an observer to understand what is happening. If I could not count on my partner to follow normative transaction rules, I could not hope to do business with her. What she might think is an acceptable way to do business, I might find offensive.[4]

[4] If the misunderstanding stems from cultural differences, it can result in the problem that frequently afflicts international business: culture clash.

Some of these "rules" seem so obvious to us as members of our own society that we take them for granted and might not be able to identify how we came to know them. Our audience or partner meets violations of the rules or norms of our social group with surprise and discomfort, and, when the violation is sufficiently severe, with castigation and ostracism (Coleman 1990).

A primary social norm underlying many of the other typically normative behaviors is that we reason rationally. Nonrational reasoning is often seen as antisocial. People realize that they ought to reason rationally. A person called on to defend preferences that others consider nonrational is likely to explain herself by describing the alternatives as she saw them and then arguing that her choices were rational in the light of these personalized alternatives. She is unlikely to defend her choice as simply an unthinking decision, one reached at random, or one reached via reasoning that violates the ordinary rules of rational thought.

The social advantages of shared norms extend to sharing the ways in which we personalize alternatives. Because comfortable interactions with others require both that we understand their personal evaluations of alternatives and that our personalizations of alternatives are intelligible to them, we want others to understand our personalizations. We therefore have personal reasons to personalize alternatives in much the same ways that they do. Since it is in society's interest for transactions to occur, society also pressures people to personalize alternatives in specific ways.

This suggests a prescriptive addition to the rules of rational choice theory (RCT): One's personalizations of alternatives should conform to those of one's society and culture, but one should then reason rationally about these personalized alternatives. The addition of this prescriptive rule to the axioms of RCT is a natural consequence of bonded rationality.

From a research perspective, bonded rationality proposes an explanation of decision-making behavior that has been ignored by many writers on nonrational decision making. Unlike the prescription of economic rationality (that expected monetary return should dominate in valuing alternatives), the prescription of bonded rationality conforms with observed decision-making behavior. Indeed, it is a social norm in Coleman's sense.

Bonded rationality argues that

- Individuals reason rationally (in terms of the axioms of Rational Choice Theory) about alternatives as they personalize the alternatives.
- Personalizations tend to deviate from the description and evaluation of alternatives that may result from an independent assessment, but tend to do so in consistent ways that are generally understood by others.
- There is a continuum of influences leading to these deviations. They may reflect:

    i. cognitive processes and limitations shared by all humans.

    ii. cognitive illusions that may be innate or learned.

    iii. heuristics that may arise independently in a variety of societies.

    iv. the psychological context of how the alternatives are presented.

    v. the social context in which the decision is made.

    vi. the cultural context of the decision maker.

- To the extent that two individuals share heuristics and context, they will tend to understand each other's personalizations, and thus find each other's decisions rational — even if they disagree on the decision itself.
- Because individuals wish to be understood as rational, they will tend toward personalizations of alternatives that conform with those favored in their culture and social context.

I describe each of the influences leading to these deviations below.

(i) Cognitive Limitations

Some personalizations of alternatives result from the mind's limited ability to process complex information. Simon (1982) observed that decision makers have cognitive limitations on the amount and complexity of the information they can process. The theory of bounded rationality identifies "in theory and in actual behavior, procedures for choosing that are computationally simpler, and that can account for observed inconsistencies in human choice patterns" (Simon 1990, 17). For example, instead of understanding probability distributions of outcomes, decision makers may use heuristic estimating procedures or adopt strategies for dealing with uncertainty that don't require a knowledge of probability.

Boundedly rational decisions do not generally maximize expected pecuniary value, per se, although maximizing expected return is one of many possible shortcuts a decision maker may choose. Boundedly rational decision rules "are derived from what is known about human thought and choice processes, and especially from what is known about the limits of human cognitive capacity for discovering alternatives" (Simon 1990, 15).

Some cognitive limitations appear to reflect fundamental inabilities to apply inferential strategies appropriately or to perceive aspects of the world as they would be evaluated by a disinterested observer. Nisbett and Ross (1980) observe that the helpful cognitive strategies that people use in understanding their world can be overapplied or misapplied, leading to major judgmental or inferential errors. Nisbett and Ross note that "objects and events are not always labeled accurately and sometimes are processed through entirely inappropriate knowledge structures. Without these structures stored in memory, life would be a buzzing confusion, but their clarity is helpful only in proportion to their validity and to the accuracy with which they are applied to the data at hand" (1980, 7).

For example, when people attempt to judge the relative frequency or likelihood of particular events, they may be influenced by how easily similar incidents come to mind. Such an influence is called an availability bias (Tversky and Kahneman 1974). In judging the size of a community's budget, for example, committee members may be overly influenced by expenses due to a recent calamitous flood in a neighboring locale rather than focussing on drier, probabilitistic measures that are more appropriate economic anchors. The result may be a budget weighted more heavily for disaster relief that is unlikely to be needed than for school funding whose need is certain.

(ii) Cognitive Illusions

Other cognitive limitations appear to reflect fundamental errors in perception that persist even after the individual understands the error. Gilovich (1991) calls such persistent failures of perception cognitive illusions by analogy with optical illusions. He demonstrates, for example, that the "hot hand" in basketball is an illusion held firmly even by experts and even after his demonstration that it is not true.[5] The concept of cognitive illusions is useful for describing some kinds of personalization of alternatives.

(iii) Heuristics

Tversky and Kahneman (1983) have shown that, while many decisions are made among alternatives that include chancy outcomes, people often cannot reason clearly about chance. For example, if outcome A has low probability and outcome B has high probability, most people see the compound outcome A *and* B to be more likely than the simple outcome A. (A famous example is provided in Appendix B.) Kahneman and Tversky have found that this *conjunction error* persists even when people are trained in probability reasoning, or when the alternatives are presented with little disguise, in a manner that highlights the nature of the joint probability.

Another cognitive illusion noted by Tversky and Kahneman (1974) is the *representativeness bias*, which leads to inflated estimates of the probability that one event or object is related to another because they resemble one another. Evaluations based on representativeness are not influenced by a variety of factors that should affect judgments of probability. For example, Tversky and Kahneman discuss "Steve," who is shy, helpful, and detail-oriented, but has little

[5] The "hot hand" theory holds that basketball players tend to have "hot" streaks during which they are more likely to make a basket. Gilovich shows that a player's observed streaks of successes are no longer than would be expected from knowing the player's long-run probability of success and applying elementary probability theory.

interest in people. When people are asked how likely is it that Steve is a farmer or a librarian, they rely on their stereotypes (they use the *representativeness heuristic*) to label Steve most likely to be a librarian. However, this evaluation reveals people's *insensitivity to prior probability of outcomes*, namely to the base-rate frequency of farmers and librarians in the population. That there are many more farmers than librarians in the population should enter into any reasonable estimate of the probability that Steve is a member of either occupation. However, the researchers' experiments show that considerations of the base rate rarely enter into people's estimates, unless the base rate is stated explicitly; but if base rate information competes with worthless evidence, the base rate information is ignored.

The Effect of Context

Decision makers often incorporate aspects of the context of the decision in their personalization of the alternatives. Arrow observed that context affects rational decision makers: "rationality is not a property of the individual alone, although it is usually presented that way. Rather, it gathers not only its force but also its very meaning from the social context in which it is embedded" (1990, 25).

Contextual effects can include *psychological* effects such as the regret we anticipate feeling at a loss or the sense of commitment we might feel after making an investment, *social* effects such as the value of fairness, and *cultural* effects such as the obligation to return a favor.

(iv) Psychological Context

Kahneman and Tversky (1979) note that people seem to use a reference point for making decisions under conditions of uncertainty. People act as though there is an S-shaped value function for alternatives, tending to be risk-seeking to avoid losses and risk-averse in gambles for gains.

While some researchers have seen Kahneman and Tversky's *prospect theory* as evidence of nonrational behavior, in fact it deals only with how we tend to perceive alternatives. It may not be correct from a disinterested assessment of value to view the prospect of a *loss* of amount x as more painful than the equivalent prospect of *failing to gain* the same amount, but many studies have shown that people tend to perceive alternatives in this way. Nevertheless, *having personalized the alternatives in this way*, people reason rationally about them.[6]

[6] The ingenious design of Kahneman and Tversky's experiments indicates that they assume that their subjects will reason rationally. They design questions so that subjects' personal understanding of alternatives will change according to the context. The results of these changing personalized understandings are choices that may appear to an independent observer to be nonrational *even though the subjects reason about these personalized alternatives rationally*.

The Allais paradox (1952) illustrates a similar effect. Subjects tend to prefer a *certainty* of a substantial gain (e.g., receiving $100 million for sure) to a bet with a high *probability* of a larger gain but some probability of no gain (e.g., a 10 percent chance of winning $500 million; an 89 percent chance of winning $100 million, and a 1 percent chance of winning nothing), even though, in this situation, the gamble has a higher expected value than the certainty. At the same time, in a second situation, these subjects prefer a gamble with a 10 percent chance of winning $500 million and a 90 percent chance of winning nothing, to a gamble of an 11 percent chance of winning $100 million and an 89 percent chance of winning nothing. The preference for certainty in the first situation seems to violate the axiom of monotonicity.[7] But subjects commonly explain that the regret they anticipate over sacrificing the sure gain if the bet were lost is not worth the additional expected return. Such explanation reveals a common personalization of alternatives that is understood easily by others.

Thaler's concept of "mental accounting" (1980; 1985) describes a number of related psychological phenomena including, for example, that people tend to value "sunk costs" even when it leads them to forego future gain, that gamblers who are winning tend to become more reckless (perhaps because they imagine they are playing with "house money" which they value less), and that people intentionally restrict their options to avoid behaviors they may regret (e.g., dieters don't keep desserts in the house; people prefer forced automatic savings plans). Thaler also identifies an "endowment effect," which leads us to value an item we possess more highly than we value the same item when another possesses it. This effect persists over a wide variety of objects and public goods (Thaler 1980).

While Thaler's work could be seen by traditional economists as maverick, the bonded rationality perspective suggests that it has not moved far enough from its mainstream roots. His work assumes that decisions that do not maximize objectively perceived self-interest (as economic theory demands) cannot be rational. Recognizing that the personalizations of alternatives that he observes are regular, consistent, and systematic, he dubs the reasoning behind these decisions "quasi-rational" (Thaler 1991). However, these personalizations fit comfortably into the larger framework of bonded rationality discussed here, precisely because they are regular, consistent across individuals and circumstances, and systematic.

Many writers have followed Thaler's lead, seeing decision makers' consideration of context as nonrational or quasi-rational behavior. If our goal is to maximize expected (pecuniary) return, as prescribed by economics, then consideration of context should be irrelevant, violating the RCT axiom of independence. The

---

[7] The preference for the bet with higher return in the second situation shows that a 1 percent increase in the risk of winning nothing is not itself seen as something to avoid.

prescription to maximize return is not, however, part of rational choice theory. The fact that human decision makers value other aspects of the context in addition to, or even more highly than, they value pecuniary return may make some economists uncomfortable, but it is not a failure of rationality in decision-making behavior.

(v) Social Context

People almost never personalize alternatives independent of their social context. As Barley notes, "In daily life, persons are almost always members of groups whose values and beliefs shape their behavior and cognition. People typically dispute and bargain as members of families, communities, cliques, and organizations, not as isolated actors whose judgment is unfettered by social relationships" (1991, 169).

Social context can alter the perceived value of an alternative by valuing aspects that might be thought extraneous by an independent observer. Thus, for example, a person who would ordinarily avoid a bet with even a small risk of death may volunteer as a soldier, in part to be thought a hero by society (or to avoid being judged a coward). Societies maximize this value with parades and medals.

Fairness is one social value that many people include in their personalizations of alternatives, even though it often has no pecuniary value. Fairness is a complex phenomenon with a variety of definitions and applications. For example, Kramer, Pommerenke, and Newton (1993) observed that people who share a social identity (e.g., are all members of the same MBA program) will be more concerned about the other party's outcomes, leading to a preference for greater equality. On the other hand, Loewenstein, Thompson, and Bazerman (1989) observed that people who felt wronged (*un*fairly treated) would accept a financial loss in order to hurt the person who had wronged them. Wiesenfeld and Brockner (this volume) observe that even fairness itself may be contextually defined: people have different perceptions of how fairly an organization has treated them depending on whether they are full-time or part-time employees.

Thaler (1991) proposed that game theory should change to reflect the fact that people care about acting fairly and being treated fairly. Several game theorists agree: Both Camerer and Gibbons (in separate papers in this volume) discuss some of the changes that game theory is experiencing. Their new "behavioral" game theory incorporates considerations of communication and some of the numerous shortcuts that people use on a regular basis. Gibbons et al. acknowledge, for example, that communication between players can lead to efficient outcomes where game theory predicts none. These advances are important steps in understanding the social context for how people personalize alternatives.

(vi) Cultural Context

Cultural context can also influence how people personalize alternatives. Most of what we learn about preferences in a social framework we learn from our culture.

People from different cultures may personalize alternatives differently. For example, there are cross-cultural differences in when and how people reciprocate a good deed. Americans tend to believe in tit-for-tat reciprocity, while the French, for example, would be offended by such insincerity—they expect reciprocity to occur over time, when a return favor seems appropriate (Carroll [1987], Sahlins [1972]). Cultural context can also affect a decision maker's willingness to take risks. For example, in many cultures men are expected to take risks while women are expected to avoid risks.

The effects of cultural differences on how decision makers personalize alternatives is especially important to cross-cultural interactions, including negotiations. Anthropologists and sociologists in particular have noted that an understanding of the other's cultural bases for personalizing alternatives is a prerequisite to improved social interaction.[8]

We automatically understand personalizations that depend upon social or cultural context when we share the social and cultural context of the other party. Because we tend to take our culture for granted, we may not be aware of its influence on our personalizations. When we deal with someone with whom we do not share a context, we risk overlooking this source of difference. The result could be a sense that the other party is not rational, leading to a breakdown in social interaction.

Social Utility

Someone who makes coherent choices between pairs of personalized alternatives has, thereby, defined a utility function. If the personalizations of alternatives value both social influences (such as fairness) and the social norm of common personalizations, the utility function defined by these preferences could be called a "social utility function."[9]

It is important to differentiate social and cultural effects from other kinds of biases that can affect personalizations of alternatives. Biases that are based on

---

[8] This observation can be applied to subcultures as well. For example, Tannen's (1986) work on gender differences in communication styles can be understood as showing that men and women tend to personalize alternatives differently.

[9] Loewenstein, Thompson, and Bazerman (1989) have used the term "social utility" differently. Imitating the methods of economic inquiry, they assume that personal evaluation of alternatives can be expressed in monetary terms, and fit a complex polynomial function to the subject's valuation of alternatives.

cognitive limitations, misunderstandings, misperceptions, and illusions—however consistent across individuals—are not socially based. In social interactions, it is valuable to understand the cognitive limitations of others, but that is relatively easy to do when they are similar to our own limitations. However, heuristics that many people employ to cope with these limitations may be socially-based if they are learned.

The "social heuristics" discussed by Bazerman, Gibbons, Thompson, and Valley (this volume) should be viewed not as heuristics (because they are not strategies for simplifying otherwise complex cognitive tasks) but as social aspects that are considered in personalizing alternatives by members of the society studied by these authors.

Research Directions

The approach described here synthesizes work in nonrational decision making under a unifying perspective. By focusing attention on how people personalize alternatives, this perspective provides an ordering and organization of these results, and suggests further areas of research. The rationality hypothesis is, to borrow Arrow's phrase, "by itself weak: to make it useful, the researcher is tempted into some strong assumptions" (1990, 29). The nature of these strong assumptions focuses the research that uses them on specific questions, and narrows the range of answers that may be anticipated.

While this chapter classifies common aspects of personalization into a few categories for convenience, there is a continuum of effects on these personalizations. One end of the continuum holds strictly cognitive effects that reflect the "wiring" of the human mind and are common to most humans through learned behaviors that might be shared across many cultures and situations. The other end of the continuum holds the strictly contextual effects of the culture in which we are raised and the social circumstances in which we face the decision. For example, the conjunction fallacy and availability bias described by Kahneman and Tversky, and classified here as cognitive illusions, can also be considered strategies for coping with cognitive complexity, but are unlikely to be cultural effects. The endowment effect may reflect the social prestige of ownership, as well as psychologically-based perceptions of value.

Some open questions could be answered with cross-cultural studies. It would be interesting to learn whether perceptions classified here as cognitive illusions are common to other cultures, whether cognitive limitations to complexity are roughly the same for all humans, and whether other cultures learn to cope with them in different ways.

Future research also could explore whether various contexts within a given culture affect individuals' personalization of alternatives. Reasonable candidates for such studies include the contexts of business, socioeconomic class, ethnicity, gender, friendship, or competition versus cooperation. One step has been made in this direction: Halpern (1994, 1997) has described a consistent effect of friendship on pricing. Individuals working in isolation, but told that they are negotiating with friends, show strong agreement on prices and a consistent pattern of pricing, providing evidence of the pervasive strength of cultural influences in personalizing alternatives.

Conclusion

People's decision-making behavior often does not optimize expected pecuniary return or game "points." Nevertheless, it generally can be viewed as the result of rational reasoning applied to personalized understandings of the alternatives at hand. Studies of human decision processes have elucidated some of the ways by which such personalized understandings develop. While each individual must achieve his or her own personal individuation of alternatives, as social creatures we share many personalization processes with those around us. These shared processes, which may include value for nonmonetary concerns, constitute a bonded rationality. The approach proposed here allows researchers to explore how we understand each other in a social decision-making context.

The concept of bonded rationality explicitly adds social and cultural context to considerations of psychological influences in rational decision making. It is thus both more realistic than theories of rationality that ignore context, and a fertile source of research questions. By emphasizing the importance of how decision makers personalize alternatives, bonded rationality focuses attention on the influences of psychology, sociology, and anthropology on rational decision making.

Appendix A

Examples of the Axioms of Rational Choice

1. Transitivity
   A person who likes ice cream sodas better than fruit juice and fruit juice better than milk can be expected to prefer ice cream sodas to milk.
2. Monotonicity
   A race car driver prefers to live. However, when racing, he prefers a lottery of life and death to certain life—that is, life without racing.
3. Independence
   A person who would rather go to the prom with Paul than with David (whether or not it rains that night) should prefer the option (*go to the*

prom with Paul if it rains, go with Dan if not) to the option (*go to the prom with David if it rains, go with Dan if not*).

4. Continuity

   For a person who likes ice cream sodas better than fruit juice and fruit juice better than milk, there is some probability, p, such that he is indifferent between the payoff "A probability p of ice cream soda and $(1 - p)$ of milk" and the payoff "fruit juice."

Appendix B

The Conjunction Fallacy

In a famous example, Tversky and Kahneman (1983) provide a description of Linda, a single, outspoken and bright woman who is deeply concerned with issues of discrimination and social justice. A list of occupations and avocations in which Linda might be involved follows their description, including "Linda is a bank teller;" "Linda is active in the feminist movement;" and "Linda is a bank teller and is active in the feminist movement." According to the mathematics of probability, the conjunction of "bank teller and feminist" cannot be more probable than either representative constituent. The conjunction of two outcomes cannot be more likely than either outcome alone. However, participants in studies of the Linda case rank the conjunction as more probable than its less representative constituents. Augmenting a seemingly unlikely outcome (bank teller) by combining it with a more likely outcome (feminist) seems to improve its plausibility and thus its perceived probability.

Endogenous Preferences:
A Structural Approach

David Krackhardt

This paper speaks to one of the key assumptions in the rational model as assumed by neo-classical economists. This assumption is that preferences are exogenous, that they are determined by forces outside the system, and that they are unchanging through time. In contrast, I will propose a model of endogenous preferences, one that captures the dynamics of preference formation as people interact with one another. This model preserves the mathematical simplicity and analyzability of modern economic theories and permits the derivation of an equilibrium of preferences in a complex dynamic system.

A Brief History of Exogenous Preferences

In their ground-establishing article, "De Gustibus Non Est Disputandum," Stigler and Becker make two claims about preferences: (1) individuals' basic tastes do not change over time, and (2) individuals do not differ from one to another in their tastes. To emphasize this point, they compare tastes to the Rocky Mountains: "Both [tastes and the mountains] are there, will be there next year, too, and are the same to all men" (76).

They recognize that this stand would be controversial, suggesting that a "generation of economists" will not be able to defend against the anticipated deluge

I would like to thank Steve Roehrig, Gerald Salancik, Seth Sanders, Herbert Simon and Lowell Taylor for their thoughtful comments on earlier versions of this work. I would also like to thank my lucky stars that I am at Carnegie Mellon University, where such collegial help is commonplace.

of questions and counterexamples. But they assure the reader that it is not their intent to explain all rich social phenomena via utility theory. Rather, they defend their approach as one that "offers guidance in tackling these problems—and that no other approach of remotely comparable generality and power is available" (77).

To demonstrate this power, Stigler and Becker (formalized and extended by Becker and Murphy 1988) provide an example of how "addictive" behaviors, which on the surface seem to be clear indications of changes in tastes over time, can be explained by appealing to the concept of "consumption capital." Consumption capital represents the degree to which experience with a good or service reduces the cost of that good or service. As a consumer gains experience with a good (such as heroin), it is easier to acquire and use (one knows better where to get it and better how to administer it, etc.). Thus, the cost of using it goes down as use goes up, resulting in higher marginal "profit" (gains in utility minus costs). As the marginal utility diminishes with ever-higher usage, equilibrium is reached when the diminishing marginal utility gains match the reduction in cost obtained by increases usage (i.e., increased consumption capital).

In the Becker and Murphy heroin example, they show three equilibrium points: no usage (a stable equilibrium), moderate usage (a saddle point, likely to result in movement to one of the other two equilibria), and addiction (a stable equilibrium). They note that these equilibria and predictions are consistent with what people who work with such addictions have found in the field.

The benefits of such a model, they argue, are that one does not have to resort to ad hoc explanations like "needs" or "different tastes," which are the purview of a whole bag of social scientists (Stigler and Becker [1977, 76]. They wonder aloud whether such a bag includes phrenologists right alongside the psychologists and sociobiologists): "We believe that the phenomenon Marshall is trying to explain, namely that the exposure to [some good] increases the subsequent demand for [the good] (for some persons!), can be explained with some gain in insight by assuming constant tastes, whereas to assume a change in tastes has been an unilluminating 'explanation'" (78).

There are many structural sociologists who would agree on this point about tastes constituting an unilluminating explanation. Mayhew (1980) passionately argued that social scientists of all stripes, including sociologists, too often resort to differential tastes, needs, or desires as explanations of behavior: "The individualists [social scientists who appeal to such explanations] do not seem to have grasped the elementary principle that one does not explain a set of data by simply repeating it. To say that 'people do things because they want to' is not an explanation (nor even an interpretation) of what people do: it is a restatement of the (individualist's) data. It is not different from saying that people do things because they do things" (355).

Encouraged by Becker and his colleagues, other economists have followed suit and begun to explain many social phenomena that used to be the domain of sociologists. For example, Manski (1993a) has developed a model that explains why underclass youth underestimate the return on education (thereby appearing to "value" education less) (see also Manski 1993b; 1995). Montgomery (1994) draws on the consumption capital idea to show why husbands of lower-class families would appear to "value" their families less.

Even sociologists have begun to incorporate utility-maximizing explanations as core to their models of human behavior (e.g., Coleman 1990; Burt 1982). Pertinent to the point of this paper, two political scientists (Cohen and Axelrod 1984) have suggested that people often learn that their underlying beliefs about the probabilities of outcomes are wrong. Faced with such "surprises" (defined as the difference between what they expected and what they observed), they not only modify their estimates of the probabilities, but their experience "is also used to modify the very utility function that is being maximized" (39).

Becker and his colleagues are to be commended for developing a consistent and powerful theory that does not resort to trivial logical tautologies. As shown in just these few examples, their efforts have succeeded in guiding many subsequent studies of macro social behavior. But that social phenomena *can* be explained by some theory does not imply that the theory is correct.

The Structuralist's Perspective

I now turn to an alternative, one that does not resort to setting up a tautology based on tastes, but does attempt to explain variance in tastes endogenously. It rests on the axiom that people influence each other in their beliefs, values, tastes, and virtually every other cognitive or affective process in which they engage. This axiom certainly is well-founded in the literature on social psychology and sociology, and I would argue is at least as robust as the utility-maximizing assumption about rational behavior. It is not my purpose here to argue this axiom, but only to state it as a starting point, from which I derive the following formal model about preferences.

To state that people influence each other is too general. I am speaking of influence that occurs as a byproduct of direct interaction.[1] Thus, not everyone influences everyone else. In fact, no one influences everyone else. While some of

---

[1] I will ignore the indirect kind of influence that may occur at a global level, for example, the effect that my congressperson might have on me even though I have never talked to her. Nor am I referring to indirect ripple effects that rumors might have on individuals. No doubt these social influences can affect one's preferences, but they are outside the scope of the model I am developing here.

my colleagues at Carnegie Mellon University influence me a great deal, others do not. Nonetheless, what I value, what I like, and what I aspire to, are all in part influenced by particular others in my social history.

The exact form of this influence is difficult to specify and is the appropriate object of empirical research, but I will start with simplifying assumptions about the form to make the models tractable. I will develop a dynamic model that suggests an equilibrium state for preferences within a given influence structure. The model suggests how to assess the extent to which preferences, and other variables of interest to social scientists, are affected by the social influence process I am proposing.

Equilibrium within an Influence Structure

Consider the case where one's preference at time t (designated as $U_t(i)$ for person i, or U_t for all persons) for a good, service, outcome, or whatever, is influenced by the preferences of a set of actors in the system (including self).[2] Let us further assume that the extent to which any other actor j influences person i is given by some weight, w_{ij}. To this point, I have not stipulated exactly how this influence might take place, except to say that it is a joint function of the opinions of all actors in the system, weighted by $\mathbf{W}$. So, for an individual,

$$U_t(i) = \sum w_{ij}U_{t-1}(j). \tag{1}$$

For the entire set of individuals, these equations can be represented in matrix notation as:

$$U_t = \mathbf{W}U_{t-1}$$

The question is, what is the nature of $\mathbf{W}$? That is, how are utilities affected through associations with others?

The truth is, $\mathbf{W}$ could take on many forms, each of which would depend on a social theory of preference influence. I will restrict myself in this paper to a theory premised on the following two assumptions:

Assumption 1: Principle of Interaction. The degree of influence person j has on person i's preferences is proportional to the amount of time i and j spend interacting with each other.

That is, the more time i and j spend interacting, the more they will influence each other in their changes in preferences over time. I also assume here that a

---

[2] I will, for the moment, constrain U_t to be positive real. An extreme value of 0 would represent indifference to the good, while increasing positive values would represent increasingly positive value placed on the good.

person can influence herself ($= w_{ii}$). This parameter represents a person's obstinacy, or what psychologists might call the individual's personality. To the extent that these diagonal elements are large relative to the off-diagonal values in **W**, we are assuming that preferences are exogenous and relatively stable over time, untempered by the preferences of others. In the extreme case, if $w_{ii} = 1$ for all i and $w_{ij} = 0$ for all $i \neq j$, then we are reduced to the model that Becker claims: preferences are exogenous and stable over time. To the extent that the w_{ii}'s are small, individuals are assumed to be quickly influenced by their social neighbors.

This is a very reasonable assumption, one that has much support in the social psychological science literature (e.g., Festinger 1954; Friedkin and Johnsen 1990; Marsden 1981). It has appeal in that it shows how people are both dependent on and independent of each other.

But it also assumes symmetry, that is, it assumes that when two people interact, they influence each other to the same extent. We can increase the sophistication of this model by recognizing that some people *respond* differently to the same amount of interaction with others. It would be tempting here to suggest that such responses are personality-based ("bad chemistry," for example), but to do so would be to fall into the same trap that Mayhew warned us against, that of explaining the outcome by describing the outcome. Instead, I will use a structural assumption about how people respond differently to the amount of time they spend with each other.

Assumption 2: Principle of Reflected Exclusivity. The degree of influence person j has on person i's preferences is *inversely* proportional to the amount of time person j spends with all others (including self).

This assumption requires somewhat more explanation. For illustration, let us assume that Stephen interacts for the same amount of time with two people, Sheila and Josephine. According to Assumption 1, Sheila and Josephine each should contribute equally to Stephen's re-formulation of his preferences. But, suppose further that Sheila is a gregarious individual, and that she interacts with everyone. Suppose that Josephine, on the other hand, confides solely in Stephen. He sees Josephine's interactions as focused on him, singling him out as someone worth investing in. Thus, while both women objectively spend just as much time with Stephen, he weighs more heavily the investment that Josephine makes in him. Therefore, Josephine has more influence on Stephen's views of the world than does Sheila.

There are two separate rationales for this assumption, one emphasizing the target of influence, and one emphasizing the source. For the first, there is an appreciation of the time devoted by the actor. Stephen recognizes that Sheila's time investment in him is not particularly aimed at him, but that Josephine's is indeed special to him. That is, the actor recognizes the relative investment on the part of the other (Josephine), and in exchange for this devotion is willing to be influenced by the other's view more readily. The second rationale is that the other who has not squandered her time on a plethora of targets can formulate a more relevant, focused and effective presentation to the target. Thus, it is likely to be more effective in its delivery, and more influential in its outcome.

With these two assumptions in place, we can complete the model. If we assume that the degree of interaction between all actors in the system is given by **X**, then we can incorporate both of the above assumptions above in determining **W**:

$$w_{ij}^{'} = \frac{x_{ij}}{\sum_{k=1}^{N} x_{kj}} \tag{2}$$

The question remains, what is the distribution of U_t as t approaches infinity in equation (1)? That is, do the utilities converge to an equilibrium? The answer is yes, under most reasonable conditions for **W**.[3] In this simple model, then, we are able to draw the following conclusion: *The structure of* **W** *determines the distribution of preferences U at equilibrium, and this distribution is independent of the initial values U_0.* This is true even if people are very stubborn individualists (i.e., w_{ii} are all large), as long as there is at least a modicum of interaction among parties (i.e., not all $w_{ij} = 0$).

Thus, we have established a model wherein we make specific predictions about the distribution of preferences based solely on the influence network among the system of actors. And the solution to this distribution is independent of the initial conditions of the set of preferences held by the actors; whatever their initial preferences, they will move toward a stable equilibrium of preferences relative to others in the system with whom they have strong contacts. Preferences are truly endogenous, without having to resort to either tasteless tautologies or rational behavior on the part of the actors.

Discussion

In a footnote, Stigler and Becker rhetorically ask the question why Jews were Jews, Christians were Christians, and Moslems were Moslems. This model answers that question: Jews are Jews because they are influenced by others who are

---

[3] It is easy to see in equation (2) that **W** is column stochastic, with each column summing to 1, and each element is nonnegative. Thus, the matrix is Markov. This is sufficient to show that U_t in equation (1) reaches an equilibrium as t —> ∞, with the steady state being proportional to the first eigenvector of **W**.

Jews; and the same is true for Christians and Moslems. Furthermore, this model predicts that Jews will convert to non-Judaism to the extent that their assimilation into a larger non-Jewish community reduces their contacts with other Jews (the same is true for Moslems and Christians). Thus, the structure of contacts (and the resulting influence that goes with such contacts) will change the distribution of even the most personal and strongly held preferences.

Becker's quote that began this paper, dedicating his work to the four prominent Chicago economists from whom he "learned" the "economic approach," raises a parallel question: Why are Chicago economists Chicago economists? Why do they seem to believe in this model with such enthusiasm? The answer to this question underscores several possible ways to approach the problem I address in this paper.

First, of course, the model suggested in this paper is that Gary Becker and other Chicago economists are the product of the social forces around them at the University of Chicago. Their daily interactions, mutual reinforcements of ideas and values, and simple time invested in discussing these models moved their group to believe in what became known as the "Chicago School." Those most active in these discussions became the most fervent believers and proselytizers. But this explanation is only one of several that could be offered for the same phenomena.

For example, it could be proposed that these four luminaries provided *information* to Becker, and that Becker, being of sound intelligence, could discern the wisdom in this information and in the logic behind the model. This information argument, however, is not sufficient. Such models are readily available in print, discussed at length in prominent journals such as *American Economic Review*, and read by almost every economist trained in this country, whether or not they have any Chicago association. They all have access to the same information that Gary Becker had. Yet, they do not all buy into the Chicago model. The argument that they may not be as discerning as Gary Becker is not sufficient, either. No one could accuse Herb Simon of lacking in intellectual horsepower; yet few would describe him as a Chicago School economist (even though his Ph.D. is from the University of Chicago).

However, even if we do interpret "influence" as merely the absorption of information, the model in this paper still holds; it only changes the interpretation. That is, if we assume that information flows throughout a system in a manner dominated by the interaction patterns described in **X**, and we assume that this new information permits the user to alter estimates of costs and benefits of the good, we can still apply the assumptions of interaction and reflected exclusivity. In this case, interaction would increase the amount of information relevant to a good, and reflected exclusivity would affect the source's ability to present a strong and convincing case about the good. The results of the model, then, would be the same. "Revealed preferences" would be a function of the structure in **X**, not independent evaluations.

Another possible explanation for the concentration of Chicago economists at the University of Chicago is selection. That is, only those economists who subscribe to the Chicago School philosophy are likely to seek admission to the club known as the University of Chicago; and even those "mistakes" who did not self-select themselves out were weeded out through the Ph.D. exam process or through the tenure-granting process.

There are two responses to this argument. First, the argument is valid. Certainly such selection processes hold, and the more dominant the Chicago School is in the University, the stronger the selection process will be. In sociology, the argument is termed "homophily," that is, those who believe, value, and act alike will seek others out (McPherson and Smith-Lovin 1987). Birds of a feather will flock together.

The second response is that such selection cannot be the whole story. If we take Becker at his word, that he "learned" about the Chicago School from these four luminaries, then presumably Becker did not hold such beliefs ahead of time. The causal direction implied in his statement was the other way around: First, he encountered his teachers, then he learned about the "economic approach." If selection were the whole story, no one would change their mind, no one would learn.

A reasonable alternative to the present model, however, is that both processes occur simultaneously. That is, people influence each other through their interactions, and at the same time people seek out others of like-mindedness to interact with. That is, they are the product of their structural environment and they also cause changes in the structure (cf., Burt 1992, chapter 7).

The advantage of the current model proposed in this paper is that the equilibrium for the distribution of utilities is derivable analytically with simple linear algebra. By including the additional assumption that the structure of interaction systematically changes to increase homophily, one is faced with a far more complex model that probably cannot be solved analytically.

Nonetheless, such a complex model has intuitive appeal. The most formidable approach to such non-linear feedback systems, however, is to set aside the simplicity and elegance of mathematics and resort to computational modeling. Some scholars have already pursued such models, and with some success. For example, Kathleen Carley's (1990) computational model on group formation and stability draws on both sets of assumptions and demonstrates under what conditions homophilic groups will persist and under what conditions they will fall apart. For those of us who wish to push this model further, the course paved by Carley and others from the computational school is most likely to lead to fruitful insights into the complexity inherent in such social processes.

Conclusion

I began by discussing the modern economists' models of rational utility theory. Modern economists appear to hold two meta-assumptions about their models. First, they assume that people are utility-maximizing. This assumption has been the object of many years of derision by behavioral decision theorists, who have demonstrated empirically that this assumption is false. But some have argued that the question has been rather moot, since it has also been shown that many results in economic theory do not rely on utility-maximizing players (Becker 1962; Gode and Sunder 1993). Perhaps more important, behavioral decision theorists have failed to replace the neoclassical model with an alternative, equally powerful model from which equilibria in social economic systems might be derived.

I prefer to concentrate on the other major assumption in economic theory, that people act atomistically. At a minimum, relaxing this assumption has profound implications on any empirical results, since such an assumption lies behind virtually all econometric techniques. Violations of this assumption can have devastating effects on statistical tests (e.g., Krackhardt 1988; Doreian 1980). But more importantly, my point is not simply to say that economists are wrong in this assumption. Nihilism is not productive, in my view. My point is that structuralists have an alternative assumption that can be formalized and can produce its own set of predictions, ones that may be empirically tested and may shed light on social/economic processes. From within this kind of formal structure, perhaps economists and structuralists could communicate on common ground, and build a new overriding model of human behavior.

References

Adams, J. S. 1965. Inequity in social exchange. In L. Berkowitz, ed., *Advances in Experimental Social Psychology* 2: 267–299. New York: Academic Press.

Akerlof, G. A. 1970. The market for 'lemons': Quality uncertainty and the market mechanism. *Quarterly Journal of Economics* 89: 488–500.

Akerlof, G. A., and J. L. Yellen. 1990. The fair wage-effort hypothesis and unemployment. *Quarterly Journal of Economics* 105 (May): 255–283.

Alchian, A. 1961. *Some economics of property.* RAND D-2316. Santa Monica: RAND Corporation.

Alchian, A., and H. Demsetz. 1972. Production, information costs and economic organization. *American Economic Review* 62 (December): 777–795.

Alchian, A., and S. Woodward. 1987. Reflections on the theory of the firm. *Journal of Institutional and Theoretical Economics* 143 (March): 110–136.

Allais, M. 1952. The foundations of a positive theory of choice involving risk and a criticism of the postulates and axioms of the American school. (English translation.) In M. Allais and O. Hagen, eds. 1979. *Expected utility hypotheses and the Allais' Paradox: Contemporary discussions and rational decisions under uncertainty with Allais' rejoinder.* Dordrecht: Reidel.

——. 1990. Allais Paradox. In J. Eatwell, M. Milgate, and P. Newman, eds. *The new Palgrave: A dictionary of economics: Utility and probability.* New York: W.W. Norton.

Altman, I., and D. A. Taylor. 1973. *Social penetration: The development of interpersonal relationships.* New York: Holt, Rinehart and Winston.

Amabile, T., B. Hennessey, and B. Grossman. 1986. Social influences on creativity: The effects of contracted-for reward. *Journal of Personality and Social Psychology* 50: 14–23.

Ansberry, C. 1993. Hired out: Workers are forced to take more jobs as contingency laborers with meager benefits. *Wall Street Journal,* 11 March: A1, A9.

Aoki, M. 1988. *Information incentives, and bargaining in the Japanese economy.* New York: Cambridge University Press.

——. 1990. Toward an economic model of the Japanese firm. *Journal of Economic Literature* 28 (March): 1–27.

——. 1992. The Japanese firm as a system of attributes: A survey and research agenda, unpublished manuscript.

Apple, W., L. A. Streeter, and R. M. Krauss. 1979. Effects of pitch and speech rate on personal attributions. *Journal of Personality and Social Psychology* 37: 715–727.

Appelbaum, E. 1991. What's driving the growth of contingent employment? Proceedings from the Conference on the Changing Workforce, Washington, D.C.

Argyris, C. 1960. *Understanding organizational behavior.* Homewood, Ill.: Dorsey Press.

Argyris, C., and D. Schon. 1978. *Organizational learning: A theory of action perspective.* Reading, Mass.: Addison-Wesley.

Arrow, K. 1974. *The limits of organization.* 1st ed. New York: W. W. Norton.

——. 1982a. Risk perception in psychology and economics. *Economic Inquiry* 20: 1–9.

——. 1982b. Innovation in large and small firms. In J. Ronen, ed., *Entrepreneurship.* Lexington, Mass.: Heath.

——. 1990. Economic theory and the hypothesis of rationality. In J. Eatwell, M. Milgate, P. Newman, eds., *The new Palgrave: A dictionary of economics: Utility and probability,* 25–37. New York: W. W. Norton.

Arrow, K., and F. Hahn. 1972. *General competitive analysis.* Amsterdam: North-Holland.

Arrow, K., R. Mnookin, L. Ross, A. Tversky, and R. Wilson, eds. 1993. *Barriers to conflict resolution.* New York: Norton.

Arthur, B. 1989. Competing technologies, increasing returns, and lock-in by historical events. *Economic Journal* 99 (March): 116–131.

——. 1990. Positive feedbacks in the economy. *Scientific American* (February): 92–99.

Asanuma, B. 1989. Manufacturer-supplier relationships in Japan and the concept of relationship-specific skill. *Journal of Japanese and International Economies* 3: 1–30.

Ashford, S. J., C. Lee, and P. Bobko. 1989. Content, causes, and consequences of job insecurity: A theory-based measure and substantive test. *Academy of Management Journal* 32: 803–829.

Austin, W. 1980. Friendship and fairness: Effects of type of relationship and task performance on choice of distribution rules. *Personality and Social Psychology Bulletin* 6: 402–408.

Axelrod, R. 1976. *The structure of decision: The cognitive maps of political elites.* Princeton: Princeton University Press.

——. 1984. *The evolution of cooperation.* New York: Basic Books.

Babcock, L., and G. Loewenstein. 1997. Explaining bargaining impasse: The role of self-serving biases. *Journal of Economic Perspectives* II: 109–126.

Babcock, L., G. Loewenstein, S. Issacharoff, and C. Camerer. 1995. Biased judgments of fairness in bargaining. *American Economic Review* 85:1337–1343.

Bacon, F. 1625. Of revenge. In *The Essays: Or, counsels civil and moral, 1882,* with an introductory dissertation and notes by J. Devey, 66–70. Chicago: Standard.

Bain, J. 1956. *Barriers to new competition.* New York: John Wiley & Sons.

Baker, G. 1992. Incentive contracts and performance measurement. *Journal of Political Economy* 100: 598–614.

Baker, G., R. Gibbons, and K. J. Murphy. 1994. Subjective performance measures in optimal incentive contracts. *Quarterly Journal of Economics* 109: 1125–1156.

——. 1997. Implicit contracts and the theory of the firm. Unpublished manuscript. Cornell University.

Ball, S. B., M. H. Bazerman, and J. S. Carroll. 1991. An evaluation of learning in the bilateral winner's curse. *Organizational Behavior and Human Decision Processes* 48: 1–22.

Banerjee, A. 1992. A simple model of herd behavior. *Quarterly Journal of Economics* 107: 797–817.

Barley, S. R. 1991. Contextualizing conflict: Notes on the anthropology of disputes and negotiations. In M. H. Bazerman, R. J. Lewicki, and B. H. Sheppard, eds. *Research on Negotiation in Organizations* 3: 165–202. Greenwich, Conn.: JAI Press.

Barnard, C. 1938. *The functions of the executive.* Cambridge: Harvard University Press (15th printing, 1962).

Barnett, W., and G. Carroll. 1993. How institutional constraints affected the organization of the early American telephone industry. *Journal of Law, Economics, and Organization* 9 (April): 98–126.

Baron, J., and M. Hannan. 1994. The impact of economics on contemporary sociology. *Journal of Economic Literature* 32 (September): 1111–1146.

Baumeister, R. F. 1982. A self-presentational view of social phenomena. *Psychological Bulletin* 91: 3–26.

Bazerman, M. H. 1990. *Judgment in managerial decision making.* 2d ed. New York: John Wiley.

Bazerman, M. H., and J. S. Carroll. 1987. Negotiator cognition. In B. A. Staw and L. L. Cummings, eds., *Research in organizational behavior* 9: 247–288. Greenwich, Conn.: JAI Press.

Bazerman, M. H., T. Magliozzi, and M. A. Neale. 1985. Integrative bargaining in a competitive market. *Organizational Behavior and Human Performance* 34: 294–313.

Bazerman, M. H., and M. A. Neale. 1982. Improving negotiation effectiveness under final offer arbitration: The role of selection and training. *Journal of Applied Psychology* 67: 543–548.

Bazerman, M. H., R. Gibbons, L. Thompson, and K. Valley. 1998. Can negotiators outperform game theory. In J. J. Halpern and R. N. Stern, eds., *Debating rationality: Nonrational aspects of organizational decision making.*

Beard, T. R., and R. O. Beil, Jr. 1994. Do people rely on the self-interested maximization of others? *Management Science* 40 (February) 40: 252–262.

Becker, G. S. 1962. Irrational behavior and economic theory. *Journal of Political Economy* 70: 1–13.

——. 1964. *Human capital.* New York: NBER.

——. 1971. *Economic theory.* New York: Alfred Knopf.

——. 1976. *The economic approach to human behavior.* Chicago: University of Chicago Press.

——. 1993. Nobel lecture: The economic way of looking at behavior. *Journal of Political Economy* 101 (June): 385–409.

Becker, G. S., M. Grossman, and K. Murphy. 1992. Rational addiction and the effect of price on consumption. In G. Lowenstein and J. Elster, eds., *Choice over time.* New York: Russell Sage Foundation.

Becker, G. S., and K. Murphy. 1988. A theory of rational addiction. *Journal of Political Economy* 96 (4): 675–700.

Bell, D., H. Raiffa, and A. Tversky. 1988. Descriptive, normative and prescriptive interactions in decision making. In D. Bell, H. Raiffa, and A. Tversky, eds., *Decision Making.* New York: Cambridge University Press.

Belmonte, T. 1989. *The broken fountain*. 2d ed. New York: Columbia University Press.

Benartzi, S., and R. H. Thaler. 1995. Myopic loss aversion and the equity premium puzzle. *Quarterly Journal of Economics*, 110:173–192.

Benedict, R. 1934. *Patterns of culture*. Boston: Houghton Mifflin.

Berglof, E. 1989. Capital structure as a mechanism of control: A comparison of financial systems. In A. Masahiko, B. Gustafsson, and O. Williamson, eds. *The Firm as a Nexus of Treaties*, 237–262. London: Sage.

Bhide, A., and H. Stevenson. 1991. Why be honest if honesty doesn't pay? *Harvard Business Review* (September-October): 121–129.

Bies, R. J. 1987. The predicament of injustice: The management of moral outrage. In L. L. Cummings, and B. M. Staw, eds., *Research in Organizational Behavior* 10: 213–255. Greenwich, Conn: JAI Press.

Bies, R. J., C. Martin, and J. Brockner. 1993. Just laid off but still a "good citizen"? Only if the process is fair. *Employee Responsibilities and Rights Journal* 6: 227–238.

Bies, R. J., and J. Moag. 1986. Interactional justice: Communication criteria of fairness. In R. J. Lewicki, B. H. Sheppard, and M. H. Bazerman, eds., *Research on Negotiations in Organizations* 1: 83–99. Greenwich, Conn.: JAI Press.

Blau, P. 1964. *Exchange and power in social life*. New York: John Wiley.

Blau, P., and W. R. Scott. 1962. *Formal organizations: A Comparative approach*. San Francisco, Calif.: Chandler.

Blount, S. 1994. The role of causal attributions and elicitation mechanisms in the trade-off between absolute and comparative payoffs in social decision making. University of Chicago Center for Decision Research (working paper).

Bolton, G. 1991. A comparative model of bargaining: Theory and evidence. *American Economic Review* 81: 1096–1136.

Bonin, J., and L. Putterman. 1987. *Economics of cooperation and labor-managed economies*. New York: Cambridge University Press.

Bowles, S., and H. Gintis. 1993. The revenge of homo economicus: Contested exchange and the revival of political economy. *Journal of Economic Perspectives* (Winter): 83–102.

Bowman, D., D. Minehart, and M. Rabin. In press. Loss-aversion in a savings model. *Economic Journal*.

Bradach, J., and R. Eccles. 1989. Price, authority, and trust. *American Review of Sociology* 15: 97–118.

Brams, S. 1993. *Theory of moves*. New York: Cambridge University Press.

Brass, D. J. 1985. Men's and women's networks: A study of interaction patterns and influence in an organization. *Academy of Management Journal* 28: 327–343.

Braver, S. L., and L. Wilson. 1984. A laboratory study of social contracts as a solution to public goods problems: Surviving on the lifeboat. Paper presented at the Western Social Science Association, San Diego, April.

Brehmer, B. 1990. Strategies in real time, dynamic decision making. In R. Hogarth, ed., *Insights in Decision Making*, pp. 262–279. Chicago: University of Chicago Press.

Bridgeman, P. 1955. *Reflections of a Physicist*. 2d ed. New York: Philosophical Library.

Brockner, J. 1988. The effects of work layoffs on survivors: Research theory, and practice. In B. Staw and L. L. Cummings, eds., *Research in Organizational Behavior* 10: 213–255. Greenwich, Conn.: JAI Press.

———. 1990. Scope of justice in the workplace: How survivors react to co-worker layoffs. *Journal of Social Issues* 46: 95–106.

Brockner, J., R. L. DeWitt, S. Grover, and T. Reed. 1990. When it is especially important to explain why: Factors affecting the relationship between managers' explanations of a layoff and survivors' reactions to the layoff. *Journal of Experimental Social Psychology* 26: 389–407.

Brockner, J., and J. Greenberg. 1990. The impact of layoffs on survivors: An organizational justice perspective. In J. Carroll, ed., *Advances in Applied Social Psychology: Business Settings*, 45–75. Hillsdale, New Jersey: Erlbaum.

Brockner, J., S. Grover, T. Reed, and R. L. DeWitt. 1992. Layoffs, job insecurity, and survivors' work effort: Evidence of an inverted-U relationship. *Academy of Management Journal* 35: 413–425.

Brockner, J., M. Konovsky, R. Cooper-Schneider, R. Folger, C. Martin, and R. J. Bies. 1994. The interactive effects of procedural justice and outcome negativity on victims and survivors of job loss. *Academy of Management Journal* 37: 397–409.

Brockner, J., B. Wiesenfeld, and C. Martin. 1995. Decision frame, procedural justice, and survivors' reactions to job layoffs. *Organizational Behavior and Human Decision Processes* 63: 59–68.

Bromley, D. 1989. *Economic interests and institutions.* New York: Basil Blackwell.

Bull, C. 1983. Implicit contracts in the absence of enforcement and risk. *American Economic Review*: 658–671.

———. 1987. The existence of self-enforcing implicit contracts. *Quarterly Journal of Economics* 102: 147–159.

Burt, R. S. 1982. *Toward a structural theory of action.* New York: Academic Press.

———. 1992. The social structure of competition. In N. Nohria and R. Eccles, eds., *Networks and organizations: Structure, form, and action*, 57–91. Boston, Mass.: Harvard Business School Press.

Buxbaum, R. 1985. Modification and adaptation of contracts: American legal developments. *Studies in Transnational Law* 3: 31–54.

Cachon, G., and C. F. Camerer. 1996. Loss-avoidance and forward induction in experimental coordination games. *Quarterly Journal of Economics* 110, 165–194.

Caldwell, J. R., S. Cobb, M. D., Dowling, and D. De Jongh. 1970. The drop-out problem in antihypertensive therapy. *Journal of Chronic Disease* 22: 579–592.

Camerer, C. F. 1990. Behavioral game theory. In R. Hogarth, ed., *Insights in decision making.* Chicago: University of Chicago Press.

———. 1992. The rationality of prices and volume in experimental markets. *Organizational Behavior and Human Decision Processes* 51: 237–272.

———. 1995. Individual decision making. In J. Kagel and A. Roth, eds., *Handbook of experimental economics.* Princeton: Princeton University Press.

———. 1997. Progress in behavioral game theory. *Journal of Economic Perspectives*, forthcoming.

———. 1998. Behavioral economics and organizational decision making. In J. J. Halpern and R. N. Stern, eds., *Debating rationality: Nonrational aspects of organizational decision making.*

Camerer, C. F., L. Babcock, G. Lowenstein, and R. Thaler. 1997. Labor supply of New York City cab drivers: One day at a time. *Quarterly Journal of Economics*, forthcoming.

Camerer, C. F., B. Blecherman, and D. Goldstein. 1994. The experimental study of mutual rationality and learning: The "electronic mail" game (working paper).

Camerer, C. F., E. J. Johnson, T. Rymon, and S. Sen. 1993. Cognition and framing in sequential bargaining for gains and losses. In K. Binmore, A. Kirman, and P. Tani, eds., *Contributions to game theory*. Cambridge, Mass.: MIT Press.

Camerer, C. F., and R. Karjalainen. 1993. Ambiguity-aversion and non-additive beliefs in non-cooperative games: Experimental evidence. In B. Munier and M. Machina, eds. *Models and experiments on risk and rationality*. Dordrecht: Kluwer.

Camerer, C. F., and M. Knez. 1997. Coordination in organizations: A game-theoretic perspective. In Z. Shapira, ed., *Organizational decision making*. New York: Cambridge University Press.

Camerer, C. F., G. F. Loewenstein, and M. Weber. 1989. The curse of knowledge in economic settings: An experimental analysis. *Journal of Political Economy* 97: 1232–1254.

Camerer, C. F., and R. H. Thaler. More ultimatum and dictator games. *Journal of Economic Perspectives*, in press.

Capen, E., R. Clapp, and W. Campbell. 1971. Competitive bidding in high risk situations. *Journal of Petroleum Technology* 23: 641–653.

Carley, K. M. 1990. Structural constraints on communication: The diffusion of the homomorphic signal analysis technique through scientific fields. *Journal of Mathematical Sociology* 15 (3–4): 207–246.

Carroll, G., and J. R. Harrison. 1992. Chance and rationality in organizational evolution, unpublished manuscript.

Carroll, J. S. 1995. Incident reviews in high-hazard organizations: Sense making and learning under ambiguity and accountability. *Industrial and Environmental Crisis Quarterly* 9: 175–197.

Carroll, J. S., M. H. Bazerman, and R. Maury. 1988. Negotiator cognitions: A descriptive approach to negotiators' understanding of their opponents. *Organizational Behavior and Human Decision Processes* 41: 352–370.

Carroll, J. S., C. Perin, and A. A. Marcus. 1992. *Organization and management of nuclear power plants for safe performance: 1992 Annual Report*. Cambridge, Mass.: MIT Energy Lab.

Carroll, R. 1987. *Cultural misunderstandings: The French-American experience*. Trans. Carol Volk. Chicago: University of Chicago Press.

Castro, J. 1993. Disposable workers. *Time* (March 29): 43–47.

Chatterjee, K., and W. Samuelson. 1983. Bargaining under incomplete information. *Operations Research* 31: 835–851.

Clark, M. S., and J. Mills. 1979. Interpersonal attraction in exchange and communal relationships. *Journal of Personality and Social Psychology* 37: 12–24.

Coase, R. H. 1937. The nature of the firm. *Economica* 4: 386–405.

——. 1959. The Federal Communications Commission. *Journal of Law and Economics* 2 (October): 1–40.

——. 1960. The problem of social cost. *Journal of Law and Economics* 3 (October): 1–44.

——. 1964. The regulated industries: Discussion. *American Economic Review* 54 (May): 194–197.

——. 1972. Industrial organization: A proposal for research. In V. Fuchs, ed., *Policy issues and research opportunities in industrial organization*, 59–73. New York: National Bureau of Economic Research.

——. 1984. The new institutional economics. *Journal of Institutional and Theoretical Economics* 140 (March): 229–231.

Cohen, M., and R. Axelrod. 1984. Coping with complexity: The adaptive value of changing utility. *American Economic Review* 74: 30–42.

Cohen, M., and J. March. 1974. *Leadership and ambiguity: The American college president*. New York: McGraw-Hill.

Cohen, M., J. G. March, and J. P. Olsen. 1972. A garbage can model of organizational choice. *Administrative Science Quarterly*, 17: 1–25.

Coleman, J. S. 1982. *The asymmetric society*. Syracuse, N.Y.: Syracuse University Press.

———. 1990. *The foundations of social theory*. Cambridge, Mass.: Harvard University Press, Belknap Press.

Colson, E. 1979. In good years and in bad: Food strategies of self-reliant societies. *Journal of Anthropological Research* 35: 18–29.

Commons, J. R. 1924. *Legal foundations of capitalism*. New York: Macmillan.

———. 1934. *Institutional economics*. Madison: University of Wisconsin Press.

Conlon, E., and J. McLean Parks. 1990. The evolution of compensation agreements in principal/agent dyads: An experiment. *Academy of Management Journal* 33: 603–622.

Cooper, R., D. DeJorge, R. Forsythe, and T. Ross. 1990. Communication in the battle of the sexes game. *Rand Journal of Economics* 21.

———. 1994. Forward induction in the battle of the sexes game. *American Economic Review*.

Cosmides, L., and J. Tooby. 1987. Evolutionary psychology and the generation of culture, Part II: Case study: A computational theory of social exchange. *Ethology and Sociobiology* 10: 51–97.

Coughlin, R. 1992. Interdisciplinary nature of socio-economics, unpublished manuscript.

Cropanzano, R. and M. A. Konovsky. 1995. Resolving the justice dilemma by improving the outcomes: The case of employee drug screening. *Journal of Business and Psychology* 10: 221–243.

Crawford, V. P. 1982. Compulsory arbitration, arbitral risk, and negotiated settlements: A case study in bargaining under imperfect information. *Review of Economic Studies* 155: 69–82.

Crawford, V. P., and J. Sobel. 1982. Strategic information transmission. *Econometrica* 50: 1431–1451.

Crocker, K., and K. Reynolds. 1993. The efficiency of incomplete contracts: An empirical analysis of Air Force engine procurement. *Rand Journal of Economics* (Spring): 126–146.

Crozier, M. 1964. *The bureaucratic phenomenon*. Chicago: University of Chicago Press.

Cummings, L., and R. Anton. 1990. The logical and appreciative dimensions of accountability. In S. Srivastra and D. Cooperider, eds., *The functioning of executive appreciation*. San Francisco: Jossey-Bass.

Cyert, R. M., and J. G. March. 1963. *A behavioral theory of the firm*. Englewood Cliffs, N.J.: Prentice-Hall.

Dahrendorf, R. 1970. On the origin of inequality among men. In Laumann, Siegel and Hodge, eds., *The logic of social hierarchies*, 3–29. Chicago: Markam.

Daly, J. P., and P. D. Geyer. 1993. Good times, bad times: Procedural fairness and organizational commitment under conditions of growth and decline. Paper presented at the Academy of Management Conference, Atlanta.

Dasgupta, P. 1988. Trust as a commodity. In D. Gambetta, ed., *Trust: Making and breaking cooperative relations*, 47–72. New York: Blackwell,.

David, P. 1985. Clio in the economics of QWERTY. *American Economic Review* 75 (May): 332–337.

———. 1986. Understanding the economics of QWERTY: The necessity of history. In W. N. Parker, ed., *Economic History and the Modern Economist*. New York: Basil Blackwell.

——. 1992. Heroes, herds, and hypteresis in technological history. *Industrial and Corporate Change* 1: 129–180.

Davis, G. F., and W. W. Powell. 1992. Organization-environment relations. In M. Dunnette, ed., *Handbook of industrial and organizational psychology*, 2d ed., 3: 315–375. New York: Consulting Psychologists Press.

Davis, L. E., and D. C. North. 1971. *Institutional change and American economic growth.* Cambridge, Eng.: Cambridge University Press.

Dawes, R. M. 1988. *Rational choice in an uncertain world.* Orlando: Harcourt Brace Jovanovich.

Deaton, A. 1987. Life-cycle models of consumption: Is the evidence consistent with the theory? In T. F. Bewley, ed., *Advances in econometrics: Fifth world congress*, Vol 2. New York: Cambridge University Press.

DeBondt, W. F. M., and R. Thaler. 1985. Does the stock market overreact? *Journal of Finance* 40: 793–805.

Demsetz, H. 1967. Toward a theory of property rights. *American Economic Review* 57 (May): 347–359.

——. 1969. Information and efficiency: Another viewpoint. *Journal of Law and Economics* 12 (April): 1–22.

DePaulo, B. 1993. Nonverbal behavior and self presentation.

DePaulo, B., J. I. Stone, and G. D. Lassiter. 1985. Telling ingratiating lies: Effects of target sex and target attractiveness on verbal and nonverbal deceptive success. *Journal of Personality and Social Psychology* 48: 1191–1203.

Diehl, E., and J. D. Sterman. 1995. Effects of feedback structure on dynamic decision making. *Organizational Behavior and Human Decision Processes* 62 (2): 198–215.

Diesenhouse, S. 1993. In a shaky economy, even professionals are 'temps'. *New York Times* (May 16): 5.

DiMaggio, P., and W. Powell. 1983. The iron cage revisited: Institutional isomorphism and collective rationality in organizational fields. *American Sociological Review* 48: 147–160. (Reprinted as Chapter 3 in Powell and DiMaggio 1991.)

——. 1991. Introduction. Chapter 1 in W. Powell and P. DiMaggio, eds., *The new institutionalism in organizational analysis*, 1–38. Chicago: University of Chicago Press.

Dixit, A. 1980. The role of investment in entry deterrence. *Economic Journal* 90 (March): 95–106.

Dixit, A., and B. Nalebuf. 1991. *Thinking strategically: The competitive edge in business, politics, and everyday life.* New York: Norton.

Donaldson, L. 1990. The ethereal hand: Organizational economics and management theory. *Academy of Management Review* 15: 369–381.

Dore, R. 1983. Goodwill and the spirit of market capitalism. *British Journal of Sociology* 34 (December): 459–482.

Doreian, P. 1980. Linear models with spatially distributed data: Spatial disturbances or spatial effects? *Sociological Methods and Research* 9: 29–66.

Eccles, R. 1981. The quasifirm in the construction industry. *Journal of Economic Behavior and Organization* 2: 335–357.

Edgeworth. 1881. *Mathematical Psychics: An essay on the application of mathematics to the moral sciences.* London: Kegan Paul; New York: A. M. Kelley, 1967.

Edwards, W. 1954. The theory of decision making. *Psychological Bulletin* 51: 380–417.

Ehrenberg, R., and M. L. Bognanno. 1990. Do tournaments have incentive effects? *Journal of Political Economy* 98: 1307–1324.

Eisenhardt, K. 1989. Agency theory: An assessment and review. *Academy of Management Review* 14: 57–74.

Ekman, P., and W. V. Friesen. 1974. Detecting deception from the body or face. *Journal of Personality and Social Psychology* 29: 288–298.

Ekman, P., W. V. Friesen, and K. Scherer. 1976. Body movements and voice pitch in deceptive interaction. *Semiotics* 16: 23–27.

Ellsberg, D. 1961. Risk, ambiguity, and the savage axioms. *Quarterly Journal of Economics* 75: 643–669.

Emerson, R. 1962. Power-dependence relations. *American Sociological Review* 27: 31–41.

——. 1972. Exchange theory, part I: Psychological basis for social exchange. In J. Berger, M. Zelditch and B. Anderson, eds., *Sociological Theories in Progress*, 38–57. Boston: Houghton Mifflin.

——. 1981. Social exchange theory. In M. Rosenberg and R. Turner, eds., *Social Psychology: Sociological Perspectives*, 30–65. New York: Basic Books, Inc.

Enz, C. A. 1988. The role of value congruity in intraorganizational power. *Administrative Science Quarterly* 33: 284–304.

Etzioni, A. 1961. *A comparative analysis of complex organizations.* New York: Free Press.

——. 1988. *The moral dimension: Toward a new economics.* New York: Free Press.

Faludi, S. 1990. Safeway LBO yields vast profits but exacts a heavy human toll. *Wall Street Journal* (May 16): 1 ff.

Fama, E. 1980. Agency problems and the theory of the firm. *Journal of Political Economy* 88: 288–307.

Farnsworth, E. A. 1968. Disputes over omissions in contracts. *Columbia Law Review* 68 (May): 860–891.

——. 1982. *Contracts.* Boston: Little, Brown.

Farrell, J., and R. Gibbons. 1989. Cheap talk can matter in bargaining. *Journal of Economic Theory* 48: 221–237.

——. 1995. Cheap talk about specific investment. *Journal of Law, Economics, and Organization* 11: 313–334.

Feldman, D. C. 1981. The multiple socialization of organization members. *Academy of Management Review* 6: 309–318.

Feldman, M., and J. March. 1981. Information in organizations as signal and symbol. *Administrative Science Quarterly* 26: 171–186.

Fernandez, R., and J. Glazer. 1991. Striking for a bargain between two completely informed agents. *American Economic Review* 81: 240–252.

Festinger, L. 1954. A theory of social comparison processes. *Human Relations* 7: 117–140.

Flynn, V. 1992. The evolution of Du Pont's corporate maintenance leadership team. DuPont Publications.

Foa, U., and E. Foa. 1975. *Resource theory of social exchange.* Morristown, N.J.: General Learning Press.

Folger, R., and R. J. Bies. 1989. Managerial responsibilities and procedural justice. *Employee Responsibilities and Rights Journal* 2: 79–90.

Forrester, J. W. 1961. *Industrial Dynamics.* Cambridge: MIT Press.

——. 1971. Counterintuitive behavior of social systems. *Technology Review* 73 (3): 52–68.

Forsythe, R., J. L. Horowitz, N. E. Savin, and M. Sefton. 1994. Fairness in simple bargaining experiments. *Games and Economic Behavior* 6:347–369.

Frank, R. 1985. *Choosing the right pond: Human behavior and the quest for status.* New York: Oxford University Press.

———. 1988. *Passions within reason: The strategic role of the emotions.* New York: W. W. Norton.

———. 1992. Melding sociology and economics. *Journal of Economic Literature* 30 (March): 147–170.

Freedman, A. 1986. Jobs: Insecurity at all levels. *Across the Board.* January, 4–5.

Friedkin, N. E., and E. C. Johnson. 1990. Social influence and opinions. *Journal of Mathematical Sociology* 15: 193–205.

Friedland, R., and R. Alford. 1991. Bringing society back in: Symbols, practices, and institutional contradictions. In W. Powell and P. DiMaggio, eds., *The new institutionalism in organizational analysis,* 232–266. Chicago: University of Chicago Press.

Friedlander, F. 1983. Patterns of individual and organizational learning. In S. Srivastva and Associates, eds., *The Executive Mind,* 192–215. San Francisco: Jossey-Bass.

Friedman, M. 1953. *Essays in positive economics.* Chicago: University of Chicago Press.

Fudenberg, D., and E. Maskin. 1986. The folk theorem in repeated games with discounting or with incomplete information. *Econometrica* 54: 532–54.

Fuller, L. 1978. The forms and limits of adjudication. *Harvard Law Review* 93: 353–409.

Fuller, L. L. 1981. Human interaction and the law. In K. I. Winston, ed., *The principles of social order: Selected Essays of Lon L. Fuller,* 212–246. Durham, N.C.: Duke University Press.

Funke, J. 1991. Solving complex problems: Exploration and control of complex systems. In R. Sternberg and P. Frensch, eds., *Complex problem solving: Principles and mechanisms.* Hillsdale, N.J.: Lawrence Erlbaum Associates.

Furubotn, E., and S. Pejovich. 1974. *The economics of property rights.* Cambridge, Mass.: Ballinger.

Furubotn, E., and R. Richter. 1991. *The new institutional economics.* College Station: Texas A&M University Press.

Gargiulo, M. 1993. Two-step leverage: Managing constraint in organizational politics. *Administrative Science Quarterly* 38: 1–19.

Geertz, C. 1963. *Peddlers and princes: Social change and economic modernization in two Indonesian towns.* Chicago: University of Chicago Press.

Gentner, D., and A. L. Stevens, eds. 1983. *Mental models.* Hillsdale, N.J.: Erlbaum.

Gergen, K. J., P. Ellsworth, C. Maslach, and M. Seipel. 1975. Obligation, donor resources, and reactions to aid in three cultures. *Journal of Personality and Social Psychology* 31: 390–400.

Gerlach, M. 1992. *Alliance capitalism.* Berkeley: University of California Press.

Gibbons, R. 1992. Game theory for applied economists. Princeton: Princeton University Press.

———. 1997a. Incentives and careers in organizations. In D. Kreps and K. Wallis, eds., *Advances in economic theory and econometrics,* Vol. 3, Chap. 1. New York: Cambridge University Press.

———. 1997b. Taking Coase seriously. *Administration Science Quarterly.*

Gilligan, C. 1982. *In a different voice: Psychological theory and women's development.* Cambridge: Harvard University Press.

Gilligan, C., J. V. Ward, and J. M. Taylor. 1988. *Mapping the moral domain.* Cambridge: Harvard University Press.

Gilovich, T. 1991. *How we know what isn't so: The fallibility of reason in everyday life.* New York: Free Press.

Gode, D. K., and S. Sunder. 1993. Allocative efficiency of markets with zero-intelligence traders: Market as a partial substitue for individual rationality. *Journal of Political Economy* 101: 119–137.

Goffman, E. 1959. *The presentation of self in everyday life.* Garden City, New York: Doubleday.

Goranson, R. E., and L. Berkowitz. 1966. Reciprocity and responsibility reactions to prior help. *Journal of Personality and Social Psychology* 3: 227–232.

Gouldner, A. W. 1954. *Industrial bureaucracy.* Glencoe, Ill.: Free Press.

———. 1960. The norm of reciprocity: A preliminary statement. *American Sociological Review* 25: 161–179.

Graham, J. 1991. An essay on organizational citizenship behavior. *Employee Responsibilities and Rights Journal* 4: 249–270.

Graham, J., and D. Organ. 1993. Commitment and the covenantal organization. *Journal of Management Issues* 5: 483–502.

Granovetter, M. 1985. Economic action and social structure: The problem of embeddedness. *American Journal of Sociology* 91 (November): 481–501.

———. 1988. The sociological and economic approaches to labor market analysis. In G. Farkas and P. England, eds., *Industries, Firms, and Jobs*, 187–218. New York: Plenum.

———. 1990. The old and the new economic sociology: A history and an agenda. In R. Friedland and A. F. Robertson, eds., *Beyond the marketplace.* New York: Aldine.

Greenberg, J. 1994. Using socially fair treatment to promote acceptance of a work site smoking ban. *Journal of Applied Psychology* 79: 288–297.

Greenberg, M. S., and D. M. Frisch. 1972. Effects of intentionality on willingness to reciprocate a favor. *Journal of Experimental Social Psychology* 8: 99–111.

Greenhalgh, L., and D. Chapman. 1993. *Interdependence in joint decision making.* Presented at the Academy of Management Meetings, Atlanta.

Greenhalgh, L., and Z. Rosenblatt. 1984. Job insecurity: Toward conceptual clarity. *Academy of Management Review* 9: 438–448.

Grief, A., P. Milgrom, and B. Weingast. 1994. Coordination, commitment, and enforcement: The case of the merchant guild. *Journal of Political Economy* 102: 745–776.

Gross, N., W. Mason, and A. W. McEachern. 1958. *Explorations in role analysis.* New York: Wiley.

Grossekettler, H. 1989. On designing an economic order: The contributions of the Freiburg School. In Donald Walker, ed. *Perspectives on the history of economic thought*, 2: 38–84. Aldershot, Eng.: Edward Elgar.

Grossman, S., and O. Hart. 1986. The costs and benefits of ownership: A theory of vertical and lateral integration. *Journal of Political Economy* 94: 691–719.

Güth, W., R. Schmittbergher, and B. Schwarze. 1982. An experimental analysis of ultimatum bargaining. *Journal of Economic Behavior and Organization* 3: 367–388.

Guzzo, R. A., G. L. Nelson, and K. A. Noonan. 1992. Commitment and employer involvement in employees' nonwork lives. In S. Zedeck, ed., *Work in families and organizations*: 236–281. San Francisco: Jossey-Bass.

Hall, D. T., and J. Richter. 1990. Career gridlock: Baby boomers hit the wall. *Academy of Management Executive* 4: 7–22.

Halpern, J. J. 1992. the effect of friendship on bargaining: Experimental studies of personal business transactions. In J. L. Wall and L. R. Jauch, eds., *Best Paper Proceedings*, 64–68. Academy of Management.

———. 1994. The effect of friendship on personal business decisions. *Journal of Conflict Resolution* 38 (4): 647–664.

———. 1997. The transaction index: A method for standardizing comparisons of transaction characteristics across different contexts. *Group Decision and Negotiation* 6 (6):557–572.

Hamilton, G., and N. Biggart. 1988. Market, culture, and authority. *American Journal of Sociology* (Supplement) 94: S52–S94.

Hansmann, H. 1988. The ownership of the firm. *Journal of Law, Economics, and Organization* 4: 267–303.

Harding, S. 1987. *Feminism and methodology*. Bloomington: Indiana University Press.

Harding, S., and J. O'Barr. 1987. *Sex and scientific inquiry*. Chicago: University of Chicago Press.

Hart, O. 1990. An economist's perspective on the theory of the firm. In Oliver Williamson, ed., *Organization theory*, 154–171. New York: Oxford University Press.

Hayek, F. 1945. The use of knowledge in society. *American Economic Review* 35 (September): 519–530.

Heath, C., M. Knez, and C. F. Camerer. 1993. The strategic management of the entitlement process in the employment relationship. *Strategic Management Journal* 14: 75–93.

Hechter, M. 1987. *Principles of group solidarity*. Berkeley: University of California Press.

Heide, J., and G. John. 1988. The role of dependence balancing in safeguarding transaction-specific assets in conventional channels. *Journal of Marketing* 52 (January): 20–35.

Held, V. 1990. Mothering versus contract. In J. J. Mansbridge, ed., *Beyond self-interest*, 287–304. Chicago: University of Chicago Press.

Helper, S., and D. I. Levine. 1992. Long-term supplier relations and product-market structure. *Journal of Law, Economics, and Organization* 8 (October): 561–581.

Hickson, D. J., C. R. Hinings, C. A. Lee, R. H. Schneck, and J. M. Pennings. 1971. A strategic contingencies theory of intraorganizational power. *Administrative Science Quarterly* 16: 216–229.

Hinds, M. 1990. Issues in the introduction of market forces in Eastern European socialist economies. The World Bank. Report No. IDP-0057.

Hinings, C. R., D. J. Hickson, J. M. Pennings, and R. H. Schneck. 1974. Structural conditions of intraorganizational power. *Administrative Science Quarterly* 23: 22–44.

Hirsch, P. 1990. Rational choice models for sociology: Pro and con. *Rationality and Society* 2: 137–141.

Hirschman, A. L. 1970. *Exit, voice, and loyalty*. Cambridge: Harvard University Press.

Hirschman, A. O. 1986. *Rival views of market society*. New York: Viking Press.

Ho, T., C. F. Camerer, and K. Weigelt. In press. Iterated dominance and iterated best-response in experimental p-beauty contests. *American Economic Review*.

Hofstaeder, D. 1983. Metamagical themas. *Scientific American* 248: 14–28.

Hogan, R., and N. Emler. 1980. Retributive justice. In M. Lerner and S. Lerner, eds., *The justice motive in social behavior: adapting to times of scarcity and change*, 125–143. New York: Plenum.

Hogarth, R. M. 1980. *Judgement and choice: The psychology of decision*. Chichster, Eng.: John Wiley.

Holmstrom, B. 1979. Moral hazard and observability. *Bell Journal of Economics* 10: 74–91.

——. 1982. Managerial incentive problems—A dynamic perspective. In *Essays in economics and management in honor of Lars Wahlbeck*. Helsinki: Swedish School of Economics.

Holmstrom, B., and P. Milgrom. 1991. Multitask principal-agent analyses: Incentive contracts, asset ownership, and job design. *Journal of Law, Economics, and Organization* 7: 24–52.

Homans, G. 1961. *Social behavior: Its elementary forms.* New York: Harcourt, Brace, and World.

Horvat, B. 1991. Review of *The road to a free economy* by Janos Kornai. *Journal of Economic Behavior and Organization* 15 (May): 408–410.

Hovenkamp, H. 1988. Telephone conversation with Dr. Herbert Hovenkamp, Law School, University of Iowa, November, 1988.

Huseman, R., J. Hatfield, and E. Miles. 1987. A new perspective on equity theory: The equity sensitivity construct. *Academy of Management Journal* 12: 222–234.

Hushbeck, J., V. Gottlick, and E. Shaffer. 1991. Ensuring pension coverage and portability for contingent workers. Proceedings from the Conference on the Changing Workforce, Washington, D.C.

Hutchison, T. 1984. Institutional economics old and new. *Journal of Institutional and Theoretical Economics* 140 (March): 20–29.

Ibarra, H., and S. B. Andrews. 1993. Power, social influence, and sense making: Effects of network centrality and proximity on employee perceptions. *Administrative Science Quarterly* 38: 277–303.

Institute for Nuclear Power Operations (INPO). 1985. *Japan's nuclear power operations: A U.S. nuclear utility report.* Atlanta: INPO.

International Atomic Energy Agency (IAEA). 1991. *Safety culture.* A report by the International Nuclear Safety Advisory Group. Vienna: International Atomic Energy Agency. Safety Series No. 75–INSAG-4.

Isaacs, W., and P. Senge. 1992. Overcoming limits to learning in computer-based learning environments. *European Journal of Operational Research* 59 (1): 183–196.

Iwanek, M. 1991. Issues of institutions transformations, and ownership changes in Poland. *Journal of Institutional and Theoretical Economics.*

Jencks, C. 1990. Varieties of altruism. In J. J. Mansbridge, ed., *Beyond self-interest,* 54–67. Chicago: University of Chicago Press.

Jensen, M. 1983. Organization theory and methodology. *Accounting Review* 50 (April): 319–339.

———. 1989. Eclipse of the public corporation. *Harvard Business Review* September–October: 61–74.

———. 1993. The modern industrial revolution, exit, and the failure of internal control systems. *Journal of Finance* 48 (May): 831–880.

Jensen, M., and W. Meckling. 1976. Theory of the firm: Managerial behavior, agency costs, and ownership structure. *Journal of Financial Economics* 3: 305–360.

Joskow, P. L. 1985. Vertical integration and long-term contracts. *Journal of Law, Economics, and Organization* 1 (Spring): 33–80.

———. 1988. Asset specificity and the structure of vertical relationships: Empirical evidence. *Journal of Law, Economics, and Organization* 4 (Spring): 95–117.

Jungermann, H., and M. Thuring. 1988. The labyrinth of experts' minds: Some reasoning strategies and their pitfalls. *Annals of Operations Research* 16: 117–130.

Kahn, C., and G. Huberman. 1988. Two-sided uncertainty and 'up-or-out' contracts. *Journal of Labor Economics* 6: 423–44.

Kahneman, D., J. Knetsch, and R. Thaler. 1986a. Fairness and the assumptions of economics. *Journal of Organizational Behavior* 59 (4): s285–s300.

———. 1986b. Fairness as a constraint on profit seeking: Entitlements in the market. *American Economic Review* 76: 728–741.

———. 1990. Experimental tests of the endowment effect and the Coase Theorem. *Journal of Political Economy* 98: 1325–1348.

Kahneman, D., and D. Lovallo. 1993. Timid choices and bold forecasts: A cognitive perspective on risk taking. *Management Science* 39: 17–31.

Kahneman, D., and D. T. Miller. 1986. Norm theory: Comparing reality to its alternatives. *Psychological Review* 93: 136–153.

Kahneman, D., and A. Tversky. 1979. Prospect theory: An analysis of decision under risk. *Econometrica* 47: 263–291.

———. 1993. Conflict resolution: A cognitive perspective. In K. Arrow, R. Mnookin, L. Ross, A. Tversky, and R. Wilson, eds., *Barriers to conflict resolution*. New York: Norton.

———. 1996. On the reality of cognitive illusions: A reply to Gigerenzer's critique. *Psychological Review*.

Kaplan, S. 1989. The effects of management buyouts on operations and value. *Journal of Financial Economics* 24: 217–154.

Kaplan, S., and J. Stein. 1993. The evolution of buyout pricing and financial structure in the 1980s. *Quarterly Journal of Economics* 108 (May): 313–357.

Keeley, M. 1988. *A social contract theory of organizations*. Notre Dame, Ind.: University of Notre Dame Press.

Kerr, S. 1975. On the folly of rewarding A, while hoping for B. *Academy of Management Journal* 18: 769–783.

Keysar, B. 1992. *The illusory transparency of intention: Linguistic perspective taking in text*. University of Chicago working paper.

Keysar, B., L. E. Ginzel, and M. H. Bazerman. (1995). States of affairs and states of mind: The effect of knowledge of beliefs. *Organizational Behavior and Human Division Processes*, 64 (3): 283–293.

Kidder, D. 1993. Why aren't all jobs temporary? Proceedings, The First Organizational Studies Doctoral Students conference, Albany, N.Y., October.

Kilborn, P.T. 1993. New jobs lack the old security in a time of "disposable workers." *New York Times*, March 15, A1, A15.

Kim, D. H. 1989. Learning laboratories: Designing a reflective learning environment. In P. Milling and E. Zahn, eds., *Computer-based management of complex systems*, 327–334. Berlin: Springer Verlag.

Klein, B. 1992. Contracts and incentives: The role of contract terms in assuring performance. In L. Werin and H. Wijkander, eds., *Contract economics*. Oxford: Blackwell.

Klein, B., R. Crawford, and A. Alchian. 1978. Vertical integration, appropriable rents and the competitive contracting process. *Journal of Law and Economics* 21 (October): 297–326.

Klein, B., and K. Leffler. 1981. The role of market forces in assuring contractual performance. *Journal of Political Economy* 89: 615–641.

Koopmans, T. 1957. *Three essays on the state of economic science*. New York: McGraw-Hill.

Kornai, J. 1990. The affinity between ownership forms and coordination mechanisms: The common experience of reform in socialist countries. *Journal of Economic Perspectives* 4 (Summer): 131–147.

Krackhardt, D. 1988. Predicting with networks: A multple regression approach to analyzing dyadic data. *Social Networks* 10: 359–381.

Kramer, R. M. 1990. The effects of resource scarcity on group conflict and cooperation. In E. J. Lawler, B. M. Markovsky, C. Ridgeway, and H. A. Walker, eds. *Advances in group process* 7: 151–177.

Kramer, R. M., and M. B. Brewer. 1984. Effects of group identity on resource use in a simulated commons dilemma. *Journal of Personality and Social Psychology* 46: 1044–1057.

Kramer, R. M., P. Pommerenke, and E. Newton. 1993. The social context of negotiations:

Effects of social identity and accountability on negotiation decision making. *Journal of Conflict Resolution* 37 (4): 633–654.

Krauss, R. M., V. Geller, and C. Olson. 1976. September. Modalities and cues in the detection of deception. In Annual Meetings of American Psychological Association.

Kraut, R. E. 1978. Verbal and nonverbal cues in the perception of lying. *Journal of Personality and Social Psychology* 36: 380–391.

Kreps, D. M. 1990. Corporate culture and economic theory. In J. Alt and K. Shepsle, eds., *Perspectives on positive political economy*, 90–143. New York: Cambridge University Press.

——. 1992. (How) can game theory lead to a unified theory of organization? Unpublished manuscript. Stanford University.

Kreps, D. M., P. Milgrom, J. Roberts, and R. Wilson. 1982. Rational cooperation in the finitely repeated prisoners' dilemma. *Journal of Economic Theory* 27: 245–252.

Laibson, D. 1997. Golden eggs and hyperbolic discounting. *Quarterly Journal of Economics*, forthcoming.

Lange, O. 1938. On the theory of economic socialism. In B. Lippincott, ed., *On the Economic Theory of Socialism*, 55–143. Minneapolis: University of Minnesota Press.

Lanir, Z., and Z. Shapira. 1984. Analysis of decisions concerning the defense of rear areas in Israel: A case study in defense decision making. In Z. Lanir, ed., *Israel's security planning in the 1980s*. New York: Praeger.

Layard, R., and G. Psacharopoulos. 1974. The screening hypothesis and the returns to education. *Journal of Political Economy* 82: 985–98.

Lazear, E. P., and S. Rosen. 1981. Rank-order tournaments as optimum labor contracts. *Journal of Political Economy* 89 (1): 841–864.

Leatherwood, M., and L. Spector. 1991. Enforcements, inducements, expected utility and employee misconduct. *Journal of Management* 17: 553–570.

Ledyard, J. 1995. Public goods experiments. In J. Kegel and A. Roth, eds., *Handbook of Experimental Economics*. Princeton: Princeton University Press.

Leventhal, G. S., J. Karuza, and W. R. Fry. 1980. Beyond fairness: A theory of allocation preferences. In G. Mikula, ed., *Justice and Social Interaction*, 167–218. New York: Springer-Verlag.

Levinson, H. 1962. *Men, management, and mental health.* Cambridge, Mass.: Harvard University Press.

Levitt, B., and J. G. March. 1988. Organizational learning. *Annual Review of Sociology* 14: 319–340.

Lewis, T. 1983. Preemption, divestiture, and forward contracting in a market dominated by a single firm. *American Economic Review* 73: 1092–1101.

Liebowitz, S. J., and S. Margolis. 1990. The fable of the keys. *Journal of Law and Economics* 33 (April): 1–26.

——. 1992. Path dependency, lock-in, and history. Unpublished manuscript.

Lincoln, J. R. 1990. Japanese organization and organization theory. *Research in Organizational Behavior* 12: 255–294.

Lincoln, J. R., and J. Miller. 1979. Work and friendship ties in organizations: A comparative analysis of relational networks. *Administrative Science Quarterly* 24: 181–199.

Lind, E., and T. Tyler. 1988. *The social psychology of procedural justice.* New York: Plenum.

Litchfield, E. 1956. Notes on a general theory of administration. *Administrative Science Quarterly* 1: 3–29.

Llewellyn, K. N. 1931. What price contract? An essay in perspective. *Yale Law Journal*, 40 (May): 704–751.

Loewenstein, G., and D. Prelec. 1992. Anomalies in intertemporal choice: Evidence and interpretation. *Quarterly Journal of Economics* 107: 573–97.

Loewenstein, G., S. Blount, and M. H. Bazerman. The inconsistent evaluation of comparative payoffs in labor supply and bargaining. *Journal of Economic Behavior and Organization*, in press.

Loewenstein, G., L. Thompson, and M. H. Bazerman. 1989. Social utility and decision making in interpersonal contexts. *Journal of Personality and Social Psychology* 57: 426–441.

Loomes, G., and R. Sugden. 1987. Some implications of a more general form of regret theory. *Journal of Economic Theory* 41: 270–287.

Luce, R. D., and H. Raiffa. 1957. *Games and decisions.* New York: Wiley.

Luhman, N. 1979. *Trust and power.* New York: John Wiley.

Macaulay, S. 1963. Non-contractual relations in business: A preliminary study. *American Sociological Review*, 28: 55–67.

Machiavelli, N. 1952. *The prince.* New York: New American Library.

Macneil, I. R. 1974. The many futures of contracts. *Southern California Law Review* 47 (May): 691–816.

———. 1978. Contracts: Adjustments of long-term economic relations under classical, neoclassical, and relational contract law. *Northwestern University Law Review* 72: 854–906.

———. 1985. Relational contract: What we do and do not know. *Wisconsin Law Review*, 483–525.

Magowan, P. A. 1989. The case for LBOs: The Safeway experience. *California Management Review* 32 (Fall): 9–18.

Mainiero, L. A. 1986. Coping with powerlessness: The relationship of gender and job dependency to empowerment-strategy usage. *Administrative Science Quarterly* 31: 633–653.

Malinowski, B. 1932. *Crime and custom.* London: Paul, Trench and Trubner.

Mankiw, N. G., J. J. Rotemberg, and L. H. Summers. 1985. Intertemporal substitution in macroeconomics. *Quarterly Journal of Economics*, 225–251.

Mansbridge, J., ed. 1990. *Beyond self-interest: The rise and fall of self-interest in the explanation of political life.* Chicago: University of Chicago Press.

Manski, C. F. 1993a. Adolescent econometricians: How do youth infer the returns to schooling? In C. Clotfelter, and M. Rothschild, eds., *Studies of supply and demand in higher education.* Chicago: University of Chicago Press.

———. 1993b. Identification of endogenous social effects: The reflection problem. *Review of Economic Studies* 60: 531–542.

———. 1995. *Identification problems in the social sciences.* Cambridge: Harvard University Press.

March, J. G. 1978. Bounded rationality, ambiguity, and the engineering of choice. *Bell Journal of Economics* 9: 587–608.

———. 1988. *Decisions and organizations.* Oxford: Basil Blackwell.

———. 1994. *A primer on decision making.* New York: Free Press.

March, J. G., and J. Olson. 1976. Ambiguity and choice in organizations. Bergen, Norway: Universitetsforlaget.

March, J. G., and Z. Shapira. 1982. Behavioral decision theory and organizational decision theory. In D. Braunstein and R. Ungson, eds., *Decision making: An interdisciplinary inquiry.* Boston: Kent.

———. 1987. Managerial perspectives on risk and risk taking. *Management Science* 33: 1404–1418.

——. 1992. Variable risk preferences and the focus of attention. *Psychological Review* 99: 172–183.

March, J. G., and H. A. Simon. 1958. *Organizations*. New York: Wiley.

——. 1993. *Organizations*. 2d ed. Cambridge, Mass.: Blackwell.

Marcus, A. A. 1992. Toward a framework for managerial problem solving at nuclear power plants. Cambridge, Mass.: MIT Sloan School. Unpublished manuscript.

Marschak, J. 1968. Economics of inquiring, communicating, deciding. *American Economic Review* 58 (May): 1–18.

Marschak, J., and R. Radner. 1972. *Economic theory of teams*. New Haven: Yale University Press.

Marsden, P. V. 1981. Introducing influence processes into a system of collective decisions. *American Journal of Sociology* 86: 1203–1235.

Masten, S. 1984. The organization of production: Evidence from the aerospace industry. *Journal of Law and Economics* 27 (October): 403–418.

——. 1992. Transaction costs, mistakes, and performance: Assessing the importance of governance. *Management and Decision Sciences*.

Matthews, R. C. O. 1986. The economics of institutions and the sources of economic growth. *Economic Journal* 96 (December): 903–918.

Mauss, M. 1969. *The gift: Forms and functions of exchange in archaic societies*. London: Cohen and West.

Mayhew, B. H. 1980. Structuralism versus individualism: Part 1, shadow-boxing in the dark. *Social Forces* 59: 335–375.

McCain, R. 1977. On the optimal financial environment for worker cooperatives. *Zeitschrift für Nationalekonomie* 37: 355–384.

McCullough, D. 1992. *Truman*. New York: Simon and Schuster.

McFarlin, D. B., and P. D. Sweeney. 1992. Distributive and procedural justice as predictors of satisfaction with personal and organizational outcomes. *Academy of Management Journal* 35: 626–637.

McGuire, P., M. Granovetter, and M. Schwartz. 1992. The social construction of industry (a book prospectus).

McKelvey, R., and T. Palfrey. 1992. An experimental study of the centipede game. *Econometrica* 60: 803–836.

McLean Parks, J. 1990. *Organization contracts: The effects of contractual specificity and social distance*. Unpublished doctoral dissertation, University of Iowa.

——. 1992. The role of incomplete contracts and their governance in delinquency, inrole, and extra-role behaviors. Symposium paper presented at SIOP meetings, Montreal, Canada, May, 1992.

McLean Parks, J., and E. J. Conlon. 1989. The contract metaphor in organizational sciences. Theory paper presented at the 1989 Academy of Management Meetings, Washington, D.C., O.T. Division.

——. 1991. The effects of social distance and contractual specificity on non-contracted, citizenship behaviors: An experimental test. Paper presented at the 1991 Academy of Management Meetings, Miami.

——. 1995. Compensation contracts: Do the agency theory assumptions predict negotiated agreements? *Academy of Management Journal* 83, 3: 821–838.

McLean Parks, J., and D. Kidder. 1994. Till death us do part . . . : Changing work relationships in the 90s. In C. Cooper and D. Rousseau, eds., *Trends in organizational behavior* 1: 111–136. London: Wiley.

McLean Parks, J., and D. Schmedemann. 1992. Pine River promises: A policy capturing analysis of the legal and organizational properties of employee handbook provisions on job security. Paper presented at the 1992 Academy of Management Meetings, Las Vegas, Nevada.

———. 1994. When promises become contracts: Implied contracts and handbook provisions on job security. *Human Resources Management Journal* 33, 3: 403–423.

McLean Parks, J., and f. l. smith. 1998. Organizational contracting: A 'rational' exchange? In J. J. Halpern and R. N. Stern, eds., *Debating rationality: Nonrational aspects of organizational decision making*. Ithaca: Cornell University Press.

McPherson, J. M., and L. Smith-Lovin. 1987. Homophily in voluntary organizations: Status distance and the composition of face-to-face groups. *American Sociological Review* 52: 370–379.

Meadows, D. L. 1989. Gaming to implement system dynamics models. In P. Milling and E. Zahn, eds., *Computer-based management of complex systems*, 635–640. Berlin: Springer Verlag.

Mechanic, D. 1962. Sources of power of lower participants in complex organizations. *Administrative Science Quarterly* 7: 349–364.

Merton, R. 1936. The unanticipated consequences of purposive social action. *American Sociological Review* 1: 894–904.

———. 1940. Bureaucratic structure and personality. *Social Forces* 18: 560–68.

Messick, D. M. 1991. Equality as a decision heuristic. In B. Mellers, ed., *Psychological issues in distributive justice*.

Messick, D. M., and K. P. Sentis. 1985. Estimating social and nonsocial utility functions from ordinal data. *European Journal of Social Psychology* 15: 389–399.

Messick, D.M., and W. B. Thorngate. 1967. Relative gain maximization in experimental games. *Journal of Experimental Social Psychology* 3: 85–101.

Meyer, J. P., and N. J. Allen. 1984. Testing the "side-bet theory" of organizational commitment: Some methodological considerations. *Journal of Applied Psychology* 69: 372–378.

Meyer, J. P., and B. Rowan. 1977. Institutionalized organizations: Formal structure as myth and ceremony. *American Journal of Sociology* 83: 340–363. (Reprinted as chapter 2 in Powell and DiMaggio 1991.)

Meyer, M. 1979. Organizational structure as signaling. *Pacific Sociological Review* 22: 481–500.

Michels, R. 1962. *Political parties*. Glencoe, Ill.: Free Press.

Mikula, G., and T. Schwinger. 1978. Intermember relations and reward allocation: Theoretical considerations of affects. In H. Brandstatter, H. Davis, and H. Schuler, eds., *Dynamics of group decisions*. Beverly Hills: Sage Publications.

Miles, E., J. Hatfield, and R. Huseman. 1989. The equity sensitivity construct: Potential implications for worker performance. *Journal of Management* 15: 581–588.

Miles, R., and C. Snow. 1992. Causes of failure in network organizations. *California Management Review* 34 (Summer): 53–72.

Milgrom, P., and J. Roberts. 1988. An economic approach to influence activities in organizations. *American Journal of Sociology* 94: S154–S179.

———.1992. *Economics, organization, and management*. Englewood Cliffs, N.J.: Prentice-Hall.

Mischel, W. 1977. The interaction of person and situation. In D. Magnusson and N. Endler, eds., *Personality at the crossroads: Current issues in international psychology*, 333–352, Hillsdale, N.J.: Erlbaum.

Mitchell, W. 1988. The defeat of hierarchy: Gambling as exchange in Sepik society. *American Ethnologist*: 638–667.

Moe, T. 1990. Political institutions: The neglected side of the story: Comment. *Journal of Law, Economics, and Organization* 6 (Special Issue): 213–254.

Mokyr, J. 1990. *The lever of riches*. New York: Oxford University Press.

Montgomery, J. 1994. Revisiting Tally's corner: Mainstream norms, cognitive dissonance, and underclass behavior. *Rationality and Society* 6: 462–488.

Moorman, R. 1991. Relationship between organizational justice and organizational citizenship behaviors: Do fairness perceptions influence employee citizenship? *Journal of Applied Psychology* 76: 845–855.

Morecroft, J. D. W., and J. D. Sterman, eds. 1994. *Modelling for Learning Organizations*. Portland, Ore.: Productivity Press.

Morgan, W. R., and J. Sawyer. 1967. Bargaining, expectations, and the preference for equality over equity. *Journal of Personality and Social Psychology* 6: 139–149.

Mowday, R., L. Porter, and R. Steers. 1982. *Employee-organizational linkages: The psychology of commitment, absenteeism, and turnover*. New York: Academic Press.

Mumby, D. K., and L. L. Putnam. 1992. The politics of emotion: A feminist reading of bounded rationality. *Academy of Management Review* 17: 465–486.

Murnighan, K. 1991. *Dynamics of Bargaining Games*. Englewood Cliffs, N.J.: Prentice-Hall.

——. 1994. Game theory and organizational behavior. In L. L. Cummings and B. M. Staw, eds., *Research in organizational behavior*, 16: 83–123. Greenwich, Conn: JAI Press.

Muscarella, C., and M. R. Vetsuypens. 1990. Efficiency and organizational structure: A study of reverse LBOs. *Journal of Finance* 45: 155–191.

Myerson, R. 1979. Incentive compatibility and the bargaining problem. *Econometrica* 47: 61–73.

——. 1989. Credible negotiation statements and coherent plans. *Journal of Economic Theory* 48: 264–303.

Myerson, R., and M. Satterthwaite. 1983. Efficient mechanisms for bilateral trading. *Journal of Economic Theory* 28: 265–281.

Nader, L., and H. F. Todd, eds. 1978. *The disputing process: Law in ten societies*. New York: Columbia University Press.

Nagel, R. 1994. Unravelling in guessing games: An experimental study. *American Economic Review* 85: 1313–1326.

——. In press. An experimental survey on beauty-contest games. In D. Budescu, I. Erev, and R. Zwick, eds. *Games and human behavior*: Essays in honor of Annon Rappoport.

Neale, M. A. 1984. The effect of negotiation and arbitration cost salience on bargainer behavior: The role of arbitrator and constituency in negotiator judgment. *Organizational Behavior and Human Performance* 34: 97–111.

Neale, M.A., and M. H. Bazerman. 1985a. When will externally set aspiration levels improve negotiator performance? A look at integrative behavior in competitive markets. *Journal of Occupational Behavior* 6: 19–32.

——. 1985b. The effects of framing and negotiator overconfidence on bargainer behavior. *Academy of Management Journal* 28: 34–49.

——. 1991. *Cognition and rationality in negotiation*. New York: Free Press.

Neale, M. A., and G. B. Northcraft. 1986. Experts, amateurs, and refrigerators: Comparing expert and amateur decision making on a novel task. *Organizational Behavior and Human Decision Processes* 38: 305–317.

Nelson, R. R., and S. G. Winter. 1982. *An evolutionary theory of economic change*. Cambridge, Mass.: Harvard University Press.

Newell, A., and H. Simon. 1972. *Human problem solving*. Englewood Cliffs, N.J.: Prentice-Hall.

Nisbett, R., and L. Ross. 1980. *Human inference: Strategies and shortcomings of social judgment*. Englewood Cliffs, N.J.: Prentice Hall.

North, D. 1986. The new institutional economics. *Journal of Institutional and Theoretical Economics* 142: 230–237.

——. 1991. Institutions. *Journal of Economic Perspectives* 5 (Winter): 97–112.

North, D., and B. Weingast. 1989. Constitutions and commitment: The evolution of institutions governing public choice in seventeenth-century England. *Journal of Economic History* 49: 803–832.

Northcraft, G. B., and M. A. Neale. 1987. Expert, amateurs, and real estate: An anchoring-and-adjustment perspective on property pricing decisions. *Organizational Behavior and Human Decision Processes* 39: 228–241.

Ochs, J., and A. E. Roth. 1989. An experimental study of sequential bargaining. *American Economic Review* 79: 355–384.

Olson, M. 1965. *The logic of collective action*. New Haven, Conn.: Yale University Press.

Orbell, J. M., A. J. C. van de Kragt, and R. M. Dawes. 1988. Explaining discussion-induced cooperation. *Journal of Personality and Social Psychology* 54: 811–819.

Organ, D. W. 1988. *Organizational citizenship behavior: The good soldier syndrome*. Lexington, Mass.: Lexington Books.

——. 1990. The motivational basis of organizational citizenship behavior. In L. L. Cummings and B. M. Staw, eds., *Research in organizational behavior* 12: 43–72. Greenwich, Conn.: JAI Press.

Organ, D. W., and M. Konovsky. 1989. Cognitive versus affective determinants of organizational citizenship behavior. *Journal of Applied Psychology* 74: 157–64.

Ouchi, W. 1980. Markets, bureaucracies, and clans. *Administrative Science Quarterly*, 25: 129–140.

Paich, M., and J. D. Sterman. 1992. Boom, bust, and failures to learn in experimental markets. *Management Science* 39 (12): 1439–1458.

Palay, T. 1981. The governance of rail-freight contracts: A comparative perspective. Ph.D. diss. University of Pennsylvania.

——. 1984. Comparative institutional economics: The governance of rail freight contracting. *Journal of Legal Studies* 13 (June): 265–288.

——. 1985. The avoidance of regulatory constraints: The use of informal contracts. *Journal of Law, Economics, and Organization* 1 (Spring).

Perrow, C. 1970. Departmental power and perspective in industrial firms. In M. N. Zald, ed., *Power in organizations*, 59–89. Nashville, Tenn.: Vanderbilt University Press.

——. 1984. *Normal accidents*. New York: Basic Books.

——. 1986. *Complex organizations: A critical essay*. 3d ed., New York: Random House.

——. 1992. Review of the new competition. *Administrative Science Quarterly* 37 (March): 162–166.

Pfeffer, J. 1981. *Power in organizations*. New York: Harper Business.

Pfeffer, J., and J. Baron. 1988. Taking the workers back out: Recent trends in the structuring of employment. In B. M. Staw and L. L. Cummings, eds., *Research in organizational behavior* 10: 257–303. Greenwich, Conn: JAI Press.

Pfeffer, J., and G. R. Salancik. 1978. *The external control of organizations: A resource dependency perspective.* New York: Harper and Row.

Polanyi, M. 1962. *Personal knowledge: Towards a post-critical philosophy.* New York: Harper and Row.

Polivka, A. E., and T. Nardone. 1989. On the definition of "contingent work." *Monthly Labor Review,* December.

Posner, R. 1993. The new institutional economics meets law and economics. *Journal of Institutional and Theoretical Economics* 149 (March).

Post, R. J., and K. E. Goodpaster. 1981. H. J. Heinz Company: The administration of policy. Harvard Business School Case #382–034.

Powell, W. 1990. Neither market nor hierarchy: Network forms of organization. *Research in Organizational Behavior* 12: 295–336.

——. 1991. Expanding the scope of institutional analysis. Chapter 8 in Powell and DiMaggio, *The new institutionalism in organizational analysis.* Chicago: University of Chicago Press.

Powell, W., and P. DiMaggio. 1991. *The new institutionalism in organizational analysis.* Chicago: University of Chicago Press.

Prendergast, C. 1993a. The role of promotion in inducing specific human capital acquisition. *Quarterly Journal of Economics* 108: 523–534.

——. 1993b. A theory of 'yes men.' *American Economic Review* 83: 757–770.

Provan, K. G., J. M. Beyer, and C. Kruytbosch. 1980. Environmental linkages and power in resource-dependence relations between organizations. *Administrative Science Quarterly* 25: 200–225.

Putterman, L. 1984. On some recent explanations of why capital hires labor. *Economic Inquiry* 22: 171–187.

Quiroz, F., J. Auerback, and R. Coles. 1991. Proceedings from the Conference on the Changing Workforce, Washington, D.C.

Rabin, M. 1993. Incorporating fairness into game theory and economics. *American Economic Review* 83 (December): 1281–1302.

Radner, R. 1975. A behavioral model of cost reduction. *Bell Journal of Economics* 6: 196–215.

Radner, R., and A. Schotter. 1989. The sealed-bid mechanism: An experimental study. *Journal of Economic Theory* 48: 179–220.

Rapoport, A., and D. Budescu. 1992. Generation of random series in two-person strictly competitive games. *Journal of Experimental Psychology: General* 121: 352–363.

Rasell, E., P. Connerton, D. Himmelstein, and R. McGarrah. 1991. Guaranteeing health insurance for contingent workers. Proceedings from the Conference on the Changing Workforce, Washington, D.C.

Rasmussen, J. 1979. *On the Structure of knowledge—A morphology of mental models in a man-machine system context.* Tech. Rep. No. Riso-M-2192. Roskilde, Denmark: Riso National Laboratory.

Rasmussen, J. and R. Batstone. 1991. *Toward improved safety control and risk management.* Washington, D.C.: World Bank.

Regan, D. T. 1968. *The effects of a favor and liking on compliance.* Ph.D. diss., Stanford University.

Richardson, G. P. 1991. Feedback thought in social science and systems theory. Philadelphia: University of Pennsylvania.

Richardson, G.P., and A.L. Pugh III. 1981. *Introduction to system dynamics modeling with DYNAMO.* Cambridge, Mass.: MIT.

Robbins, L., ed. 1933. *The common sense of political economy and selected papers on economic theory,* by Philip Wicksteed. London: Routledge.

Robinson, E. A. G. 1934. The problem of management and the size of firms. *Economic Journal* 44 (June): 240–254.

Robinson, S. L., M. S. Kraatz, and D. M. Rousseau. 1994. Changing obligations and the psychological contract: A longitudinal study. *Academy of Management Journal* 37: 137–152.

Robinson, S. L., and D. Rousseau. 1994. Violating the psychological contract: Not the exception but the norm. *Journal of Organizational Behavior* 15: 245–259.

Roethlisberger, F. J., and W. J. Dickson. [1939] 1964. *Management and the worker.* New York: Wiley.

Roth, A. E. 1993. Bargaining experiments. In J. Kagel and A. E. Roth, eds. *Handbook of experimental economics.* Princeton: Princeton University Press.

———. 1994. Bargaining. In J. Kagel and A. E. Roth, eds., *Handbook of experimental economics.* Princeton: Princeton University Press.

Rothschild, M., and J. Stiglitz. 1976. Equilibrium in competitive insurance markets: An essay on the economics of imperfect information. *Quarterly Journal of Economics* 80: 629–649.

Rouse, W. B., and N. W. Morris. 1986. On looking into the black box: Prospects and limits in the search for mental models. *Psychological Bulletin* 100: 349–363.

Rousseau, D. M. 1989. Psychological and implied contracts in organizations. *Employee Rights and Responsibilities Journal* 2: 121–139.

———. 1990. New hire perceptions of their own and their employer's obligations: A study of psychological contracts. *Journal of Organizational Behavior* 11: 389–400.

Rousseau, D. M., and R. Anton. 1988. Fairness and implied contract obligations in termination: A policy capturing study. *Human Performance* 1: 273–289.

———. 1991. Fairness and implied contract obligations in job terminations: The role of contributions, promises, and performance. *Journal of Organizational Behavior* 12: 287–299.

Rousseau, D. M., and K. Aquino. 1993. Fairness and implied contract obligations in job terminations: The role of remedies, social accounts, and procedural justice. *Human Performance* 6: 135–149.

Rousseau, D. M., and J. McLean Parks. 1993. The contracts of individuals and organizations. In L. L. Cummings and B. M. Staw, eds., *Research in organizational behavior* 15: 1–43. Greenwich, Conn.: JAI Press.

Roy, D. 1952. Quota restriction and goldbricking in a machine shop. *American Journal of Sociology* 57: 427–42.

Rubinstein, A. 1991. Comments on the interpretation of game theory. *Econometrica* 59: 909–924.

Sahlins, M. 1972. *Stone age economics.* Chicago: Aldine Atherton.

Salancik, G. R., and J. Pfeffer. 1974. The bases and use of power in organizational decision making: The case of a university. *Administrative Science Quarterly* 19: 453–473.

Samuelson, W. F., and M. H. Bazerman. 1985. Negotiating under the winner's curse. In V. Smith, ed., *Research in experimental economics* 3. Greenwich, Conn.: JAI Press.

Savage, L. 1954. *The foundations of statistics.* New York: John Wiley.

Scharfstein, D., and J. Stein. 1990. Herd behavior and investment. *American Economic Review* 80: 465–477.

Schaubroeck, J., D. R. May, and F. W. Brown. (1994). Procedural justice explanations and employee reactions to economic hardship: A field experiment. *Journal of Applied Psychology* 79: 455–460.

Schein, E. H. 1976. *Organizational psychology.* 2d ed., Englewood Cliffs, N.J.: Prentice- Hall.

———.1985. *Organizational culture and leadership.* San Francisco: Jossey-Bass.

Schelling, T. C. 1960. *The strategy of conflict.* Cambridge: Harvard University Press.

———.1978. *Micromotives and macrobehavior.* New York: Norton.

Scherer, F. M. 1970. *Industrial market structure and economic performance.* Chicago: Rand McNally.

Schmedemann, D., and J. McLean Parks. 1994. Contract formation through employee handbooks: Legal, psychological and empirical analyses. *Wake Forest Law Review* 647–718.

Schmid, A. 1972. Analytical institutional economics. *American Journal of Agricultural Economics* 54: 893–901.

Schottes, A. 1981. *The economic theory of social institutions.* New York: Cambridge University Press.

Schotter, A., K. Weigelt, and C. Wilson. 1994. Presentation effects and choice selection: Experimental results. *Games and Economic Behavior* 16: 445–468.

Schumpeter, J. A. 1947. The creative response in economic history. *Journal of Economic History* 7: 149–159.

Schwartz, A. 1992. Legal contract theories and incomplete contracts. In L. Werin and H. Wijkander, eds., *Contract economics.* Oxford: Blackwell.

Scott, W. R. 1992. Institutions and organizations: Toward a theoretical synthesis. Unpublished manuscript.

Selznick, P. 1949. *TVA and the grass roots.* Berkeley: University of California Press.

Sen, A. K. 1990. Rational fools: A critique of the behavioral foundations of economic theory. First published in H. Harris, ed. *Scientific models and men.* London, Oxford University Press, 1978, 317–44. Reprinted in J. Mansbridge, ed. *Beyond self-interest: The rise and fall of self-interest in the explanation of political life,* 25–43. Chicago: University of Chicago Press.

Senge, P. 1990. *The fifth discipline: The art and practice of the learning organization.* New York: Doubleday.

Senge, P., and J. D. Sterman. 1991. Systems thinking and organizational learning: Acting locally and thinking globally in the organization of the future. In T. Kochan and M. Useem, eds., *Transforming organizations,* 353–370. Oxford: Oxford University Press.

Shafir, E., and A. Tversky. 1992. Thinking through uncertainty: Non-consequential reasoning and choice. *Cognitive Psychology.*

Shanteau, J., and P. Harrison. 1991. The perceived strength of an implied contract: Can it withstand financial temptation? *Organizational Behavior and Human Decision Processes* 49: 1–21.

Shapira, Z. 1995. *Risk taking: A managerial perspective.* New York: Russell Sage Foundation.

———. 1997. Introduction and overview. In Z. Shapira, ed., *Organizational decision making.* New York: Cambridge University Press.

Shapiro, C. 1989. The theory of business strategy. *Rand Journal of Economics* 20 (Spring): 125–137.

Sheard, P. 1989. The main bank system and corporate monitoring in Japan. *Journal of Economic Behavior and Organization* 11 (May): 399–422.

Shefrin, H., and R. H. Thaler. 1988. The behavioral life-cycle hypothesis. *Economic Inquiry* 26: 609–643.

Shelanski, H. 1991. *Empirical research in transaction cost economics: A survey and assessment.* Unpublished manuscript, University of California, Berkeley.

———. 1993. Transfer pricing. Ph.D. diss. University of California, Berkeley.

Shleifer, A., and L. Summers. 1988. Breach of trust in hostile takeovers. In A. Auerbach, ed., *Corporate takeovers: Causes and consequences*, Chicago: University of Chicago Press.

Siegel, S., and L. E. Fouraker. 1960. *Bargaining and group decision making: Experiments in bilateral monopoly*. New York: McGraw-Hill.

Simon, H. A. 1947. *Administrative behavior*. New York: Free Press.

———. 1955. A behavioral model of rational choice. *Quarterly Journal of Economics* 69: 99–118.

———. 1957a. 2d ed. *Administrative behavior*. New York: Macmillan.

———. 1957b. *Models of man*. New York: Wiley.

———. 1978. Rationality as a process and as product of thought. *American Economic Review* 68 (May): 1–16.

———. 1979. Rational decision-making in business organizations. *American Economic Review* 69: 493–513.

———. 1982. Models of bounded rationality. Cambridge: MIT Press.

———. 1983. *Reason in human affairs*. Stanford: Stanford University Press.

———. 1985. Human nature in politics: The dialogue of psychology with political science. *American Political Science Review* 79: 293–304.

———. 1987. Making management decisions: The role of intuition and emotion. *Academy of Management Executive* 2: 57–64.

———. 1990. Bounded rationality. In J. Eatwell, M. Milgate, and P. Newman, eds., *The new Palgrave: A dictionary of economics: Utility and probability*, 15–18. New York: W. W. Norton.

———. 1991. Organizations and markets. *Journal of Economic Perspectives* 5 (Spring): 25–44.

Smith, A. 1776. The wealth of nations. Ed. Edwin Cannon, New York: Modern Library, 1937.

Smith, A. J. 1990. Corporate ownership structure and performance: The case of management buyouts. *Journal of Financial Economics* 27: 143–164.

Smith, C. A., D. W. Organ, and J. P. Near. 1983. Organizational citizenship behavior: Its nature and antecedents. *Journal of Applied Psychology* 68: 653–63.

Smith, V. L. 1994. Economics in the laboratory. *Journal of Economic Perspectives* 8 (Winter): 113–131.

Spence, A. M. 1973. Job market signaling. *Quarterly Journal of Economics* 87: 355–374.

Starbuck, W., and F. J. Milliken. 1988. The Challenger: Fine-tuning the odds until something breaks. *Journal of Management Studies* 25: 319–340.

Staw, B., and J. Ross. 1989. Understanding behavior in escalation situations. *Science* 246: 216–220.

Sterman, J. D. 1988. *People Express management flight simulator*. Simulation Game (software), Briefing Book and Simulator Guide, Available from author, MIT Sloan School of Management, Cambridge, Mass. 02142–1347.

———. 1989a. Misperceptions of feedback in dynamic decision making. *Organizational Behavior and Human Decision Processes* 43 (3): 301–335.

———. 1989b. Modeling managerial behavior: Misperceptions of feedback in a dynamic decision making experiment. *Management Science* 35 (3): 321–339.

———. 1994. Learning in and about complex systems. *System Dynamics Review* 10 (2–3): 291–330.

Sterman, J. D., E. Banaghan, and E. Gorman. 1992. Learning to stitch in time: Building a proactive maintenance culture at E. I. Du Pont de Nemours and Co. Unpublished manuscript. Cambridge: MIT Sloan School of Management.

Stigler, G. J. 1968. *The organization of industry*. Homewood, Ill.: Richard D. Irwin.

Stigler, G., and G. Becker. 1977. De gustibus non est disputandum. *American Economic Review* 67: 76–90.

Stinchcombe, A. L. 1968. *Constructing social theories*. New York: Harcourt, Brace & World.

Straub, P. G., and J. K. Murnighan. 1992. An experimental investigation of ultimatums: Common knowledge, fairness, expectations, and lowest acceptable offers. Mimeo.

Sundaram, A., and J. S. Black. 1992. The environment and internal organization of multinational enterprise. *Academy of Management Review* 17 (October): 729–757.

Sutton, R.I., and A. L. Callahan. 1987. The stigma of bankruptcy: Spoiled organizational image and its management. *Academy of Management Journal* 3: 405–436.

Swedberg, R. 1987. Economic sociology: Past and present. *Current Sociology* 35: 1–221.

———. 1990. *Economics and sociology: On redefining their boundaries*. Princeton: Princeton University Press.

———. 1991. Major traditions of economic sociology. *Annual Review of Sociology* 17: 251–276.

Tajfel, H., and J. Turner. 1979. An integrative theory of intergroup conflicts. In W. G. Austin and S. Worchel, eds. *The social psychology of intergroup relations*, 33–47. Monterey, Calif.: Brooks/Cole.

Tannen, D. 1986. *That's not what I meant*. New York: Ballantine.

Taylor, F. 1916. The principles of scientific management. *Bulletin of the Taylor Society*, (December).

Teece, D. J. 1986. Profiting from technological innovation. *Research Policy* 15 (December): 285–305.

Telser, L. 1980. A theory of self-enforcing agreements. *Journal of Business* 53: 27–44.

Thaler, R. H. 1980. Toward a positive theory of consumer choice. *Journal of Economic Behavior and Organization* 1: 39–60.

———. 1985. Mental accounting and consumer choice. *Marketing Science* 4: 199–214.

———. 1988. The ultimatum game. *Journal of Economic Perspectives* 2: 195–206.

———. 1991. *Quasi rational economics*. New York: Russell Sage Foundation.

Thaler, R. H., and H. M. Shefrin. 1981. An economic theory of self-control. *Journal of Political Economy* 89: 392–410.

Thibaut, J., and H. Kelley. 1959. *Social psychology of groups*. New York: Wiley.

Thibaut, J., and L. Walker. 1975. *Procedural justice: A psychological analysis*. Hillsdale, N.J.: Lawrence Erlbaum Associates.

Thompson, J. D. 1967. *Organizations in action*. New York: McGraw Hill.

Thompson, L. 1990. Negotiation behavior and outcomes: Empirical evidence and theoretical issues. *Psychological Bulletin* 108: 515–532.

Thompson, L., and R. Hastie. 1990. Social perception in negotiation. *Organizational Behavior and Human Decision Processes* 47: 98–123.

Thompson, V. 1976. *Bureaucracy and the modern world*. Morristown, N.J.: General Learning Press.

Trevino, L. 1993. Unpublished data.

Turner, J. C. 1987. *Rediscovering the social group: A self-categorization theory*. Oxford: Basil Blackwell.

Tversky, A. 1975. A critique of expected utility theory: Descriptive and normative considerations. *Erkenntnis* 9: 165–173.

Tversky, A., and D. Kahneman. 1971. The belief in the law of small numbers. *Psychological Bulletin* 76: 105–110.

——. 1974. Judgment under uncertainty: Heuristics and biases. *Science* 185: 1124–1131.

——. 1981. The framing of decisions and the psychology of choice. *Science* 211: 453–458.

——. 1983. Extensional versus intuitive reasoning: The conjunction fallacy in probability judgment. *Psychological Review* 90 (4): 293–315.

——. 1986. Rational choice and the framing of decisions. *Journal of Business* 59: s251–s278.

——. 1991. Loss aversion in riskless choice: A reference-dependent model. *Quarterly Journal of Economics* 106: 1039–1061.

Tyler, T. R., and R. J. Bies. 1990. Beyond formal procedures: The interpersonal context of procedural justice. In J. Carroll, ed., *Applied social psychology and organizational settings*, 77–98. Hillsdale, N.J.: Lawrence Erlbaum Associates.

U.S. Small Business Administration. 1991. *The state of small business: A report to the president*. Washington, D.C.: U.S. Government Printing Office.

Udy, S. H., Jr. 1969. Administrative rationality, social setting, and organizational development. In A. Etzioni, ed., *A sociological reader on complex organizations*, 480–494. New York: Holt Rinehart, & Winston.

Uniform Laws Annotated. Uniform commercial code, volume 1. St. Paul, Minn.: West.

Uzzi, B. 1992. The dynamics of organizational networks: Structural embeddedness and economic behavior. *Dissertation Abstracts International*, 55, 391A, State University of New York at Stony Brook.

Valley, K. L., J. Moag, and M. H. Bazerman. 1993. Avoiding the curse: Relationships and communication in dyadic bargaining. Working paper, Johnson Graduate School of Management, Cornell University.

Van de Ven, A. 1992. The institutional theory of John R. Commons: A review and commentary, unpublished manuscript.

Van Dyne, L., J. Graham, and R. Dienesch. 1994. Organizational citizenship behavior: Construct redefinition, measurement, and validation. *Academy of Management Journal* 37: 765–802.

Velleman, J. D. 1989. *Practical reflection*. Princeton: Princeton University Press.

Von Neumann, J., and O. Morgenstern. 1944. *Theory of games and economic behavior*. Princeton: Princeton University Press.

Wageman, R., and G. Baker. 1997. Incentives and cooperation: The joint effects of task and reward interdependence on group performance. *Journal of Organizational Behavior* 18: 139–158.

Waldrop, M. M. 1992. *Complexity*. New York: Simon & Schuster.

Walzer, M. 1983. *Spheres of justice*. New York: Basic.

Wayne, C., H. Hartmann, and W. Spriggs. 1991. Boosting economic security for contingent workers: Wage parity and unemployment insurance benefits. Proceedings from the Conference on the Changing Workforce, Washington, D.C.

Weick, K. E. 1977. Re-punctuating the problem. In P. S. Goodman and J. M. Pennings, eds. *New perspectives on organizational effectiveness*, 193–225. San Francisco: Jossey- Bass.

——. 1979. *The social psychology of organizing*. Reading, Mass.: Addison-Wesley.

——. 1987. Organizational culture as a source of high reliability. *California Management Review* (Winter): 112–127.

Wiesenfeld, B., and J. Brockner. 1993. Procedural unfairness and the psychology of the contingent worker. Paper presented at the Academy of Management Meetings, August, Atlanta.

———. 1998. Towards a psychology of contingent work. In J. J. Halpern and R. N. Stern, eds., *Debating rationality: Nonrational aspects of organizational decision making.*

Wiesenfeld, B., J. Brockner, and C. Martin. 1994. Unpublished data.

Wiesenfeld, B., J. Brockner, and B. Petzall. 1994. Unpublished data.

Williamson, O. E. 1968. Economies as an antitrust defense: The welfare tradeoffs. *American Economic Review* 58 (March): 18–35.

———. 1975. Markets and hierarchies. Analysis and antitrust implications. New York: The Free Press.

———. 1979. Transaction-cost economics: The governance of contractual relations. *Journal of Law and Economics* 22 (October): 233–261.

———. 1981. The economics of organization: The transaction cost approach. *American Journal of Sociology* 87 (November): 548–577.

———. 1983. Credible commitments: Using hostages to support exchange. *American Economic Review.* 73: 519–540.

———. 1985. *The economic institutions of capitalism.* New York: Free Press.

———. 1988a. The logic of economic organization. *Journal of Law, Economics, and Organization* 4 (Spring): 65–93.

———. 1988b. The economics and sociology of organization: Promoting a dialogue. In G. Farkas and P. England, eds. *Industries, firms, and jobs,* 159–185. New York: Plenum.

———. 1989. Internal economic organization. In O. E. Williamson, S. E. Sjostrand, and J. Johanson, eds. *Perspectives on the economics of organization,* 7–48. Lund, Sweden: Lund University Press.

———. 1991a. Comparative economic organization: The analysis of discrete structural alternatives. *Administrative Science Quarterly* 36 (June): 269–296.

———. 1991b. Economic institutions: Spontaneous and intentional governance. *Journal of Law, Economics, and Organization* 7 (Special Issue): 159–187.

———. 1991c. Strategizing, economizing, and economic organization. *Strategic Management Journal* 12: 75–94.

———. 1993a. Calculativeness, trust, and economic organization. *Journal of Law and Economics* (April): 453–486.

———. 1993b. The evolving science of organization. *Journal of Institutional and Theoretical Economics* 149 (March).

———. 1996. *The mechanisms of governance.* New York: Oxford.

———. 1996. Transaction cost economics and organization theory. In J.J. Halpern and R.N. Stern, eds., *Debating rationality: Nonrational aspects of organizational decision making.*

Winter, S. 1987. Knowledge and competence as strategic assets. In D. Teece, ed., *The competitive challenge: Strategies for industrial innovation and renewal.* Cambridge, Mass.: Ballinger.

Yakura, E. K. 1995. Transferring best management practices across cultural and organizational boundaries: Japanese and U.S. nuclear power plants. *Industrial and Environmental Crisis Quarterly* 9: 198–212.

Yngvesson, B. 1978. The Atlantic fishermen. In L. Nader and H. F. Todd, eds. *The disputing process: Law in ten societies,* 59–85. New York: Columbia University Press.

Zald, M. 1987. Review essay: The new institutional economics. *American Journal of Sociology* 93 (November): 701–708.

Zeldes, S. P. 1989. Consumption and liquidity constraints: An empirical investigation. *Journal of Political Economy* 97: 305–346.

Zucker, L. 1983. Organizations as institutions. In S. Bacharach, ed., *Research in the sociology of organizations*. Greenwich, Conn.: JAI Press.

Zuckerman, M., B. M. DePaulo, and R. Rosenthal. 1981. Verbal and nonverbal communication of deception. In L. Berkowitz, eds. *Advances in experimental social psychology*, 2–60. New York: Academic Press.

Contributors

MAX H. BAZERMAN is the J. Jay Gerber Distinguished Professor of Dispute Resolution and Organizations, Kellogg Graduate School of Management, Northwestern University, Evanston, Illinois. Bazerman's research focuses on decision making, negotiation, and the natural environment. He is the author or co-author of more than a hundred research articles, and the author, co-author, or co-editor of seven books, including *Judgment in Managerial Decision Making* (New York: Wiley, 1994, now in its third edition), *Cognition and Rationality in Negotiation* with M. A. Neale (New York: Free Press, 1991), and *Negotiating Rationally*, with M. A. Neale (New York: Free Press, 1992).

JOEL BROCKNER is a Professor of Management in the Graduate School of Business, Columbia University. He received a Ph.D. in social/personality psychology from Tufts University in 1977. His research interests center on organizational and individual change, self-processes, and the escalation of commitment to a failing course of action.

COLIN F. CAMERER received an MBA in finance and a Ph.D. in decision theory from the University of Chicago Business School in 1981. He studies psychology and economics, game theory, financial markets, primarily using experimental Methods. He is the Rea and Lela Axline Professor of Business Economics at CalTech.

JOHN S. CARROLL is Professor of Behavioral and Policy Sciences at the MIT Sloan School of Management. His research on decision making focuses on how individuals, groups, and organizations interpret behavior and its consequences, for example, the review incident and corrective action process in nuclear power and chemical process plants.

ROBERT GIBBONS uses game theory to analyze employment relationships and organizational design and performance. He has been co-editor of the *Journal of Labor Economics* and is currently a member of the Advisory Board of the Citicorp Behavioral Science Research Council.

JENNIFER J. HALPERN received her Ph.D. from the University of California at Berkeley. Formerly Assistant Professor of Organizational Behavior at Cornell University, she taught negotiation, mediation, and social psychology in the workplace. She has published on the effects of social context on decision making, emphasizing the effects of friendship and gender differences. Her current interests include computer-based communication, negotiation, and decision making, and multimedia design for education in the workplace. She made the economically irrational decision to be an at-home parent.

DAVID KRACKHARDT is a Professor of Organizations and Public Policy at the Heinz School of Public Policy and Management, Carnegie Mellon University. His research addresses questions of how network analysis can be used to better understand and change organizations. His published works have appeared in journals in psychology, sociology, anthropology, statistics and management. His current research agenda includes developing models of diffusion of controversial innovations and exploring the role of Simmelian (super-strong) ties in organizations.

ALFRED A. MARCUS is Professor of Strategic Management and Organization at the University of Minnesota Carlson School of Management. His research has focused on high reliability organizations and safety in the nuclear power and other industries. He is the author of *Business and Society: Strategy, Ethics, and the Global Economy* (Irwin Press).

JUDI MCLEAN PARKS'S research focuses on the "psychological contract" between employers and employees, and how the nature of the employer/employee relationship is changing. She currently is examining the implications of broken psychological contracts in terms of disaffected workers, workplace violence, and revenge as an enactment of retributive justice.

ZUR SHAPIRA, Research Professor of Management and Organizational Behavior at the Stern School of Business, New York University, is the author of *Risk Taking: A Managerial Perspective* (New York: Russell Sage Foundation, 1995); an editor of *Organizational Decision Making* (New York: Cambridge University Press, 1977); and co-editor, with R. Garud and P. Nayyar, of *Technological Innovation: Oversights and Foresights* (New York: Cambridge University Press, 1977).

FAYE L. SMITH received her Ph.D. from the University of Iowa. Her research interests are in strategic management and macro-organizational issues. She also has experience in the social expression, banking, and fashion industries.

JOHN STERMAN is J. Spencer Standish Professor of Management and director of the System Dynamics Group at the MIT Sloan School of Management. He specializes in the development of "management flight simulators" to create learning environments for students and senior executives. His research includes the dynamics of organizational improvement programs such as reengineering and total quality management.

ROBERT N. STERN is professor of organizational behavior at the School of Industrial and Labor Relations, Cornell University, Ithaca, New York. His current research interests include corporate compliance with government regulation, labor as a social movement, industrial conflict, and employee participation in decision making. Some of these topics are addressed in *The Labor Movement: References and Resources*, with Daniel Cornfield (New York: Macmillan, 1996) and "Consultants and Workplace Democracy: Reproducing the Relations of Production" with Asaf Darr, in *Organizational Decision Making under Different Economic and Political Conditions* (Royal Netherlands Academy of Sciences, 1996). He received his Ph.D. in sociology from Vanderbilt University.

LEIGH THOMPSON (Ph.D. Northwestern University, 1988) is the John L. and Helen Kellogg Distinguished Professor of Organization Behavior at Northwestern University. Her current research, funded by the National Science Foundation, examines social judgment processes in negotiation and social relationships in group decision making. In 1991, she received an NSF Presidential Young Investigator Award, and in 1995 she was a Fellow at the Center for Advanced Study in the Behavioral Sciences. She is currently writing a book titled *Negotiation: Key Principles*.

KATHLEEN L. VALLEY is an Assistant Professor at the Graduate School of Business Administration, Harvard University. Professor Valley received her Ph.D. from the Kellogg Graduate School of Management at Northwestern University. Her research focuses on interpersonal relationships, and their role in decisions, conflict, and resource allocation within and between organizations.

BATIA M. WIESENFELD received her Ph.D. in Management from Columbia University. She is an assistant professor in the Department of Management at the Stern School of Business, New York University. Her current research focuses on self processes in organizations, the management of organizational change and group cognition and affect.

OLIVER E. WILLIAMSON is the Edgar F. Kaiser Professor of Business, Professor of Economics, and Professor of Law at the University of California, Berkeley. He is a member of the National Academy of Sciences and a fellow of the American Academy of Arts and Sciences and the Econometrics Society. His research deals with the economics of organization. His most recent book is *The Mechanisms of Governance* (Oxford; Oxford University Press, 1996).

Index

Acquiring a Company problem, 26, 29, 82
Agency theory, 29, 32, 40, 41, 131
Altruism, 137, 140, 147
Asset specificity, 41, 131, 173

Bargaining, 93, 95–98
Behavioral Decision Theory, 9, 21, 51, 58
Benchmarking, 101
Biases, 202, 231, 236
Bonded rationality, 220, 224–30
Bounded rationality, 7, 14, 21–25, 34,
    161,193, 220, 230
Bureaucracy, 165–66, 169, 183

Cognition, 6–9, 79
Cognitive illusions, 231
Collectivism, 139–40
Competition, 9
Conjunction fallacy, 236, 238
Consequential choice, 25
Consumption capital, 240
Context:
    cultural, 235
    social, 3, 10–12, 88, 134, 232, 234
Contracts, 29, 125, 159–60, 194
    communitarian, 149–50
    custodial, 150–52
    explicit, 46, 210
    exploitive, 145–49
    implicit, 45
    incomplete, 37, 47, 174
    organizational, 126–28, 131, 139, 143–45

promissory, 127–28, 130, 134
psychological, 128, 140–41, 211–12
relational, 130, 133–34, 138–47, 149
social, 127, 134, 147
spot, 137, 176
transactional, 129–34, 138–41, 145, 147, 211
violations, 129, 135, 146, 150–51
Cooperation, 180
Coupling, 109
Culture, 111
Curse of knowledge, 96–97

Deception, 95
Decision processes, 2, 13, 58, 164, 202, 214

Economics, 51, 125
    classical, 2, 135–37
    experimental, 80, 94
    institutional, 158–59
Economizing, 187–88
Embeddedness, 167–68, 193
Emotion, 150
Endowment effects, 233, 236
Equity, 89
Escalation of commitment, 35
Exchange, norm of reciprocity, 130–31, 153,
    181
Exchange transactions, 219–20
Externalities, 180

Fairness, 9, 31, 60–62, 80, 86–88, 129, 132,
    135, 149, 153–54, 228, 232, 234

Feedback, 162
Friendship, 12, 237

Gambler's fallacy 22
Game theory, 5, 8, 27, 30, 35, 51, 57–58, 63,
    81–82, 90–94, 210–12, 234
    See also Behavior Decision theory
Garbage can model, 16, 24, 38, 51
Governance, 159–61, 167, 169–70, 180

Herd behavior, 56
Heuristics, 8–9, 26, 30, 90–92, 226, 231
Human Capital Theory, 244–46

Incentives (reward), 197–98, 206, 211
Inefficiency, 54, 184–85
Informal organization, 14, 158
Information:
    private, 84–86
    search, 39, 43, 56
Institutions, 167, 192
Interdependence, 176, 225
Iron Law of Oligarchy, 163
Isomorphism, 47, 50

Job loss, 200–8
Justice, 140–41, 147, 149–50, 153–54
    distributive, 140–41, 202–3
    interactional, 140, 202–3
    procedural, 140, 202–8, 212
    retributive, 140–41, 202–3

Layoffs. See Job Loss
Learning, 112–14
Leveraged buyouts, 71–77
Loss–aversion, 69

Markets, imperfect, 219
Mental models, 100–104, 109–13, 119–20,
    233
Monitoring, 149
Motivation, 209, 214

Nash equilibrium, 64
Negotiations, 11, 80, 90, 94–96
Norms, definition, 12
    commitment, 93, 127
    shared, 22, 58, 102, 158
    social reciprocity, 92, 134–40, 145–47,
        150–53, 232, 235
Nuclear power plants, 104–11, 119

Opportunism, 139, 161, 174, 193
Organizational behavior, 13, 139, 206, 211–12
Organizational culture (corporate), 45, 102
Organizational, theory, 16, 47
    performance, 100
Outcomes, 199

Pareto optimality, 86
Path dependence, 171, 183–88
Personalization, 219–21, 224–30, 233–37
Power, 142–49, 177, 182
Preferences:
    competing, 15
    endogenous, 162, 239, 241–44
    exogenous, 239–42
    ordering, 6, 12–15, 198, 221, 224
    revealed, 4, 242
Prisoner's dilemma, 30, 78
Procedural justice, 140, 202–8, 212
Prospect theory, 88, 232
Psychology, 21, 199

Rational Choice Theory, 4, 8, 25, 29, 219, 226,
    229, 237–38
    See also Personalization
Rationality:
    adaptive, 25, 165, 193
    contextual, 25, 29
    game, 25–26
    limited, 25
    mutual, 65
    organizational, 15
    process, 25
    quasi-, 8, 233
    selected, 25
    social, 9–10, 15
    substantive, 23, 57
    See also Altruism; Bonded rationality;
        Bounded rationality; Decision processes
Reciprocity, see Norms
Reference groups, 61–62
Repeated games, 45–47
Reputation, social, 91, 137
Risk, 171
Rules, 34, 158–59, 163

Satisficing, 7, 21–24, 169
    See also Bounded Rationality
Self-interest, 3, 11, 14, 28, 51, 80, 86–89, 125,
    138–39, 147, 151, 223
Signalling, 43
Simultaneous causality, 91

Social bonding, 226
Social comparison, 61–62, 67, 80
Social identity theory, 93, 137, 197, 234
Social utility, 10
Sunk cost, 220, 225, 228, 233

Time frame, 99, 110, 120, 132, 197, 210–12, 243
Transaction cost economics, 32, 38, 128,
    156–62, 165, 169–72
    See also Asset Specificity
Trust, 135, 190–91, 212

Ultimatum games, 31, 60, 80, 87–88
Unit of analysis, 172

Utility theory, 5, 25, 54, 60, 65–67, 168–69,
    241, 247
Utility, expected, 21, 35
Utility, social, 28, 88–89, 226, 235–36, 246

Winner's curse, 26, 82
Worker self-management, 188–89
Workers:
    Allais Paradox, 223
    contingent work, 195–97, 207
    contract workers, 195
    layoff, 213
    organizational commitment, 206, 209

DATE DUE

Demco, Inc. 38-293